Test Theory for a New Generation of Tests

Test Theory for a New Generation of Tests

Edited by

Norman Frederiksen
Robert J. Mislevy
Isaac I. Bejar
Educational Testing Service

LEA LAWRENCE ERLBAUM ASSOCIATES, PUBLISHERS
1993   Hillsdale, New Jersey   Hove and London

Lawrence Erlbaum Associates, Inc., Publishers
365 Broadway
Hillsdale, New Jersey 07642

Library of Congress Cataloging-in-Publication Data

Test theory for a new generation of tests / edited by Norman
Frederiksen, Robert J. Mislevy, Isaac I. Bejar.
    p.   cm.
Includes bibliographical references and index.
ISBN 0-8058-0593-1
    1. Educational tests and measurements. 2. Ability—Testing.
3. Examinations—Interpretation. 4. Examinations—Design and
construction. I. Frederiksen, Norman. II. Mislevy, Robert J.
III. Bejar, Isaac I.
LB3051.T433 1993
371.2´6—dc20   91-39408
                                      CIP

Books published by Lawrence Erlbaum Associates are printed on acid-free
paper, and their bindings are chosen for strength and durability.

Printed in the United States of America
10 9 8 7 6 5 4 3 2 1

Contents

v

Introduction

Robert J. Mislevy
Educational Testing Service

A full century has passed since papers on statistical test theory first began to appear (Edgeworth, 1888, 1892; Spearman, 1904a, 1904b, 1907, 1910, 1913). In his 1961 review of *Measurement of Learning and Mental Abilities*, Gulliksen (1961) succinctly characterized the field as follows:

> The central problem of test theory is the relation between the *ability* of the individual and his [or her] *observed score* on the test . . . Psychologists are essentially in the position of Plato's dwellers in the cave. They can know ability levels only through the shadows (the observed test scores) cast on the wall at the back of the cave. The problem is how to make the most effective use of these shadows (the observed test scores) in order to determine the nature of reality (ability) which we can know only through these shadows. (p. 101)

Following the aforementioned work, a sequence of influential and increasingly mathematically sophisticated books followed, notable among them Thorndike's (1919) *An Introduction to the Theory of Mental and Social Measurements*, Kelley's (1927) *Interpretation of Educational Measurements*, Guilford's *(1936) Psychometric Methods*, Gulliksen's (1950/1987) own *Theories of Mental Tests*, Rasch's (1960/1980) *Probabilistic Models for Some Intelligence and Attainment Tests*, and Lord and Novick's (1968) encyclopaedic *Statistical Theories of Mental Test Scores*, which includes Birnbaum's contributions on item response theory. Why, now, *Test Theory for a New Generation of Tests*? A point of departure from Gulliksen's description portends our motivation.

We would concur with Gulliksen that the heart of test theory is connecting

FIG. 1.   The Shadow of an object in the back of a cave.

what we can observe with a more general, inherently unobservable, conception of what a student knows or can do. This is essentially a statistical problem—given a framework in which this conception is to be erected. The framework implicit in Gulliksen's description, and throughout the papers and books listed, is that of a measure of a quantity he calls *ability*. To extend Plato's analogy, inferring this number from test scores is like the inferential task of deducing the form of an object from its shadows; designing efficient tests is like configuring locations and intensities of fires to best educe shapes. Recall, however, that a two-dimensional shadow is consistent with infinitely many three-dimensional objects. Figure 1 is a shadow from one perspective; Figures (A, B, & C) could all be shadows of the same object as cast by an orthogonal light source. Our inference depends as much on our conception of what we expect to perceive as on the imperfect information we are accorded.

Ability corresponds to *reality* in Gulliksen's description. This is the correct term in the analogy, but perhaps the identification has been taken too literally. Useful as the ability level paradigm has proven in large-scale selection and prediction problems, it represents but one of many possible perspectives. Its legacy includes, most obviously, a collection of testing practices and statistical techniques suited to educational questions cast in its terms. More subtly, yet more profoundly, it has defined the universe of discourse within which discussions of

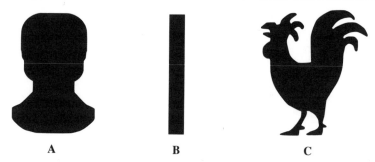

A   B   C

FIG. 2.   (A, B, C). Shadows that might appear if the object were turned 90° south.

educational options take place, at both the instructional and policy-making levels. Unrecognized assumptions underlie analyses about what should be tested, how outcomes might be used, and how the effectiveness of the effort should be evaluated.

What is missing from the conceptualization upon which standard test theory is based are models for just how people know what they know and do what they can do, and the ways in which they increase these capacities. The impetus for an examination of the foundations of test theory arises from psychologists and educators, who, as they extend the frontiers of understanding about human cognition, ask questions that fall outside the universe of discourse that standard test theory generates. The point is not that new models are true and the ability level model is false; indeed, we are inclined to argue that they are all false in the final analysis. The point is, rather, that different models are useful for different purposes, and we should develop a generalized capability to reason from observations to broader families of models of ability—models consonant with research on cognition and capable of addressing applied educational questions cast in these terms. In our view, then, test theory should be construed more broadly—as a technology of marshaling and interpreting evidence about what students know and can do—without limiting ourselves to the trait-level conceptualization of ability.

For some, perhaps many, educational applications, the kinds of information familiar tests and familiar test theory capture will remain appropriate. For others, however, broader or alternative student models will be appropriate. The chapters in this volume consider a variety of directions in which standard test theory might be extended. Chapters 1, 2, and 3, by Snow and Lohman, Mislevy, and Lohman and Ippel, along with commentary by Cole, discuss in general terms the role of test theory in the light of recent work in cognitive and educational psychology. The remaining chapters address more specific issues, including test design (Bennett's chapter 5, Marshall's chapter 7, and Bejar's chapter 13); student modeling (Embretson's chapter 6, and Haertel & Wiley's chapter 14); test analysis (Thissen's chapter 4, Masters & Mislevy's chapter 9, Gitomer & Rock's chapter 10, and Yamamoto and Gitomer's chapter 11); and the integration of assessment and instruction (Feltovich, Spiro, & Coulson's chapter 8). The reader is warned that several chapters could have been assigned into different categories in this rough categorization! Integrative discussions appear in Bert Green's commentary on chapters 4–6, Jack Carroll's commentary on chapters 7–10, and Henry Braun's commentary on chapters 11–14.

REFERENCES

Edgeworth, F. Y. (1888). The statistics of examinations. *Journal of the Royal Statistical Society*, *51*, 599–635.

Edgeworth, F. Y. (1892). Correlated averages. *Philosophical Magazine* (5th Series), *34*, 190–204.

Guilford, J. P. (1936). *Psychometric methods*. New York: McGraw-Hill.

Gulliksen, H. (1987). *Theory of mental tests*. Hillsdale, NJ: Lawrence Erlbaum Associates. (Original work published 1950)

Gulliksen, H. (1961). Measurement of learning and mental abilities. *Psychometrika, 26*, 93–107.

Kelley, T. L. (1927). *Interpretation of educational measurements*. New York: World Book.

Lord, F. M., & Novick, M. R. (1968). *Statistical theories of mental test scores*. Reading, MA: Addison-Wesley.

Rasch, G. (1980). *Probabilistic models for some intelligence and attainment tests*. Chicago: University of Chicago Press. (Original work published 1960)

Spearman, C. (1904a). The proof and measurement of association between two things. *American Journal of Psychology, 15*, 72–101.

Spearman, C. (1904b). "General intelligence" objectively determined and measured. *American Journal of Psychology, 15*, 201–292.

Spearman, C. (1907). Demonstration of formulae for true measurement of correlation. *American Journal of Psychology, 18*, 161–169.

Spearman, C. (1910). Correlation calculated with faulty data. *British Journal of Psychology, 3*, 271–295.

Spearman, C. (1913). Correlations of sums and differences. *British Journal of Psychology, 5*, 417–426.

Thorndike, E. L. (1919). *An introduction to the theory of mental and social measurements* (2nd ed.). New York: Bureau of Publications, Teachers College, Columbia University.

1

Cognitive Psychology, New Test Design, and New Test Theory: An Introduction

Richard E. Snow
Stanford University

David F. Lohman
University of Iowa

In the 1980s, much new research and discussion focused on the improvement of psychological tests in relation to their uses in education, as well as in industry and government. The implications of cognitive psychology for measurement began to be considered (see, e.g., Snow & Lohman, 1989). New proposals for using technological as well as substantive theoretical advances to develop more diagnostic forms of assessment were increasingly developed (see e.g., Frederiksen, Glaser, Lesgold, & Shafto, 1990). And psychometric theory and test design principles were reviewed and expanded, particularly by the contributors to this volume. The possibility now exists to bring new concepts and measures of aptitude, learning, development, and achievement, together with instructional innovations, to create truly diagnostic and adaptive systems. But we must learn how to use the new psychometric, substantive, and technological advances in concert to do it right. This is the main challenge for the 1990s, in our view.

We cannot here reiterate, or even summarize adequately, all of the many interesting ideas, promises, projections, cautions, and criticisms that have already been published on these topics. What we can do here is to choose, from our own writings (Lohman, 1989a; Snow, 1988, 1989, 1990; Snow & Lohman, 1989) and a few other sources, some advances in cognitive theory and research that exemplify potentials and problems to be met by new test theory and new test designs. For convenience, we group these advances under separate headings for cognitive abilities and cognitive achievements. However, we see the range across these traditional categories as continuous, especially as the integration of assessment and instruction is considered; some implications of this view

1

are summarized in a concluding section. We omit here another large and un-charted domain for new test theory and design, namely, conative and affective assessment (see Snow, 1989, 1990).

ANALYSES OF COGNITIVE ABILITIES

Research in several laboratories has sought to analyze the information-processing activities involved in performance on cognitive tasks. The tasks studied have included both the laboratory tasks of cognitive science and many of the ability tests typically used as indicants of cognitive aptitude for learning. From this work, a new kind of cognitive theory of abilities has emerged.

Some Principal Findings

It is now possible to identify at least some of the component processing skills required in ability test performance. Stimulus encoding, feature comparison, rule induction, rule application, and response justification are examples of such separa-ble processes (see e.g., Lohman, 1989a; Pellegrino & Glaser, 1982; Sternberg, 1985a, 1985b). This progress in the cognitive psychology of ability tests has been coupled with progress in measurement theory. Embretson's (1985) mul-ticomponent latent trait approach, for example, brings the separate component identifications into combination in a powerful psychometric model. Yet, as in all such models, the power is bought with strong assumptions, and these have not been fully justified. Indeed, some evidence suggests that item parameters depend on intratest psychological effects, such as variations in self-regulation and speed–accuracy trade-off, indicating that the assumptions of latent-trait models may not be met in important instances (Lohman, 1989b; Schaeffer, 1991; Snow & Lohman, 1989). A componential processing skill theory of human abili-ties may require a different test theory—one that considers the place of an item in a sequence and also indexes performance along two dimensions, speed and accuracy, rather than on one dimension only.

Evidence from cognitive analyses also suggests that a significant portion of individual difference variance reflected by ability tests arises from the strategic adaptation of information processing during performance, not just from compo-nent skill differences. Not only do individuals adopt qualitatively distinct strate-gies for performing particular tests (Sternberg & Weil, 1980), they also shift strategies as a function of item characteristics and adapt these strategies as they learn through the test (see, e.g., Bethell-Fox, Lohman, & Snow, 1984; Kyllo-nen, Lohman, & Woltz, 1984; Snow & Lohman, 1984). Mislevy and Verhelst (1986) adapted latent trait models to meet some of the problems posed by strate-gy variation in test performance; their approach allows the identification of differ-ent strategy groups on a test, but does not yet encompass strategy shifting by individuals within a test. Here then is a further problem to be addressed by new test theoretic research. The work of Kyllonen, Lohman, and Woltz (1984) and of Ippel and Beem (1987) is a start in one possible new direction. This work envisions tests designed to manipulate strategy choices and strategy shifts systematically.

Part of the problem in capturing strategy shifting in test performance is understanding the sources of item difficulty and how these change from item to item. In conventional tests, sources of difficulty are not systematically controlled by item writers. One important contribution of cognitive psychology is the identification of these sources. Butterfield and his colleagues (Butterfield, Nielsen, Tangen, & Richardson, 1985) showed how cognitive analyses can lead to computerized item generation procedures designed to control the various sources of item difficulty—in effect, to control the cognitive psychology of the test more precisely and more adaptively than human item writers do. The result should be test designs that help diagnose disabilities associated with particular types of difficulty, as well as test designs that systematically manipulate, and thus diagnose, individual facility for strategy choice and adaptation. However, the psychometric model needed for such tests must accommodate an adaptive diagnostic process in which the succession of items is shaped for each person on substantive grounds; the appropriate model will likely not assume a single underlying ability continuum for all items and persons. Furthermore, although faceted tests can provide much information, it remains to be seen whether practically useful tests of broad abilities can be constructed by systematically varying a few sources of item difficulty. In some domains, tests of broad abilities that are not easily coached and that show good predictive validities may require a wider sampling of sources of difficulty (see Humphreys, 1985). Other test designs are possible, and some—such as nested designs in which each examinee attempts a different set of items—have important advantages over the completely crossed design in which all examinees attempt all items (Cronbach, Gleser, Nanda, & Rajaratnam, 1972). These unconventional test designs, which were difficult to achieve with paper-and-pencil tests, should be easy to implement when tests are computer generated and administered.

New sources of variation in both ability and learning task performance have been identified in addition to skill and strategy differences; examples are the attentional requirements of such tasks, and the degree to which consistent processing becomes automatic with practice, thus changing the attentional requirements (see, e.g., Ackerman, 1987, 1989; Hunt & Lansman, 1982). Also, direct training of ability components to produce these changes is now a distinct possibility (Sternberg, 1986). If the ability construct underlying a test changes qualitatively with practice or training on the test, then the measurement model must somehow accommodate this fact. Conventional test theory has not addressed such effects. Assuming the same underlying ability continuum at different points in time, with some computation of a "difference" score, will not suffice.

Work on fluid reasoning abilities suggests not only that multiple strategies are available to many individuals but that adaptiveness and flexibility in problem solving involve the assembly and reassembly of workable strategies as difficulty and novelty vary in complex tasks. In effect, fluid reasoning is interpreted as rapid learning in the test, at least in part (Snow, 1981; Snow & Lohman, 1984). However, this description of fluid ability is not yet well understood. Nor is the question of how to measure directly the adaptive assembly and control processes involved. A particular difficulty is how to understand and identify novelty in test problems and transfer relations among test problems for particular persons. Novelty is in some degree person specific.

Many new analyses of spatial ability tests show that psychometric understanding of these abilities has been particularly superficial (Lohman, 1988). It appears that spatial abilities also involve multiple strategies, some of which are not at all "spatial"; these strategies vary with task demands and can be altered with seemingly minor variations in such demands. Some new techniques have been suggested for the measurement of spatial abilities, but the changes in test theory and design associated with these techniques need much more investigation.

An improved theory of verbal ability has been constructed that posits many subprocesses involved in the representation of word meaning and the nature and speed of word processing in verbal comparison tasks (Hunt, 1985b). The theory accounts for the acquisition of word meaning from context using contextual cues to guide encoding, combination, and comparison processes to produce schemata that then are used in verbal comprehension (Sternberg & Powell, 1983). It also helps explain why verbal tests often correlate highly with reasoning tests, and identifies some of the item facets that control this relation (Marshalek, 1981).

What emerges from all this is a description of perceptual, memory, reasoning, verbal, and spatial ability tests, and increasingly also of learning and problem-solving tasks, in terms of dynamic microprocessing models. In effect, the research provides a new and elaborated form of construct validation for ability assessments (Embretson, 1983; Messick, 1989).

Further Issues

There are many other new issues to be addressed by measurement theory and research in this direction. One further issue is how best to incorporate into new tests the experimental techniques that identify the component information-processing skills associated with these abilities (see Embretson, 1985). Another is how to combine error and latency measures in this pursuit (see Lohman, 1989b). Another concerns the measurement scales to be used in these procedures and their potential advantages over the linear, norm-referenced scales of conventional tests. Still another is the continuing identification of aspects of these abilities not directly measured in paper-and-pencil tests, but perhaps important in the complex learning and problem-solving situations the ability tests are designed to predict.

Finally, one can imagine new batteries of closely articulated tasks designed to identify and contrast component processes and strategies in reasoning, verbal, spatial, and various special ability constructs. A unified theory of intelligence might then be built to show what organization of task process models reproduces the hierarchical or radex structure of psychometric test correlations typically found (see Snow, Kyllonen, & Marshalek, 1984). It will need to be shown, however, that profiles or other descriptions derived from such batteries are more diagnostically useful than conventional tests for instructional purposes.

Examples

Two example projects suggest that such improvements can indeed be realized. The two, noted only briefly here, are particularly important because they address abilities fundamental to instructional learning—reading, mathematical, and fluid reasoning abilities—and because they suggest how some cognitive and psychometric approaches can be combined.

J. Frederiksen's (1981, 1982; see also Frederiksen, Warren, & Roseberg, 1985a, 1985b) work on reading ability is one example. He distinguished three types of information-processing skills: word analysis processes (e.g., encoding single and multiletter units, translating graphemic units into phonological units, and activation of appropriate lexical categories); discourse analysis process (e.g., retrieving and integrating word meanings, comprehending basic propositions underlying sentences, integrating processes across sentences, resolving problems of reference, and inferring nonexplicit but essential relations by elaborating to prior knowledge); and integrative processes (e.g., generating extrapolations from the text models, combining information from perceptual and contextual sources). These three types of component processes interact because they share processing resources and work on a common database. Components also differ in the degree to which they have been automatized; skilled readers show more and better component automatization than less skilled readers.

Frederiksen has developed measures for eight of these component processes, tested several models for component interactions, and also correlated the component measures with a range of reference ability tests. His analysis indicates that conventional tests of reading speed, vocabulary, and comprehension do not include some important discourse-processing skills.

The construction and validation of such a battery proceeds in several steps. First, tasks hypothesized to require particular components are selected. Second, stimulus variables are identified that can be manipulated to alter processing difficulty of the designated components. Third, contrasts among task conditions are computed for each person to represent the extent to which performance is degraded as stimulus variables are manipulated. Predicted declines in performance constitute a first-level validation of the task and its process model. Convergent and discriminant validity of individual contrast scores constitutes the second level of validation. This is accomplished through the formation and testing of a set of structural equations using LISREL.

With the initial battery thus assembled, Frederiksen selected three of the eight components for training. Selection was based on two criteria: Performance on the component should influence higher-level components, and automatic performance of the component should significantly reduce the drain on processing resources required by other components. Components thus selected were perception of multiletter units within words, decoding orthographic patterns to phonological units of speech, and context utilization. Computer games were then devised to train each skill. Extensive study of poor readers showed that training was effective for at least some learners on some components. Frederiksen's work is ongoing and will need to be strengthened by larger validation and training studies. Nevertheless, it is a prime example of the sort of assessment designs that can be produced by combining sophisticated measurement models with detailed cognitive theory.

Another example is the work of Brown and Campione, and their colleagues, on a scripted tutoring procedure for diagnosing and promoting mathematical and reasoning abilities (see Brown & Campione, 1986; Brown & Ferrara, 1985; Campione & Brown, 1984, 1987, 1990; Ferrara, 1987). Their procedure is to administer sets of problems in arithmetic, for example, and then to provide hints to the learner where difficulties occur. The hints are organized in a hierarchy from general to specific to assess the amount and kind of instruction needed by each individual to solve a problem. The arithmetic tasks are carefully chosen to reflect skills and distinctions shown to be important in prior cognitive analyses of arithmetic operations. There is a pre- and postknowledge test involving number–word sequences in counting, appreciation for the context of counting, and actual counting operations. The tasks also embody a transfer continuum from original learning and maintenance through three levels of near to far transfer. A "learning efficiency" score is derived from the hint hierarchy as the inverse of the explicitness of help the learner needs in order to progress. A "transfer propensity" score is also obtained to indicate the distance across the range of increasingly novel problems the learner can negotiate.

The Brown–Campione results show that learning and transfer measures are related to conventional ability tests, but are better predictors of independently measured pre–post gains in achievement, and provide diagnostic information for further instruction that is not available from the conventional tests. It appears, furthermore, that measures of flexible or "far" transfer offer particularly useful prediction and diagnosis. The work further implicates the importance of metacognitive thinking skills in this sort of learning and transfer. Transfer performance, in particular, is seen as dependent on the operation of effective self-regulatory functions, such as planning, monitoring one's own progress, questioning and checking, and devising repair strategies when things go wrong.

Similar results have been obtained in studies in which progressive matrices and letter-series tasks, typical measures of fluid reasoning ability, have been used. Again, in addition to evidence that skills involved in these tasks can be improved, the learning and transfer measures derived from them seem to offer unique prediction and diagnosis not obtainable from conventional forms of these measures.

The Brown–Campione program is also ongoing. There are attempts to apply the procedure in other instructional domains, to investigate motivational and personality measures in relation to the cognitive assessments, and to mesh the quantitative measures with think–aloud protocols and other qualitative descriptions of performance.

The initial success of both the Frederiksen and Brown–Campione approaches should motivate associated psychometric research. The psychometric properties of Frederiksen's contrast scores and skill interaction models, or the learning and transfer measures of Brown and Campione, are not yet well understood. The problems of measurement scale, error estimation, and difference scores need study in these contexts. In particular, alternative measurement models that do not rely on gain scores should be investigated.

ANALYSES OF COGNITIVE ACHIEVEMENT

Cognitive analyses have also sought to understand the declarative and procedural knowledge assembled by learners during formal instruction, the kinds of errors learners make during as well as after instruction, and the various forms of preconceptions they may harbor that interfere with learning progress. Much of the research has been done on mathematics and science learning, but there are beginnings in other school subjects. What emerges from this work are models of knowledge structure and its acquisition that constitute new theories of achievement (Glaser & Bassok, 1989).

Some Principal Findings

One product of cognitive psychology is a much richer view of knowledge organization, both its acquisition and its structure, than was extant when standardized achievement tests took the form they still display today. This view distinguishes phases of knowledge and skill acquisition. The accretion of new information and its chunking, elaboration, and connection to existing knowledge are followed by restructuring, through which new knowledge organizations are formed to replace or reformulate old concepts and relations, and then by the tuning or adaptation and practice of the new structures in particular uses (Norman, 1982). In skill development, the parallel phases are declarative knowledge acquisition, compilation or proceduralization, and automatization (Anderson, 1985).

The new research further posits several different forms of knowledge structure that such learning might produce. Among these are semantic networks, schemata, scripts, prototypes, images, and mental models; each has its special uses in describing knowledge structure, and evidence from different kinds of tasks suggests some validity for each.

Such knowledge structures are not only formed during learning; they are also used to reason about what is being learned, to recall what has been learned, and to solve problems. Their effects are thus sometimes detectable in task performance. There are many measurement possibilities, although they have so far been studied only in piecemeal, small-scale attempts with little attention to psychometric underpinnings (Snow & Lohman, 1989). Using interview or teach-back procedures it is possible to detect degree and kind of restructuring and elaboration after learning, and to measure chunk size. Scoring templates for qualitatively different kinds of structure can be imposed on the protocols (Marshall, 1988; Marton, 1983; Pask, 1976). Because different kinds of knowledge structure should produce different patterns of responses, and particular kinds of errors, tests might be designed to elicit different error patterns from different structures (Mandler, 1984). At least in narrow domains, bug libraries can be assembled for error diagnosis (Brown & Burton, 1978). Resnick's (1984) work suggests how strategic inventions during learning might be used to assess understanding. Greeno and Mayer (1975) demonstrated the use of faceted achievement tests to detect qualitative differences in cognitive structure. Various word-association, graphing, card-sorting, interview, and questionnaire techniques have also been tried (see, e.g., McKeachie, Pintrich, & Lin, 1985; Naveh-Benjamin, McKeachie, Lin & Tucker, 1986; Pines, Novak, Posner, & Van Kirk, 1978). There are many other ideas about achievement assessment in this line of research (see, e.g., Glaser, Lesgold, & Lajoie, 1987). Research on the training of learning strategies is also suggestive of methods for assessing knowledge structuring and related approaches to learning (O'Neil, 1978; O'Neil & Spielberger, 1979; Weinstein, Goetz, & Alexander, 1988).

Domain-relevant conceptual organization prior to learning has been recognized as an important further target for measurement. The evidence shows that learners come to instruction with preconceived notions about natural phenomena, in science for example, that can be impediments to new learning (see Strauss, 1988). These beliefs also seem difficult to change. In other domains, learners appear to progress through a series of increasingly sophisticated beliefs about the world. Using techniques similar to those noted earlier, however, key aspects of these alternative conceptions in a domain might be delineated, suggesting how diagnostic tasks might be designed to detect them.

Delineation of the several aspects of skilled performance also suggests multiple indicators for assessment. Among these are understanding principles underlying the skill, as opposed to mindless execution; rapidity of execution with minimal disruption by concurrent tasks; smoothness of execution, with steps organized as a unit; the range of skill transfer; appropriate action control and self regulation; reduction in mental effort and fatigue associated with skilled performance; reduction of skill deterioration during stress; and display of expert points of view (see Snow & Lohman, 1989).

Further Issues

Beyond the development of situation- or time-specific measures of the sorts noted previously, there is need for the assessment of learner trajectory, from prior states of knowledge and skill through one or more courses of instruction to advanced competence. The psychometric models of such trajectory will likely be growth models rather than traditional time-point models (Rogosa, 1991). They will also need to provide diagnosis of qualitative as well as quantitative change. We have little experience with such measurement models.

This problem raises many other issues. It is one thing to demonstrate that prior learning has produced misconceptions, malrules, or other errorful forms of cognitive functioning. It is quite another to build diagnostic assessments of them that usefully guide instruction, and still another to detect whether instruction has resulted in qualitative change in them. Conceptual misunderstandings, in particular, may be both deep-seated and so specific as to require detailed concept-by-concept analysis of each instructional level in a domain, before it is clear what particular categories of misconception imply for instruction or for trajectory. The work to date seems best able to support the design of new assessments of knowledge and skill, and their use in instruction, in the intermediate ranges of achievement—beyond the chaotic performance of extreme novices.

Cognitive research has also begun to look beyond the achievement goals of given units or courses of instruction to ask, in mathematics for example, what it means to think mathematically—to exhibit the kinds of expertise that mathematicians possess (Greeno, 1986). Research on the nature of expertise in a domain may help suggest test blueprints that capture the knowledge and skills of well-educated persons. However, there is much controversy at present about both the nature of expertise and its development (Dreyfus & Dreyfus, 1986). Again, it seems that assessment design for time-point diagnosis and for trajectory is now attainable in the middle range but not in the extremes.

Perhaps the most difficult issues involve assessments of transfer, due no doubt to the persistent difficulties in demonstrating and understanding the phenomena of transfer. In some narrowly defined domains, one can build graduated transfer continua and obtain useful measures, as Brown and Campione have done. However, transfer seems to require the analysis of novel situations, the representation of situations by some cognitive structure (such as mental models), and the use of such structures to support relational reasoning (such as reasoning by analogy) among them, and between them and the specifics of situations. The situatedness of cognition and the need for person–situation relational concepts to deal with learning and transfer are problems that have only begun to be considered (Greeno, 1989; Snow, 1991).

All these issues argue for educational assessments that go well beyond what is specifically taught in some instructional program. One cannot assess relevant prior knowledge and skill, or the development of expertise, or transfer to novel situations without including a range of cognitive and situational specifications, as well as content specifications, in the test blueprint.

Examples

Research on computerized instruction and computerized testing is now evolving into research on systems that integrate instructional and assessment functions. Some of these systems, such as intelligent tutors, operate on a microadaptive level, where instructional decisions based on measurements occur from minute to minute. Some are designed to cover whole courses of instruction as complements to human teaching at a macroadaptive level, over days and weeks (see Snow & Mandinach, 1991).

One good example of how both aptitude and achievement assessments can be used interactively in microadaptive tutoring comes from the work of Lesgold and his colleagues (see Lesgold, 1988; Lesgold, Bonair, & Ivill, 1987). An instructional system on electricity builds up a model of learner knowledge through close cycles of instruction and testing. The model is based on a curriculum goal structure and shows an achievement profile, that is, the state of each goal acquisition for that learner, at each point in time. There are rules to choose which part of the profile to work on next. As instruction proceeds, a diagnostic cycle sweeps through the student profile to identify the parts that should next be tested and to produce test problems suited to that student according to a list of constraints on item type or format. These constraints are based partly on an aptitude profile and partly on the need to detect bugs or misconceptions so that they can be corrected before instruction proceeds. One example of an item design decision might be "Test use of Ohm's Law in diagrammed circuits next, but use simple computations because this student is still weak in numerical skill." In other words, because instruction cannot work on the whole achievement profile at once, it sidesteps some weaknesses while instructing and testing others. The system of microadaptive rules thus coordinates instruction and test design and suggests a way to integrate aptitude and achievement diagnosis in the service of improved adaptive instruction.

Research on another example tutor, also in electricity, goes further to suggest that such systems can be designed to formulate simulation models of student problem-solving skills and learning strategies as well as student domain knowledge (see Frederiksen & White, 1990). Learning is here seen as a progression through qualitatively different mental models in a domain—as successive approximations to a target model. The instructional sequence introduces problems that cannot be solved with the student's present model and that require new concepts and reasoning involved in the next, more complex model. At any point in time, student achievement is represented by the list of models in the progress space that have so far been mastered. Instructional options also support multiple learning strategies and assess their preferred use and effectiveness by different students.

An example of macroadaptive instructional assessment is the learning progress system envisioned by Bunderson and his colleagues (see Bunderson, Inouye, & Olson, 1989; Murphy & Bunderson, 1988). Here, a network of reference tasks is designed to blanket a course of instruction, with particular tasks focused on important learning milestones or targets of difficulty. Each such task is designed to test as well as to instruct some present learner capability and to provide diagnostic information of use in choosing among alternative next steps in the domain. Learners can take different routes through the network, and teachers can use the diagnostic information provided to guide intervening instruction.

These examples suggest a nest of important further problems for test design and test theory. One concerns the nature of the classification decisions such systems use to identify the present state of a student model. Deciding whether a student performance displays one mental model or another is a qualitative classification, not a more–less distinction. As such, it has the character of medical diagnostic decisions that classify cases into distinct categories based on multivariate indicators. Furthermore, for instructional purposes such decisions have two facets: diagnosis of present state, and choice of next instructional step. The latter decision requires validation using the logic of the aptitude–treatment interaction paradigm, applied on a microadaptive scale. Except in the decision theoretic view of tests (Cronbach & Gleser, 1965; van der Linden, 1981, 1984), psychometric theory has not addressed these sorts of classification problems.

A related matter concerns the detection of different types of misconceptions, or alternative conceptions that may apply only to a limited portion of the cognitive domain of instructional concern. Specific errors may be detectable, and degree of fit between a simulation model of the student and the performance indicators may be estimated. Beyond this, however, tests aimed at uncovering deep-seated student beliefs may need to be designed to produce particular patterns of errors. Again, classification psychometrics are needed. In all of the aforementioned, furthermore, new kinds of configural scoring may be needed to transform the multivariate indicators produced from the records of computerized learning episodes into a form that human diagnosticians and teachers can understand and use (see Kyllonen & Shute, 1989).

CONCLUSION AND CHALLENGE

We have tried to point to various findings and examples of cognitive psychological research that raise issues and opportunities for new test theory and test design. We also have pointed to some apparent limitations of present day psychometrics in this regard. Rather than summarize this mere introductory collection, however, we conclude with an abstract view of mental testing that suggests a more general challenge for test theory and design. This view is not new, and it remains vague. However, cognitive theory and research are beginning to flesh it out.

Beyond their biological substrata, human capabilities can be seen to develop gradually from a stream of multifaceted learning experience. Knowledge, skills, understandings, beliefs, and attitudes are acquired, structured, and tuned through experience in the progression of learning situations that define each individual's stream, so individual development is to some degree idiosyncratic. However, important facets can be defined in the population of learning situations and of persons that shape the resulting cognitive capabilities for each person, both quantitatively and qualitatively. To note just a few of these facets, learning situations may be simple or complex in their information-processing demands; broad or narrow in their knowledge and skill demands; and familiar or novel in relation to the individuals' previous experience. They may be informally imposed on individuals by everyday life in a culture, or formally imposed by other individuals and institutions, or chosen or contrived by individuals themselves. The resulting capabilities may be generalized across facets or specialized within facets as a function of similarity relations existing within the population of learning situations experienced by some segment of the person population. In this sense, each capability is a psychological construct interpreting individual cognitive developments in a population of persons, produced by similarities and differences in their respective learning histories and in the organization and functioning of their brains.

It is the result of a particular psychometric history that mental tests and their associated constructs are still sharply distinguished as reflecting "abilities" versus "achievements," interpreted as "total amounts possessed." Any such test is a task inserted into the experiential stream to draw off a sample of what some persons can think and do at a particular point in their development. The task and thus the sample may be simple or complex, broad or narrow, familiar or novel, and may be designed to sample knowledge and skill for which there is a definable instructional program of preparation, or for which there is not. We typically think of "ability" tests as sampling facets not explicitly taught or that transect facets defined by content or common experience, and distinguish crystallized and fluid intelligence using the familiar–novel facet; general and special abilities are distinguished using the broad–narrow and complex–simple facets. We typically think of "achievement" tests designed to sample facets explicitly taught and thus familiar. General and special achievements are distinguished by tests designed to be broad or narrow, whether simple or complex.

However, cognitive psychology is now teaching us that to understand a particular individual's performance on a particular task, one must delve more deeply into its constituents—the configurations of knowledge, skill, understanding, belief, and attitude that underly particular responses. A richer, denser, more sensitive description is especially needed if tests are to be designed for diagnosis and classification in guiding instruction, rather than for summary selection and evaluation purposes only. This would seem to require test theories that use multivariate categorical as well as interval scale indicators and that apply to time series, not just to single-point assessments.

However, the design of test items, the methods by which they are organized into tests, and the rules by which scores are assigned to responses must be guided by the purposes of testing. A test designed to sample factual knowledge in a domain will differ from one designed to identify personal theories, perhaps in the items administered, but more importantly in the way scores are assigned to responses. In other words, the observation design (i.e., the design that describes items, their organization, and the type of response required) and the measurement model (i.e., the rules that describe how performances are scored or classified) both depend on the purposes of testing (i.e., the inferences that will be made from scores). Modern theories of cognition and learning have described new, potentially useful constructs for measurement. Some of these may be defined by summing scores or averaging latencies over items; others, however, require completely different types of measurement models. One of the more important challenges for new test theory and design, then, is to explore the measurement properties of these new scores. The temptation will be to understand these new scores by using familiar statistical and psychometric techniques, but these new scores should also sometimes force us to investigate unfamiliar techniques and to develop new ones.

Psychometric theory and test design might be made to meet the challenges of new understandings and new uses suggested from cognitive psychology by extending from its present bases in particular mathematical models. This is a constructive though conservative response. It might also look for radically different mathematical bases that better fit the shape of these new understandings and uses. We believe that both approaches warrant attention in the years to come, but we emphasize the latter because it remains the minority view.

REFERENCES

Ackerman, P. L. (1987). Individual differences in skill learning: An integration of psychometric and information processing perspectives. *Psychological Bulletin, 102*, 3–27.

Ackerman, P. L. (1989). Individual differences and skill acquisition. In P. L. Ackerman, R. J. Sternberg, & R. Glaser (Eds.), *Learning and individual differences* (pp. 164–217). New York: W. H. Freeman.

14   SNOW AND LOHMAN

Anderson, J. R. (1985). *Cognitive psychology and its implications* (2nd ed.). New York: W. H. Freeman.

Bethell-Fox, C. E., Lohman, D. F., & Snow, R. E. (1984). Adaptive reasoning: Componential and eye movement analysis of geometric analogy performance. *Intelligence, 8,* 205–238.

Brown, A. L., & Campione, J. C. (1986). Psychological theory and the study of learning disabilities. *American Psychologist, 41,* 1059–1068.

Brown, A. L., & Ferrara, R. A. (1985). Diagnosing zones of proximal development. In J. Wertsch (Ed.), *Culture, communication and cognition: Vygotskian perspectives* (pp. 273–305). Cambridge: Cambridge University Press.

Brown, J. S., & Burton, R. R. (1978). Diagnostic models for procedural bugs in basic mathematical skills. *Cognitive Science, 2,* 155–192.

Bunderson, C. V., Inouye, D. K., & Olson, J. B. (1989). The four generations of computerized educational measurement. In R. L. Linn (Ed.), *Educational measurement* (3rd ed., pp. 367–407). New York: Macmillan.

Butterfield, E. C., Nielsen, D., Tangen, K. L., & Richardson, M. B. (1985). Theoretically-based psychometric measures of inductive reasoning. In S. E. Embretson (Ed.), *Test design: Developments in psychology and psychometrics* (pp. 77–148). Orlando, FL: Academic Press.

Campione, J. C., & Brown, A. L. (1984). Learning ability and transfer propensity as sources of individual differences in intelligence. In P. H. Brooks, C. McCauley, & R. Sperber (Eds.), *Learning and cognition in the mentally retarded* (pp. 265–293). Hillsdale, NJ: Lawrence Erlbaum Associates.

Campione, J. C., & Brown, A. L. (1987). Linking dynamic assessment with school achievement. In C. S. Lidz (Ed.), *Dynamic assessment* (pp. 82–115). New York: Guilford Press.

Campione, J. C., & Brown, A. L. (1990). Guided learning and transfer: Implications for approaches to assessment. In N. Frederiksen, R. Glaser, A. Lesgold, & M. Shafto (Eds.), *Diagnostic monitoring of skill and knowledge acquisition* (pp. 141–172). Hillsdale, NJ: Lawrence Erlbaum Associates.

Cronbach, L. J., & Gleser, G. G. (1965). *Psychological tests and personnel decisions.* Urbana, IL: University of Illinois Press.

Cronbach, L. J., Gleser, G., Nanda, H., & Rajaratnam, N. (1972). *The dependability of behavioral measures: Theory of generalizability for scores and profiles.* New York: Wiley.

Dreyfus, H. L., & Dreyfus, S. E. (1986). *Mind over machine.* New York: The Free Press.

Embretson, S. E. (1983). Construct validity: Construct representation versus nomothetic span. *Psychological Bulletin, 93,* 179–197.

Embretson, S. E. (Ed.). (1985). *Test design: Developments in psychology and psychometrics.* New York: Academic Press.

Ferrara, R. A. (1987). *Learning mathematics in the zone of proximal development: The importance of flexible use of knowledge.* Unpublished doctoral dissertation, University of Illinois, Urbana, Champaign.

Frederiksen, J. R. (1981). Sources of process interaction in reading. In A. M. Lesgold & C. A. Perfetti (Eds.), *Interactive processes in reading* (pp. 361–386). Hillsdale, NJ: Lawrence Erlbaum Associates.

Frederiksen, J. R. (1982). A componential theory of reading skills and their interactions. In R. J. Sternberg (Ed.), *Advances in the psychology of human intelligence* (Vol. 1, pp. 125–180). Hillsdale, NJ: Lawrence Erlbaum Associates.

Frederiksen, J. R., Warren, B. M., & Roseberg, A. S. (1985a). A componential approach to training reading skills: Part I. Perceptual units training. *Cognition and Instruction, 2,* 91–130.

Frederiksen, J. R., Warren, B. M., & Roseberg, A. S. (1985b). A componential approach to training reading skills: Part 2. Decoding and use of context. *Cognition and Instruction, 2,* 271–338.

Frederiksen, J. R., & White, B. Y. (1990). Intelligent tutors as intelligent testers. In N. Frederiksen, R. Glaser, A. Lesgold, & M. Shafto (Eds.), *Diagnostic monitoring of skill and knowledge acquisition* (pp. 1–25). Hillsdale, NJ: Lawrence Erlbaum Associates.

Frederiksen, N., Glaser, R., Lesgold, A., & Shafto, M. (1990). *Diagnostic monitoring of skill and knowledge acquisition.* Hillsdale, NJ: Lawrence Erlbaum Associates.

Glaser, R., & Bassok, M. (1989). Learning theory and the study of instruction. *Annual Review of Psychology, 40,* 631–666.

Glaser, R., Lesgold, A., & Lajoie, S. (1987). Toward a cognitive theory for the measurement of achievement. In R. R. Ronning, J. G. Glover, J. C. Conoley, & J. C. Witt (Eds.), *The influence of cognitive psychology on testing and measurement* (pp. 41–85). Hillsdale, NJ: Lawrence Erlbaum Associates.

Greeno, J. G. (1986, April). *Mathematical cognition: Accomplishments and challenges in research.* Invited address to the American Educational Research Association, San Francisco.

Greeno, J. G. (1989). Situations, mental models, and generative knowledge. In D. Klahr & K. Kotovsky (Eds.), *Complex information processing: The impact of Herbert A. Simon* (pp. 285–318). Hillsdale, NJ: Lawrence Erlbaum Associates.

Greeno, J. G., & Mayer, R. E. (1975). *Structural and quantitative interaction among aptitudes and instructional treatments.* Unpublished manuscript, University of Michigan, Ann Arbor.

Humphreys, L. G. (1985). General intelligence: An integration of factor, test, and simplex theory. In B. B. Wolman (Ed.), *Handbook of intelligence: Theories, measurements, and applications* (pp. 331–360). New York: Wiley-Interscience.

Hunt, E. (1985a). Cognitive research and future test design. In E. E. Freeman (Ed.), *The redesign of testing for the 21st century* (pp. 9–24). Princeton, NJ: Educational Testing Service.

Hunt, E. (1985b). Verbal ability. In R. J. Sternberg (Eds.), *Human abilities: An information-processing approach* (pp. 31–58). New York: W. H. Freeman.

Hunt, E., & Lansman, M. (1982). Individual differences in attention. In R. J. Sternberg (Ed.), *Advances in the psychology of human abilities* (Vol. 1, pp. 207–254). Hillsdale, NJ: Lawrence Erlbaum Associates.

Ippel, M. J. & Beem, L. A. (1987). A theory of antagonistic strategies. In E. DeCorte, H. Lodewijks, R. Parmentier, & P. Span (Eds.), *Learning and instruction: European research in an international context* (Vol. 1, pp. 111–121). Oxford, UK: Pergamon Press.

Kyllonen, P. C., Lohman, D. F., & Woltz, D. J. (1984). Componential modeling of alternative strategies for performing spatial tasks. *Journal of Educational Psychology, 76,* 1325–1345.

Kyllonen, P. C., & Shute, V. J. (1989). A taxonomy of learning skills. In P. L. Ackerman, R. J. Sternberg, & R. Glaser (Eds.), *Learning and individual differences* (pp. 117–163). New York: W. H. Freeman.

Lesgold, A. (1988). Toward a theory of curriculum for use in designing intelligent instructional system. In H. Mandl & A. Lesgold (Eds.), *Learning issues for intelligent tutoring systems* (pp. 114–137). New York: Springer-Verlag.

Lesgold, A., Bonar, J., & Ivill, J. (1987). *Toward intelligent systems for testing* (Tech. Rep. No. LSP-1). Pittsburgh: University of Pittsburgh, Learning Research and Development Center.

Lohman, D. F. (1988). Spatial abilities as traits, processes, and knowledge. In R. J. Sternberg (Ed.), *Advances in the psychology of human intelligence* (Vol. 4, pp. 181–248). Hillsdale, NJ: Lawrence Erlbaum Associates.

Lohman, D. F. (1989a). Human intelligence: An introduction to advances in theory and research. *Review of Educational Research, 59,* 333–373.

Lohman, D. F. (1989b). Individual differences in errors and latencies on cognitive tasks. *Learning and Individual Differences, 1,* 179–202.

Mandler, J. M. (1984). *Stories, scripts, and scenes: Aspects of schematic theory.* Hillsdale, NJ: Lawrence Erlbaum Associates.

Marshalek, B. (1981). *Trait and process aspects of vocabulary knowledge and verbal ability* (Tech. Rep. No. 15). Stanford, CA: Stanford University, Aptitude Research Project, School of Education. (NTIS No. AD-A102 757)

Marshall, S. P. (1988). *Assessing schema knowledge* (Tech. Rep.). San Diego, CA: San Diego State University, Center for Research in Mathematics and Science Education.

Marton, F., (1983). Beyond individual differences. *Educational Psychology, 3,* 291–305.

McKeachie, W. J., Pintrich, P. R., & Lin, Y-G. (1985). Teaching learning strategies. *Educational Psychologist, 20,* 153–160.

Messick, S. J. (1989). Validity. In R. L. Linn (Ed.), *Educational measurement* (3rd ed., pp. 13–103). New York: Macmillan.

Mislevy, R. J., & Verhelst, N. (1986). *Modeling item responses when different subjects employ different solution strategies.* Princeton, NJ: Educational Testing Service.

Murphy, J., & Bunderson, C. V. (1988). *An update on the concepts and status of mastery assessment systems.* Princeton, NJ: Educational Testing Service.

Naveh-Benjamin, M., McKeachie, W. J., Lin, Y-G., & Tucker, D. G. (1986). Inferring students' cognitive structures and their development using the "Ordered Tree Technique." *Journal of Educational Psychology, 78,* 130–140.

Norman, D. (1982). *Learning and memory.* San Francisco: W. H. Freeman.

O'Neil, H. F. Jr. (Ed.). (1978). *Learning strategies.* New York: Academic Press.

O'Neil, H. F., Jr. & Spielberger, C. D. (Eds.). (1979). *Cognitive and affective learning strategies.* New York: Academic Press.

Pask, G. (1976). Styles and strategies of learning. *British Journal of Educational Psychology, 46,* 128–148.

Pellegrino, J. W., & Glaser, R. (1982). Analyzing aptitudes for learning: Inductive reasoning. In R. Glaser (Ed.), *Advances in instructional psychology* (Vol. 2, pp. 269–345). Hillsdale, NJ: Lawrence Erlbaum Associates.

Pines, A. L., Novak, J. D., Posner, G. J., & Van Kirk, J. (1978). *The clinical interview: A method for evaluating cognitive structure* (Res. Rep. No. 6). Ithaca, NY: Cornell University, Department of Education.

Resnick, L. B. (1984). Beyond error analysis: The role of understanding in elementary school arithmetic. In H. N. Cheek (Ed.), *Diagnostic and prescriptive mathematics: Issues, ideas and insights* (1984 Research Monograph, pp. 2–14). Kent, OH: Research Council for Diagnosis and Prescriptive Mathematics Research.

Rogosa, D. (1991). A longitudinal approach to ATI research: Models for individual growth and models for individual differences in response to instruction. In R. E. Snow & D. E. Wiley (Eds.), *Improving inquiry in social science: A volume in honor of Lee J. Cronbach* (pp. 221–248). Hillsdale, NJ: Lawrence Erlbaum Associates.

Schaeffer, E. L. (1991). *Understanding context effects: Test-taker processes and test situation demands.* Unpublished doctoral dissertation, Stanford University, Stanford, CA.

Snow, R. E. (1981). Toward a theory of aptitude for learning: Fluid and crystalized abilities and their correlates. In M. P. Friedman, J. P. Das, & N. O'Connor (Eds.), *Intelligence and learning* (pp. 345–362). New York: Plenum.

Snow, R. E. (1988). Progress in measurement, cognitive science and technology that can change the relation between instruction and assessment. In E. E. Freeman (Ed.), *Assessment in the service of learning: Proceedings of the 1987 ETS Invitational Conference* (pp. 9–25). Princeton, NJ: Educational Testing Service.

Snow, R. E. (1989). Toward assessment of cognitive and conative structures in learning. *Educational Researcher, 18*(9), 8–14.

Snow, R. E. (1990). New approaches to cognitive and conative assessment in education. *International Journal of Educational Research, 14,* 455–473.

Snow, R. E. (1991). The concept of aptitude. In R. E. Snow & D. E. Wiley (Eds.) *Improving inquiry in social science: A volume in honor of Lee J. Cronbach* (pp. 249–284). Hillsdale, NJ: Lawrence Erlbaum Associates.

Snow, R. E., Kyllonen, P. C., & Marshalek, B. (1984). The topography of ability and learning correlations. In R. J. Sternberg (Ed.), *Advances in the psychology of human intelligence* (Vol. 2, pp. 47–104). Hillsdale, NJ: Lawrence Erlbaum Associates.

Snow, R. E., & Lohman, D. F. (1984). Toward a theory of cognitive aptitude for learning from instruction. *Journal of Educational Psychology, 76,* 347–376.

Snow, R. E., & Lohman, D. F. (1989). Implications of cognitive psychology for educational measurement. In R. Linn (Ed.), *Educational measurement* (3rd ed., pp. 263–331). New York: Macmillan.

Snow, R. E., & Mandinach, E. B. (1991). Integrating assessment and instruction: A research and development agenda (Research Rep. No. RR-91-8). Princeton, NJ: Educational Testing Service.

Sternberg, R. J. (1985a). *Beyond IQ: A triarchic theory of human intelligence.* Cambridge: Cambridge University Press.

Sternberg, R. J. (1985b). Cognitive approaches to intelligence. In B. B. Wolman (Ed.), *Handbook of intelligence: Theories, measurements, and applications* (pp. 59–118). New York: Wiley-Interscience.

Sternberg, R. J. (1986). *Intelligence applied.* Orlando, FL: Harcourt Brace Jovanovich.

Sternberg, R. J., & Powell, J. S. (1983). Comprehending verbal comprehension. *American Psychologist, 38,* 878–893.

Sternberg, R. J., & Weil, E. M. (1980). An aptitude-strategy interaction in linear syllogistic reasoning. *Journal of Educational Psychology, 72,* 226–234.

Strauss, S. (Ed.). (1988). *Ontogeny, phylogeny, and historical development.* Norwood, NJ: Ablex.

Van der Linden, W. J. (1981). Using aptitude measurements for the optimal assignment of subjects to treatments with and without mastery scores. *Psychometrika, 46,* 257–274.

Van der Linden, W. J. (1984). *The use of test scores for classification decisions with threshold utility.* Unpublished report, Twente University of Technology, Enschede, The Netherlands.

Weinstein, C. E., Goetz, E. T., & Alexander, P. A. (Eds.). (1988). *Learning and study strategies.* San Diego, CA: Academic Press.

2

Foundations of a New Test Theory

Robert J. Mislevy
Educational Testing Service

It is only a slight exaggeration to describe the test theory that dominates educational measurement today as the application of 20th century statistics to 19th century psychology. Sophisticated estimation procedures, new techniques for missing-data problems, and theoretical advances into latent-variable modeling have appeared—all applied with psychological models that explain problem-solving ability in terms of a single, continuous variable. This caricature suffices for many practical prediction and selection problems because it expresses patterns in data that are pertinent to the decisions that must be made. It falls short for placement and instruction problems based on students' internal representations of systems, problem-solving strategies, or reconfigurations of knowledge as they learn. Such applications demand different caricatures of ability—more realistic ones that can express patterns suggested by recent developments in cognitive and educational psychology. The application of modern statistical methods with modern psychological models constitutes the foundation of a new test theory.

INTRODUCTION

Educational measurement faces today a crisis that would appear to threaten its very foundations. The essential problem is that the view of human abilities implicit in standard test theory—item response theory as well as classical true-score theory—is incompatible with the view rapidly emerging from cognitive and educational psychology. Learners increase their competence not by simply

19

accumulating new facts and skills, but by reconfiguring their knowledge structures, by automating procedures and chunking information to reduce memory loads, and by developing strategies and models that tell them when and how facts and skills are relevant. The types of observations and the patterns in data that reflect the ways that students think, perform, and learn cannot be accommodated by traditional models and methods. To some it would seem that psychometrics has little to offer in the quest to apply this new knowledge to the practical educational problems of the individual, the classroom, or the nation (Hunt & MacLeod, 1978).

I concur that the standard methods of test theory do not suffice for solving many problems cast in the framework of what we are learning about how people acquire knowledge and competence. I cannot agree that psychometrics has nothing to offer.

Standard test theory evolved as the application of statistical theory with a simple model of ability that supports important selection and placement decisions that are common in mass educational systems. Broader educational options, based on insights into the nature of learning and supported by more powerful technologies, demand a broader range of models of capabilities—still simple compared to the realities of cognition, but capturing patterns that inform a broader range of alternatives. A new test theory can be brought about by applying to well-chosen cognitive models the same general principles of statistical inference that led to standard test theory when applied to the simple model.

The first half of this chapter sketches the evolution of standard test theory, highlighting the challenges that spurred each new advance. The challenges that cognitive and educational psychology present today are then discussed, and a framework for responding to that challenge is outlined. Directions for needed development are exemplified with current work.

THE EARLY CONTEXT
OF EDUCATIONAL DECISIONS

The kinds of decisions that shaped the evolution of classical test theory were nearly universal in education at the beginning of this century, and dominate practice yet today. They were born of the constraints educators encountered as they launched their campaign to provide education on a broader scale than had ever been attempted hitherto:

the demand for tests arose during the period when school attendance was made compulsory and when higher education was developing its strengths. Educators faced the unprecedented dilemma of dealing with the range and diversity of abilities and backgrounds that individuals bring to schooling. They needed ways of determining which children and youths would be able to profit from some form of instruction as given in ordinary school and college practices as designed essentially for the majority of the population. (Glaser, 1981, p. 924)

Educators were confronted with selection or placement decisions for large numbers of students. Resources limited the information they could gather about each student, constrained the number of options they could offer, and precluded tailoring programs to individual students once a decision was made.

A first example is selecting applicants into a college that presents the same material in the same way to all students. There is only one treatment, and the alternatives are to accept or reject. It is preferable to accept those who are likely to succeed. When resources permit more than one decision option, the usual generalization of the accept/reject paradigm is to offer a sequence of alternatives, each more demanding than the next. Placing high school freshmen into academic tracks is an example of this latter type. Problems of selection into a single program and of placement into a single sequence are both decisions about *linearly ordered options*; that is, the options are ordered with respect to their demands or their skill and/or knowledge prerequisites.

Exposing a diverse group of students to a uniform educational treatment typically produces a distribution of outcomes (Bloom, 1976). An individual's degree of success depends on how his or her unique skills, knowledge, and interests match up with the equally multifaceted requirements of the treatment.

At costs substantially lower than personal interviews or performance samples, responses to multiple-choice test items provide information about certain aspects of this matchup. What is necessary is that each item tap some of the skills required for success. Even though a single item might require only a few of the relevant skills and offer little information in its own right, a tendency to provide correct answers over a large number of items supports some degree of prediction of success (Green, 1978). If all candidates are administered the same items, and one wishes to predict success in linearly ordered options, their number-correct scores can be used (Dawes & Corrigan, 1974). Even though the several students at a given score level possess different constellations of skills, abilities, and backgrounds, making the same decision for all of them among the available alternatives is often about as well as can be done with the available data (see Cronbach & Gleser, 1965, on the theory of personnel decision making in this context).

Once the test and the linearly ordered options are specified, making decisions from test performances requires nothing more complicated than adding up numbers of correct responses. Two different tests constructed for the same decision, however, invariably line up examinees differently as they draw upon different particular skills from the myriad of those potentially informative. Additional statistical machinery is required to guide one in constructing tests and evaluating their quality. Classical test theory was a first response to these needs.

CLASSICAL TEST THEORY

Charles Spearman (1904a, 1904b, 1907, 1910, 1913) is generally credited with the central idea of classical test theory (CTT): a test score can be viewed as the sum of two components, a true score and a random error term. Two similar parallel tests are considered to reflect the same true score, but disagree about an examinee's observed scores because of the error components—the variance of which can, under the assumptions of CTT, be driven to zero by just making the tests long enough. Ideally decisions would be based on true scores; in practice they must be based on observed scores. *Reliability*, the degree to which the unobservable true scores account for the variance in observed scores, gauges the accuracy with which a test lines up a group of examinees—a reasonable criterion for the quality of a test if it is assumed that the items tap appropriate skills and scores will be used to decide among linearly ordered options.

Upon these notions was founded a practicable testing methodology. Reliability became a paramount measure of the quality of a test, although of course reliability had to be complemented with validity measures such as the correlation between test scores and subsequent performance. Validity studies had less influence on test construction, however, because they arrive too late in the process—only after the test has been administered and examinees have been followed over time. To obtain high reliability, one uses items that would be answered correctly by about half the examinees, for example, and avoids items that would have low correlations with the total test scores.

Note that these dicta could guide test construction solely from counts and patterns of right and wrong responses to candidate test items—ignoring both the content of the items and the contemplated decision alternatives. Of course, good test construction does consider the knowledge, skill, and strategy requirements of items. The point is that these considerations lie outside the realm of the classical test theory. Test developers use them independently of, and sometimes in contradiction to, what test theory tells them.

Building upon Spearman's foundation, psychometricians developed a vast armamentarium of techniques for building and using tests (Gulliksen, 1950), such as approximating reliability from the internal consistency of items within a test (Kuder & Richardson, 1937) and estimating validity without knowing subsequent performances of rejected examinees (Kelley, 1923). Over time, a rigorous axiomatic foundation was laid for statistical inference under the aegis of CTT (Lord, 1959; Novick, 1966; Lord & Novick, 1968). The simple partitioning of observed scores into true and error components was generalized to multiple sources of variation from items, persons, and observational settings, and the full power of analysis of variance was brought to bear upon decision-making problems using test scores (Cronbach, Gleser, Nanda, & Rajaratnam, 1972; Lord & Novick, 1968).

A source of dissatisfaction with CTT early on was that its characterizations of examinees, such as total score and percentile rank, and of items, such as percent-correct and item-test correlation, are confounded descriptions of the particular items that constitute a test and a particular group of examinees who takes it (Wright, 1968). If one test consists of easier items than a second otherwise similar test, examinees' scores on the two tests are not directly comparable and score distributions have different shapes. If a test is administered to groups of examinees that differ in proficiency, item percents-correct and item-test correlations differ. When many tests could be constructed for the same purpose, differing perhaps in difficulty or length, should not there be a way to characterize examinees independently of the test they took, and items independently of the examinees who took them?

In attitude measurement, where agreements to a topic are analogous to correct answers to test questions, L. L. Thurstone (1928) expressed the following desideratum: "If a scale is to be regarded as valid, the scale values of the statements should not be affected by the opinions of the people [whose responses] help to construct it." Thurstone (1925) and E. L. Thorndike (Thorndike, Bregman, Cobb & Woodyard, 1926) pioneered efforts to relate test scores to psychological traits, using item percents-correct and assumptions about distributions of traits to transform scores from different tests onto the same scale.

Thurstone and Thorndike scaling, despite allusions to an underlying trait, remained essentially theories for scores, albeit transformed (with the aid of untestable assumptions) to permit comparisons across nonparallel tests. Psychological traits per se appear as explicit parameters in the models of Ferguson (1942), Lawley (1943), and Tucker (1946). These researchers studied test construction problems within CTT by making an assumption beyond those of CTT proper: namely, that aside from random factors, item responses were driven by a unobservable ability variable. A second generation of test theory began to take form as attention shifted from test scores per se as the object of inference, to unobservable variables hypothesized to have produced them.

ITEM RESPONSE THEORY

Item response theory (IRT), or "latent trait theory," as it was called at the time, appears as a test theory in its own right in the work of Frederic Lord (1952) and Georg Rasch (1960). Like classical test theory, IRT concerns examinees' overall proficiency in a domain of tasks. Whereas CTT makes no statement about the genesis of performance, IRT posits a single, unobservable, proficiency variable.

At the heart of IRT is a mathematical model for the probability that a given person will respond correctly to a given item, a function of that person's proficiency parameter and one or more parameters for the item. The item's parameters express properties such as difficulty or sensitivity to proficiency. The item response, rather than the test score, is the fundamental unit of observation. If an IRT model holds, responses to any subset of items support inferences on the same scale of measurement.

This conceptualization opens the door to solving many practical testing problems that were difficult under CTT, such as:

- Test construction (Birnbaum, 1968; Theunissen, 1985). If item parameters are available for a collection of items, tests can be constructed for optimal performance in specific applications, such as minimizing classification errors in the context of linearly ordered options.
- Adaptive testing (Lord, 1980, Chapter 10; Weiss, 1984). An adaptive testing scheme selects the best item to administer next to an examinee, based on the amount of information that various available items would provide and a provisional estimate of the examinee's proficiency from responses to items given thus far.
- Large-scale educational assessment (Bock, Mislevy, & Woodson, 1982; Choppin, 1976; Messick, Beaton, & Lord, 1983). Large-scale educational assessments gauge proficiencies at the level of populations rather than individuals, to evaluate programs and monitor trends. IRT makes it possible to establish a stable measurement scale while allowing assessment instruments to evolve over time.

This work assumed, for the most part, that the IRT model was known and correct, and that true values or accurate estimates of item parameters were available. Current IRT research emphasizes integrating IRT into the general framework of statistical inference, and acquiring an understanding of just when and how IRT models are appropriate.

STATISTICAL INFERENCE
IN ITEM RESPONSE THEORY

Early applications of IRT were designed more to demonstrate its potential than to solve actual measurement problems. Data were gathered with tests written according to CTT dicta; the same long tests were administered to many examinees, and each item had passed CTT quality checks. Illustrative purposes were served adequately by rough estimation procedures that treat point estimates of examinee and item parameters as if they were the parameters themselves, ignoring the uncertainty associated with the estimates. These approximations break down when IRT is applied beyond the usual limits of CTT testing, as when examinees are presented only, say 15 items in adaptive testing or five in educational assessments (Mislevy, 1991). In response, IRT researchers have turned to two active lines of research in statistics: missing data methods and Bayesian estimation.

Missing data methods are relevant because a latent variable such as an IRT examinee proficiency parameter can be viewed as a datum whose value is missing for everyone. General results on estimating parameters when some data are missing, such as Dempster, Laird, and Rubin's (1977) EM algorithm, have led to methods of item parameter estimation that are at once rigorous and efficient (e.g., Bock & Aitkin, 1980; Tsutakawa, 1984). Results on statistical information in missing data problems yield insights into the uncertainty structures of IRT parameters (Mislevy & Sheehan, 1989; Mislevy & Wu, 1988) and offer ways of increasing accuracy by exploiting collateral information about items and examinees (Mislevy, 1987, 1988).

The Bayesian perspective confronts uncertainty head on, expressing what is known about parameters as probability distributions. When these distributions are concentrated, the expedient of using point estimates as if they were the true parameters can give acceptable results in subsequent analyses. However, when the distributions are diffuse, one must propagate the uncertainty into subsequent analyses to obtain correct inferences. Statistical reasoning along these lines was proposed as far back as 1927 by Kelley (1927), and championed by Novick in the 1970s (e.g., Novick & Jackson, 1974), but only now are the ideas gaining currency. In this framework, one can determine when the standard, simpler, approximations suffice, but use (admittedly more complex) correct analyses when they don't. For examples in IRT estimation problems, see Bock and Aitkin (1981) on item parameters, Mislevy (1984) on proficiency distributions, and Tsutakawa and Soltys (1988) on individuals' proficiencies.

THE QUESTION OF MODEL FIT

Of course, the IRT model is never exactly correct. A single variable that accounts for all nonrandomness in examinees' responses is not a serious representation of cognition, but a caricature that can solve applied problems when it captures the patterns that are salient to the job. The pattern that CTT and IRT can capture is examinees' tendencies to give correct responses, which can usefully inform decisions about linearly ordered alternatives. IRT was a practical advance beyond CTT because it provides information about overall proficiencies in more flexible ways. It was a conceptual advance because it provides a framework for detecting anomalies in the ''overall proficiency'' paradigm. This can be illustrated with Rasch's (1960) model for right/wrong items, supposing for convenience all examinees are presented the same test. Under CTT, all examinees with a given total score would be treated alike. Under the Rasch model, all examinees with the same score would receive the same ability estimate, and might also be treated alike—depending on an analysis of model fit. Combining an examinee's proficiency estimate with an items' difficulty estimate, the Rasch model states how likely a correct response would be if the single-proficiency conception of ability were true. The items that high scorers missed should usually be hard ones, and the items low scorers got right should be easy ones. Finding that these patterns hold supports making the same decisions about people with same scores, because, to an approximation, they got the same items right and the same ones wrong. Total scores, and thus Rasch ability estimates, convey nearly everything these data have to say about comparing these examinees.

To the extent that high-scoring examinees miss items that are generally easy and low-scoring examinees get hard ones right, neither total scores nor IRT ability estimates may be capturing all the systematic information in the data. Analyses of an individual's unexpected responses can reveal misconceptions or atypical patterns of learning (Mead, 1976; Smith, 1986; Tatsuoka, 1983). To understand these patterns one must look beyond the simple universe of the IRT model—to the content of the items, the structure of the learning area, the pedagogy of the discipline, and the psychology of the problem-solving tasks the items demand.

Now, patterns in responses other than overall level proficiency can have educational and psychological meaning but yet hold no salience for a particular decision. If overall proficiency in a domain of items suffices for a particular decision, as can be the case with linearly ordered educational options, cross-current patterns constitute data variation that need not be explicated. This is the essence of statistical modeling: expressing the patterns that are dominant and meaningful in terms of model parameters, and allowing for departures from these patterns in terms of distributions of residuals. However, if the decision does depend on the cross-current patterns, in addition to or instead of overall proficiency, neither CTT nor standard IRT may be the right tool for the job.

The issue of model fit, then, is more pragmatic than statistical, since lack of fit must be judged in practice by the nature and the magnitude of the errors it causes. An IRT model might be satisfactory for selecting honors math students, for example, if people with similar scores have similar chances of success—even though examinees with similar scores have different profiles of skills and knowledge. The profile differences could be modeled as "noise" without harm for the selection decision—but probably not for advising individual examinees which topics to study to maximally increase their scores.

Measuring learning is one application where IRT models can fail, because their characterization is complete for only a highly constrained type of change: an examinee's chances of success on all items must increase or decrease by exactly the same amount (in an appropriate metric). A single IRT model applied to pretest and posttest data cannot reveal how different students learn different topics to different degrees—patterns that could be at the crux of an instructional decision.

TESTING AND LEARNING

Making good "macro-level" decisions to place students into appropriate educational programs is the traditional route to increasing the quality of education, but it is neither the only nor necessarily the best way to do so. Tracking individual students as they progress opens the door to finer-grained micro-level decisions to enhance learning along the way. Good decision making at this level requires an inferential framework built around an understanding of how students learn.

A picture of a learner that is consistent with standard test theory is that of a collector of facts and skills, adding each to his repertoire more or less independently of others. Recent developments in psychology sketch a markedly different picture, reflecting the astounding capabilities and the surprising limitations of the mind—lightning-fast recognition of stored patterns and creative applications of heuristic strategies, on the one hand, yet with short-term memory capacities of only about seven elements and an inability to perform more than one attention-demanding task at a time. Performance is to be understood through the availability of well-practiced procedures that no longer demand high levels of attention (*automaticity*); strategies by which actions are selected, monitored, and, when necessary, switched (*metacognitive skills*); and the mental structures that relate facts and skills (*schemas*). Learning is to be understood through the automatization of procedures; the acquisition and enhancement of metacognitive skills; and the construction, revision, and replacement of schemas.

Comparing the performances of novices and experts offers insights into the nature of performance and learning. A first, unsurprising, difference is that experts command more facts and concepts than novices, and have richer interconnections among them. Interconnections overcome limitations of short-term memory; while the novice may work with seven distinct elements, the expert works with seven constellations that embody relationships among many elements ("chunking"). Moreover, experts often organize their knowledge in schemas possessing not simply more connections, but qualitatively different ones. The advanced concepts that college physics students acquire, for example, can be organized around informal associations or naive misconceptions (Caramazza, McCloskey, & Green, 1981). These novices tackle physics problems in less effective ways than expert physicists, whose more appropriate schemas lead them to the crux of the matter (Chi, Feltovich, & Glaser, 1981). Experts also differ from novices by having automatized, through study and practice, procedures that were once slow and attention-consuming, allowing them to focus on novel aspects of a problem, look from different perspectives, and more efficiently monitor and guide their efforts as they work (Lesgold & Perfetti, 1978). The challenge to education is to discover what experiences help a learner with a given configuration of propositions, skills, and connections to reconfigure that knowledge into a more powerful arrangement. Vosniadou and Brewer (1987) point to Socratic dialogue and analogy as mechanisms that facilitate such learning. To apply them effectively, one must take into account not simply target configurations, such as the experts' model, but the individual learners' current configurations. The challenge to test theory is to provide models and methods to assess knowledge, and to guide instruction, as seen in this new light.

To what extent can standard test theory meet this challenge? Recall that standard test theory characterizes performance only as to overall level of proficiency, and learning only as to change in overall proficiency. Cronbach and Furby (1970) note the inadequacy of such measures of change when applied with conventional broad range educational tests:

> Even when [test scores] X and Y are determined by the same operation [e.g., scored in accordance with the same CTT or IRT model], they often do not represent the same psychological processes (Lord, 1958). At different stages of practice or development different processes contribute to performance of a task. Nor is this merely a matter of increased complexity; some processes drop out, some remain but contribute nothing to individual differences within an age group, some are replaced by qualitatively different processes. (p. 76)

Standard test scores can be connected more closely with cognition if they summarize performance over only tasks that are very homogeneous in their requirements (Glaser, 1963), and this specificity marked the criterion-referenced testing movement of the 1960s and 1970s. Merely defining testing areas very narrowly, however, is not sufficient to make test scores instructionally relevant (Glaser, 1981). A list of scores in narrowly defined areas ignores the interconnections among scores induced by the knowledge, skills, and strategies they tap in pairs, in triples, or in hierarchies of the specific behaviors—yet it is at just this level that instructional relevance must be sought.

NEW TESTS, NEW TEST THEORY

A learner's state of competence at a given point in time is a complex constellation of facts and concepts, and the networks that interconnect them; of automatized procedures and conscious heuristics, and their relationships to knowledge patterns that signal their relevance; of perspectives and strategies, and the management capabilities by which the learner focuses his efforts.

There is no hope of providing a complete description of such a state. Neither is there a need to. But the new pedagogy does need to identify communalities among states of competence that can be linked to instructional actions that facilitate changes to preferable states. Distinctions need not be made among all possible states, but only among classes of states with different instructional implications (extending Cronbach & Snow's [1977] Aptitude-by-Treatment Interaction theory). The new tests to inform instructional decisions do need to present tasks that learners in the different states are likely to carry out in observably different ways: not only correctly as opposed to incorrectly, but perhaps at what speed, with what intermediate products, or with which incorrect response; not simply as independent pieces of information from distinct items, but in patterns of similarity, dissimilarity, or independence across tasks that probe knowledge structures and problem-solving strategies. And the new test theory does need to provide models whose parameters are capable of expressing the salient patterns, and inferential procedures upon which to base instructional decisions in the presence of uncertainty.

Foundations of the new pedagogy are to be found in the union of analyses of key concepts in a substantive area, research into the cognitive psychology of the area, and detailed observations of learners as they progress. Greeno (1976) argues that the tools and the perspectives of cognitive and educational psychology have developed to a point at which they can be used to generate instructional objectives in this manner. He provides detailed illustrations in three substantive domains at increasing levels of complexity and sophistication: fourth-grade fractions, high-school geometry, and college-level auditory psychophysics.

Foundations of the new theory of test construction are similarly to be found in educational and cognitive psychology (Embretson, 1985a; Messick, 1984). Standard vocabulary items suffice to ascertain the breadth of a learner's familiarity with concepts in a substantive area, but tasks based on analogies probe the interconnections among concepts. Speed of response is more informative than correctness about the automaticity of procedures, and is hence a better guide to assigning additional practice on a currently conscious process. Designing appropriate measures demands familiarity with the substantive field, not just about the knowledge structures of the expert but about the incomplete or inaccurate structures novices often use. For an overview of how the requisite cognitive and substantive analyses might be carried out, and how tasks that differentiate among learners at different states of competence might then be constructed, the reader is referred to Snow and Lohman (1989). Specific examples can be found in Curtis and Glaser (1983) concerning reading achievement, and in Marshall (1985) concerning "story problems" in arithmetic.

Foundations of the new test theory are to be found in the general principles that led to the development of item response theory. The examinee will be characterized by parameters that express tendencies to act in accordance with the various continuous levels or discrete states in simplified models of cognition. Tasks will be characterized by parameters that indicate the extent to which they tap different aspects of knowledge structures, procedures, or strategies. As in IRT, individual differences among examinees that are not salient to the decision will be modeled as random—this not as a psychologically tenable assertion, but as a practically useful expedient.

Beyond "Low-to-High Proficiency"

The breadth of problems to which standard test theoretic models have been usefully employed, despite their limited low-to-high conception of proficiency, suggests a certain robustness of modeling. It is not necessary that models account for all possible ways students might approach a test, but it is necessary that they can capture instructionally relevant patterns. A test must be designed to highlight the pertinent patterns, and analyzed with a model capable of expressing them.

The idea of building test items around cognitive principles can be traced back at least as far as to Guttman's facet design tests (Guttman, 1970). Guttman worked out analytic methods for analyzing data from such tests within the framework of classical test theory. Scheiblechner (1972) and Fischer (1973), with their "linear logistic test model," expressed item difficulty parameters in the Rasch IRT model as functions of psychologically salient features of test items, but still characterized examinees in terms of overall proficiency. More recently, test theory models built around patterns other than overall proficiency have begun to appear in the psychometric literature.

"Tectonic plate" Models. Increasing competence in a substantive area need not be reflected as uniformly increasing chances of success on all tasks. Patterns of smooth increase may be observed for certain people on certain sets of tasks, in certain phases of development; standard test theory will give good summaries of change in these neighborhoods. Discontinuous patterns of change begin to appear as the scope of tasks becomes broader, as the range of development becomes greater, and as the range of experiences of examinees becomes more diverse. *Tectonic plate* models generalize IRT by allowing for a limited number of predetermined, theory-driven discontinuities in item response patterns. In tectonic plate geological models, points within a given land mass, or plate, maintain their relative positions, but the plates move with respect to one another. In tectonic plate psychometric models, items tapping the same set of skills maintain their difficulties relative to one another, but the difficulties of the *groups* of items change with respect to other groups as learners acquire new skills or concepts.

Wilson's (1985, 1989) Saltus model extends the Rasch IRT model to development with discontinuous jumps. An example is Siegler's (1981) rule-learning analysis of balance-beam tasks, where students can increase their competence either by using the rules they know more effectively (continuous change) or by learning new rules (discontinuous change). Sometimes students who learn a new rule begin to miss a type of problem they used to get right, because their previous, less complete, set of rules gave the right answers for the wrong reasons. This pattern flouts standard test theory. The Saltus model assumes that each examinee is in one of a number of unobservable stages of development. Items are classified so that all items in a class have the same relationship to developmental stages. One set of item parameters expresses relative difficulties among items *within* item classes, which, like Rasch item difficulty parameters, are the same for people in all stages. A second set of parameters quantifies patterns that the Rasch model cannot express: differences in relative difficulties *between* item classes for people in different stages, such as the difficulty reversals mentioned above. Saltus is effectively a mixture of standard Rasch models.

Mislevy and Verhelst (1990) discussed mixture models more generally, listing assumptions, laying out general models, and suggesting estimation procedures. They emphasize situations in which different subjects follow different strategies, pointing out that instructional decisions can depend on *how* students solve problems, not just *how many* they solve. The salient features of items are those that can differentiate among users of different strategies, mental models, or conceptions about key relationships. An examinee is characterized by the probabilities that she employed the various alternative strategies, and a conditional estimate of proficiency under each. Measurement with such a model can indicate change that is either quantitative (e.g., the examinee employed Strategy A on both occasions, but more effectively at the second) or qualitative (e.g., she used Strategy A before instruction but Strategy B afterward). Despite this beginning step, modeling strategy usage must be extended further, in light of evidence that examinees can switch strategies within the period of observation, often in reaction to characteristics of tasks (see, for example, Kyllonen, Lohman, & Snow, 1984)

Latent Class Models. Although models with continuous latent variables have dominated educational measurement, Lazarsfeld (1950) introduced models with categorical latent variables nearly half a century ago. Most educational applications of latent class models have been in "mastery" testing: one attempts to infer an examinee's unobservable state—master or nonmaster—on the basis of observable responses (Macready & Dayton, 1977, 1980). In the more recent *binary skills* models (Haertel, 1984), examinees are classified in terms of which of a set of skills they possess. This "true" classification is unobservable. Items are classified according to which of the skills they require for solution. This classification is known. Ideally, an examinee would respond correctly to only and exactly those items that require skills he or she possesses. The stochastic parameters of the model reflect departures from this ideal.

Except in the special case of mastery testing, computational constraints have limited applications of latent class models to no more than about 10 items until recently. Information about skill profiles in groups can be gleaned from such data, but individuals' skills could not be inferred accurately. Improved computational procedures have opened the door to applications with 50 or 60 items (e.g., Paulson, 1986; Yamamoto, 1987), and work with structurally similar models in expert systems holds promise of handling much larger problems (Lauritzen & Spiegelhalter, 1988). Progress in this direction is vital to educational applications, because these inferences demand more data than low-to-high proficiency inferences. Moreover, adaptive testing, which made IRT measurement more efficient, will be able to make latent class measurement practicable (Macready & Dayton, 1989; Falmagne & Doignon, 1988).

Componential Models. The models just described were introduced with right/wrong test items, which, if constructed carefully, yield response patterns that differentiate examinees who tackle them in different ways. Richer information can be accumulated if it is possible to track intermediate products of solution. Consider, for example, a situation in which the binary skills model applies. Inferences about skill profiles can be stronger if one can see which subtasks were attempted and their outcomes: overall correctness can result from one sequence of correct operations or another, or a fortuitous mixture of correct and incorrect operations; overall incorrectness can be caused by a poor plan of attack, or a flawed execution of a good plan. Early implementations of these ideas have been worked out by Embretson (1983, 1985b) and Samejima (1983).

All of the models discussed above—tectonic plate, latent class, and componential models—exhibit the same cardinal feature: they support inferences about proficiencies other than just low-to-high ability because, and only because, the user specifies theoretically salient patterns of response other than just less-to-more correct answers. Current implementations require expertise in statistics as well as in the substantive area. Test theory researchers must embed these approaches in generally applicable computer routines, or shells, so that a broader range of users can put them into practice in the substantive areas.

Beyond Right/Wrong, Multiple-Choice Items

Currently, IRT is used predominantly to draw inferences about a low-to-high proficiency variable from responses to multiple-choice test items. The preceding section discussed how, even with multiple-choice data, one can found inferences upon radically different conceptions of proficiency. Inferences can be made yet stronger, and decision making more efficient, if different kinds of data can be collected.

We have mentioned the possibility of exploiting the identity of incorrect responses to multiple-choice items, for when particular misconceptions are probed in more than one item and we wish to infer how an examinee is approaching tasks. IRT models that distinguish among incorrect alternatives have been discussed by Bock (1972), Masters (1982), Samejima (1979), and Thissen and Steinberg (1984). These papers show how to connect observations more complex than right/wrong to the standard psychological model of low-to-high proficiency. The same machinery for the observational aspect of modeling can be used when the psychological aspect is an alternative cognitive model. Embretsen (1983, 1985b) and Masters (Masters & Mislevy, chap. 9, this volume) have taken some initial steps in this direction.

Because data collected on computers can provide response time routinely, response latency can also be exploited. Response latencies are particularly pertinent to inferences about automaticity; a correct answer arrived at through a laborious conscious process can have different instructional implications than the same response obtained through automatized processes. Response latencies can also be used in conjunction with correctness to design items that differentiate among examinees who use different strategies. Many quantitative items in the SAT, for example, can be solved either by a "brute force" calculation or by a simple calculation if a key relationship is recognized; "correct and fast" suggests the insightful solution. Scheiblechner (1985) and Thissen (1983) show how to use response times to measure low-to-high proficiency (also see Lohman, 1989, on the psychology of the speed–accuracy trade-off). Their methods of linking observed responses to expected responses could be applied with an alternative cognitive model for expected responses.

Beyond Tester-Controlled Observational Settings

Traditional educational tests present small, closed-form problems, isolated and packaged more neatly than the problems people encounter in life. Real-world tasks require one to recognize a problem space; to plan strategies, to take initial steps, and gather additional information; and, observing preliminary results, to determine which direction to proceed. Controlling the observational setting in testing to some degree is probably unavoidable in a decision-making system applied routinely to many learners. Controlled simulation tasks strike a compromise between the rigid, tester-controlled observational setting of traditional tests and the wholly unstructured observation of performance in natural settings.

The most work in this area has been carried out in the arena of medical education in the form of patient management problems, or PMPs (Assmann, Hixon, & Kacmarek, 1979). A simulated patient (through a written or oral dialogue, or as a live actor or a computer model) presents the examinee with initial symptoms; the examinee requests tests, considers their results, prescribes treatments, and monitors their effects, generally attempting to identify and treat the initially unknown disease. Despite their appeal as evocators of critical problem-solving skills, PMPs do not seem to provide reliable data from the perspective of standard test theoretic techniques (McGuire, 1985). For the same amount of testing time, reliability coefficients of PMP scores prove disappointingly low compared with multiple-choice tests.

A possible explanation of this result is that standard test theory analyses of PMP data are not looking for the right patterns. They look at simple additive combinations of single outcomes, rather than relationships that might suggest associations among facts in examinees' schema, or indicate the use of effective or ineffective problem-solving strategies. A distinct stream of medical research, however, does address these relationships: "expert systems" that help health care workers with diagnostic problems (e.g., Pope, 1981; Shortliffe, Axline, Buchanan, Merigan, & Cohen, 1973).

An expert system representation of a diagnostic area is built around associations among unobservable disease states, observable symptoms and test results, and outcomes of treatments. Some expert systems express these associations through "fuzzy logic" (Zadeh, 1983) or "belief functions" (Shafer, 1976), but ones based on probabilitistic reasoning (see Pearl, 1988, and Spiegelhalter, 1986) are extensions of the latent class models discussed above. In an educational setting, associations would be delineated among substantive concepts, strategies, observable outcomes, and prescribed instruction (Clancey, 1988). The reader is referred to Mislevy, Yamamoto, and Anacker (in press) for a discussion of this approach to assessing students' knowledge.

There are two levels at which such an approach could be implemented in educational settings. The first appears more amenable to end-of-course or macro-level decision making, while the second seems better suited to an ongoing instructional system.

In the first, simpler, approach, a system is built only for a "correct" model. An examinee's responses are evaluated in terms of their efficacy at each decision point as compared with the best possible action given present information. If scores were also available from a standard multiple-choice test of knowledge, one could distinguish performance problems caused by strategic errors from those caused by knowledge deficiencies.

In the second, more ambitious, approach, not only would a correct expert system be built, but examinees' possibly "inexpert systems" would be inferred. Perhaps the best known example of this type is Anderson's (Anderson & Reiser, 1985) computer-programming tutor. Although more individualized instructional prescriptions can be made in this way, inferring even selected aspects of examinees' schemas and strategies requires far more data than does comparing performance to a fixed expert model. A successful system of this type would probably require a more constrained problem space and more extensive interactions of the learner with the simulation.

CONCLUSION

Einstein's theory of relativity revolutionized physics, but it extended rather than supplanted Newton's laws of motion. Classical mechanics still works just fine for building bridges, planning billiards shots, and figuring out how to stand up from a overstuffed easy chair. And as long as educators are called upon to make the macro-level, linearly ordered decisions that engendered standard test theory, standard test theory will continue to be useful and will continue to be used. Recent developments in technology, however, provide opportunities for decision making at the micro-level more frequently and for larger numbers of students than ever before; recent developments in education and psychology give us conceptions of competence and learning that can be used to guide these decisions.

Researchers in education and psychology have begun to lay the theoretical groundwork to link testing with the cognitive processes of learning. Meanwhile, researchers in measurement and statistics have made breakthroughs in inferential procedures for the models of standard test theory. To inform modern educational decisions requires drawing together the insights from these two strands of research—the twin foundations of a new test theory.

ACKNOWLEDGMENT

This work was supported in part by Contract No. N00014-88-K-0304, R&T 4421552, from the Cognitive Science Program, Cognitive and Neural Sciences Division, Office of Naval Research.

REFERENCES

Anderson, J. R., & Reiser, B. J. (1985). The LISP tutor. *Byte, 10*, 159–175.

Assmann, D. C., Hixon, S. H., & Kacmarek, R. M. (1979). *Clinical simulations for respiratory care workers.* Chicago: Year Book Medical Publishers.

Birnbaum, A. (1968). Some latent trait models and their use in inferring an examinee's ability. In F. M. Lord & M. R. Novick, *Statistical theories of mental test scores* (pp. 395–479). Reading, MA: Addison-Wesley.

Bock, R. D. (1972). Estimating item parameters and latent ability when responses are scored in two or more nominal categories. *Psychometrika, 37*, 29–52.

Bock, R. D., & Aitkin, M. (1981). Marginal maximum likelihood estimation of item parameters: An application of an EM-algorithm. *Psychometrika, 46*, 443–459.

Bock, R. D., Mislevy, R. J., & Woodsen, C. E. M. (1982). The next stage in educational assessment. *Educational Researcher, 11*, 4–11, 16.

Bloom, B. S. (1976). *Human characteristics and school learning.* New York: McGraw-Hill.

Caramazza, A., McCloskey, M., & Green, B. (1981). Naive beliefs in "sophisticated" subjects: Misconceptions about the trajectories of objects. *Cognition, 9*, 117–123.

Chi, M. T. H., Feltovich, P., & Glaser, R. (1981). Categorization and representation of physics problems by experts and novices. *Cognitive Science, 5*, 121–152.

Choppin, B. (1976). Recent developments in item banking. In D. N. de Gruijter & L. J. van der Kamp (Eds.), *Advances in psychological and educational measurement* (pp. 233–245). London: Wiley.

Clancey, W. J. (1988). The role of qualitative models in instruction. In J. Self (Ed.), *Artificial intelligence and human learning: Intelligent computer-aided instruction* (pp. 49–68). London: Chapman and Hall.

Cronbach, L. J., & Furby, L. (1970). How should we measure "change"—Or should we? *Psychological Bulletin, 74*, 68–80.

Cronbach, L. J., & Gleser, G. C. (1965). *Psychological tests and personnel decisions* (2nd ed.). Urbana, IL: University of Illinois Press.

Cronbach, L. J., Gleser, G. C., Nanda, H., & Rajaratnam, N. (1972). *The dependability of behavioral measurements: Theory of generalizability for scores and profiles.* New York: Wiley.

Cronbach, L. J., & Snow, R. E. (1977). *Aptitudes and instructional methods: A handbook for research on interactions.* New York: Irvington.

Curtis, M.E., & Glaser, R. (1983). Reading theory and the assessment of reading achievement. *Journal of educational measurement, 20,* 133–147.

Dawes, R. M., & Corrigan, B. (1974). Linear models in decision making. *Psychological Bulletin, 81,* 95–106.

Dempster, A. P., Laird, N. M., & Rubin, D. B. (1977). Maximum likelihood from incomplete data via the EM algorithm (with discussion). *Journal of the Royal Statistical Society, Series B, 39,* 1–38.

Embretson, S. E. (1983). A general latent trait model for response processes. *Psychometrika, 49,* 175–186.

Embretson, S. E. (Ed.) (1985a). *Test design: Developments in psychology and psychometrics.* Orlando, FL: Academic Press.

Embretson, S. E. (1985b). Multicomponent latent trait models for test design. In S. E. Embretson (Ed.), *Test design: Developments in psychology and psychometrics* (pp. 195–218). Orlando, FL: Academic Press.

Falmagne, J.-C., & Doignon, J.-P. (1988). A class of stochastic procedures for the assessment of knowledge. *British Journal of Mathematical and Statistical Psychology, 41,* 1–23.

Ferguson, G. A. (1942). Item selection by the constant process. *Psychometrika, 7,* 19–29.

Fischer, G. H. (1983). Logistic latent trait models with linear constraints. *Psychometrika, 48,* 3–26.

Glaser, R. (1981). The future of testing: A research agenda for cognitive psychology and psychometrics. *American Psychologist, 36,* 923–936.

Glaser, R. (1963). Instructional technology and the measurement of learning outcomes: Some questions. *American Psychologist, 118,* 519–521.

Green, B. F. (1978). In defense of measurement. *American Psychologist, 33,* 664–670.

Greeno, J. G. (1976). Cognitive objectives of instruction: Theory of knowledge for solving problems and answering questions. In D. Klahr (Ed.), *Cognition and instruction* (pp. 123–159). Hillsdale, NJ: Lawrence Erlbaum Associates.

Gulliksen, H. (1950). *Theory of mental tests.* New York: Wiley.

Guttman, L. (1970). Integration of test design and analysis. *Proceedings of the 1969 Invitational Conference on Testing Problems.* Princeton, NJ: Educational Testing Service.

Haertel, E. H. (1984). An application of latent class models to assessment data. *Applied Psychological Measurement, 8,* 333–346.

Hunt, E., & MacLeod, C. M. (1978). The sentence-verification paradigm: A case study of two conflicting approaches to individual differences. *Intelligence, 2,* 129–144.

Kelley, T. L. (1923). *Statistical methods.* New York: Macmillan.

Kelley, T. L. (1927). *Interpretation of educational measurements.* New York: World Book.

Kuder, G. F., & Richardson, M. W. (1937). The theory of the estimation of test reliability. *Psychometrika, 2,* 151–160.

Kyllonen, P. C., Lohman, D. F., & Snow, R. E. (1984). Effects of aptitudes, strategy training, and test facets on spatial task performance. *Journal of Educational Psychology, 76,* 130–145.

Lauritzen, S. L., & Spiegelhalter, D. J. (1988). Local computations with probabilities on graphical structures and their application to expert systems (with discussion). *Journal of the Royal Statistical Society, Series B, 50,* 157–224.

Lawley, D. N. (1943). On problems connected with item selection and test construction. *Proceedings of the Royal Society of Edinburgh, Section A, 61,* 273–287.

Lazarsfeld, P. F. (1950). The logical and mathematical foundation of latent structure analysis. In S. A. Stouffer, L. Guttman, E. A. Suchman, P. F. Lazarsfeld, S. A. Star, & J. A. Clausen (Eds.), *Studies in social psychology in World War II, Vol. 4: Measurement and Prediction* (pp. 362–412). Princeton, NJ: Princeton University Press.

Lesgold, A. M., & Perfetti, C. A. (1978). Interactive processes in reading comprehension. *Discourse Processes, 1,* 323–336.

Lohman, D. F. (1989). Estimating individual differences in information processing using speed-accuracy models. In R. Kaufer, P. L. Ackerman, & R. Cudeck (Eds.), *Abilities, motivation, and methodology: The Minnesota symposium on learning and individual differences* (pp. 119–164). Hillsdale, NJ: Lawrence Erlbaum Associates.

Lord, F. M., (1952). A theory of test scores. *Psychometrika Monograph No. 7, 17* (4, Pt. 2).

Lord, F. M. (1958). Further problems in the measurement of growth. *Educational and Psychological Measurement, 18,* 437–454.

Lord, F. M. (1959). Statistical inference about true scores. *Psychometrika, 24,* 1–18.

Lord, F. M. (1980). *Applications of item response theory to practical testing problems.* Hillsdale, NJ: Lawrence Erlbaum Associates.

Lord, F. M., & Novick, M. R. (1968). *Statistical theories of mental test scores.* Reading, MA: Addison-Wesley.

Macready, G. B., & Dayton, C. M. (1977). The use of probabilistic models in the assessment of mastery. *Journal of Educational Statistics, 2,* 99–120.

Macready, G. B., & Dayton, C. M. (1980). The nature and use of state mastery models. *Applied Psychological Measurement, 4,* 493–516.

Macready, G. B., & Dayton, C. M. (1989, March). *The application of latent class models in adaptive testing.* Paper presented at the annual meeting of the American Educational Research Association, San Francisco, CA.

Marshall, S. P. (1985, December). *Using schema knowledge to solve story problems.* Paper presented at the Office of Naval Research Contractors' Conference, San Diego, CA.

Masters, G. N. (1982). A Rasch model for partial credit scoring. *Psychometrika, 47,* 149–174.

McGuire, C. H. (1985). Medical problem-solving: A critique of the literature. *Journal of Medical Education, 60,* 587–595.

Mead, R. J. (1976). *Analysis of fit to the Rasch model.* Unpublished doctoral dissertation, University of Chicago.

Messick, S. (1984). The psychology of educational measurement. *Journal of Educational Measurement, 23,* 147–156.

Messick, S., Beaton, A. E., & Lord, F. M. (1983). *National Assessment of Educational Progress reconsidered: A new design for a new era* (NAEP Rep. 83-1). Princeton, NJ: National Assessment for Educational Progress.

Mislevy, R. J. (1984). Estimating latent distributions. *Psychometrika, 49,* 359–381.

Mislevy, R. J. (1987). Exploiting auxiliary information about examinees in the estimation of item parameters. *Applied Psychological Measurement, 11,* 81–91.

Mislevy, R. J. (1988). Exploiting auxiliary information about items in the estimation of Rasch item difficulty parameters. *Applied Psychological Measurement, 12,* 281–296.

Mislevy, R. J. (1991). Randomization-based inferences about latent variables from complex samples. *Psychometrika, 56,* 177–196.

Mislevy, R. J. & Sheehan, K. M. (1989). The role of collateral information about examinees in item parameter estimation. *Psychometrika, 54,* 661–679.

Mislevy, R. J., & Verhelst, N. (1990). Modeling item responses when different subjects employ different solution strategies. *Psychometrika, 55,* 195–215.

Mislevy, R. J., & Wu, P-K. (1988). *Inferring examinee ability when some item responses are missing* (ETS Res. Rep. RR-88-48-ONR). Princeton, NJ: Educational Testing Service.

Mislevy, R. J., Yamamoto, K. & Anacker, S. (in press). Toward a test theory for assessing student understanding. In R. A. Lesh & S. Lamom (Eds.), *Assessments of authentic performance in elementary mathematics.* Washington, D.C.: American Association for the Advancement of Science.

Novick, M. R. (1966). The axioms and principle results of classical test theory. *Journal of Mathematical Psychology, 3,* 1–18.

Novick, M. R., & Jackson, P. H. (1974). *Statistical methods for educational and psychological research.* New York: McGraw-Hill.

Paulson, J. A. (1986). *Latent class representation of systematic patterns in test responses* (Tech. Rep. ONR-1). Portland, OR: Psychology Department, Portland State University.

Pearl, J. (1988). *Probabilistic reasoning in intelligent systems: Networks of plausible inference.* San Mateo, CA: Kaufmann.

Pople, H. E. (1981). Heuristic methods for imposing structure on ill-structured problems: The structuring of medical diagnostics. In P. Szolovitz (Ed.), *Artificial intelligence in medicine* (pp. 119-185). Boulder, CO: Westview Press.

Rasch, G. (1960). *Probabilistic models for some intelligence and attainment tests.* Copenhagen: Danish Institute for Educational Research.

Samejima, F. (1979). *A new family of models for the multiple-choice item* (ONR Res. Rep. 79-4). Knoxville, TN: University of Tennessee.

Samejima, F. (1983). *A latent trait model for differential strategies in cognitive processes* (ONR Res. Rep. 83-1). Knoxville, TN: University of Tennessee.

Scheiblechner, H. (1972). Das lernen und Lösen komplexer denkaufgaben [The learning and solution of complex cognitive tasks]. *Zeitschrift für experimentalle und Angewandte Psychologie, 19,* 476-506.

Scheiblechner, H. (1985). Psychometric models for speed-test construction: The linear exponential model. In S. E. Embretson (Ed.), *Test design: Developments in psychology and psychometrics* (pp. 219-244). Orlando, FL: Academic Press.

Siegler, R. S. (1981). *Developmental sequences within and between concepts.* Monograph of the Society for Research in Child Development, *46* (Serial No. 189).

Shafer, G. (1976). *A mathematical theory of evidence.* Princeton, NJ: Princeton University Press.

Shortliffe, E. H., Axline, S. G., Buchanan, B. G., Merigan, T. C., & Cohen, S. W. (1973). An artificial intelligence program to advise physicians regarding antimicrobial therapy. *Computers in Biomedical Research, 6,* 544-560.

Smith, R. (1986). Person fit in the Rasch model. *Educational and Psychological Measurement, 46,* 359-372.

Snow, R. E., & Lohman, D. F. (1989). Implications of cognitive psychology for educational measurement. In R. L. Linn (Ed.), *Educational measurement* (3rd ed., pp. 263-331). New York: American Council on Education/Macmillan.

Spearman, C. (1904a). The proof and measurement of association between two things. *American Journal of Psychology, 15,* 72-101.

Spearman, C. (1904b). "General intelligence" objectively determined and measured. *American Journal of Psychology, 15,* 201-292.

Spearman, C. (1907). Demonstration of formulae for true measure of correlation. *American Journal of Psychology, 18,* 161-169.

Spearman, C. (1910). Correlation calculated with faulty data. *British Journal of Psychology, 3,* 271-295.

Spearman, C. (1913). Correlations of sums and differences. *British Journal of Psychology, 5,* 417-426.

Spiegelhalter, D. J. (1986). Probabilistic reasoning in predictive expert systems. In L. W. Kanal & J. Lemmer (Eds.), *Artificial intelligence and statistics* (pp. 47-68). Amsterdam: North-Holland.

Tatsuoka, K. K. (1983). Rule space: An approach for dealing with misconceptions based on item response theory. *Journal of Educational Measurement, 20,* 345-354.

Theunissen, T. J. J. M. (1985). Binary programming and test design. *Psychometrika, 50,* 411-420.

Thissen, D. (1983). Timed testing: An approach using item response theory. In D. J. Weiss (Ed.), *New horizons in testing: Latent trait test theory and computerized adaptive testing* (pp. 179-203). New York: Academic Press.

Thissen, D., & Steinberg, L. (1984). A response model for multiple choice items. *Psychometrika, 47,* 201-214.

Thorndike, E. L., Bregman, E. O., Cobb, M. V., & Woodyard, E. (1926). *The measurement of intelligence.* New York: Columbia Teachers College, Bureau of Publications.

Thurstone, L. L. (1925). A method of scaling psychological and educational tests. *Journal of Educational Psychology, 16,* 433-451.

Thurstone, L. L. (1928). The measurement of opinion. *Journal of Abnormal and Social Psychology, 22*, 415–430.

Tsutakawa, R. K. (1984). Estimation of two-parameter logistic item response curves. *Journal of Educational Statistics, 9*, 263–276.

Tsutakawa, R. K., & Soltys, M. J. (1988). Approximation for Bayesian ability estimation. *Journal of Educational Statistics, 13*, 117–130.

Tucker, L. R. (1946). Maximum validity of test with equivalent items. *Psychometrika, 11*, 1–13.

Vosniadou, S., & Brewer,W. F. (1987). Theories of knowledge restructuring in development. *Review of Educational Research, 57*, 51–67.

Weiss, D. J. (1984). Application of computerized adaptive testing to educational problems. *Journal of Educational Measurement, 21*, 361–376.

Wilson, M. R. (1985). *Measuring stages of growth: A psychometric model of hierarchical development* (Occasional Paper No. 19). Hawthorne, Australia: Australian Council for Educational Research.

Wilson, M. R. (1989). Saltus: A psychometric model of discontinuity in cognitive development. *Psychological Bulletin, 105*, 276–289.

Wright, B. D. (1968). Sample-free test calibration and person measurement. In *Proceedings of the 1967 Invitational Conference on Testing Problems* (pp. 85–101). Princeton, NJ: Educational Testing Service.

Yamamoto, K. (1987). *A model that combines IRT and latent class models.* Unpublished doctoral dissertation, University of Illinois, Champaign-Urbana.

Zadeh, L. A. (1983). The role of fuzzy logic in the management of uncertainty in expert systems. *Fuzzy Sets and Systems, 11*, 199–227.

3

Cognitive Diagnosis: From Statistically Based Assessment Toward Theory-Based Assessment

David F. Lohman
University of Iowa

Martin J. Ippel
University of Leiden

INTRODUCTION

The measurement of individual differences in intellectual functioning is well found-ed in mental test theory and has gained social significance through an impres-sive array of instruments that predict socially important criterion achievements, such as job performance and learning outcomes. Yet despite its high level of statistical and methodological sophistication, the differential approach to human intelligence never assumed a central role in the development of psychology as a science, even though intelligence tests are often hailed as one of psycholo-gy's greatest practical triumphs. The increasing isolation of differential psychology from the mainstream of psychology during the first half century of scientific study of individual differences was in large measure due to the fact that differential psychology was unable to achieve one of its central goals: the identification of the mental processes that underlie intelligent functioning. Instead, differential psychology produced theories that described the organization of individual differ-ences in traits thought to comprise human intelligence. Furthermore, despite the fact that some differential psychologists have long recognized the need to identify the mental processes that produce intelligent behavior (Cronbach, 1957; Freeman, 1926; McNemar, 1964; Spearman, 1927; Thurstone, 1947), it was only recently that many in the field acknowledged that a research program domi-nated by factor analyses of test intercorrelations was incapable of producing an explanatory theory of human intelligence.

In this chapter, we discuss the general features of a theory for measurement of cognitive processes. This theory presents three related theoretical propositions. Our first thesis is that the failure to identify the processes of intelligence stemmed from the failure to identify and to take into account aspects of tasks that have measurable impacts on task performance. Our second thesis is that the generally accepted idea of test theory as applied statistics precluded the development of a structural theory of measurement needed for the measurement of processes. Our third thesis is that it is useful to distinguish between tests as observation designs and test scores as reflections of particular measurement models. We discuss this distinction in some detail, and then summarize the general features of methods that have been proposed to identify mental processes. Attempts to use these methods to study individual differences were sometimes successful, but more often sobering. We believe that this was because (a) we had either not foreseen or had underestimated the impact of several thorny, methodological issues, (b) we had focused our efforts on the measurement of component processes rather than on the measurement of qualitative differences in knowledge or strategy, and (c) we had applied our efforts to the wrong types of cognitive tasks. Here the basic claim is that a cognitive approach to measurement is most useful when applied to tasks designed to elicit responses that reveal qualitative differences between individuals in knowledge or strategy. Unfortunately, neither tests modeled after experimental tasks studied by cognitive psychologists nor experimental tasks modeled after ability tests studied by differential psychologists were designed to evoke such individual differences or to reveal them when they occur. We conclude with a discussion of the types of tasks and measurement methodologies that seem more likely to exploit the strengths of a cognitive approach to measurement.

IDENTIFICATION OF MENTAL PROCESSES

Individual Differences as a Main Road to Process

During the first half century of scientific study of intelligence, research was guided by the assumption that the analysis of individual differences through factor analysis provided "an avenue of approach to the study of the processes which underlie these differences" (Thurstone, 1947, p. 55). This assumption derived its plausibility from the fact that patterns of intercorrelations among test scores appeared to be replicable across studies. These patterns were thought to reflect the action of a much smaller set of cognitive functions. In fact, in his first paper on factor analysis, Spearman (1904) used the terms *factor* and *function* interchangeably. Thurstone (1947) also spoke of *functional unities* and argued that "in the interpretation of mind we assume that mental phenomena can be identified in terms of distinguishable functions, which do not all participate equally in everything the mind does"(p. 57).

Twenty years later, in what was probably one of the best summaries of research on human abilities, Guilford (1967) made the same argument. In discussing the proper interpretation of factors, he noted: "It is only by correlating [scores on a test] with [scores on] other tests that we can test any hypothesis as to what it measures psychologically" (p. 42). Further, factors identified from correlation matrices of aptitude tests were, in fact, mental functions: "In our search for the meaning of aptitude factors, we can take one more easy but very significant step, for it ties factors . . . to psychological theory. This step is to say that such a factor is also a psychological function" (p. 42). Thus, Guilford made explicit Spearman's assumption that factor and function were interchangeable concepts.

Gradually, though, this assumption was challenged. It appeared that factor analysis was apt to produce an ever-proliferating series of new factors rather than a parsimonious list of mental functions. Furthermore, although factor analysis did produce useful "functional unities," it did not provide a better understanding of mental processes. McNemar (1964) captured the impasse:

> these studies of individual differences never come to grips with the *process* or operation, by which a given organism achieves an intellectual response. Indeed, it is difficult to see how the available individual difference data can be used even as a starting point for generating a theory as to the process nature of general intelligence or of any other specified ability. (McNemar, 1964, p. 881)

Thus, the main problem with the individual difference approach to the study of intelligence was that it did not have a clear conception of what a "process" might be, or how particular aspects of a test might elicit those processes.

Mental Processes as Information Processes

For a long time, then, the basic problem for a process analysis of intelligence was that the concepts "mental processes" or "mental activities" were but vague notions, devoid of technical meaning. Questions such as "What is a process?" or "What are the elementary units of a process theory?" had no clear answers. This situation changed with the emergence of the information-processing approach.

The information-processing approach that now dominates cognitive psychology treats mental activities as different operations performed on symbols and symbol structures. The approach does not provide for a model in the strict sense. Rather, it provides a general framework for theorizing about the mental events that are presumed to underly overt behavior. A general characterization of the information-processing approach would be that it studies mental processes as behavioral phenomena. Because these mental processes are not open to direct observation, certain assumptions are required about the nature of the processes so that they can be investigated. A central assumption is that mental activities can be thought of as decomposable into a series of relatively independent processes or operations. Further, it is also assumed that for each mental operation a set of task conditions exists that, if varied, will exert a selective influence on these particular mental processes. Finally, it is assumed that, when used, each of these internal processes may produce externally observable effects on behavior. These represent core assumptions of the information processing approach. The approach does not provide a particular methodology for experimentation, and in fact spawned a variety of research methods, some of which are discussed later. But first we must take a brief detour into measurement theory.

MEASUREMENT AS A STRUCTURAL THEORY

By the early 1970s, the idea that measurement was fundamentally a statistical adventure seemed well accepted. This period was marked by the publication of a series of major works that established test theory as applied statistics (Cronbach, Gleser, Nanda, & Rajaratnam, 1972; Fischer, 1974; Lord, 1980; Lord & Novick, 1968; Rasch, 1960). Amidst this comfortable mutual consent, Guttman (1971) delivered his presidential address at the annual meeting of the Psychometric Society. In this address, he argued against treating measurement theory as a statistical theory.

Observations versus Measurements

The concept of a measurement theory proposed by Guttman emphasized the distinction between *observations* and *measurements*. Any substantive psychological problem concerns a universe of observations. Statistical theories allow one to make inferences about aspects of this universe from samples of observations. A measurement procedure, Guttman argued, does not consist of a (random) sample of observations from this universe. Rather, it is a procedure for ordering or classifying observations according to a structural regression hypothesis. Guttman (1971) summarized this idea in the following conjecture: "A desired structural hypothesis for measurement here would help to specify, in advance of the calculations, an order amongst the categories of each variable separately that might yield monotone regressions" (p. 338).

We read this somewhat cryptic statement as follows: A structural hypothesis for measurement imposes an ordered set of categories on the observations such that this order will yield monotone regressions from the dependent variable(s) to the categories.

Two implications of this idea should be noted. First, the goal of collecting observations in Guttman's proposal for a theory of measurement obviously differs from current statistical test theories. In general, the goal of observation in mental testing is to compare individuals. In Guttman's proposal, the goal is to assess the structure of relationships among observations. Second, designing a procedure for classifying observations on the basis of a structural regression hypothesis introduces substantive theory (psychological or otherwise) into the domain of measurement theory. This substantive theory replaces a merely statistical justification for attaching meaning to scores.

In summary, by a set of measurements Guttman means a set of observations recorded on the basis of a regression hypothesis. The concept of "an observation" includes "a measurement" as a special case. The universe of observations may be a universe of measurements in many cases, but initially one must begin with observations which are not measurements.

Behavior Consistency

In 1971, Guttman's proposal for a measurement theory might have seemed too much a wave of the future. Most psychological research that used psychometric theories and methods for measurement were dominated by dimensional theories, such as trait theories that describe the dimensions of an individual's personality, or factor-analytic theories that describe the structure of intelligence. A crucial assumption of dimensional theories is that an individual's value on a latent dimension is a stable characteristic that explains behavior consistencies across relevant situations (Lord & Novick, 1968). No structural regression hypothesis can be derived to explain relationships among observations, because dimensional theories assume that the important latent variable remains constant across observations. For example, in generalizability theory (Cronbach et al., 1972), a person's universe score is defined as the expected value over a universe of nominally parallel items. This implies that the universe score is identical for all observation conditions.

Although the assumption of a constant universe score works well in dimensional theories such as factorial theories of intelligence, it conflicts with the assumption made in research that aims to describe how subjects achieve the responses they give. In such research, investigators carefully arrange observation conditions so that patterns of responses might reveal processes or mechanisms which generated them. Thus, information-processing approaches rest on a view of measurement that is fundamentally different from that of dimensional theories of individual differences.

This point is clearly illustrated in two studies of Ippel (1981, 1986) in which task facets of the Embedded Figures Test (EFT) were systematically manipulated. A number of different tests with embedded figures material are currently used. In all these tests, a subject is required to locate a simple geometric figure within a more complex embedding figure. In the first study (Ippel, 1981) the experiment was designed in such a way that the levels of the experimentally manipulated task facets covered the differences among existing variants of embedded figures tests. The research question was whether these different embedded figures tests could be considered equivalent measures to estimate the universe score for this problem domain. This type of question is fairly typical for statistical theories of mental testing. Generalizability theory (Cronbach et al., 1972) was used to estimate the contributions of different within-subject sources to the standard error of measurement and to the generalizability coefficient. The results of the experiment showed substantial within-subject variance. However, in traditional test theory, such within-subject variance (some of which actually represents systematic performance variation) is relegated to the residual or error term, thus inflating the standard error of measurement and attenuating generalizability coefficients. In the second experiment (Ippel, 1986), which was basically a replication of the first, it was shown that indeed a large proportion of this intraindividual variance could be understood as systematic and replicable response patterns reflecting different mental activities induced by different task demands.

In conclusion, one of the problems for a theory of process measurement is to explain intraindividual variance that results from differences in processing demands of different task conditions as systematic variance.

ELEMENTS OF TEST THEORY
FOR PROCESS MEASUREMENT

The theory to be proposed distinguishes two aspects of tests for the measurement of cognitive processes. That is, tests can be considered as observation designs, and scores on tests can be considered as the products of different measurement models. Validation of both aspects of a test is an essential element of the method we propose. However, inferences about processes depend on what processes are conceived to be and how they are estimated. In this section an informal development of our theoretical positions is presented using examples. The task used to exemplify our theoretical position is the well-known mental rotation task of Shepard and Metzler (1971). The task requires the individual to decide about the identity of three-dimensional figures differing in orientation. Items of this type have been included in psychometric tests for years. We have chosen this task because it has been much studied and because the research on it is readily understandable. A detailed description of the theory presented can be found in Ippel (1986). Throughout this section the emphasis is on conceptual issues, rather than on complex estimation problem associated with these issues.

Two Aspects of Mental Tests

A test can be viewed from two different aspects: as an observation design and as a measurement design. Any theory of test design should systematically deal with both aspects.

The observation design describes test items, their organization, and the type of responses required. The purpose of the observation design is to structure observations so that defensible inferences about theoretical constructs can be made from these observations. Construction of a test requires commitment to a particular observation design. For example, assume that a certain process model underlies the performance of a specific task and that this process model specifies a series of independent component processes. Given these assumptions, observations should be arranged in such a way that a test of the independence of these component processes is possible. One way to accomplish this would be to use a factorial design in which observation conditions are constructed to represent the cartesian product of two or more task facets.

The measurement design aspect of a test refers to it as a procedure to assign a single value to an object of measurement. The traditional object of measurement in psychometric testing is the person. However, process analyses of cognitive tasks make it possible to specify multiple objects of measurement, namely, the overall task performance of the person as well as her proficiency on any of the specified component processes. For any of these measurement objects, a measurement model is used to specify the rules that will be used to score, classify, or combine objects of observation. For example, in psychometric testing, a single score for a person can be obtained by averaging performance over items. This is consistent with a measurement model that relegates variability in performance across items to the error term. In Guttman's (1971) terms, the structural regression for each subject contains only a constant and an error term. Information-processing accounts of task performance usually result in a more complex set of measurement models, in which scores are estimated for component processes hypothesized to be used by subjects to generate answers or to choose among response options. Component scores for these models contrast performance over two or more item sets. Different measurement models can be evaluated for a given observation design by combining and contrasting performance on different item sets in different ways.

Validity

Measurement theory always implies inference from observables to theoretical concepts. Such inference must be defended or validated. Questions about mental processes used by subjects to solve test items concern the validity of inferences about the proposed process model that are made from the behavioral records evoked by the observation design. Because of this, inferences about particular processes will be more defensible for some observation designs than for others.

Questions about the breadth, fairness, or representativeness of a test also concern validation of the observation design. Psychometric accounts of mental testing usually do not offer formal solutions to this aspect of test validation. An exception is Kane's (1982) sampling model for validity based on generalizability theory. This model justifies a sort of inductive inference from observations to a universe score by assuming that observations are randomly sampled from a universe of nominally parallel items.

Guttman's (1971) proposal of measurement as a structural theory implies a systematic manipulation of task demands. The primary purpose for manipulating item difficulty or task demands is to test hypotheses about the psychology of the test. These hypotheses are made explicit in a process model that describes how subjects solve items. This process model can be tested in many different ways: for example, by writing and then running a computer program, by administering the task to subjects and asking them to think aloud, by recording subjects' eye fixations while they solve the task, by classifying the responses subjects make, or by analyzing the duration of their responses. In each case, one must find some way to compare the predictions of the model with the behavioral records obtained. When verbal protocols or eye fixations are used as data, the process of fitting model to data is relatively unstructured, so no exact statistical test of model fit is available. Model testing is most rigorous when the information-processing model can be approximated in a regression model that can be fitted to some aspect of performance, usually response latency. For example, if subjects use a mental rotation strategy to solve spatial test items, they should be less successful or respond more slowly on items that require more rather than less rotation. This hypothesis can be tested by fitting to each subject's data a regression model that tests the effect of increases in angular separation between stimuli on performance. If this model provides a reasonable account for the subject's data, then one can estimate scores that directly reflect the action of particular component processes hypothesized in the model. Thus, in addition to a score representing overall performance (estimated by averaging over-all trials or by the intercept of the regression of response latencies or errors on amount of rotation), one also obtains an estimate of the speed or efficacy of the rotation process itself.

The Construction of a Process Model

The formulation of a process model that reflects the mental activities involved in task performance is essentially the product of a conceptual analysis of this performance. In the case of a componential analysis, it is accomplished by specifying a (limited) number of component processes that together can be assumed to account for task performance. For each component process, a variable (which is often represented as a task facet) must be specified that can be assumed to exert a selective and salient influence on that particular component process.

There are several complexities here. To ensure that the proposed processes are not wholly fantasies, certain constraints on the class of possible models are required in order to allow for empirically testable predictions. These constraints include the nature and interrelationships of the elements from which a model can be composed. Tests for the validity of such a task-performance model focus on formal aspects as implied by the class of possible models as well as on substantive properties dictated by theoretical suppositions. (For a detailed treatment of these model tests, see Ippel, 1986.)

Let us—for a moment—jump to the end of the story, and suppose that we have a valid componential theory for task performance on the mental rotation task. In Fig. 3.1, a simple model of task performance for the mental rotation task is depicted. This figure also shows which task facet is thought to influence each component process. In addition to the mental rotation component, there is experimental evidence that suggests that the time required for encoding depends on the discriminability or complexity of the stimulus figures (Carpenter & Just, 1978). Also, a comparison process is assumed to check whether the remaining parts of the figure are identical under transformation. The same/different judgment is thought to influence this mental comparison process. The idea is that varying the conditions of any task facet will result in different task loads on the corresponding component process. Basically, the components shown in Fig. 3.1 are response-time components. That is, the total response time is conceived of as being composed of a train of successive component processes. In this context we would like to focus on the mental rotation component.

Shepard and Metzler (1971) were the first to discover the linear relationship between the magnitude of angular difference of two three-dimensional figures and the time it takes to compare the figure representations. This result has been replicated in several studies, for two- and three-dimensional drawings (e.g., Shepard & Cooper, 1982). This response pattern is generally interpreted as suggesting a physical-analogue process of rotating the mental images of the stimulus pairs into congruence with each other.

With this example it is possible to demonstrate the two functions of a process

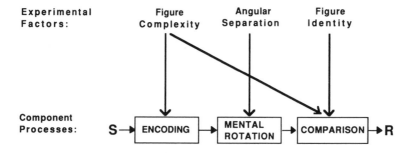

FIG. 3.1. Information-processing model for the mental rotation task. Three experimental factors of figure complexity, angular separation between figures, and figure identity (match or mismatch) are assumed to influence the three component processes of encoding, mental rotation, and comparison as shown by the arrows.

model: (a) It is a means to process inference, and (b) it can impose an ordering among categories of observations.

A Process Model as a Means for Process Inference. The function of a process model within a theory of test design is to relate observations to theoretical concepts about processes. Suppose, for example, that the response latencies for a subject were 680 msecs and 810 msecs, and that these observations were made at stimulus pairs with angular disparities of 60 and 90 degrees, respectively. It is only through application of an information-processing model that it becomes intelligible that differences in response latencies reflect a proficiency in rotating an internal representation of one figure into congruence with the other. The model supports the inference that it takes a particular person 130 msecs to rotate into congruence two mental images that differ 30 degrees in spatial orientation.

A Process Model Imposes an Ordering Among the Conditions of Observation. The process model enables the test designer to impose an ordering on the categories of observations such that it yields monotone regressions from the dependent variables to the categories of observation. Thus, the model of task performance yields a number of structural hypotheses for measurement (Guttman, 1971). Such structural hypotheses provide scores for the hypothesized cognitive (component) processes. There are some complications involved here. Ippel and Beem (1987) showed that the task load function that is specified by a structural hypothesis is specific for a particular processing strategy. Different processing strategies imply different task load functions.

Objects of Measurement

The typical purpose of psychological measurement has been to differentiate among individuals. Therefore, the object of measurement in mental test theories is the *person*. The construction of component scores that reflect a person's sensitiveness for changes in task demands implies a more complicated class of measurement objects. In the case of current mental test theory, an observed score of a person on a test of mental rotation simply is the mean of all item scores, or some function of it. This is because theories of psychological measurement assume an equivalence of the observations of a person's performance. Accordingly, performance variation across observations is relegated to the residual or error variance. As a consequence, the scores corresponding with "person" as object of measurement only roughly reflect the performance of each subject in every observation condition of the task facet (i.e., angular disparity). The differential impact of levels of the task facets on a person can only be investigated by taking pairs of person and observation conditions of a certain task as objects of measurement, and finding ways to estimate this differential impact.

The measurement of cognitive processes thus implies a different view of tests and test items than the traditional psychometric approach to mental testing. Psychometric accounts of mental testing treat items as independent elements of behavior. For example, the sampling model of generalizability theory implies that items are primitives in the sense that they can be identified, indexed, and catalogued as members of a well-defined population. This conception has been criticized as invalid (Loevinger, 1965; Rozeboom, 1978). In formulating a process model for certain cognitive tasks, this criticism is met, because this validity model does not require that items be considered primitives. Instead, items are viewed as realizations of a process model that only in the aggregate can give information concerning certain properties of that model. As for the inference of these properties, the aggregate (i.e., the test) cannot be obtained through random sampling. The choice of observations or items should be strictly controlled by reference to the requirement to manipulate the task loads of certain component processes and to make the effects of variations in task load measurable. Therefore, the testing of cognitive processes involves the replacement of the conception of a test as a random sample of items by an alternative conception of a test as a structured collection of items. The guiding principle of item selection is the process model.

The Process Model as Target Variable

The discussion to this point has focused on component processes. However, the nature of the process model itself can also be the target variable. If subjects solve a task in different ways, then they can be classified on the basis of the information-processing model that best describes their performance. If these categories can be ordered by another model, then the classification scheme becomes a new measurement model. For example, R. Sternberg (1977) distinguished among four different validity models for analogical reasoning tasks. In Model I, all component processes were self-terminating, whereas in Model IV all component processes were exhaustive. Models II and III distinguished intermediate cases. Performance of adult subjects was generally well fit by Models III or IV. In later work with children, Sternberg discovered that the performance of younger children was better fit by models with self-terminating processes, whereas that of older children was generally better fit by models that hypothesized more exhaustive processing (R. Sternberg & Rifkin, 1979). Thus, categories could be *ordered* by amount of exhaustive processing required. Category score in this measurement model was thus shown to be correlated with age or developmental level.

Developmental theories provide the most straightforward examples of how such second-order measurement models can be used to explain systematic variation in how individuals solve tasks (i.e., first-order process models). This is because they usually posit a single dimension along which information processing models may be classified. Sometimes more than one dimension is required, such as in attempts to relate strategy differences on cognitive tasks to ability constructs identified in dimensional theories (e.g., Kyllonen, Lohman, & Woltz, 1984).

APPLICATIONS OF THE THEORY

Methods for Inferring Component Processes from Response Latencies

Information-processing models that purport to describe how component processes are organized into strategies must somehow estimate the action of each process that is postulated. However, mental processes are unobservable. They must be inferred from patterns of responses across items presumed to require different amounts of different processes. Various observation designs have been proposed for accomplishing this task. Some differences among observation designs reflect different assumptions about the nature of a mental process embedded in the information-processing model, such as what constitutes a stage of processing, the order of stage execution, and whether stages are allowed to influence one another or are presumed to function independently. In this section, we briefly review these methods. Our aim is not to provide an exhaustive treatment of this rather complex topic, but rather to set the stage for a discussion of the problems these methods encounter when individual differences are the object of investigation.

Subtractive Method. A simple method for estimating the duration of processing stages was proposed by Donders (1868/1969). A series of two or more nested tasks must be developed, in which each successive task is presumed to require all of the processing stages required by previous tasks, plus an additional processing stage. The duration of each stage is then estimated by subtraction.

The subtraction method is not without its problems, particularly the assumptions that cognitive processing may be modeled as a sequence of fixed "stages," that these stages are executed serially, and that new stages may be inserted without affecting prior or subsequent processing (see Taylor, 1976).

Additive Factors Method. S. Sternberg (1969) proposed a set of techniques, known as the additive factors method, that tests the assumption of stage independence without assuming that a stage may be completely deleted with impunity or that stages are executed serially. In essence, one attempts to induce subjects to execute a particular process longer or repeatedly by manipulating some experimental variable. An important assumption, then, is that one can identify a task variable (or set of variables) that exerts a selective and salient influence on a particular stage. S. Sternberg generalized the model to include more than one stage, but kept strictly within the analysis-of-variance framework in which task variables hypothesized to influence processing for different stages in the model were kept uncorrelated. For example, if two stages are hypothesized, then at least two independent variables must be postulated. Response time (T) would then be hypothesized to be a linear function of these two independent variables (X_1 and X_2):

$$T = b_0 + b_1X_1 + b_2X_2 + b_3X_1X_2 \quad \text{where Cov}(X_1, X_2) = 0.$$

The interaction term (b_3) in the model tests for the independence of stages 1 and 2.

The fact that independent variables are constrained to be orthogonal is at once an important strength and an important weakness of this model. The model meshes easily with faceted tests and generalizability theory. Estimates of model parameters are stabler and more easily interpreted than when model predictors covary. However, models that posit multiple cognitive processes often do not fit neatly into an orthogonal mold. In such cases, weaker models that allow for correlations among predictors may be more appropriate.

Combined Methods.   Clark and Chase (1972) provided one of the first examples of modeling latencies using a weaker model that contained correlated predictor variables. Independent variables were entered into the regression equation in the presumed order in which corresponding processes in their sentence comprehension task were executed. However, because Clark and Chase (1972) were not interested in individual differences, data were averaged over subjects before modeling.

R. Sternberg (1977) suggested that the type of regression model proposed by Clark and Chase (1972) could be performed separately for each individual, and that model parameters could then be taken as estimates of the speed or accuracy with which subjects executed particular component processes. Sternberg (1977) also suggested that this sort of model could be combined with the subtractive method of Donders (1868/1969) to unconfound otherwise confounded component processes.

There are several ways to unconfound correlated predictors, all of which use some variant of the subtractive method. These methods have been summarized by Sternberg (1985). One method is called precuing. Here, the subject first examines a part of the problem for as long as necessary, then signals readiness to see the remainder of the item. Two latencies may be obtained: time taken to view the precue, called a cue latency (which is sometimes discarded), and time taken to solve the remainder of the problem, called a solution latency).

Precuing has probably been less frequently used than simply decomposing a complex task into two or more consecutively presented steps. Latencies for the two or more task steps can then be appended into a single dependent variable (R. Sternberg, 1977) or modeled separately (e.g., Kyllonen et al., 1984). The major steps in performing a componential analysis are: (a) Formulate two or more competing information processing models. (b) Identify variables that influence each component process in each model. If possible, create an observation design in which these variables are varied orthogonally. This will often be impossible if the process model is complex. (c) If desired, unconfound independent variables for different components that are highly correlated by precuing, task decomposition, or some other method. (d) Test process models by regressing dependent variables (usually latencies) on the independent variables. (e) Revise process models or their operationalization after examining residuals by adding new component processes, altering assumptions about how processes are executed (e.g., is mode of execution self-terminating or exhaustive?), or whether all component processes enter into the solution of all items.

Poor model fits (usually judged by R-square or root-mean-square error) challenge the validity of the information-processing model or the way it has been operationalized. A good model fit indicates that the chosen model or any model whose predictions are correlated with the chosen model would explain the data. Thus, validation of process models requires evidence other than model fit statistics (such as introspective reports or correlations between model parameters and similar model parameters derived from analyses of other tasks). And as with psychological theories more generally, process models for tasks gradually gain credence by prevailing in tests against plausible rival models.

Examples of Component Scores

Faceted Tests and Component Scores. Faceted tests in which sources of difficulty are varied orthogonally have many desirable properties. Subscores may be formed by collapsing over some task facets and not others, thereby creating scores with predictably different properties. Indeed, the symmetry of factorial designs makes it possible to use every source of variance as a class of measurement objects. For example, in one spatial assembly and rotation task, Lohman (1979) varied five sources of difficulty: the number of stimuli to be assembled, the average complexity of these stimuli, the complexity of the new stimulus that would be formed by combining the stimuli in the initial set, the amount of rotation performed on the assembled stimulus, and the identity of the probe (positive or negative). Subscores were formed by averaging over particular facets of the design. It was hypothesized that these scores would capture individual differences in different spatial abilities identified in factor-analytic investigations. In fact, subscores formed by averaging over particular facets did show systematic relationships with reference ability factors. For example, correlations between accuracy and scores on a reference Spatial Visualization factor increased from $r = .21$ to $r = .43$ to $r = .55$ as the number of to-be-combined stimuli increased from one to three. An added advantage of this sort of analysis is that dependability of subscores can be easily estimated using generalizability theory (Cardinet, Tourneur, & Allal, 1981; Cronbach et al., 1972) or related procedures (Mellenberg, 1977).

Faceted tests can also be used to estimate component scores for subjects. In the simplest method, one subscore is simply subtracted from another. For example, in the spatial task previously described, Lohman (1979) computed scores that contrasted performance on two or more subscores. Thus, the rotation facet contained two levels: 90-degree rotation and 180-degree rotation. A contrast score was computed for each subject in which performance on 90-degree rotation trials was subtracted from performance on 180-degree rotation trials. For errors, this contrast correlated $r = -.52$ with a Visual Memory ability factor; for latency, the contrast correlated $r = .46$ with a Verbal ability factor. In other words, it appeared that high verbal subjects had the slowest rate of rotation, and subjects who scored well on the visual memory tests had the smallest increase in errors between 90-degree and 180-degree items.

These are but brief samples of the sort of results we have obtained using contrast score or faceted tests to estimate component processes. For other examples, see Ippel (1986), Lohman (1988), Snow and Peterson (1985), and Irving, Dann, and Anderson (1990).

Regression Estimates of Component Scores. Other methods must be used when independent variables are not or cannot be varied orthogonally. In such cases, information-processing models are tested and component scores for subjects are estimated by fitting a regression model to latency or error data. Independent variables in the model estimate particular sources of difficulty hypothesized to affect the amount or difficulty of component processes. Unstandardized regression coefficients from the within-subject analyses are then used as estimates of component scores for individuals. R. Sternberg (1977) gave examples of this procedure and of attempts to correlate component scores across different tasks.

Problems with Component Scores

Component models have had an enormous appeal; they are elegant and rely on generally familiar statistical procedures such as analysis of variance and multiple regression. However, proper use of these models rests on assumptions that are often implausible when individual differences are the object of investigation, rather than something that is relegated to the error term.

Statistical Problems

Component scores are difference scores, whether computed by subtracting mean performance at one level of a facet from mean performance at another level of that facet, or by using orthogonal polynomials and thereby combining several simple difference scores in a weighted average, or by regressing performance on a noncategorical variable. Difference scores present many problems. First, raw scores are often bounded, and so magnitude of the difference is often systematically related to the general average of the scores. For example, latencies have a lower bound. Subjects who respond rapidly on one type of item can show less reduction in response latency on other items than can subjects who respond slowly to the first item type. Second, within-cell variances often show systematic relationships with cell means, especially when response latency is the dependent variable. Thus, scores that contrast performance in two cells tend to reflect the rank order of individuals in the cell with the greater variance. Third, beta weights can be unstable if independent variables in a regression model are highly correlated.

All of these problems have been recognized by those who have proposed techniques for estimating component scores for individuals. However, other problems have received less attention, and so we discuss them in greater detail.

The Accuracy–Latency Problem

The second type of problem is deceptively simple. It is one that many researchers do not consider seriously until it is time to analyze the data. The problem has two faces. When latencies are the dependent variable, it is "What shall I do with latencies for error responses?" And, less commonly, when errors are the dependent variable, it is "How shall I equate subjects on response latency?" Since one problem is the inverse of the other, we discuss only the problem of error-response latencies.

Error-response latencies often differ systematically from correct response latencies. On simple tasks, error responses are often faster than correct responses, perhaps reflecting fast guesses or other incomplete types of processing. On complex tasks, they are often slower, as when subjects make several attempts at a problem, but sometimes faster, as when subjects do not appreciate the difficulty of a problem or abandon it after initial inspection. The goal of obtaining clean latencies for modeling is thus compromised when subjects do not solve all trials. Experimental psychologists usually cope with this problem by (a) simplifying the task so that errors are infrequent, (b) discarding or repeating trials on which subjects err, and (c) discarding subjects who cannot attain relatively error-free levels of responding. Alas, these remedies are not available to the psychologist interested in individual differences. This is because errors on a task can reflect (a) systematic ability differences, (b) the speed–accuracy trade-off adopted by subjects, or (c) other, usually nonsystematic, influences such as fluctuations in attention and guessing. Discarding subjects or trials only applies to the third type of error. Such errors certainly occur, but they are overshadowed by errors due to ability differences and errors due to speed–accuracy trade-off.

Errors due to Ability Differences. Simplifying a task invariably changes the abilities required for solution of the task. Furthermore, subjects differ systematically in the number of errors they make on exceedingly simple tasks where average error rates are low (Lohman, 1989a), and so discarding error trials throws away different portions of the data for different subjects. This means that models fitted to each subjects' data may represent very different portions of a task, especially for the subjects who err most and least. Unfortunately, subsequent analyses of individual differences (such as correlations between model parameters and other variables) depend most on the comparability of subjects at the extremes of the ability and score distributions.

Errors due to Speed–Accuracy Trade-Off. Differences between latencies or errors across conditions in an experiment may simply reflect differences in the average speed or accuracy emphasis subjects adopt in that condition. This is an important, but frequently ignored, problem in experimental research in which individual differences are consigned to the error term. It is an even greater problem when subjects are a factor in the design. The assumption that all subjects in an experiment adopt the same speed–accuracy trade-off for all items is contradicted by much evidence. Subjects differ enormously in the speed or accuracy emphasis they adopt, even in those rare cases in which they are given explicit instructions about what speed or accuracy emphasis to adopt. Furthermore, small, statistically nonsignificant differences in error rate between subjects or within subjects across item types can be associated with massive changes in response latency. Yet most investigators fail to recognize this problem, or, if they recognize it, dismiss it because of inappropriate statistical tests. In particular, it is common practice to test for a speed–accuracy trade-off by estimating the correlation (over subjects) between response accuracy and response latency. Unfortunately, the presence or absence of such a correlation usually gives little clue as to the presence or absence of a speed–accuracy trade-off (Lohman, 1989b).

Multivariate Methods. Some have attempted to sidestep these problems that arise from attempts to model either errors or latencies by including both variables in the model. Although often more informative than univariate analyses, standard multivariate analyses offer no panacea. There are two problems with such methods. One is that they usually confuse the within-subject speed–accuracy trade-off (or accuracy–latency relationship) with the between-subject speed–accuracy trade-off. These functions may be completely independent (Wickelgren, 1977). Second, statistical controls for the effects of errors on latencies and vice versa cannot somehow equate subjects on speed–accuracy trade-off. In other words, the cognitive processes used by a fast inaccurate subject are not somehow made more comparable to those used by a slow accurate subject by such analyses. A better procedure is to vary this trade-off experimentally for each subject on each trial type by controlling stimulus exposure. One then discards the (impossible) goal of obtaining pure latencies (or errors) and, instead, tries to determine how these two aspects of performance covary. Although several studies using these methods show promise (see Lohman, 1989a), such studies require even more observations than the typical experiment. Effects of practice, attention, and fatigue loom even larger than in typical information-processing studies that use a self-paced procedure to administer trials.

The Strategy Problem

The percent of variance accounted for by a model (i.e., R^2) can be disappointingly low, even if the model accurately describes performance on some, even most, items. Suppose, for example, that subjects can solve rotation items in two different ways: by using a rotation strategy or by using an analytic strategy. If subjects use a rotation strategy, then latency is assumed to be perfectly predicted by the amount of rotation required, but independent of stimulus complexity. If they use an analytic strategy, then latency is assumed to be perfectly predicted by the complexity of the stimulus figure, but independent of amount of rotation required. Assume that these two task facets (stimulus complexity and amount of rotation) are varied orthogonally in task construction. What happens if a subject solves some items by a rotation strategy and other items by the analytic strategy?

Case 1. In the simplest case, assume the subject solves half of the items using the rotation strategy, and the remaining items by the analytic strategy. Assume further that the effects of angular separation on response latency are the same as the effects of stimulus complexity on response latency, and that there is no error of measurement. Although the subject solves only half of the items by each strategy, we do not know how to sort the items. Therefore, we then test each model separately on all the data by regressing either angular separation or stimulus complexity on latencies. For both models $R^2 = .25$.

Case 2. We make the same assumptions as before, but this time assume that the effects for the rotation strategy (i.e., the slope for the regression of latency on amount of rotation) are 10 times greater than the effects for the analytic strategy (i.e., the slope for the regression of latency on stimulus complexity). Now $R^2 = .145$ for the rotation strategy and $R^2 = .00145$ for the analytic strategy.

In both cases, we have two models, each of which perfectly predicts performance on half of the items, yet model fits (R^2) can be quite poor. Fits would be better if we could find some third variable that predicted which items were solved by each strategy. This is the purpose of the strategy-shift models developed by Kyllonen et al. (1984) and Ippel and Beem (1987).

Strategy-Shift Models. Suppose, for example, that two strategies were postulated for a given task. Strategy A is represented by independent variables a_1, a_2, and a_3 and strategy B is represented by independent variables b_1, b_2, and b_3. Single-strategy models could be tested by regressing the dependent variable (Y) on variables a_1, a_2, and a_3, and then, in a separate analyses, by regressing Y on b_1, b_2, and b_3. A "mixed" model (e.g., Sternberg, 1977) could be formed by regressing Y on all six independent variables, a_1, a_2, a_3, b_1, b_2, and b_3. A strategy-shift model would also regress Y on these six independent variables, but would require that only three predictors (a_1, a_2, and a_3, or b_1, b_2, and b_3) have nonzero values for any one item. Thus, performance on some items would be predicted by Strategy A, whereas performance on other items would be predicted by Strategy B. Further, one must hypothesize some variable that will predict strategy shifting (e.g., overall problem difficulty), and must then specify a value of that variable (the "shift point") at which the subject is hypothesized to change strategies. For example, Subject 1 might solve most items using strategy A and only a few items using strategy B, whereas Subject 2 might show the reverse pattern. Thus, several types of information must be evaluated for each subject: the nature of the best-fitting model (single strategy or strategy shift), the goodness of fit of that model compared to other models and to an absolute standard (since even the best model for a subject may account for only trivial variation in the task), and the value of the shift variable (i.e., the ratio of items solved by each strategy).

Effects on Component Scores. Within- and between-person differences in strategies present one further complication for the goal of estimating component scores for subjects. Even if the best-fitting models for different subjects contain a common core of component processes, items used to estimate these components will vary across persons, and so component scores are not comparable. For example, the componential models Kyllonen et al. (1984) tested differed in the percent of items on a form board task subjects were presumed to have synthesized. Thus, component scores for the synthesis "component" were based on all items for some subjects and the easiest 25% of the items for other subjects.

Increasingly, investigators are noting these and other perils of modeling response latencies (Pellegrino & Goldman, 1989; Siegler, 1989). The basic problem for testing information-processing models is that performance on different items should not be combined unless items are solved in the same way. If items are not exchangeable, then models fitted to them may be seriously misleading, especially if data are averaged before models are tested (Pellegrino & Goldman, 1989).

In summary, the goal of estimating scores for individual subjects that reflect the action of particular component processes is greatly compromised when all subjects do not solve all items in the same way.

Resolving Residual Variation into Component Scores

General Statement of the Problem. The problems of error-response latencies, speed-accuracy trade-offs, and within-person strategy shifts destroy the symmetry of the observation design. Large pieces of the design generate missing or ambiguous data for some individuals and not others. The faceted test is literally shot full of holes—nonrandomly. But component scores are not what they seem even in the ideal case where all subjects solve all items, all use the same strategy for each item, and all adopt the same speed–accuracy trade-off.

The basic problem is this: Any task of psychological interest requires more than one component process. In a componential analysis, one decomposes task performance into two or more component processes and then estimates scores for each individual on the various components. It is thus easy to think that one has also thereby decomposed individual differences captured in a total score on the task into smaller chunks, each of which corresponds to a different mental process. This is not the case. Individual differences in overall task performance are not decomposed. Instead, component scores merely salvage new individual difference variance from the residual. Consider a simple example: n_p subjects are administered n_i mental rotation problems. Each item shows two stimuli. The task is to determine if one stimulus can be rotated into congruence with the other or if they are mirror images. The dependent measure is response accuracy. Thus, we have a simple person-by-item data matrix with n_p rows and n_i columns. Assuming that both the person facet and the item facet are random, we can estimate three variance components: the person component (p), the item component (i), and a residual component that confounds the person × item interaction and other disturbances (pi, e).

Suppose an individual difference researcher attempts to go beyond a mean score for each subject and, instead, derives component scores that better reflect the process of mental rotation for each subject. To this end, he applies the model of Shepard and Metzler (1971) and computes the linear regression of response accuracy on the angular separation between stimuli. The slope of this function estimates the rate at which accuracy declines with increases in rotation. The intercept estimates the accuracy of all nonrotation processes (encoding, comparison, and response). Assume that the investigator fits this model to the data for each subject and that estimates of model fit are relatively high. Armed with two component scores for each subject, the slope and the intercept, he correlates them with other variables, expecting that the slope score will better represent spatial processing than will a score that also contains other components. Instead, he finds that the intercept shows relatively high correlations with other variables, whereas the slope score (i.e., the rotation component) shows weak or inconsistent relationships with other variables.

The reason for this becomes clear when we examine what part of the variance is explained by component scores. In terms of generalizability theory, component scores salvage systematic individual differences from the residual (pi, e) variance. These differences are ignored when performance for each subject is represented by a score that averages performance over all items. A part of this residual represents individual differences in slopes. Average effects of amount of rotation required on response latencies (i.e., the average slope) are captured by the i component. Individual differences in slope certainly exist, but they are usually overshowed by average differences between persons (p component) and the average effects of items (the i component). Thus, mean scores for subjects (the p component) can show high correlations with other variables, and model fits to item means (the i component) can be excellent, but the process parameters derived from the task show no dependable relationships with other variables.

Some have recognized this problem but assumed that it merely reflected the well-known fact that individual differences in gain scores (whether constructed from two-wave or multiple-wave data) are unreliable. The implication is that if one somehow had more reliable measures, component scores would be more useful. On the contrary, one could have error-free measurement of component scores and yet fail to find relationships between component scores and other variables.

This is shown clearly in the model that is fitted to each subject's data:

$$Y_{pi} = I_p + B_p X_i \tag{1}$$

where Y_{pi} is the score for person p on item i, I_p is the intercept for person p, B_p is the slope for person p, and X_i is the angular separation between stimuli on item i. With a little algebra, this can be rewritten as:

$$Y_{pi} = \bar{Y}_{p\cdot} + B_p (X_i - \bar{X}.). \tag{2}$$

Here $\bar{Y}_{p\cdot}$ is the mean score on dependent measure Y for person p, B_p is the slope for person p, and $X_i - \bar{X}.$ is the deviation between the rotation required by a given trial and the average amount of rotation required for all trials. The upper limit for variability across individuals in slopes (B_p values) is given by the size of the pi variance component.[1] When this component is large relative to the p component, then there may be large variations in slope across individuals. However, when the pi interaction is relatively small, then there is little variability to be explained. Highly homogeneous tasks—such as the mental rotation task—typically show good internal consistency, that is, a large p component and a small pi, e component. When this is the case, the mean score for each person

---

[1]This is because the interaction may have nonlinear components as well; further, the pi component will often be confounded with e, as in the present example.

($\bar{Y}_{p.}$) will capture most of the systematic individual differences and will be highly correlated with the intercept, I_p, as a comparison of Equations 1 and 2 shows. In other words, individual component scores can explain only that portion of the individual difference variance ordinarily relegated to the residual when a total (or mean) score is reported, and do not explain or decompose the typically much larger variance captured by the person component, that is, the variability due to overall performance on the task.

Information-processing analysis of tasks contributes important information about how subjects attempted to solve items on the task. Component scores are of secondary importance. Such measures do not decompose and therefore do not help explain individual differences in overall task performance.

BEYOND CORRELATES AND COMPONENTS

Limitations of Tests as Tasks and of Tasks as Tests

When things are not going well, it is often useful to examine basic assumptions. One assumption of both experimental and differential psychologists was that the tests or tasks most familiar to them would provide useful vehicles for understanding individual differences in abilities. For differential psychologists, the assumption was that cognitive tests were cognitive tasks that could be studied in the same way that experimental psychologists studied other tasks. Furthermore, unlike tasks taken directly from the laboratory, these testlike tasks had the important advantage that individual differences on them had known relationships with other mental tests and with criterion tasks.

However, these advantages were often lost or at least compromised in the transition from test to laboratory task. For example, test items were rarely studied experimentally in exactly the same form as they had appeared on source tests. At the very least, items were taken off the printed page and administered one at a time. Time limits were usually removed and replaced with instructions emphasizing speed, accuracy, or both. Difficult items were often eliminated in an effort to improve the interpretability of response latencies. Formats were usually altered, for example, by requiring subjects to process the stem before examining response alternatives, or, more commonly, by reducing the number of alternatives. Most often, however, the experimental task was completely reconstructed so that variables hypothesized to influence different processes within the task could be manipulated systematically, and, if possible, independently. For example, the source test may have contained 10–20 items that varied greatly in difficulty, with many different variables influencing item difficulty. These sources would be identified and then reduced to a number that could be varied orthogonally in the design of the experimental task. Thus, the experimental task might contain hundreds of trials, many of which would be unlike anything that appeared on the source test.

But perhaps the most important limitation was that although psychometric tests were generally designed to provide efficient vehicles for estimating individual differences, such tests were not composed of items designed to reveal interesting individual differences in processes.

Two Types of Cognitive Tasks. It is perhaps no accident that qualitative advances in our understanding of the mental processes that produce intelligent performances have more often come from those who study the development of intelligence rather than from those who have attempted to describe organization of individual differences at a particular point in time. Much of this can be explained by a closer examination of the type of task typically studied by the developmentalist.

All scientific measurements of intelligence that we have at present are measures of some product produced by the person or animal in question, or of the way in which some product is produced. A is rated as more intelligent than B because he produces a better product, essay written, answer found, choice made, completion supplied or the like, *or produces an equally good product in a better way, more quickly or by inference rather than by rote memory, or by more ingenious use of the material at hand.* (E. L. Thorndike, Bregman, Cobb, & Woodyard, 1926, p. 11–12, emphasis added)

Thorndike et al. (1926) described two types of tasks: tasks that support inferences about ability from individual differences in the average quality or correctness of responses given (a quantitative judgment), and tasks that permit inferences about ability from the type of response made (a qualitative judgment). We claim that process theories of ability constructs will be difficult to derive from analyses of tasks designed to represent ability in an ''amount solved'' score. On the other hand, we see much promise in tasks that everyone can solve, but that allow inferences about ability from the nature of the response given.

There are two sources of evidence for this claim: (a) the growing realization that traditional methods of defining ability as individual differences in number correct on some task or group of tasks are often incompatible with experimental methods used to define ability by individual differences in the way information is processed, and (b) the corresponding realization that investigations of process give considerable insight when applied to tasks that are explicitly designed to admit a variety of solution methods, especially when these different solution methods can be inferred from the type of response given, that is, when the investigator is more interested in classifying responses than in scoring them.

Early efforts to develop tests which provided a qualitative assessment of intelligence, such as the tests of Healy and Fernald (1911) or even the Binet scale of 1908, "did not emphasize the objective score which the child made so much as his general behavior and the way in which he went about the tasks which were set him" (Freeman, 1926, p. 108). For example, Binet and Simon (1908/1916) extoled the virtues of a picture presentation task "of exceptional value" for diagnosing intelligence. "We place [this task] above all others, and if we were obliged to retain only one, we should not hesitate to select this one" (p. 189). The task consists of three pictures, all showing one or more persons and containing a theme. The child is shown a picture and asked "What is this?" or "Tell me what you see here." Three types of responses are distinguished: (a) an enumeration response ("a man, and a cart," etc.) (b) a descriptive response ("There is an old man and a little boy pulling a cart"), and (c) an interpretive response ("There is a poor man moving his household goods"). Thus, all children are shown the same stimuli, all respond, and intellectual levels are inferred from the quality of the response given. This is the type of task favored by Piaget and many other developmental psychologists. However, it was not the type of task chosen by Terman, Yerkes, Thorndike, and others who strove to solve the practical problem of assessing intelligence. They realized that judgments about process were less dependable than judgments about whether the subject gave a keyed response, or, with the introduction of group tests, whether the subject selected the keyed response, and so qualitative assessments of process were quickly displaced by quantitative assessments of product. Tests that provided a score that could be unambiguously compared with scores for other individuals better fit the requirements for standardization of a burgeoning test industry that was more interested in identifying who was intelligent than in understanding what intelligence was.

By the 1970s, however, cognitive psychologists had developed new methods for testing inferences about process, methods that were more sophisticated and objective than clinical judgments. Rather ironically, many of us attempted to apply these sophisticated methods of detecting process to a class of tasks pruned of interesting individual differences in processes through 50 years of item and factor analyses. It is a tribute to the power of these new methods of analysis that they found anything interesting at all.

Strategies as Substance. The most important contribution of an information-processing analysis of a particular task is information on how subjects solved the task. This information is most useful when there are interesting and important differences in the way subjects solve a task that might be discovered by such analyses. Differences in the way subjects solve tasks are particularly interesting if they can be systematically related to other indices of learning or cognitive development.

Unfortunately, these are not the sort of differences we are likely to find by studying performance on test-like tasks modeled after homogeneous ability tests or laboratory tasks. For example, studies of how subjects solve test-like tasks modeled after the mental rotation problems of Thurstone (1938) or Shepard and Metzler (1971) tell us that a major source of difficulty on such tasks is the speed or accuracy with which subjects can accomplish the rotation transformation. Did anyone seriously doubt this? What is news is when we find that some subjects appear *not* to use a rotation strategy, or when we find that subjects perseverate in rotating stimuli in one direction (e.g., clockwise) when rotation in the opposite direction would be shorter (Ippel & Beem, 1987; Rust, 1988), or when we find that some subjects make several attempts to rotate problems whereas others require only a single attempt (Lohman, 1988). However, such differences are difficult to detect, simply because these tasks were not designed to reveal them. Like all ''point-scale'' tasks, they were designed to reflect individual differences in ability by estimating how far up a ladder one can climb or how many steps can be climbed in a fixed time. More importantly, though, these differences in strategy often do not tell us much about the ability construct we hope to understand. In other words, they caution our interpretation of tests scores by informing us that even homogeneous tasks may represent different abilities for different subjects. However, they do not go very far in telling us what those abilities might be.

The argument, then, is that ability tests often do not make informative cognitive tasks. Furthermore, the chief contribution of cognitive analyses of such tasks ought to be to determine when subjects are attempting to solve items in ways that compromise the interpretation of their scores. For example, analyses of errors made by children on analogical reasoning tests of the type ''A is to B as C is to—'' suggest that less able and younger subjects sometimes attempt to solve items by finding an alternative that looks like or is in some other way associated with one of the terms in the problem stem, usually the ''C'' term (Heller, 1979). Such subjects are not engaged in analogical reasoning at all, and so their scores should not be interpreted as such. Test items should be designed in such a way that they eliminate (or at least do not encourage) such methods of responding, or can reveal them when they occur.

In passing, it is worth noting that analyses that aim to explain individual differences in response latencies generally have little to say about these sorts of differences in strategy, because latencies can be modeled only when error rates are low for all subjects. Models that focus on errors do a better job, although a careful item analysis is often equally informative.

Rule-Based Assessment

What sort of tasks might be more informative? We have already mentioned the example of the picture interpretation task used by Binet and given general guidelines. Specifically:

1. Tasks should admit a variety of answers, not simply a single correct an-

swer. This point concerns the observation design. It is often more a function of how tasks are administered and thus of what type of responses are elicited than of anything else. Forced-choice formats are often least informative, multiple-choice formats of intermediate value, and free-response formats generally most informative. Furthermore, tasks themselves often structure responses in ways that make response classification a less arduous problem than, say, the classification of open-ended essay questions (see, e.g., Anderson's adaptation of Piaget's balance beam task, discussed next; for an interesting scheme for classifying open-ended essays, see Biggs & Collis, 1982).

2. There should be a systematic relationship between responses given and the way in which the subject attempted to solve problems. This point concerns the relationship between the observation design and the different information-processing models that are hypothesized. Observation designs defined by the cartesian product of different aspects of items are particularly powerful, especially when different facets are systematically related to different measurement models. For example, if one method for solving a task uses (among other processes) component process A whereas another method uses component process B, then it may be possible to distinguish between these methods if independent variables that influence component processes A and B can be varied independently. This is often not the case, and so many tasks that are otherwise interesting either do not elicit interesting differences in solution strategy or elicit strategies that are difficult to disentangle.

3. Individual differences in solution strategy should show systematic relationships with ability constructs defined in a traditional "amount solved" score or with other criterion measures. This last point concerns the relationship between the classification scheme imposed on subjects by the different process models fitted to their data and external constructs. In other words, many tasks elicit qualitative differences in solution strategy. Such differences gain import if these strategies can themselves be ordered by another measurement model, for example, a model derived from a theory of learning or development. Thus, the goal is to invent tasks that elicit qualitatively different types of responses (or response patterns) for individuals who differ quantitatively on some other dimension. Good theory and psychological insight are probably the best guides here.

Many of the tasks invented by Piaget satisfy all of these criteria to one degree or another, particularly the first and the last. One particularly interesting example is the balance scale task of intuitive physics (Inhelder & Piaget, 1955/1958). The apparatus for the task consists of a two-arm balance with four pegs spaced at equal intervals on each side of the fulcrum. In the forced-choice version of the task, metal disks of equal weight are placed on the pegs on both sides of the fulcrum. The scale is prevented from tipping by blocks under each arm. The subject's task is to predict what would happen if the blocks were removed.

Siegler (1976) claimed that subjects use four different rules when solving balance-scale problems and that rule usage is systematically related to cognitive development. Subjects using Rule 1 consider only weight. Those using Rule 2 incorporate information about distance from the fulcrum, but only when weights are equal. Subjects using Rule 3 consider both weight and distance, but in a series of binary decisions based on one dimension at a time. These subjects fail to solve conflict problems in which one side has greater weight and the other greater distance. Finally, subjects using Rule 4 consider both weight and distance, and use the correct weight × distance product rule when confronted with conflict problems.

Siegler infers which rule subjects use by administering a set of diagnostic test problems. Problems are constructed so that the consistent use of different rules will produce predictably different patterns of response over the sequence of test problems. Results have generally shown that most subjects administered a standard 24-item test can be classified as using one of the four rules.

Although the balance-scale task exemplifies at least some of the characteristics of a task rich in interesting process differences, Siegler's rule-assessment procedures have been challenged. Several problems have been noted, particularly by Wilkening and Anderson (1982). First, the decision-tree methodology Siegler uses has no way to assess whether deviations from a rule are real or random occurrences. In other words, "because it lacks an error theory to handle response variability, the decision tree methodology [of Siegler] tends to impose itself on the data" (Wilkening & Anderson, 1982, p. 225). Second, the method is unable to detect integration of attributes, if such occurs. For example, if subjects solve balance-scale problems by combining weight and distance by some additive rule, then their performance will generally be diagnosed by Siegler as following a nonadditive, decision-tree rule. Third, the forced-choice methodology may itself impose a strategy of sequential processing, and may thus lead one to infer that knowledge is represented by rules that correspond to decision points in binary trees used to model a sequence of choice responses. The same critique applies to production-system representations of knowledge. According to Wilkening and Anderson (1982), the important point is not that such systems are wrong, but that they are unable to recognize when they are wrong. They claim that Anderson's "functional measurement methodology" provides a better way to infer what type of rules subjects use.

Functional Measurement Methodology

Functional measurement was developed by Anderson (1981, 1982) as a part of information integration theory, which attempts to answer the question: How do subjects combine information from different sources to form an overall judgment? Experimental studies in many areas suggest that subjects often integrate information using simple algebraic rules (such as addition or multiplication) when asked to make an overall judgment.

The first step is to gather data using a free-response rather than a forced-choice procedure. For example, in one free-response version of the balance-scale task, the investigator manipulates weights and distance on one arm, and subjects adjust the distance and/or weight on the other arm to the point where they think that the two sides will balance. An adjustment procedure of this sort was also used in the original Inhelder and Piaget (1955/1958) studies.

Like S. Sternberg's additive-factors method, functional measurement uses analysis of variance on factorially designed experiments to infer different types of integration rules. For example, suppose weight and distance of objects placed on the left side of the fulcrum are varied in a factorial design, and subjects indicate their responses by moving all weights the same distance along the right arm of the balance scale. Thus distance is taken as the dependent measure. Those subjects using a simple addition rule to combine information about weight and distance should show main effects for each factor, but no interaction. Those combining weight and distance according to a multiplication rule should show the fan pattern typical of linear interaction.

Our aim here is not to advocate the use of functional measurement instead of other rule-assessment procedures. Indeed, functional measurement has its critics as well (e.g., Simon, 1976). Rather, our goal is to suggest that those who are drawn to the symmetry of faceted tests need not restrict themselves to the study of response latencies on fast-process tasks, or errors on complex tasks, or some mixture of latencies and errors on tasks of intermediate complexity. This is important, given the many problems we have noted for these dependent variables. Further, while we see much promise in rule-based assessment, it seems critical to employ methods that allow formal testing (and thus rejection) of models that specify different processing strategies.

SUMMARY AND CONCLUSIONS

The purpose of this chapter was to present the general features of a theory for measurement of cognitive processes, to show how it has been applied, and to suggest how future applications might be more productive. We began by arguing that the failure to identify the processes of intelligence originated in the failure to identify and to take into account aspects of a test that have measurable impacts on performance during test taking. Indeed, the generally accepted idea of test theory as applied statistics seems to have precluded the development of a structural theory of measurement needed for the measurement of processes. Following Guttman (1971), we claimed that tests could be viewed as observation designs, and scores on tests as the products of particular measurement models. We then showed how scores for mental process could be estimated using componential models. We claimed that a focus on component scores had not been terribly productive, primarily because such scores do not decompose the major source of individual differences on tasks. Instead, the nature of the process model itself appeared to be a more useful target variable. Because of this, we claimed that a cognitive approach to measurement would be most fruitful if applied to tasks designed to reveal qualitative differences between individuals in knowledge or strategy. We then described the general features of such tasks, and related these features to the measurement theory proposed earlier in the paper. We also noted that neither tests modeled after experimental tasks studied by cognitive psychologists nor experimental tasks modeled after ability tests studied by differential psychologists were designed to evoke or to reveal such individual differences. But such tasks do exist, and many have been studied by developmental psychologists. The balance-scale task is one example. We conclude with a discussion of this task and of two different methods that have been used to study it.

REFERENCES

Anderson, N. H. (1981). *Foundations of information integration theory.* New York: Academic Press.
Anderson, N. H. (1982). *Methods of information integration theory.* New York: Academic Press.
Biggs, J. B., & Collis, K. F. (1982). *Evaluating the quality of learning: The SOLO Taxonomy.* New York: Academic Press.
Binet, A., & Simon, T. (1916). The development of intelligence in the child. In H. Goddard (Ed.) (E. S. Kate, Trans.), *The development of intelligence in children* (pp. 181–273). Baltimore: Williams & Wilkins. (Reprinted from *L'Annee Psychologique*, 1908, *14*, 1–94).
Cardinet, J., Tourneur, Y., & Allal, L. (1981). Extensions of generalizability theory and its applications in educational measurement. *Journal of Educational Measurement, 18*, 4, 183–204.
Carpenter, P. A., & Just, M. A. (1978). Eye fixations during mental rotation. In J. W. Senders, D. F. Fisher, & R. A. Monty (Eds.), *Eye movements and higher psychological functions* (pp. 115–134). Hillsdale, NJ: Lawrence Erlbaum Associates.
Clark, H. H., & Chase, W. G. (1972). On the process of comparing sentences against pictures. *Cognitive Psychology, 3*, 472–517.
Cronbach, L. J. (1957). The two disciplines of scientific psychology. *American Psychologist, 12*, 671–684.
Cronbach, L. J., Gleser, G. C., Nanda, H., & Rajaratnam, N. (1972). *The dependability of behavioral measurements.* New York: Wiley.
Donders, F. C. (1969). On the speed of mental processes. *Acta Psychologica, 30*, 412–431. (Translated by W. G. Koster from the original in *Onderzoekingen gedaan in het Physiologisch Laboratorium der Utrechtsche Hoogeschool, 1868, Tweede reeks,* II, 92–120).
Fischer, G. H. (1974). *Einfuhrung in die theorie psychologischer tests. Grundlagen und anwendungen.* Bern: Hans Huber.
Freeman, F. N. (1926). *Mental tests: Their history, principles and application.* Boston: Houghton Mifflin.
Guilford, J. P. (1967). *The nature of human intelligence.* New York: McGraw-Hill.
Guttman, L. (1971). Measurement as structural theory. *Psychometrika, 36*, 329–347.
Healy, W., & Fernald, G. M. (1911). Tests for practical mental classification. *Psychological Monographs, 13*(2).

Heller, J. I. (1979). Cognitive processing in verbal analogy solution (Doctoral dissertation, University of Pittsburgh). *Dissertation Abstracts International, 40*, 2553A.

Inhelder, B., & Piaget, J. (1958). *The growth of logical thinking from childhood to adolescence* (A. Parsons & S. Milgram, Trans.). New York: Basic Books. (Originally published 1955)

Ippel, M. J. (1981). Generalizability of performance scores on embedded figures material. *Educational and Psychological Measurement, 41*, 315–331.

Ippel, M. J. (1986). *Component-testing: A theory of cognitive aptitude measurement.* Amsterdam: Free University Press.

Ippel, M. J., & Beem, A. L. (1987). A theory of antagonistic strategies. In E. De Corte, H. Lodewijks, R. Parmentier, & P. Span (Eds.), *Learning and instruction: European research in an international context* (Vol. 1, pp. 111–121). Oxford, UK: Leuven University Press and Pergamon Press.

Irving, S. H., Dann, P. L., & Anderson, J. D. (1990). Towards a theory of algorithm-determined cognitive test construction. *British Journal of Psychology, 81*, 173–195.

Kane, M. T. (1982). A sampling model for validity. *Applied Psychological Measurement, 6, 2*, 125–160.

Kyllonen, P. C., Lohman, D. F., & Woltz, D. J. (1984). Componential modeling of alternative strategies for performing spatial tasks. *Journal of Educational Psychology, 76*, 1325–1345.

Loevinger, J. (1965). Person and population as psychometric concepts. *Psychological Review, 72*, 143–155.

Lohman, D. F. (1979). *Spatial ability: Individual differences in speed and level* (Tech. Rep. No. 9). Stanford, CA: Stanford University, Aptitude Research Project, School of Education. (NTIS No. AD-A075 973.)

Lohman, D. F. (1988). Spatial abilities as traits, processes, and knowledge. In R. J. Sternberg (Ed.), *Advances in the psychology of human intelligence* (Vol. 4, pp. 181–248). Hillsdale, NJ: Lawrence Erlbaum Associates.

Lohman, D. F. (1989a). Estimating individual differences in information processing using speed-accuracy models. In R. Kaufer, P. L. Ackerman, & R. Cudeck (Eds.), *Abilities, motivation, and methodology: The Minnesota symposium on learning and individual differences* (pp. 119–164). Hillsdale, NJ: Lawrence Erlbaum Associates.

Lohman, D. F. (1989b). Individual differences in errors and latencies on cognitive tasks. *Learning and Individual Differences, 1*, 179–202.

Lord, F. M. (1980). *Applications of item response theory to practical testing problems.* Hillsdale, NJ: Lawrence Erlbaum Associates.

Lord, F. M., & Novick, M. (1968). *Statistical theories of mental test scores.* Reading, MA: Addison-Wesley.

McNemar, Q. (1964). Lost: Our intelligence? Why? *American Psychologist, 19*, 871–882.

Mellenbergh, G. J. (1977). The replicability of measures. *Psychological Bulletin, 34, 2*, 378–384.

Pellegrino, J. W., & Goldman, S. R. (1989). Mental chronometry and individual differences in cognitive processes: Common pitfalls and their solutions. *Learning and Individual Differences, 2*, 203–227.

Rasch, G. (1960). *Probabilistic models for some intelligence and attainment tests.* Cophenhagen, Denmark: Danmarks Paedagogiske Institute.

Rozeboom, W. W. (1978). Domain validity—why care? *Educational and Psychological Measurement, 38*, 81–88.

Rust, T. S. (1988). *Strategy shifting on a spatial rotation task.* Unpublished master's thesis, University of Iowa, Iowa City.

Shepard, R., & Metzler, J. (1971). Mental rotation of three-dimensional objects. *Science, 171*, 701–703.

Shepard, R. N., & Cooper, L. A. (1982). *Mental images and their transformations.* Cambridge, MA: MIT Press.

Siegler, R. S. (1976). Three aspects of cognitive development. *Cognitive Psychology, 8*, 481–520.

Siegler, R. S. (1989). Hazards of mental chronometry: An example from children's subtraction. *Journal of Educational Psychology, 81,* 497–506.

Simon, H. A. (1976). Discussion: Cognition and social behavior. In J. S. Carroll & J. W. Payne (Eds.), *Cognition and social behavior* (pp. 253–267). Potomac, MD: Lawrence Erlbaum Associates.

Snow, R. E., & Peterson, P. (1985). Cognitive analyses of tests: Implications for redesign. In S. E. Embretson (Eds.), *Test design: Developments in psychology and psychometrics* (pp. 149–166). Orlando, FL: Academic Press.

Spearman, C. (1904). "General intelligence," objectively determined and measured. *American Journal of Psychology, 15,* 201–293.

Spearman, C. E. (1927). *The abilities of man.* London: Macmillan.

Sternberg, R. J. (1977). *Intelligence, information processing, and analogical reasoning: The componential analysis of human abilities.* Hillsdale, NJ: Lawrence Erlbaum Associates.

Sternberg, R. J. (1985). *Beyond IQ: A triarchic theory of human intelligence.* Cambridge: Cambridge University Press.

Sternberg, R. J., & Rifkin, B. (1979). The development of analogical reasoning processes. *Journal of Experimental Child Psychology, 27,* 195–232.

Sternberg, S. (1969). Memory-scanning: Mental processes revealed by reaction time experiments. *American Scientist, 57,* 421–457.

Taylor, D. A. (1976). Stage analysis of reaction time. *Psychological Bulletin, 83,* 161–191.

Thorndike, E. L., Bregman, E. O., Cobb, M. V., & Woodyard, E. (1926). *The measurement of intelligence.* New York: Columbia University, Teachers College.

Thurstone, L. L. (1938). Primary mental abilities. *Psychometric Monographs, 1.*

Thurstone, L. L. (1947). *Multiple factor analysis.* Chicago: University of Chicago Press.

Wickelgren, W. A. (1977). Speed-accuracy tradeoff and information processing dynamics. *Acta Psychologica, 41,* 67–85.

Wilkening, F., & Anderson, N. H. (1982). Comparison of two rule-assessment methodologies for studying cognitive development and cognitive structure. *Psychological Bulletin, 92,* 215–237.

Comments on Chapters 1-3

Nancy S. Cole
Educational Testing Service

INTRODUCTION

Testing is a field in the process of being re-created. For half a century, the field has focused on measuring individual differences on major, global proficiencies. The power of this approach has not only defined testing but also inhibited its expansion to the wide range of other important possibilities for which testing technology is useful and needed. In the first three chapters, and in this book as a whole, we get a glimpse of this burgeoning new field of testing.

Some of my early views of this new field of testing came through efforts to understand differences in group responses to test items, which were then being studied under the rubric "item bias." I came to appreciate how much more than a global score was present in today's tests, and to realize that "much more" was important to our understanding of individual differences as well as group differences. In fact, I was so bold as to predict a decade ago that the greatest long-term contribution of item bias studies would be to push our field toward "understanding the subtle differences in the content of a stimulus (such as a test item) to which individuals react differently, and . . . understanding the conceptual and psychological implications of statistical differences in items" (Cole, 1981).

The first three chapters of this book indicate that I was right about the field reaching a point of far greater understanding of differences in task or item features to which individuals respond, and in the psychological meaning of such differences. The chapters also illustrate that I was wrong about studies of item bias being a sole or primary impetus for change. The impetus for these increased understandings has come from a surprising breadth of perspectives and interests. It has included educators trying to understand features of student performance for decisions about next instructional steps, educational psychologists trying to build educational–psychological theories, cognitive psychologists building theories of mental processes, and more.

My understanding in the aforementioned quote was incomplete in another way. I characterized the differences in task features that we saw in test-bias studies as subtle (and, in different language in the same article, "small" effects that are "not obvious"). Whereas they were subtle in the context of the global measures of proficiency we were studying, they can take on an important life of their own when they are the target of interest. Mislevy (chapter 2) made the distinction between interest in overall proficiency and interest in "the cross-current patterns." As he noted in his chapter, if the decision of interest depends on the cross-current patterns, then the cross-current patterns (the subtleties I referred to) are not subtleties at all but the patterns of interest. In a broad test of high-school mathematics, for example, correct answers to an item on the Pythagorian theorem and to another on the volume of a sphere might be considered exchangeable if the goal is to predict success in introductory calculus. The distinction is crucial, however, for deciding in which of the topics a student requires instruction.

A decade ago, I was trying to understand accidents of current test design. I thought of my task as understanding the accidents that happened to be present in item features rather than recognizing the important gains that could come to be if we theorized about the cross-current patterns and designed tasks to test those theories. When seeking to understand psychological processes or educational features of various types, tests must be designed to elicit the patterns of interest. Some of these task features I called "subtle" properly became the primary focus of concern and central to the design of the test.

This set of chapters illustrates the importance of the layer of patterns in human responses just underneath the global proficiencies that have so dominated testing. They illustrate as well several key issues in approaching the task of understanding this important new layer of concern. Snow and Lohman in chapter 1 ("Cognitive Psychology, New Test Design, and New Test Theory: An Introduction") survey many of the important aspects of this important layer that we need to understand, even approaching from the traditional interest in cognitive abilities and cognitive achievement. As we begin to understand the constituents of students' capabilities—their individual configurations of knowledge, skill, understanding, belief, and attitude—how can we develop observational settings that capture critical distinctions among students? Mislevy in chapter 2 ("Foundations of a New Test Theory") provides a perspective on the past development of testing and the prospects for the future. If we wish to assess key features of students' skill and knowledge configurations, how can statistical theory be employed to guide inferences and make decisions? Lohman and Ippel in chapter 3 ("Cognitive Diagnosis: From Statistically Based Assessment Toward Theory-Based Assessment") address the requirements of testing for building theories—understanding in testable ways the intellectual processes that underlie performances. After modeling the processes that underly performance in a class of problems, how can we design measures of students' capabilities and devise test items to effectively inform those measures? Together, the chapters point us toward what will be needed in re-creating the field of testing for a higher level of understanding and use.

DIVERSITY OF PURPOSES

Several common threads of these three chapters by Snow and Lohman, Mislevy, and Lohman and Ippel set the tone for the book as a whole. The first thread, and perhaps the most striking, is the fact that the efforts for creating a new generation of tests beyond the traditional global measures of proficiency are coming from many directions and interests. Some interests come out of the educational arena. There the global measures have assumed increasing importance for increasing numbers of purposes, with dissatisfaction in their use for many of those new purposes. Snow and Lohman and Mislevy bring that educational perspective to their chapters, often trying, for practical educational purposes, to understand more than global proficiency.

In addition, Snow and Lohman address the need to understand better, both theoretically and practically, even the general-level cognitive skills that have been the traditional focus of tests. They attend closely to the underlying skills and processes for the traditional global proficiencies, apparently not to reject the global but to understand it better. Snow and Lohman's approach conjures up the image of layers of an onion in which the traditional measurement has been a thick outer layer, and now they are seeking to look below that outer layer to understand more thoroughly other layers. Different layers represent different questions—whether to understand educational implications or educational–psychological theories.

Lohman and Ippel illustrate well the theory building purpose. They wish to understand intellectual processes in ways well beyond those with which traditional measures can help. They approach the problem of examining cognitive process theories and types of observation designs and measurement models needed for that purpose. Their purpose is to build a theory of component cognitive processes, not to make immediate practical decisions (although in their minds a good theory of cognitive processes would relate to other important characterizations of intellectual functioning). Theory-building is the purpose, and their chapter can be seen as an effort to think through what their own theoretical area must do with testing to use it effectively for building better theories.

It is important to note the diversity of purpose in these three chapters because it suggests that this period of re-creating testing will not be driven by a small number of new questions but by a large and diverse set of questions and purposes. It is also important to note the implications of this diversity of purpose for test design and statistical models to which these three chapters point.

NEW TEST DESIGNS

Another important thread of the three chapters concerns the implications of the different purposes for test design. It is hardly revolutionary to recognize that the use of the observations or measurements must determine the appropriate nature of the tasks and the design of the task observations, if their intended purpose is to be met. However, in the traditional testing of major proficiencies, test design has received less attention than have the statistical theories designed to handle the scores produced. Perhaps measuring the global proficiencies came so easy that test design became a hidden feature. Design considerations do exist for present tests, but more informally than their statistical counterparts. Today's test design is not based on a well-explicated design theory; tomorrow's likely will need to be.

This requirement for new approaches to test design is implicit to the Snow and Lohman chapter, and more explicit but not as developed in Mislevy's chapter. Design receives the greatest attention in the chapter by Lohman and Ippel; it is also a major contribution not only of that chapter but of the approach of cognitive psychology to testing. The message I derive from all three is that purpose will determine the test design. The diversity of purposes already noted implies to me that we will see many new test designs for new purposes. Test design will become an important and visible part of the technical and theoretical base of testing of the future.

THEORY OF SUBSTANCE
AS WELL AS OF TECHNOLOGY

The third thread of great interest in these chapters is the extent to which substantive theory of the characteristic being measured will be central to each new observation/measurement direction. The traditional measurement approach has certainly used the expertise of the particular field in creating test questions and understanding what is important to measure. However, it has been characterized by a set of technologies widely applicable to a range of substantive fields and little affected by differences among the fields. As long as global proficiency was the target, the testing approach worked.

By contrast, as these chapters indicate, when the focus is on an educational decision or a psychological theory or a more fine-grained understanding of the global proficiency, development of a theory of the situation cannot be avoided. In fact, such a theory shapes the very approach to the observation and measurement. Testing of the future will include intricately the theory of the field of use as well as the technology of the testing. In the past, we have often thought of testing technology as a field unto itself and of testing as a discipline for separate study. The chapters make clear the extent to which, if that has not already changed, it will change in the future. Testing of the future will be a theory-based activity grounded in the substantive theory of the characteristics being tested. Statistical theories will be needed, but they will be driven from the substantive fields.

This combination of substantive theory and technological capabilities, common in most arenas of scientific endeavor, will be the combination of future testing.

NEW STATISTICAL TEST THEORIES

Traditional testing that has served as the base and point of contrast for these chapters has used predominantly objective exercises that contribute (perhaps in a host of complex and not-well-understood ways) to a fairly global set of proficiencies that are important to decisions of several types because of their relation to subsequent important events. A complex of statistical models has grown up over the years to address this situation, and they have been applied in a fairly wide range of situations with minimal differences from situation to situation. One of the implications of these chapters and the previous points noted in this commentary is that testing of the future will involve multiple test theories in ways more diverse than the statistical theoretical approaches of today. Each theory will start from the features of the substantive field and its theoretical base, and will diverge in ways from other theories and starting points. Some parts will be relatively universal, and technical theories from one field may be adapted or adopted by some others, but the assumption of a single statistical theory for all testing will not exist.

It is interesting to speculate on some of the characteristics of the new statistical theories. In some arenas where the underlying substantive theories are strong, they may require more highly explicated models of expected behavior than we now use. The test designs will be more fine-grained in these situations, and the models of expected data more complexly stated. These will most likely be the theory-building uses of testing rather than the practical applications. In other arenas where the immediate goal is to try to help students learn better, the theories are as yet less precise, and test designs with the level of control needed for theoretical work have not yet been achieved. Here it seems likely that the starting models will be cruder, with the first level of learning fo-

cused on the characteristics of test design most helpful for instructional decisions, and the next level of learning attending to statistical models for measuring those characteristics. The challenges are exciting and great in both types
of arenas.

CONCLUSION

A field in transition and on the verge of new possibilities is an exciting field.
Testing is such a field. These chapters point to several of those exciting possibilities, as do the chapters that follow. The challenges, however, are great. The
diversity of purposes and the resulting need for different test designs, a better
base in the theory of the field being tested, and more diverse statistical models
pose problems for several decades ahead. The revolution ahead is not a small
one. In solving these problems, we will be re-creating the field of testing.

REFERENCE

Cole, N. S. (1981). Bias in testing. *American Psychologist, 36,* 10, 1067–1077.

4

Repealing Rules That No Longer Apply to Psychological Measurement

David Thissen
University of North Carolina at Chapel Hill

Item response theory (IRT) has gained considerable acceptance as a basis for item analysis and test scoring in the field of educational measurement, and IRT is gaining a foothold in social measurement as a structural model for the responses to survey questions. However, with the notable exception of the development of computerized adaptive testing, the advent of item response theory has not changed the appearance of tests—the theory has been applied almost exclusively to existing material. Even within the new context of computerized adaptive testing, IRT has been used to provide a scoring mechanism for old tests presented on a computer screen, one item at a time. It does not have to be this way.

In this chapter we will discuss some of the forms a new generation of psychological tests and measurement instruments may take, given item response theory. We will discuss some ways in which IRT may permit the format of psychological tests to be the servant of psychological theory, rather than its master. The concepts will be illustrated using an unconventional scoring method for a test of numerical knowledge in preschool children, a combination rule for data on mental health admissions, and a questionnaire measuring risk for eating disorders among college-age women.

Item response theory is about the processes involved when a person responds to a question (an item). The theory is conceptually based on early work by Thurstone (1925, 1927) on the concept of the response process and by Lazarsfeld (1950) and Lord (1952) on the relationship of latent (unobserved) variables with item responses and test scores. There have been contributions by many others between and since; IRT now provides elegant procedures for item analysis and test construction.

Application of IRT provides numerical summaries of the performance of each item, called item parameters; the item parameters define "trace lines" (Lazarsfeld, 1950, p. 363) showing the relationship between the probability of a particular item response and the latent variable being measured. In the examples that follow, we illustrate the use of several different item response models; in all of these models the item responses depend on a single continuous latent variable.

Our first topic of discussion is, "What is an item?" It is not necessary, within the context of item response theory, that the items upon which measurement is based be the same as the questions the respondent answers. Conjunctive or disjunctive (or, indeed, any) combinations of the answers to the questions may provide the basis for the test scores.

THE "ITEMS" DO NOT HAVE TO BE "ITEMS"
I: PRESCHOOL NUMERICAL KNOWLEDGE

In their description of the use of latent class models for the validation of the structure of knowledge domains, Bergan and Stone (1985) report a number of analyses of the data in Table 4.1. The data were collected as the responses to four items measuring the numerical knowledge of a sample of preschool children in the Head Start program. The first two items required the children to identify numerals (3 or 4), and the second two items required the children to match a numeral (again, 3 or 4) represented by an array of blocks.

For the analysis reported here,[1] we redefine the items as two pseudoitems, each of which has four response categories. The first of these pseudoitems is denoted Identify and has four categories of response: correctly identifying neither numeral, only 3, only 4, or both. The second pseudoitem is called Match, with the same four response categories. The pseudoitems are equivalent to "testlets" as defined by Wainer and Kiely (1987): they are clusters of items between which conditional independence may reasonably be expected. In this case, it is unlikely that anyone wants to measure "identifying knowledge" and "matching knowledge"; we are interested in the knowledge of the children about the concept of number. Knowledge of the numerical properties of 3 and 4 implies that the children should be able both to identify the numerals and to match them to the number of objects that they represent.

Put another way, in a structural model for the data, we presume that the reason that many of the same children correctly identify both numerals and correctly match those numerals to the blocks is because they really understand the numerical meaning of 3 and 4. We also presume that for some preschool children, knowledge of the meaning of these numerals is not yet perfectly reliable; they may be able to respond correctly under some circumstances and not

---

[1]The data analysis discussed in this section is also described by Thissen and Steinberg (1988).

TABLE 4.1
Observed and Expected Frequencies
for the Preschool Numerical Knowledge Pseudoitems

Identify	Match	Observed	Expected	EAP[θ]	(S.D.)
Neither	Neither	71	70.2	−1.0	(0.7)
	3 only	34	32.9	−0.8	(0.7)
	4 only	30	32.9	−0.8	(0.7)
	3 and 4	38	37.1	−0.2	(0.6)
3 only	Neither	30	29.6	−1.0	(0.7)
	3 only	13	13.9	−0.8	(0.7)
	4 only	15	13.9	−0.8	(0.7)
	3 and 4	15	15.7	−0.2	(0.6)
4 only	Neither	13	15.1	−0.5	(0.6)
	3 only	4	8.2	−0.4	(0.6)
	4 only	15	8.2	−0.4	(0.6)
	3 and 4	19	19.4	0.2	(0.6)
3 and 4	Neither	43	42.1	0.1	(0.6)
	3 only	30	28.0	0.2	(0.6)
	4 only	25	28.0	0.2	(0.6)
	3 and 4	197	196.9	0.9	(0.7)

others. Other children may have no real knowledge of the numerical concepts involved in 3 and 4, but may still have some (nonnumerical) knowledge that will result in some correct responses (guesses). Our structural analysis is an attempt to characterize these beliefs quantitatively.

The trace-line model used for these data is the nominal model proposed by Bock (1972), in which the trace line for the response in category $x = 1, 2, \ldots,$ m is

$$T_x(\theta) = \frac{\exp(a_x\theta + c_x)}{\sum_{k=1}^{m} \exp(a_k\theta + c_k)}$$

where θ is the latent variable, and $\{a_k, c_k\}$, $k = 1, 2, \ldots, m$, are category parameters; $m = 4$ for both pseudoitems. Under the assumption of local independence, the model for the proportion observed with response pattern $\mathbf{x}$ $= [x_1, x_2]$ is

$$P(\mathbf{x}) = \int_{-\infty}^{+\infty} \prod_{i=1}^{nitems} T_{x_i}(\theta) \, \phi(\theta) \, d\theta, \qquad (1)$$

where the number of items, $nitems$, may (in general) be greater than two, and $\phi(\theta)$ is the distribution of the underlying latent variable in the population. Here we assume $\phi(\theta)$ is N[0,1]. The constraints

$$a_1 = c_1 = 0$$

are imposed to identify the model. We also impose the constraints $a_2 = a_1$ for Identify and $a_3 = a_2$ and $c_3 = c_2$ for Match because there is no evidence in the data that these parameters are significantly different from each other. [The likelihood ratio test of the (joint) null hypothesis that $a_2 = a_1$ for Identify and $a_3 = a_2$ and $c_3 = c_2$ for Match is $G^2(3) = 0.3$, $p = 0.95$. The test statistic is obtained by fitting the model with and without the constraints—the difference between the two goodness-of-fit statistics is a test of the null hypothesis that the constrained parameters do not differ.]

The likelihood ratio goodness-of-fit statistic indicates that the model fits the data: $G^2(6) = 8.5$, $p = 0.2$. The parameter estimates are shown in Table 4.2, and the results of the analysis are visible in the trace lines in Fig. 4.1. The θ axis in Fig. 4.1 represents (latent) numerical knowledge. For both Identify and Match, the trace line for "3 and 4" rises steeply, indicating that two correct responses discriminate sharply between those with low numerical knowledge and those with higher numerical knowledge. The curve for "Match 3 and 4" is offset somewhat to the right with respect to the curve for "Identify 3 and 4"; in traditional terms, that means that matching is more difficult than identification.

In the case of both matching and identification, "neither" correct has a decreasing trace line over numerical knowledge (θ), as would be expected. Surprisingly, "Identify 3 only" has a trace line that is proportional to the trace line for "neither." The implication is that children who identify 3 correctly, but not 4, are among those of relatively low numerical knowledge. Presumably, their "correct" identification of 3 (with a probability of about .3) arises from something other than knowledge about the properties of numbers or numerals. Very few children correctly identify 4 but not 3. The trace line indicates that this

TABLE 4.2
Preschool Numerical Knowledge Item Parameters

	Identify		
a_1	a_2	a_3	a_4
0.0	0.0	1.18	2.91
c_1	c_2	c_3	c_4
0.0	-0.86	-0.67	0.69
	Match		
a_1	a_2	a_3	a_4
0.0	0.32	0.32	2.04
c_1	c_2	c_3	c_4
0.0	-0.46	-0.46	0.53

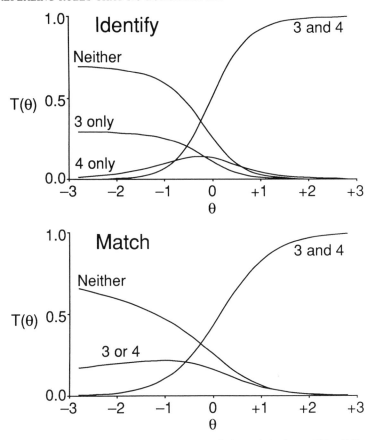

FIG. 4.1. Trace lines for the preschool numerical knowledge items: "identify" in the upper panel, and "match blocks" in the lower panel.

response may be associated with moderate levels of numerical knowledge: They know (weakly?), but err (by accident?) on 3. For the Matching pseudoitem, in contrast to identification, the trace lines for "3 only" and "4 only" are coincident in the model that fits these data. This implies that for the matching task, unlike simple identification, there is no particular difference between the properties of 3 and 4.

This all makes psychological sense. Experienced teachers (or parents or researchers) questioning children in an effort to ascertain their knowledge very rarely settle for a response to a single question. If we ask a child to identify the numeral 3, we realize that a correct answer may reflect some knowledge of number; it may also reflect the fact that the child watches a television show that has a repetitive opening logo making extensive use of the sequence 1-2-3, or that the child has just celebrated a third birthday with much discussion of that numeral. So we ask a second question, under the intuitive assumption that two correct answers in a row are less likely to arise by chance. For these two pseudoitems about identifying and matching 3 and 4, the trace-line analysis agrees with (and extends the precision of) this kind of intuition.

AN ASIDE: HOW DO WE ESTIMATE TRACE LINES?

The trace lines form the core of the IRT item analysis of this little test; how are they obtained? The trace lines are defined by the item parameters, which in turn are estimated from the observed item response data (in this case) by a maximum likelihood procedure described in technical detail elsewhere (Bock & Aitkin, 1981; Thissen & Steinberg, 1984; Thissen, 1988). The curves in Fig. 4.2 may be used to illustrate the essential aspects of the process.

The top panel of Fig. 4.2 describes the population distribution of (latent) numerical knowledge among preschool children; it is assumed to be standard normal. The middle panel of Fig. 4.2 shows the trace lines for "identifying 3 and 4" and "matching 3 and 4." According to the model, the distribution of children correctly performing all four tasks is the product of the population distribution in the upper panel and the two trace lines in the middle panel; that product is shown in the lower panel.

The population distribution is not changed during the process of item parameter estimation, which is also the process of "choosing trace lines." The trace lines, however, are chosen from among many possibilities to their left or right, and steeper or less steep so that the area of the product (in the lower panel in Fig. 4.2) corresponds closely to the percentage of children who actually responded correctly. Related trace lines for the other response categories produce fitted values for the observed counts for all of the other response patterns.

When trace lines have been chosen so that the modeled probabilities for each response pattern correspond most closely to the observed proportions, the parameters associated with those trace lines are the maximum likelihood estimates. The goodness of fit of the model to the data is evaluated by the closeness of the correspondence between the observed and fitted proportions. Here, the fit of the model is quite good; the expected values from the fitted model are included in Table 4.1.

The IRT model, as illustrated in Fig. 4.2, is essentially an explanation of the fact that many of the same children "identify 3 and 4" and "match 3 and 4." The idea is that they are relatively high in the distribution of numerical knowledge, and the trace lines indicate that correct responses are very likely from such children.

The curve in the lower panel of Fig. 4.2 is also used in the computation of IRT scale scores. A commonly used scale score in IRT is the mean, or "expected value" of the product shown in the lower panel; Bock and Mislevy (1982)

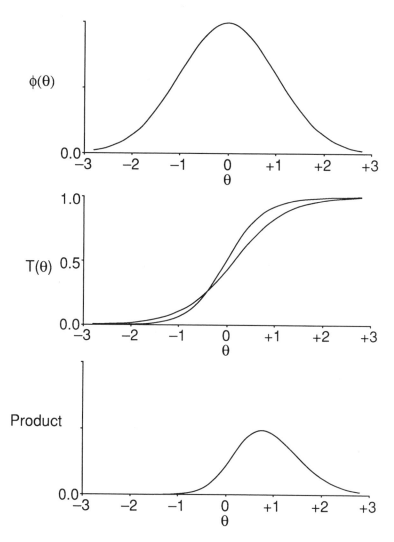

FIG. 4.2. The population distribution (upper panel), trace lines (middle panel), and their product (lower panel) characterizing numerical knowledge for children correctly identifying 3 and 4 and matching 3 and 4.

called this the Expected a posteriori score, or EAP[θ]. All of the response patterns have similarly constructed products, and the means of those products may be used in IRT as "test scores." The values of EAP[θ] are also shown in Table 4.1.

The point here is not how IRT works; it does. It might have been easier to say "you get the trace lines and scale scores by using a computer program," which is also true. The point here is that IRT is a very flexible system for item analysis and test scoring, and it is made much more flexible when we remember that we can recast the definition of the "items" to suit our purposes in psychological measurement. The "items" are not necessarily the same as the "questions."

THE "ITEMS" DO NOT HAVE TO BE "ITEMS"
II: MENTAL HEALTH ADMISSIONS

Klassen and O'Connor (1987) conducted a prospective study of predictors of violence in adult male mental health admissions. Participants in their study were considered "potentially violent" when admitted to a mental health center, due to a history of violence toward others or a presenting problem involving violence. The goal of the research was the development of a system to aid in the prediction of subsequent violent behavior. To this end, Klassen and O'Connor collected a large amount of data on the participants, and followed up later to determine who was, in fact, subsequently violent.

One combination of possible predictors of subsequent violence involved data readily available in mental health center records: The number of prior (inpatient) admissions and age at the first such admission. Both a large number of previous admissions and a young age at first admission are considered possible predictors of subsequent violence, presumably because both reflect more serious psychological problems.

In acquiring the interview data, Klassen and O'Connor divided both age at first admission and number of prior admissions into four categories. Table 4.3 shows the observed frequencies in the resulting 4 × 4 contingency table. The two variables do not really appear to be test items. However, they are related to each other, in an obvious sort of way: Those whose first admission was at a relatively young age tend to have had more previous admissions [$G^2(9) = 16.4, p = 0.05$ for independence]. From the point of view of the item response theorist, the fact that these two "items" are not independent is explained by their common relationship to an underlying variable: the "long-term nature" or "seriousness" of the mental health problems for which the person is being admitted. From the point of view of the researchers attempting to predict subsequent behavior, estimates of individual values on that underlying continuum may be more useful than either of the two observed variables alone.

IRT requires only that the nonindependence, or covariance, among the observed data may be explained by the relationship of the observed variables to some underlying variable. It does not require that the "items" be questions on a test. In this case, we have fitted the data in Table 4.3 with Samejima's (1969) item response model for graded data (or data in ordered categories). The model describes the trace line for the probability of a response in category x or above as

TABLE 4.3
Observed and Expected Frequencies for the Mental Health Admissions "Items"

Age at First Admission	Number of Prior Admissions	Observed	Expected	EAP[θ]	(S.D.)
>34	None	28	28.0	-1.0	(0.9)
	1-3	15	15.1	-0.5	(0.8)
	4-9	8	6.2	-0.2	(0.8)
	10 or more	5	6.7	0.1	(0.9)
25-34	None	35	35.3	-0.6	(0.8)
	1-3	23	24.7	-0.2	(0.8)
	4-9	12	11.5	0.1	(0.8)
	10 or more	15	13.4	0.4	(0.8)
18-24	None	43	40.0	-0.2	(0.8)
	1-3	35	36.9	0.2	(0.8)
	4-9	19	20.5	0.5	(0.8)
	10 or more	29	28.5	0.8	(0.8)
<18	None	6	8.9	0.1	(0.9)
	1-3	14	10.1	0.5	(0.8)
	4-9	6	6.6	0.9	(0.8)
	10 or more	11	11.4	1.2	(0.9)

$$T_x^*(\theta) = \frac{1}{1 + \exp[-a(\theta - b_{x-1})]},$$

and

$$T_1^* = 1 \qquad T_{m+1}^* = 0$$

for an item with m categories (in this case, $m = 4$). The trace line for category x is

$$T_x(\theta) = T_x^*(\theta) - T_{x+1}^*(\theta).$$

Using Samjima's graded model in place of Bock's nominal model in Equation 1 and fitting the model to the data as in the previous illustration, we obtain parameter estimates. The model fits the data in Table 4.3 very well; the expected frequencies are shown with the data, and the likelihood ratio is $G^2(7) = 4.2$, $p = 0.75$. This result does not particularly depend on the use of the logistic version of Samejima's (1969) graded model; the normal-ogive version fits as well. An easy way to fit what amounts to the normal-ogive graded model to two items is to use what Muthén (1987) calls the chi-square test of "the polychoric model"; that gives a Pearson $X^2(8) = 3.5$, $p = 0.9$. The parameter estimates for both models are shown in Table 4.4; those for the logistic model were computed using the Bock and Aitkin (1981) MML algorithm in MULTI-

TABLE 4.4
Mental Health Admissions Item Parameters

	Age			
	a	b_1	b_2	b_3
Logistic	0.87	-1.96	-0.20	2.57
Normal	0.95	-1.85	-0.19	2.39
	Admissions			
	a	b_1	b_2	b_3
Logistic	1.01	-0.64	0.77	1.66
Normal	0.95	-0.69	0.82	1.75

LOG (Thissen, 1988), and for the normal ogive by direct maximum likelihood using LISCOMP (Muthén, 1987).[2] The parameters are so similar that they give indistinguishable trace lines. The upper panel of Fig. 4.3 shows the trace lines for the categories of age at first admission, and the lower panel of Fig. 4.3 shows the trace lines for the categories of number of prior admissions. With these trace lines, we may estimate IRT scale scores for each combination of "age at first admission" and "number of prior admissions." Expected a posteriori (EAP) estimates of θ are shown in Table 4.3 for each combination. IRT provides a way to rationally combine these two indicators into a single score.

Of course, some free-spirited practitioners of traditional test theory would be willing to code age-at-first-admission and number-of-prior-admissions from one to four and add the codes to develop a predictive index. In this case, that would serve most purposes, although it would not give quite the same results as the IRT-scale scores. The trace line scores differ slightly for different response patterns with the same total score; but the IRT-scale scores for patterns with the same summed score never differ by more than about 0.1 standard score units. Using the numbers from one to four in an additive fashion makes all those slightly unequal differences equal; that has little effect on, say, the correlations of the scores with other variables. We ultimately used the summed scores for the predictive research, for ease of computation and explication to nonquantitative audiences. The IRT analysis served primarily as a justification for summed scores using this particular categorization.

So what is an item? IRT provides a coherent justification for using non-items like these as "items": The IRT analysis indicates when that may be

---

[2]The parameters for the normal-ogive model listed in Table 4.4 have been transformed onto the scale of the logistic function. The "polychoric model," as fitted by LISCOMP, estimates only the polychoric correlation between the two items in place of the two distinct slopes estimated for the logistic. This has been interpreted as a constraint that the items have equal slopes in Table 4.4.

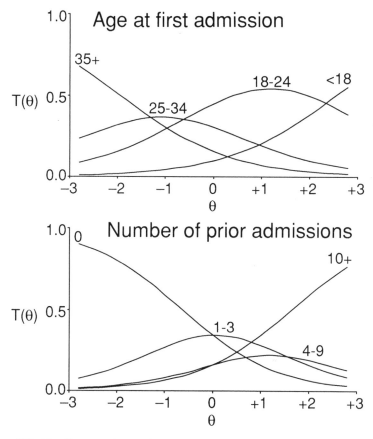

FIG. 4.3. Upper panel: trace lines for age at first inpatient mental health admission, categorized as 35 and older, 25–34, 18–24, and less than 18. Lower panel: trace lines for number of prior admissions, categorized as none, 1–3, 4–9, and 10 or more.

useful, and when it is not. As we noted in the context of the first example, it is also not necessary that the items used for measurement be the same as the questions for the respondent. Conjunctive or disjunctive (or, indeed, any) combinations of the responses to the questions may provide the "items" that are the basis for the scores. Other scales constructed for the violence-prediction project used concatenated responses from several interview questions for purposes of item analysis and test scoring. We also used IRT models to rationalize scores based on combinations of binary items with four- and nine-category Likert-type scale items. Indeed, the ability to do measurement with mixed item types is the next topic of this chapter.

THE ITEMS DO NOT HAVE TO HAVE SIMILAR
FORMATS: RISK FOR EATING DISORDERS

In the context of traditional test theory, there is an implicit requirement that the items on a test have the same format. Because the test score is the sum of points associated with each response, those points must appear to have equal value. There are few tests that have a variety of item types.

Item response theory imposes the less restrictive requirement that each item response (or category of responses) must have a specifiable relationship with the construct(s) being measured. These relationships may have different forms for different items. In principle, we are free to use item formats that fit our psychological purposes, even if this leads to variability in the appearance of items on a single instrument. Very few existing psychological tests or questionnaires mix item types. To some extent, that is natural; however, it may also be because tests using mixed item formats are very difficult to score using the classical theory. Exceptions arise, however, sometimes unintentionally. This section illustrates the IRT analysis of such an unintentional mixture of response formats.

In research related to the subject of eating disorders among college women, Irving (1987) used a questionnaire called the BULIT, a 36-item index created to identify individuals with, or at risk for developing bulimia (Smith & Thelen, 1984). All of the items on the scale have five response alternatives; most are ordered or Likert-type items, like the following two items selected for illustrative purposes:

14. I don't like myself after I eat too much.
    A. Always (5)
    B. Frequently (4)
    C. Sometimes (3)
    D. Seldom or never (2)
    E. I don't eat too much (1)
10. How much are you concerned about your eating binges?
    A. I don't binge (1)
    B. Bothers me a little (2)
    C. Moderate concern (3)
    D. Major concern (4)
    E. Probably the biggest concern in my life (5)

The questionnaire was developed to be scored by adding the numbers (from 1 to 5) associated with each response; high scores imply high risk. The data Irving (1987) obtained with these two items are also summarized very well with the graded-model (Samejima, 1969) trace lines for Likert-type responses shown in Figs. 4.4 and 4.5. In both cases, each numerically higher response (indicating a higher risk for eating disorders) is associated with a trace line (mostly) located to the right of lower responses.

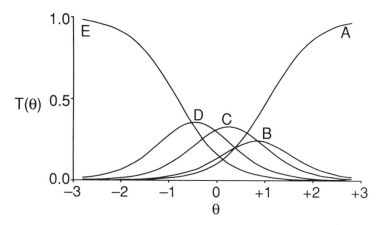

FIG. 4.4. Trace lines for BULIT item 14.

The BULIT also includes items for which the responses are not so obviously ordered. One of these is

5. I prefer to eat:
   A. At home alone (5)
   B. At home with others (4)
   C. In a public restaurant (3)
   D. At a friend's house (2)
   E. Doesn't matter (1)

Conventional scoring of the questionnaire includes in the summed score the numerical values for each of the responses for this item (in parentheses, above).

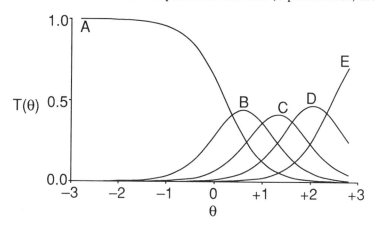

FIG. 4.5. Trace lines for BULIT item 10.

However, it is not really clear that the five possible responses to item 5 have any obvious order. The fastidious might be inclined to remove the item from the scale.

Using item response theory an alternative course of action is available. Because the responses to the item are not ordered, a model for ordered responses will not fit the data. Some other model must be used; again, we use Bock's (1972) nominal model. Here the constraints

$$\sum_k a_k = \sum_k c_k = 0$$

are imposed to identify the model. The model was further constrained, to give $a_1 = a_2 = a_4$. When this model is combined with the graded model for the other two items using Equation 1, and fitted to the proportions observed with each response pattern, the fit to the data is very good. For the $5 \times 5 \times 5$ table arising from the cross-classification based on the three items described here, the graded model for items 10 and 14 and the nominal model for item 5 give $G^2(108) = 100.7$, $p = 0.6$. The trace lines for item 5 are shown in Fig. 4.6, and the parameter estimates for all three items are in Table 4.5.

It is clear that the trace lines in Fig. 4.6 are not like those for the ordered responses shown in Figs. 4.4 and 4.5. There is no (left–right) order among responses B, D, and E; there is only a vertical separation, because those three trace lines are proportional to each other. Most of those at low risk for eating disorders say it "doesn't matter" (E); a few choose "at home with others" (B) and almost no one chooses a "friend's house" (D). The trace line for response A, "at home alone" rises sharply with risk for eating disorders, which is expected because one diagnostic feature of such disorders is an inclination to eat inconspicuously, which is easy when alone (L. M. Irving, personal com-

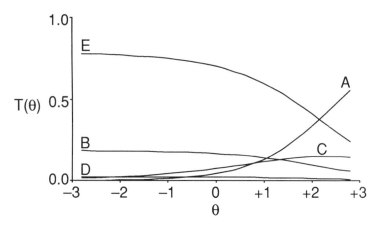

FIG. 4.6.   Trace lines for BULIT item 5.

TABLE 4.5
BULIT Item Parameters

		Item 5		
a_1	a_2	a_3	a_4	a_5
-0.39	-0.39	0.24	-0.39	0.93
c_1	c_2	c_3	c_4	c_5
2.02	-1.49	-0.26	0.57	-0.83
		Item 10		
a	b_1	b_2	b_3	b_4
2.57	0.23	0.97	1.66	2.46
		Item 14		
a	b_1	b_2	b_3	b_4
2.02	-0.83	-0.09	0.59	1.08

munication, July 1987). Response C, "in a public restaurant," is increasingly likely for those at moderate-to-high risk, apparently because it may include the possibility of eating inconspicuously.

While the trace lines in Fig. 4.6 are not those of ordered responses, they summarize the item response data well, so the model provides useful item analysis. And the trace lines may be used to characterize the risk of individuals for eating disorders, by using the five (nongraded) trace lines in the computation of an IRT scale score. The EAP scale scores are shown with the observed item response patterns and frequencies in Table 4.6.

The point is that although most of the items in this scale have ordered, Likert-type response alternatives, an item may be included that has strictly nominal responses. The inclusion of such an item has no deleterious effect on the scale overall, as long as item response theory is used to provide the item analysis and scale scores.

CONCLUDING REMARKS

This chapter has illustrated the ideas that the "items" to which the models of item response theory may be applied may not be individual questions, they may not even appear to be "test items," and they may vary in format within a single measurement instrument. Implicit rules to the contrary may be repealed. A further change to common practice in psychological measurement is suggested by the implicit message in all three illustrations: Using IRT, tests do not have to be long. We have taken (moderately) seriously "tests" of two and three

TABLE 4.6
BULIT Data: Patterns Are the Item Responses for Items 5, 10, and 14, where
1 = low and 5 = high in the Original Scoring Scheme

Pattern	Observed	Expected	EAP[θ]	(S.D.)
111	72	76.9	−1.09	(0.69)
112	47	48.2	−0.52	(0.52)
113	36	33.1	−0.22	(0.57)
114	15	14.4	0.03	(0.58)
115	10	13.0	0.22	(0.60)
121	4	7.6	−0.15	(0.58)
122	18	12.4	0.14	(0.52)
123	21	17.2	0.38	(0.41)
124	8	11.7	0.50	(0.37)
125	17	14.7	0.71	(0.49)
131	3	2.1	0.16	(0.62)
132	3	4.4	0.40	(0.51)
133	8	7.6	0.60	(0.45)
134	8	6.4	0.79	(0.50)
135	10	13.1	1.16	(0.52)
141	2	0.5	0.38	(0.70)
142	2	1.2	0.63	(0.60)
143	2	2.4	0.87	(0.56)
144	5	2.6	1.12	(0.53)
145	7	8.5	1.48	(0.47)
154	1	0.6	1.31	(0.56)
155	3	3.0	1.87	(0.61)
211	3	2.3	−1.09	(0.69)
212	1	1.4	−0.52	(0.52)
214	1	0.4	0.03	(0.58)
223	1	0.5	0.38	(0.41)
225	1	0.4	0.71	(0.49)
233	1	0.2	0.60	(0.45)
235	1	0.4	1.16	(0.52)
311	4	4.4	−0.81	(0.65)
312	1	3.7	−0.35	(0.53)
313	4	3.1	−0.03	(0.56)
314	3	1.6	0.22	(0.53)
315	2	1.6	0.43	(0.57)
322	3	1.4	0.29	(0.47)
323	2	2.3	0.47	(0.38)
324	3	1.7	0.59	(0.39)
332	2	0.6	0.56	(0.50)
333	3	1.2	0.74	(0.49)
334	1	1.1	0.96	(0.52)
335	1	2.9	1.31	(0.47)
344	1	0.6	1.28	(0.48)
345	4	2.3	1.62	(0.48)
411	25	18.1	−1.09	(0.69)

(Continued)

94

TABLE 4.6
(Continued)

Pattern	Observed	Expected	EAP[θ]	(S.D.)
412	9	11.3	−0.52	(0.52)
413	5	7.8	−0.22	(0.57)
414	3	3.4	0.03	(0.58)
415	6	3.1	0.22	(0.60)
422	3	2.9	0.14	(0.52)
423	3	4.1	0.38	(0.41)
425	5	3.4	0.71	(0.49)
433	2	1.8	0.60	(0.45)
434	2	1.5	0.79	(0.50)
435	6	3.1	1.16	(0.52)
445	1	2.0	1.48	(0.47)
455	1	0.7	1.87	(0.61)
511	4	1.6	−0.53	(0.62)
512	1	1.8	−0.15	(0.55)
515	3	1.4	0.66	(0.58)
522	2	1.1	0.43	(0.43)
523	1	1.9	0.57	(0.38)
524	2	1.5	0.72	(0.45)
525	4	2.7	1.07	(0.55)
534	2	1.3	1.14	(0.50)
535	4	4.3	1.45	(0.43)
544	1	0.8	1.42	(0.43)
545	3	4.2	1.79	(0.52)
553	1	0.1	1.55	(0.61)
555	4	2.8	2.35	(0.59)

items. Note that the parameter estimates and goodness-of-fit statistics were computed for the data in the 4×4 and $5 \times 5 \times 5$ cross-classifications in Tables 4.1, 4.3, and 4.6. It is true that very short tests do not usually produce the precise measurement that longer tests do; the Spearman–Brown formula is still an accurate prophecy. However, IRT handles very small numbers of items as well as long tests, and very few items are sufficient for informative item analysis. Indeed, the assumption of unidimensionality involved in conventional IRT is much more likely to be appropriate for small numbers of items than for long tests. Because research psychologists are frequently actually interested in the answers to a few questions, that is useful: It is now possible to apply test theory to small numbers of questions as well as long tests. We can do item analysis, item selection, and measurement with a handful of items where that is appropriate. And we can tailor the format of each item individually to our goals in psychological measurement.

What might the future hold? Computerized adaptive testing (CAT) may be an idea whose time is about to come in many areas of psychological research. To date, CAT has been used primarily in an effort to shorten tests in the educational domain. However, the psychological measurement instruments that most need shortening may lie in the areas of social and personality measurement and the assessment of pathology; there, the wide range of individual differences and large numbers of constructs to be measured have fostered the creation of very long tests and batteries, that could well be shortened by tailored testing strategies. Adaptive testing requires scaled scoring, and that requires some form of IRT calibration. That is currently feasible.

It is not currently practical to explore the underlying structure of potentially multidimensional sets of nominal-response items. If we restrict ourselves to the possibility that a single underlying variable accounts for the observed nominal item responses, we may examine the goodness of fit of Bock's (1972) (unidimensional) nominal model, as we did in the preceding section. However, there is currently no practical way to consider a multidimensional latent-variable model for nominal responses analogous to standard factor analysis models for continuous or ordered responses. Therefore, if we find that the unidimensional IRT model does not fit, we cannot straightforwardly consider the fit of a two-factor model. Psychological research has many strictly nominal indices that may reflect variation on underlying continua. Methods for examining the fit of underlying latent variable models for nominal data could be quite useful. We can go little further than that without serious research on the problem.

We have considered some relatively simple topics with modest sets of data, involving only measurement. Measurement is, after all, only a small part of any applied research program. However, measurement is an important part of any research program, and contemporary theory has much to offer psychological researchers.

REFERENCES

Bergan, J. R., & Stone, C. A. (1985). Latent class models for knowledge domains. *Psychological Bulletin, 98*, 166–184.

Bock, R. D. (1972). Estimating item parameters and latent ability when the responses are scored in two or more nominal categories. *Psychometrika, 37*, 29–51.

Bock, R. D., & Aitkin, M. (1981). Marginal maximum likelihood estimation of item parameters: An application of an EM algorithm. *Psychometrika, 46*, 443–459.

Bock, R. D., & Mislevy, R. J. (1982). Adaptive EAP estimation of ability in a microcomputer environment. *Applied Psychological Measurement, 6*, 431–444.

Irving, L. M. (1987). *Mirror images: Effects of the standard of beauty on women's self and body esteem.* Unpublished master's thesis, University of Kansas.

Klassen, D., & O'Connor, W. A. (1987, October). *Predicting violence in mental patients: Cross-validation of an actuarial scale.* Paper presented at the annual meeting of the American Public Health Association, New Orleans.

Lazarsfeld, P. F. (1950). The logical and mathematical foundation of latent structure analysis. In S. A. Stouffer, L. Guttman, E. A. Suchman, P. F. Lazarsfeld, S. A. Star, & J. A. Clausen (Eds.), *Measurement and Prediction* (pp. 362–412). New York: Wiley.

Lord, F. M. (1952). A theory of test scores. *Psychometric Monographs* (Whole No. 7).

Muthén, B. O. (1987). *LISCOMP: Analysis of linear structural equations using a comprehensive measurement model*. Mooresville, IN: Scientific Software, Inc.

Samejima, F. (1969). Estimation of latent ability using a response pattern of graded scores. *Psychometrika Monographs, 34* (4, Pt. 2, Whole No. 17).

Smith, M. C., & Thelen, M. H. (1984). Development and validation of a test for bulimia. *Journal of Consulting and Clinical Psychology, 52*, 863–872.

Thissen, D. (1988). *MULTILOG user's guide*. Mooresville, IN: Scientific Software, Inc.

Thissen, D., & Steinberg, L. (1984). A response model for multiple choice items. *Psychometrika, 49*, 501–519.

Thissen, D., & Steinberg, L. (1988). Data analysis using item response theory. *Psychological Bulletin, 104*, 385–395.

Thurstone, L. L. (1925). A method of scaling psychological and educational tests. *Journal of Educational Psychology, 16*, 433–449.

Thurstone, L. L. (1927). A law of comparative judgment. *Psychological Review, 34*, 278–286.

Wainer, H., & Kiely, G. L. (1987). Item clusters and computerized adaptive testing: A case for testlets. *Journal of Educational Measurement, 24*, 185–201.

5

Toward Intelligent Assessment: An Integration of Constructed-Response Testing, Artificial Intelligence, and Model-Based Measurement

Randy Elliot Bennett
Educational Testing Service

Any book on a new test theory must include consideration of new testing conceptions. This chapter concerns one such conception, intelligent assessment. The chapter outlines a formulation and rationale for this conception, describes progress toward realizing it, and offers some ideas on practical applications, including ones related to large-scale standardized testing programs.

INTELLIGENT ASSESSMENT

Intelligent assessment is conceived of as an integration of three research lines, each dealing with cognitive performance from a different perspective: constructed-response testing, artificial intelligence, and model-based measurement. This integration is envisioned as producing assessment methods consisting of tasks closer to the complex problems typically encountered in academic and work settings. These tasks will be scored by automated routines that emulate the behavior of an expert, providing a rating on a partial credit scale for summative purposes as well as a qualitative description designed to impart instructionally useful information. The driving mechanisms underlying these tasks and their scoring are cognitively grounded measurement models that may dictate what the characteristics of items should be, which items from a large pool should be administered, how item responses should be combined to make more general inferences, and how uncertainty should be handled.[1]

---

[1] Bunderson, Inouye, and Olsen (1989) offer a different view of intelligent assessment as the application of artificial intelligence to any of the subprocesses of educational measurement: test development, test administration, and test analysis and research.

It is important to stress that the emphasis is on assessment that facilitates instruction, rather than on instruction that embeds assessment, as some intelligent tutoring systems at least implicitly do (J. R. Frederiksen & White, 1988). This emphasis was chosen to encourage developments that might result in near-term, incremental improvements to major standardized testing programs (such as achievement and admissions programs), in more sophisticated environments for preparing for such tests, and, in the longer term, in more effective assessment modules for intelligent tutoring systems (Wenger, 1987).

Complex Constructed-Response Tasks

A constructed-response task can be thought of as any task for which the space of examinee responses is not limited to a small set of presented options. As such, the examinee is forced to formulate, rather than recognize, an answer. This definition implies a substantial range in the complexity of the responses, from an item that calls for rearranging the sentences in a paragraph to one that requires performing a musical piece (Bennett, Ward, Rock, & LaHart, 1990). In this chapter, interest is focused toward responses of greater complexity. Hence, a *complex* constructed-response item is one for which scoring decisions cannot typically be made immediately and unambiguously, using mechanical application of a limited set of explicit criteria, but rather require some degree of expert judgment. Fig. 5.1 presents examples of such items in the algebra and computer programming domains.

The use of such items may engender many difficulties. Surely, more multiple-choice questions can be completed per unit time than complex constructed responses. Tests composed of the latter item type will often have reduced content coverage and, potentially, lower reliability and validity (as seen from the traditional test theoretic perspective). Scoring constructed responses for any large-scale testing program is a major undertaking: detailed, defensible scoring keys must be produced; human judges trained, housed, and fed while scoring is underway; and rater performance must be constantly monitored to maintain interjudge agreement and scale stability.

Given these difficulties, why be interested in such items at all? For one, these items are likely to measure processes different from those tapped by multiple-choice tests (Ackerman & Smith, 1988; Ward, N. Frederiksen, & Carlson, 1980). Because constructed responses may more closely represent real-world tasks, they should more readily engage many of the higher-order cognitive processes required in academic and work settings. As a result, important constructs that are presumably not measured by multiple-choice tests are more likely to be assessed. Such increases in construct validity may, in turn, lead to enhanced predictive value (N. Frederiksen & Ward, 1978), especially when constructed responses are combined with multiple-choice items (Breland, Camp, Jones, Morris, & Rock, 1987).

a. On a 600-mile motor trip, Bill averaged 45 miles per hour for the first 285 miles and 50 miles per hour for the remainder of the trip. If he started at 7:00 a.m., at what time did he finish the trip (to the nearest minute)?

Example Correct Response:

Time 1 = 285 miles / 45 miles per hour
Time 1 = 6.33 hours
Distance 2 = 600 miles - 285 miles
Distance 2 = 315 miles
Time 2 = 315 miles / 50 mile per hour
Time 2 = 6.3 hours
Total time = 6.33 hours + 6.3 hours
Total time = 6 hours 20 min + 6 hours 18 min
Total time = 12 hours 38 min
End time = 7:00 am + 12 hours 38 min
End time = 7:38 pm

Answer: 7:38 pm

b. Write a procedure that rotates the elements of an array s with n elements so that when the rotation is completed, the old value of s[1] will be in s[2], the old value of s[2] will be in s[3],..., the old value of s[n-1] will be in s[n], and the old value of s[n] will be in s[1]. Your procedure should have s and n as parameters. You may assume that the type Item has been declared and s is of type List which has been declared as List = array[1..Max] of Item.

Example Correct Response:

```
program foo (input,output);                     {initialize program}
const
  max = 100;
type
  item = integer;
  list = array[1..max] of item;
var
  PassedAsS : list;
  PassedAsN : integer;
Procedure RotateArray(var s:list; var n:integer);
  var                                           {initialize local variables}
    temp : integer;
    i : 1..max;
  begin
    temp := s[n];                               {move last element to temporary storage}
    for i := n downto 2 do                      {move each element to the right}
      begin
        s[i] := s[i-1];
      end;
    s[1] := temp;                               {move last element from temporary storage to the first position}
  end;
begin
  RotateArray(PassedAsS,PassedAsN);
end.
```

FIG. 5.1. Complex constructed-response items in algebra and programming (with example correct responses).

A second argument for using complex constructed-response items is that the responses provide a window onto the strategies examinees use in arriving at a solution. This window facilitates the gathering of diagnostic information not easily attainable in the multiple-choice format (Birenbaum & Tatsuoka, 1987).

Third, it has been argued that constructed response questions play an important role in making the outcomes of instruction more clearly visible (Breland,

et al., 1987; J. R. Frederiksen & Collins, 1989). As implied, multiple-choice
tests in many instances attempt to measure skill using a format different from
those commonly encountered in real-world tasks. Even when substantially similar
cognitive operations underlie the two formats, instruction would seem less efficient as teachers (and students) use one format to achieve the objectives of
the curriculum and the other to prepare for the test. The real danger comes
in those situations where the multiple-choice format requires a substantially different (and less valued) set of operations than the criterion performance, and test
preparation is emphasized over curricular achievement (J. R. Frederiksen &
Collins, 1989; N. Frederiksen, 1984)—as, in high-stakes testing situations, it
inevitably will be. The result might be a class of students good at recognizing
isolated facts but poor at integrating the knowledge, skill, and strategies needed for more involved tasks. Complex constructed-response items should
eliminate this conflict by focusing both instruction and assessment on the same
criterion tasks.

Finally, because it looks different from—and more mechanical than—real-world
tasks, the multiple-choice format is easily characterized as irrelevant and trivial
(e.g., Fiske, 1990). The persistency and frequency with which these characterizations have been made would seem to reduce the credibility of conventional testing programs. Such characterizations would be much less convincing if
the test and the criterion tasks were more similar.

The research literature underlying these purported advantages of complex
constructed-response is quite limited, leading to few definitive conclusions (Bennett, in press). Though there is, for example, evidence that different abilities
are sometimes demanded by multiple-choice and free-response items, the nature of these differences is not clearly understood (Traub & MacRury, 1990).
Even so, the arguments for constructed response appear logically and often theoretically well grounded, justifying continued exploration of this format as, at
the least, a potential supplement to multiple-choice items.

Scoring

The second feature in the proposed conception of intelligent assessment is evaluative feedback approximating the analyses of an expert. For summative purposes, an expert would be expected to rate a complex constructed response
on a partial-credit scale. To help the learner, a qualitative analysis of the response
should also be provided.

Why score responses on a partial-credit scale? Though partial-credit models
for scoring multiple-choice items have been proposed (Millman & Greene, 1989),
standardized tests have traditionally treated responses to these items as right
or wrong. With a complex response, dichotomous scoring throws a rich database away, thereby potentially reducing test reliability and validity.

Fig. 5.2 presents several incorrect answers generated by GRE General Test

On a 600-mile motor trip, Bill averaged 45 miles per hour for the first 285 miles and 50 miles per hour for the remainder of the trip. If he started at 7:00 a.m., at what time did he finish the trip (to the nearest minute)?

Response #1:

1. 285 miles/45 miles per hr = 6.33 hrs
2. 6.33 hrs = 6 hrs 20 min
3.
4. 600 - 285 = 415 miles
5.
6. 415 miles/50 miles per hr = 8.3 hrs
7. 8.3 hrs = 8 hrs 18 min
8.
9. 6 hrs 20 min + 8 hrs 18 min = 14 hrs 38 min
10.
11. 7:00 + 14 hrs 38 min = 9:38 pm

Answer: 9:38 pm

Response #2

1. 285/x = 45/60
2. 285/x = 3/4
3. 285/4 = 71.25
4. 71.25 * 3 = 213.75
5. 213.75/60 = 3.56
6.
7. 315/x = 50/60
8. 315/x = 5/6
9. 315/6 = 52.5
10. 52.5 * 5 = 262.5
11. 262.5/60 = 4.375
12.
13. 3.56 hours + 4.38 hours = 7.94

Answer: approximately 3 pm

Response #3

1. On a 600 mile motor trip
2. 285 miles = 45 miles/hr
3.
4. 285 + 315 = 600
5.
6. 315 = 50 miles/hr
7.
8. 45 * 50 = 22.50 = 22:50 minutes

Answer: 22:50 minutes

FIG. 5.2. Wrong answers to a complex constructed-response item.

examinees to an algebra word problem (Sebrechts, Bennett, & Rock, 1991). One means of decomposing the problem is in terms of the following goals: (a) find the time for the first part of the trip, (b) find the missing distance for the second part, (c) find the time for the second part, (d) add the two times, and (e) add the total trip time to the starting time. The first response recapitulates this decomposition exactly. The answer is wrong only because a minor computational error is made in finding the missing distance for the second part (line 4).

In the second response, three of the five goals are correctly structured. The missing distance is generated (as implied from its use in line 7), the two travel times (though incorrectly derived) are summed (line 13), and the total is added (implicitly) to the start time to produce a finish time. Structural flaws are present, however, in finding the travel times (lines 1–5 and 7–11).[2]

The last response is the most seriously wrong. This response achieves only one of the five goals, find the missing distance, which is indicated on line 4.

These three responses differ considerably in the extent to which they approach a correct problem solution, as well as in the understanding of the problem they imply. Yet each result would have been treated equivalently under a dichotomous scoring scheme.

In addition to partial credit, an expert would be expected to generate a qualitative analysis to give individual examinees an indication of where they went wrong in solving the problem. In applications of intelligent assessment within major standardized testing programs, this feedback might simply serve as a more complete explanation of test performance than scores can provide. In a test preparation system, such feedback would hopefully have more tangible value, giving examinees the information needed to modify their solution strategies.

Fig. 5.3 gives examples of item responses that, while very close to a correct solution, contain qualitatively different errors. Response 1 contains only a simple computational error (line 4). In Response 2, the error is in considering 6.3 to be the same as 6 and 1/3 (lines 7 and 9). Response 3's error is in lines 10–11 where 6.30 hours is mistakenly transformed to 6 hours, 30 minutes.

Cognitively Motivated Measurement Models

Although statements about what an examinee did incorrectly on a given item might be helpful, it would seem that far greater instructional value would accrue from more general diagnostic statements based on commonalities in performance across items. Such commonalities are more likely to be indicative of stable errors associated with particular skill deficiencies. To guide aggregations across items, a model, or general set of rules applicable to a class of assessment purposes, can be used. Measurement models guided primarily by the semantics of the domain should offer more efficient and psychologically meaningful statements than ad hoc approaches to aggregation (Masters & Mislevy, chapter 9, this volume). In addition, they might suggest, among other things, the cognitive and psychometric characteristics of items, which of a large pool of items should be administered, the order in which they should be given, and how noise in the data should be dealt with.

---

[2]The examinee's error in computing the travel times was in dividing when a multiplication was called for (lines 3 and 9) and multiplying when division was required.

On a 600-mile motor trip, Bill averaged 45 miles per hour for the first 285 miles and 50 miles per hour for the remainder of the trip. If he started at 7:00 a.m., at what time did he finish the trip (to the nearest minute)?

Response #1:

1. 285 miles/45 miles per hr = 6.33 hrs
2. 6.33 hrs = 6 hrs 20 min
3.
4. 600 - 285 = 415 miles
5.
6. 415 miles/50 miles per hr = 8.3 hrs
7. 8.3 hrs = 8 hrs 18 min
8.
9. 6 hrs 20 min + 8 hrs 18 min = 14 hrs 38 min
10.
11. 7:00 + 14 hrs 38 min = 9:38 pm

Answer: 9:38 pm

Response #2

1. 600 mile - 285 = miles at 50 mi/hr
2.
3. time at 45 mi/hr = 285 mi * 1 hr/45 mi
4. time at 45 mi/hr = 6 and 1/3 hrs
5.
6. time at 50 mi/hr = 315 * 1 hr/ 50 mi
7. time at 50 mi/hr = 6.3
8.
9. total time = 12 + 2/3 hrs
10. 2/3 hr = 2/3 hr * 60 min/hr
11. total time = 12 hrs 40 min

Answer: 7:40 pm

Response #3

1. 600 - 285 = 315
2.
3. 45 : 285
4. 50 : 315
5.
6. 285 mi /45 mi per hr = 6.33
7. 315 /50 = 6.30
8.
9. 6.33 hrs : 285 miles
10. 6.30 hrs : 315 miles
11. 6 hrs 20 min + 6 hrs 30 min = 12 hrs 50 min
12.
13. 7 am + 12 hrs 50 min = 7:50 pm

Answer: 7:50 pm

FIG. 5.3.   Responses of similar correctness but containing qualitatively different errors.

PROGRESS TOWARD INTELLIGENT ASSESSMENT

Scoring[3]

Perhaps the greatest problem in operationalizing intelligent assessment lies in scoring. Complex constructed-response items are used routinely in some large-scale testing programs (e.g., the College Board's Advanced Placement Program). In these programs, responses are scored by human experts. This method is extremely expensive because judges must be trained, fed, housed, and paid. Because of the tremendous volume (responses in the hundreds of thousands for the Advanced Placement Program), scoring is time-consuming, taking hundreds of experts a week or more to complete. Qualitative analyses are not included and, given the additional time this analysis would take, it is unlikely that they ever could be. Finally, an appreciable degree of error is introduced in part because even if a reasonably objective scoring rubric can be established, judges' accuracy in consistently applying this rubric often changes during an operational grading (Braun, 1988). These difficulties argue for attempts to create machine-based methods for scoring complex tasks. Machine-scorable tasks would reduce the operational expense associated with human grading, speed up the scoring process, permit the introduction of qualitative analyses, and eliminate within-judge inconsistency (because the machine would apply its rules the same way every time).

Our work toward developing machine-scorable, complex, constructed-response tasks is proceeding in two domains, computer programming and algebra, using two major standardized testing programs, the College Board's Advanced Placement Computer Science (APCS) Examination and the Graduate Record Examinations (GRE) General Test, as settings. In both instances, the underlying scoring mechanism is an expert system—a computer program that emulates one or more aspects of the behavior of a master judge. Both systems were originally built as research tools within the field of intelligent tutoring (Sleeman & Brown, 1982; Wenger, 1987). Because it is centrally concerned with issues related to individualizing instruction, this field has initiated some extremely provocative approaches to instructional diagnosis, offering useful bases for building intelligent assessment.

Computer Programming. The expert system used in our work in this domain has been MicroPROUST, a derivative of PROUST (Johnson, 1986; Johnson & Soloway, 1985).[4] PROUST was developed to study the conceptual er-

---

[3]The work described in this section builds on many years of effort by our principal collaborators, Elliot Soloway and Marc M. Sebrechts, and several years of our own work, with central contributions by Henry I. Braun and Donald A. Rock.

[4]The system descriptions in this and the next section are condensed and consequently simplified.

rors made by students in learning to program in Pascal. MicroPROUST was built as a portable demonstration of the concepts embodied in PROUST and, consequently, is less powerful in its analytical techniques.

MicroPROUST attempts to find nonsyntactic bugs in Pascal programs. The system has knowledge to reason about selected programming problems within a framework called intention-based diagnosis (Johnson, 1986; Johnson & Soloway, 1985). Intention-based diagnosis is derived from an extended research program on the development of programming expertise (e.g., Soloway & Ehrlich, 1984; Soloway & Iyengar, 1986). This research suggests that in debugging programs, experts first attempt to map the program into a deep-structure goal-and-plan representation. Goals are the objectives to be achieved in a program, whereas plans are stereotypical means (i.e., step-by-step procedures) for achieving those goals. Following the lead of experts, MicroPROUST attempts to "understand" student solutions by identifying the goals and plans that the student intended to realize in the program, and the bugs produced. The term *bug* takes its traditional meaning of programming error and is conceptualized as an unsuccessful or incorrectly realized plan for satisfying a goal. Bugs located are verbally described to the student in hope of preventing similar errors and of stimulating thinking about how to approach the problem correctly.

To analyze a problem, MicroPROUST must have what is in essence a reasonably deep understanding of the problem domain. Developing this understanding involves a labor-intensive cognitive analysis. For each problem, student responses are analyzed to derive one or more goal decompositions, correct plans for achieving the goals, and bug rules representing faulty plan implementations.

In evaluating a student solution, MicroPROUST first reads the problem specification contained in its knowledge base. This specification identifies the goals the student should be attempting to achieve in solving a particular problem. The system uses this goal specification, its plan and bug rule knowledge bases, and the student's code to construct the solution intended by the student. For example, the specification for the "rotate array" problem (see Figure 5.1b) includes the goal, "shift each array element to the right." The system would use this goal to locate in its knowledge base a set of plans to achieve the desired result. MicroPROUST's knowledge base has 24 such plans, which vary in their loop control structures, how they accomplish the shift (using a single array, a pair of arrays, or a pair of temporary variables), and so on.

Next, the system would attempt to match one of these plans to a portion of the student's code. If a match is found, inferences about the student's intentions with respect to this code segment can be made, for instance, what meaning to attribute to particular variables. On the basis of these inferences, the system can predict how these variables will be used in achieving the next goal needed to satisfy the problem specification and, in addition, where in the program relative to the current segment that next goal should reside. If an appropriate code segment cannot be found for achieving that next goal, an attempt is made to match the segment using "buggy plan" rules. This goal plan matching strategy provides considerable leverage; correct plans and bug rules can be juxtaposed in different combinations to handle the variety of responses generated by novice programmers.

Our first study with MicroPROUST examined the extent of agreement between the program and human readers in diagnostically and numerically scoring solutions to each of two APCS programming problems (Bennett, Gong, et al., 1990). Each problem asked the student to write a short program or procedure to satisfy a given specification (see the problem statement in Fig. 5.1b). The rules employed by the high-school and college teachers who operationally grade the APCS exam were used to develop a rubric for MicroPROUST that deducted points depending upon the particular bug detected. Solutions were graded by MicroPROUST and by a sample of teachers drawn from the grading pool. MicroPROUST was able to produce an analysis for approximately 70% of the solutions (it offered no analysis on the remaining papers), and for those programs it could analyze, its performance was indistinguishable from human readers for one problem and not dramatically different from them for the second (the correlations between the machine and mean rater scores for the two problems were .96 and .75). In a cross-validation sample, however, the percentage of papers the program was able to analyze was considerably lower at 42%, though, again, its scores were very similar to a human judge's.

To improve MicroPROUST's performance, especially with respect to the percentage of solutions analyzed, several approaches might be tried. Our second study looked at one such approach, constraining the constructed-response task (Braun, Bennett, Frye, & Soloway, 1990). The subjects for this study were examinees taking the APCS examination who were subsequently given one of the same problem specifications used in the previous study, accompanied by an incorrect solution to the problem. The task was to correct the faulty program instead of writing it *ab initio*. The corrected programs were scored by MicroPROUST (without any change to its knowledge base to adapt it to this new problem type). Results showed, first, a substantial increase in the percentage of solutions analyzed—from 42% to 83%. Second, those solutions that MicroPROUST could not analyze were almost always incorrect: 93% had one or more bugs. Third, reasonable agreement was found between MicroPROUST's scores and a human rater—the product-moment correlation was .86. Finally, whereas agreement on scores was good, agreement with the rater on bug diagnosis was more moderate: The two agreed on the exact nature and location of individual bugs in 56% of cases. Further work to identify the causes of this disagreement needs to be undertaken.

Our third study focused on the construct validity of MicroPROUST's scores for the constrained free-response item, specifically on whether this item functioned more like multiple-choice or free-response questions (Bennett, Rock, et al., 1990). This issue is important because our goal was to produce an item type that, although machine scorable, retained the cognitive demand characteristics of free response. To address this issue, data from the previous study were analyzed. (In that study, examinees were divided into two samples and assigned constrained free-response items that differed in the number of seeded bugs: 1 vs. 3.) Confirmatory factor analysis (Joreskog & Sorbom, 1988) was applied to the data to estimate the relationships among the three item types (multiple choice, free response, constrained free response). Results suggested that the proficiency information distilled from the three item types was essentially the same in the sample taking the 1-bug constrained free-response, implying that this question type might constitute a reasonable supplement to the two existing APCS item formats.

Our ongoing work in computer programming is directed at several goals. The first is to understand better the reasons for the functional similarity of the three item types by undertaking additional studies of their structural relations and cognitive demand characteristics. Second, the APCS Practice System (Bennett, Sack, & Soloway, 1991), is being developed to permit issues related to intelligent assessment to be more easily studied. The APCS system contains more items and item formats, and larger knowledge bases, than MicroPROUST. Rather than operating in "batch" mode as MicroPROUST does, the APCS System incorporates a standard programming editor, thereby forming an interactive system that presents programming problems, accepts responses, and provides immediate feedback. Finally, tools are being built to make constructing knowledge bases easier, so that greater coverage of student solutions—and higher analysis rates—can be efficiently achieved.

Algebra. Our work in this domain is centered upon building constructed-response formats for algebra word problems adapted from the GRE General Test. Student solutions to these problems differ fundamentally from programming solutions (Sebrechts & Schooler, 1987). First, steps are frequently left out because they can be mentally computed. Second, syntax is considerably looser: Students use assignment to values, include free (unbound) expressions, and occasionally use multiple symbols to represent the same variable or the same symbol to represent different variables. Finally, the algebraic expressions that compose a solution typically culminate in a single, easily verifiable result. The nearest analogue in programming is an output, which varies as a function of the input and which cannot be generated without compiling the solution. These characteristics of students' algebra problem solutions make the task of scoring and diagnosis significantly different from that in programming.

To score solutions to algebra word problems, GIDE is being used (Sebrechts, LaClaire, Schooler, & Soloway 1986). In keeping with the nature of students' solutions, GIDE was constructed to accept productions in relatively unconstrained forms.[5] Solutions must be written linearly (though not in a strict order), any names can be used to identify variables or constants, and there is no restriction on the degree to which examinees are allowed to deviate from a correct solution path. Though this lack of constraint makes solutions substantially more difficult to interpret, it appears to be more consistent with the ways in which problems are solved in real-world settings.

Like MicroPROUST, GIDE can only analyze responses to problems about which it is knowledgeable. GIDE's algebra word problem knowledge presently is enough to handle responses to several variants of five basic problems (see Fig. 5.1a for an example). The knowledge base for these problems was developed by asking Educational Testing Service (ETS) mathematics test developers to specify correct and incorrect problem solutions, and by analyzing the written solutions and think-aloud protocols of university undergraduates.

GIDE's evaluation of responses is guided by several strategies. As with MicroPROUST, these strategies help it to build an understanding of the response in terms of a goal-plan structure. For example, consider the "rate × time" problem in Figure 5.1a, which can be decomposed into the following goals:

1. Find the time for the first part of the trip.
2. Find the missing distance for the second part.
3. Find the time for the second part.
4. Add the times for the two parts to get a total time.
5. Add the total trip time to the starting time.

In determining whether a goal is satisfied, GIDE will attempt to match one of the several plans it has for that goal to a portion of the examinee's solution. GIDE does this by matching plans for the form and numerical value of equations (e.g., for Goal 2, part 2 distance = 600 miles – 285 miles, 315 = 600 – 285), for free-standing expressions (e.g., 315 appearing in isolation as the result of a mental computation), and for groups (e.g., when a goal consists of a list of elements that can take on any order, such as group of numbers to be summed). As a result of this matching, values as well as names used by the examinee to represent variables or constants are bound to GIDE's internal representations. These bindings are available for use in analyzing subsequent goals.

As part of GIDE's analyses, it attempts to separate conceptual from computational errors. It does this by noting instances in which erroneous values are associated with correct symbolic forms and then carrying these computational errors through to subsequent goals. So, for example, in Response 1 in Fig. 5.3,

---

[5]GIDE was originally designed to diagnose student errors in statistics and automotive mechanics problems.

the examinee incorrectly computed the distance for part 2. GIDE would assign the result of this incorrect computation (i.e., 415) to its internal representation of the part 2 distance for all remaining computations. In this way, GIDE is able to determine if the rest of the solution is conceptually correct and if a wrong answer was produced only because of a low-level mistake.

These strategies are successful as long as plans representing conceptually correct solutions to the active goal can be matched to portions of the examinee's solution. If such a plan cannot be matched to the examinee's solution, GIDE attempts to match to the solution plans that incorporate conceptual errors commonly made in achieving that goal or bug rules that, in GIDE, represent more general errors.

In some cases, however, none of these plans or rules match an examinee solution. When this occurs, GIDE searches the proposed solution for a name it has associated with the current active goal to find a clue as to what the examinee was doing. For Goal 2 of this problem (the distance for part 2), such names might include "part 2 distance," "distance 2," "missing distance," and "dist 2." If such a name is found, GIDE checks the associated expression and result to see if they can reasonably be considered deviations from a correct plan for that goal.

In those cases where GIDE is not able to account for how the examinee has attempted to satisfy the goal through either correct or incorrect plans, GIDE waits to see if satisfaction of subsequent goals will fulfill the currently active goal implicitly. Implicit matching is triggered when explicit matching has failed and a dependency link is active; that is, a goal presumes the satisfaction of one or more prior goals. So, for example, in this problem, if plans for Goals 1–3 (find the missing distance and calculate the times for the two parts) are not matched—perhaps because the examinee did the computations mentally—but a plan satisfying Goal 4 is matched (add the two times together), Goals 1–3 would be matched implicitly.

Finally, when no plan, buggy or correct, can be matched to a portion of the solution, the goal is considered missing. GIDE, in essence, "understands" this solution component to be physically absent, a presumption that will likely be correct if the domain analysis has been well done.

After completing its analysis, GIDE issues a brief bug report and a partial-credit score. The bug report identifies the errors detected. Because of its experimental nature, GIDE's algebra bug reports are relatively unrefined, giving only enough detail to permit verification of an error's existence by an independent source. In any operational implementation, these descriptions would need to be carefully crafted to communicate clearly the nature of the error and perhaps a method for resolving it.

GIDE's partial credit scores are derived from goal plan analysis. This linkage is meant to give the scores a principled, cognitive basis. The rubric awards full credit if all goals are achieved, suggesting that the student was able to decompose the problem, correctly structure each goal, and compute its solution. Credit is deducted differentially, depending on the errors detected for each goal. The largest deduction is made for missing goals because these absences suggest the student was unaware that addressing the goal was necessary to achieving a correct result. Less credit is deducted for conceptual bugs because such bugs suggest both recognition of the goal's importance and a coherent, though incorrect, attempt to solve the goal. The smallest deduction is for computational errors that imply only trivial procedural slips.

Because students may approach a problem using an alternative decomposition (see Fig. 5.4), GIDE has the capability to process solutions against such alternatives. The mechanisms for handling alternatives are, however, largely ad hoc and represent one area for the program's further development.

GIDE's performance has been evaluated using algebra word problems adapted from the GRE General Test (Sebrechts, Bennett, & Rock, 1991). Twelve problems were drawn from three content classes (rate × time, work, interest). Agreement was evaluated for each item separately by comparing the system's scores to the mean scores taken across five content experts, with the mean conceptualized as an approximation of the examinee's "true" score on the item. In contrast with MicroPROUST, GIDE produced scores for *all* responses, in part because it was able to capitalize on domain characteristics (e.g., the presence of a single, easily verifiable result) not available to MicroPROUST. Further, GIDE duplicated the judgments of raters with reasonable accuracy; the 12 correlations between the system and human scores ranged from .74 to .97, with a median value of .88. In a second study, the relationship of GIDE's scores to performance on the GRE General Test's quantitative section, an established mathematical reasoning measure, was assessed (Bennett, Sebrechts, & Rock, 1991). Results showed the factors represented by the two tests to be highly related, thus supporting GIDE's scores as indicators of quantitative proficiency.

```
The active ingredient is 0.25 percent of a 3-ounce dose of a certain cold remedy.
What is the number of doses a patient must take before receiving the full 3 ounces
of the active ingredient?

Correct Answer = 400 doses

a.   1.  0.25% = .0025
     2.  Active Ingredient per dose = .0025 * 3 oz
         Active Ingredient per dose = .0075 oz
     3.  Number of doses required = 3 oz/.0075 oz per dose
         Number of doses required = 400 doses

b.   1.  .25%x dose = 100% dose
         x dose = 100% dose/.25% dose
         x = 400 doses
```

FIG. 5.4. Alternative goal decompositions for an algebra word problem.

Cognitively Motivated Measurement Models

In their current experimental states, GIDE and MicroPROUST produce analyses only for item-level responses. That is, scores and diagnostic comments are restricted to performance on a single item. These scores and comments have potential value for describing how an examinee did on that item and perhaps for helping him or her avoid those same mistakes next time. However, as noted, more dependable statements about an examinee's skills might be derived from model-based aggregations of performance made across constructed-response tasks.

Several approaches can be taken to response modeling. In psychometrics, methods like item response theory (Lord, 1980) have been built on purely statistical foundations. As Mislevy notes (chapter 2, this volume), these approaches work well for some assessment purposes (e.g., selection) and far less well for others (e.g., instructional diagnosis).

Intelligent tutoring, in contrast, has focused on developing models incorporating an understanding of the domain in which responses are to be aggregated (Wenger, 1987). As a result, these models promise interpretations of performance that are more clearly tied to instructional decisions. At the same time, however, these deterministic formulations generally do not deal well with the inconsistency that often characterizes human performance (Wenger, 1987).[6]

Given this situation, it would seem sensible to work toward some combination of probabilistic methods and the cognitively based diagnosis exemplified by intelligent tutoring. As suggested by Masters and Mislevy (chapter 9, this volume), the probabilistic methods should be subservient to cognitive considerations: Domain semantics should shape the model's application in any given case.

Several recent measurement models attempt to fill this requirement, including the Hierarchically Ordered Skills Test (HOST) model (Rock & Pollack, 1987), the HYBRID model (Yamamoto, 1987), and Masters' Partial Credit Model (Masters & Mislevy, chapter 9, this volume).[7] A brief summary of the first two models will be given here as introduction to how they might be applied in intelligent assessment (for more complete descriptions see Gitomer & Rock, chapter 10; and Yamamoto & Gitomer, chapter 11, this volume).

In the HOST model, groups of items are written to represent levels of proficiency, with each succeeding level requiring one or more new cognitive operations in addition to those of the preceding level. If the model fits, standing on the scale denotes what operations the examinee is and is not able to perform. Because individuals often come to proficiency in an area by different paths, the

---

[6]Unfortunately, there have been relatively few attempts within intelligent tutoring to address this issue, and, as a consequence, no generally applicable models capable of efficiently handling uncertainty have emerged.

[7]Masters and Mislevy (chapter 9, this volume) offer examples of other appropriate models.

model provides a measure of fit for each examinee. When the model does not fit an examinee's performance, that performance can usually be placed on a more general ability scale. In addition to measures of individual fit, the model provides estimates of the probabilities associated with being at particular skill levels. These probabilities have proven particularly useful for measuring individual change because the probabilities seem less sensitive than other metrics to the ceiling and floor effects that have perennially hampered attempts to measure individual growth (Rock & Pollack, 1987).

Rock has studied the fit of the HOST model to mathematics achievement data from the 1980 sophomore High School and Beyond (HS&B) cohort and from the population taking the SAT (Rock & Pollack, 1987; Gitomer & Rock, chapter 10, this volume). In these studies, the overwhelming majority of examinees fit the model: 90% for the HS&B sample and 96–98% for the SAT sample. Further, the model fit equally well for males and females, and for majority and minority examinees.[8]

The second approach, Yamamoto's (1987) HYBRID model, combines latent class models with item response theory (IRT). Latent class models are built on the idea of a categorical latent variable (Lazarsfeld, 1960). Because a hierarchy of classes is not required, information can be provided about unordered qualitative states that characterize examinees (e.g., a tendency toward a specific error type). In addition, the probability that an examinee's response pattern belongs to a given class is provided.

In practice, not all examinee response patterns can be captured by a limited set of classes. More classes may exist than are reflected in the model, or individuals may respond in an extremely inconsistent fashion. Performance that does not fit one of the hypothesized latent classes may be represented by a continuous model that makes no assumptions about examinees' qualitative understandings. The HYBRID model accounts for this eventuality by scaling these examinees along a general dimension underlying a problem set, while simultaneously providing diagnostic information for those individuals who fit a latent class.

The performance of the HYBRID model has been assessed using data on electronic technicians' ability to interpret logic gate symbols (Gitomer & Yamamoto, 1991). Five latent classes were represented based on specific errors commonly made by technicians. The model's latent class portion was able to capture 25% of the response patterns, a respectable performance given the specificity of the error classes. In addition, for individuals picked up by the latent classes, the distinction among error classes given particular response patterns was quite sharp, making class assignments very clear. Finally, the probability of belonging to any latent class was unrelated to overall ability estimates, supporting the model's capacity to represent qualitative states.

---

[8]In both the HS&B and SAT studies, the HOST model was fit to a specially chosen subset of items rather than to the complete mathematical scale.

Depending upon the domain and the assessment purpose. either the HOST or the HYBRID models might be used. Alternatively, they might be employed together to provide complementary aggregations of item information. Fig. 5.5 shows four algebra item formats hypothesized to form a hierarchical ordering by Bennett, Sebrechts, and Yamamoto (1991). The formats are *open-ended* (only the problem stem is presented), *goal specification* (the problem stem, a list of givens, and a list of unknowns, or goals, is presented), *equation setup* (the problem stem and the equations, or plans, needed to derive the unknowns are given), and *faulty solution* (the stem and an incorrect response are presented for the examinee to correct). The problems presented in each format are isomorphs (i.e., the same solution process can be applied to all four problems). A theoretical justification of the hierarchy is presented in Fig. 5.6 as a list of cognitive operations suggested to underlie each proficiency level. If the HOST model fit a complete test built around this illustration, examinees who successfully completed items in the open-ended format would generally succeed with the other formats (though the reverse would not necessarily be true). The operations underlying the levels would form the basis for diagnostic statements that might be made about individuals whose performance fit the model.

The Hybrid model might be used on this same test to give information about the latent error class to which an examinee's performance belongs. As with HOST, this classification is semantically driven: Latent classes derive from the domain and the nature of examinee performance, not directly from the measurement model. Bennett, Sebrechts, and Yamamoto (1991) suggest four theoretically motivated error categories that can serve as the basis for such classes. *Mathematical errors* involve a failure to execute a low-level operation (e.g., by inappropriately shifting a decimal). *Specific plan errors* are incorrect procedures for solving a goal linked to a particular problem (e.g., confusing the rates for different trip segments). *General plan errors* suggest more universal failures to formulate procedures, with the same malformation having the potential to occur across problems (e.g., dividing when multiplication is called for). Finally, *missing goals* suggest the omission of a critical solution component. From these error categories, latent classes can be formed to represent those individuals who consistently tend to make only one of these error types, as well as those examinees who make particular error combinations. Individuals whose response patterns place them into one of the classes can be identified as needing a specific type of attention if success in the domain is to be achieved.

Using a 12-item test, Bennett, Sebrechts, and Yamamoto (1991) explored the fit of the HOST and HYBRID models to the hypothesized cognitive structures previously described. In a sample of GRE General Test examinees, they found that—contrary to expectation—the faulty solution items proved harder than the other formats (perhaps because examinees solved the faulty problems in a way similar to the open-ended items, but with the added step of comparing their

a. On a 600-mile motor trip, Bill averaged 45 miles per hour for the first 285 miles and 50 miles per hour for the remainder of the trip. If he started at 7:00 a.m., at what time did he finish the trip (to the nearest minute)?

_____
_____
_____

ANSWER:_____

b. 800 gallons of a 2,400 gallon tank flow in at the rate of 75 gallons per hour through a clogged hose. After the hose is unclogged, the rest of the tank is filled at the rate of 250 gallons per hour. At what time to the nearest minute will the filling of the tank be finished if it starts at 5:30 a.m.?

Givens
Tank Capacity   = _____
Filling Rate 1   = _____
Filling Amount 1   = _____
Filling Rate 2   = _____
Start Time for Filling   = _____

Unknown
Filing Time 1   = _____
Filling Amount 2   = _____
Filling Time 2   = _____
Total Filling Time   = _____
Ending Time for Filling = _____

ANSWER:_____

c. Of the 720 pages of printed output of a certain program, 305 pages are printed on a printer that prints 15 pages per minute and the rest are printed on a printer that prints at 50 pages per minute. If the printers run one after the other and printing starts at 10 minutes and 15 seconds after the hour, at what time to the nearest second after the hour will the printing be finished?

Equations that Will Provide a Solution:

Time for Printing on Printer 1 = Number of Pages on Printer 1 / Printing Rate of Printer 1
Number of Pages on Printer 2 = Total Number of Pages - Number of Pages on Printer 1
Time for Printing on Printer 2 = Number of Pages on Printer 2 / Printing Rate of Printer 2
Total Printing Time = Time for Printing on Printer 1 + Time for Printing on Printer 2
Time Print Job Finished = Starting Print TIME + Total Printing Time

Your Solution:

_____
_____
_____
_____

ANSWER:_____

d. A Department of Transportation road crew paves 15 mile city portion of a 37.4 mile route at the rate of 1.8 miles per day and paves the rest of the route, which is outside the city, at a rate of 2.1 miles per day. If the Department of Transportation starts the project on day 11 of its work calendar, on what day of its work calendar will the project be completed?

Time for Portion 1 = 15 miles/1.8 miles per day
Time for Portion 1 = 8 and 1/3 days
Time for Portion 2 = 37.4 miles/2.1 miles per day
Time for Portion 2 = 17.81 days
Total Time = 8.30 days + 17.81 days
Total Time = 26.11 days
Completion Day = 27

Your Corrected Solution:

_____
_____
_____
_____

ANSWER:_____

FIG. 5.5. Four item formats hypothesized to form a hierarchical ordering: (a) open-ended, (b) goal specification, (c) equation setup, (d) faulty solution. (Print size is reduced, space for writing solutions shortened, and page arrangement modified for publication purposes.) From Bennett, Sebrechts, and Yamamoto, 1991. Copyright © 1991, Educational Testing Service. Used by permission.

Level	Format	Operations
4	Open ended	Identify givens and unknowns. Create representation for problem based on knowns and unknowns. Map equations onto problem statement. Solve equations. Check solution, detect error(s), and recover.
3	Goal specification	Create representation for problem based on knowns and unknowns. Map equations onto problem statement. Solve equations. Check solution, detect error(s), and recover.
2	Equation setup	Map equations onto problem statement. Solve equations. Check solution, detect error(s), and recover.
1	Faulty solution	Check solution against problem statement, detect error(s), and recover.

FIG. 5.6. Operations suggested to underlie a proposed hierarchical arrangement of item formats. From Bennett, Sebrechts, and Yamamoto, 1991. Copyright © 1991, Educational Testing Service. Used by permission.

solutions to the erroneous given ones). Analyses with the HYBRID model showed examinees to make relatively few errors overall and to fall into one of two classes: missing-goal errors and inconsistent patterns better captured by the unidimensional IRT model. Although the posited cognitive structures were not confirmed, this study illustrates an initial step in making such model-based characterizations from the constructed responses of examinees. Clearly, additional work is needed to refine the postulated structures and then reevaluate fit using these measurement models.

POTENTIAL APPLICATIONS

The three components of intelligent assessment—complex constructed response, intelligent scoring, and cognitively driven measurement models—are in different states of readiness for operational use. Complex constructed response has, of course been employed for quite some time in large-scale testing programs such as the College Board's Advanced Placement Program. As a result, much practical experience has accumulated about the item type's development, administration, and scoring using human judges. As noted, however, the item format's measurement characteristics have not been fully explored. Though these items are unarguably more "direct" measures of the constructs schools aim to teach (J. R. Frederiksen & Collins, 1989), whether they are in reality more valid measures of these constructs remains an open question (Traub & MacRury, 1990).

Methods for automatically scoring complex constructed responses are generally not ready for operational use. For example, neither GIDE nor MicroPROUST can accurately score all the responses encountered. Other scoring systems are in a similar state (e.g., see Bejar, 1988; Freedle, 1988). Due to the diversity of human performance, perfect accuracy may be far in the future.

Finally, the cognitively motivated measurement models and in-depth understandings of domain performance required to support this notion of assessment are only beginning to emerge (Mislevy, chapter 2, this volume). Thus, a considerable period of research will likely be required before these models begin to see widespread use.

Even though the foundations for intelligent assessment are not yet firmly established, enough progress has been made to justify building some initial applications, the study of which should begin to provide the knowledge to support operational realizations. Three ideas are discussed, ranging from a heavily constrained implementation that could be quickly built to a fully featured intelligent assessment system that may take many years to construct. Each idea is structured so as to explore some of the central issues in intelligent assessment.

The least ambitious idea requires as context a computer delivered testing program. Several such programs exist (e.g., the College Board's Computerized Placement Tests), and more are under development ("ETS research plan," 1989). Many of these programs will be computerized adaptive tests (Wainer et al., 1990). Computerized adaptive tests dynamically home in on the estimated skill level of the examinee, presenting fewer but more informative items than conventional tests. Consequently, they take less time to administer while maintaining the content coverage and reliability of paper-and-pencil analogues.

One profitable way to use some of this saved time might be to supplement the multiple-choice item pool with a small number of intelligently-scored complex constructed-response items, such that each examinee encounters one or two of them. In the event that the constructed responses were found to measure the same trait as the rest of the test, a plausible occurrence in some instances (Bennett, Rock et al., 1990; Traub & Fisher, 1977; Ward, 1982), all items might be placed on the same IRT scale using, for example, the Partial Credit Model (Masters & Mislevy, chapter 9, this volume). Item parameters not only would be used to select constructed responses appropriate to the examinee's skill level, but also might be employed in scoring the test. Though chosen adaptively, the constructed response items would be presented last to avoid the cognitive and conative disruption that might occur from mixing item formats. If, after analyzing the solution, the expert system was able to account for each goal, a report of the examinee's constructed response performance would be displayed. This application leaves content coverage intact and provides the examinee with information beyond the total test score. The effects of any potential scoring inaccuracy are mitigated because item-level feedback is provided (and factored into overall test score) only if all parts of the examinee's production are explained. Finally, the application gives some visibility (though far less than deserved) to the behaviors that should be the focus of instruction, a feature particularly important for achievement, college admissions, and other large-scale programs that can influence school curricula.

A second potential application is a self-assessment intended to help develop skills and prepare students for a particular standardized test. The self-assessment should make visible the standards for domain performance so that the student can internalize and use them for judging his or her own productions (J. R. Frederiksen & Collins, 1989). In the APCS program, such an assessment might be built around the APCS Practice System (Bennett, Sack, & Soloway, 1991) and contain a large pool of free-response and constrained free-response programming problems that students could access on demand. For incorrect solutions, the application would print not only a diagnostic analysis and a partial-credit score, but a goal-plan decomposition and the rules for judging the item using that decomposition. The student might then be given two tasks: (a) to verify that the system's analysis was correct and (b) to revise the solution utilizing the system's comments and the problem's goal-plan decomposition. For instances in which the system was not able to produce an analysis, the goal-plan decomposition would be printed with a direction to consult the classroom teacher (or perhaps a more skilled peer). Student and teacher might then collaboratively analyze the solution to see how it diverged from the goal-plan decomposition, bringing to light other legitimate approaches to the problem or rare errors beyond the system's understanding. In this instance, the system's inability to flawlessly analyze all responses is a virtue: It forces the student to seek others' counsel, hopefully encouraging both collaborative problem solving and the internalization by student and teacher of goal-plan analysis as one approach to problem solution.

The last potential application is a model-governed intelligent assessment system for instructional diagnosis. Such a system might complement the College Board's Computerized Placement Tests (CPTs), which are used to select students needing remedial instruction from the freshman class entering an institution.

At the front end of this system would be an adaptive, multiple-choice assessment module. This module's purpose would be to estimate efficiently the examinee's general skill level in the domain so that appropriate constructed response tasks could be presented. Accurate assignment is critical not only because responses to overly difficult items will almost invariably be wrong, but because those responses will usually be severely flawed and, as a result, indecipherable by an expert scoring system. Responses to items that are too easy will likely be correct, and, though decipherable, will contribute no useful information. This module would not need to be used if a skill estimate were already available from a companion test, such as the CPTs.

The second component, the constructed response module, would need to be built from a deep understanding of the domain. It would be composed of problems requiring the application and integration of key knowledge and skill.

On top of this domain structure would rest a measurement model, like HOST or HYBRID, able to generate diagnostically useful information. On the basis of constructed response performance, the model would generate hypotheses about the examinee's proficiency. Both because of inconsistencies in examinee performance and because any expert scoring system will sometimes fail to understand a production, these hypotheses would in some cases be based on incomplete or contradictory information. To reduce uncertainty, the constructed response module would pass its list of competing, plausible hypotheses to a verification module.

The verification module would be composed of two parts, called upon as necessary. One part would consist of a series of testlets, homogeneous multiple-choice item clusters focused on a specific skill (Wainer & Kiely, 1987). The contents of these testlets would derive from the same comprehensive analysis of the domain that formed the basis for the constructed response module. Only those testlets that might serve to confirm or disconfirm an active diagnostic hypothesis would be administered. A second module component would ask the examinee for an estimate of his or her understanding of the skills in question and use this estimate in the verification process, a strategy used in rudimentary ways in several intelligent tutors (Wenger, 1987).

In addition to indicating whether a student is in fact behaving consistently, this verification process might also confirm whether consistently manifested errors (e.g., converting 10.63 hours to 11 hours, 3 minutes) represent slips or real misunderstandings (Matz, 1982). In one case, simply pointing out the error to the examinee might resolve it; in the other, a more extended explanation would be required. An assessment system with such verification and feedback capabilities begins to take on J. R. Frederiksen and Collins' (1989) notion of *systemic validity* by helping students improve the skills it is attempting to test.

CONCLUSION

This chapter presented a conceptualization of intelligent assessment as an integration of constructed-response testing, scoring methods based on artificial intelligence, and cognitively motivated measurement models. To illustrate progress toward this conception, two intelligent scoring systems—Micro-PROUST and GIDE—and two measurement models—HOST and HYBRID—were described. It is worth emphasizing that these approaches take particular perspectives, especially the scoring systems, which derive from the same theoretical base. Other approaches to both scoring and response modeling exist, and it is likely to be some time before any individual method becomes generally accepted.

Second, it should be evident that many unresolved issues are associated with intelligent assessment. The development of even the least ambitious realization implies a considerable effort—in domain understanding and knowledge-base development, item writing, scoring rules, feedback contents and processes, programming, pilot testing, and validation research, among other things—with no certainty that the result will prove substantially better than current testing approaches. But the purpose of this chapter, the work it describes, and research generally is to develop and test new ideas, to discover their effects and the conditions under which they manifest. Only through this inquiry process will we be able to build the innovative assessment approaches needed to help shape an educational system that meets the demands of an increasingly complex world.

REFERENCES

Ackerman, T. A., & Smith, P. L. (1988). A comparison of the information provided by essay, multiple-choice, and free-response writing tests. *Applied Psychological Measurement, 12*, 117–128.

Bejar, I. I. (1988). A sentence-based automatic approach to assessment of writing: A feasibility study. *Machine-Mediated Learning, 2*, 321–332.

Bennett, R. E. (in press). On the meanings of constructed response. In R. E. Bennett & W. C. Ward (Eds.), *Construction vs. choice in cognitive measurement*. Hillsdale, NJ: Lawrence Erlbaum Associates.

Bennett, R. E., Gong, B., Kershaw, R. C., Rock, D. A., Soloway, E., & Macalalad, A. (1990). Assessment of an expert system's ability to automatically grade and diagnose students' constructed-responses to computer science problems. In R. O. Freedle (Ed.), *Artificial intelligence and the future of testing* (pp. 293–320). Hillsdale, NJ: Lawrence Erlbaum Associates.

Bennett, R. E., Rock, D. A., Braun, H. I., Frye, D., Spohrer, J. C. & Soloway, E. (1990). The relationship of constrained free-response items to multiple-choice and open-ended items. *Applied Psychological Measurement, 14*, 151–162.

Bennett, R., E., Sack, W., & Soloway, E. (1991). *The Advanced Placement Computer Science Practice System*. Princeton, NJ: Educational Testing Service.

Bennett, R. E., Sebrechts, M. M., & Rock, D. A. (1991). Expert system scores for complex constructed-response quantitative items: A study of convergent validity. *Applied Psychological Measurement, 15*, 227–239.

Bennett, R. E., Sebrechts, M. M., & Yamamoto, K. (1991). *Fitting new measurement models to GRE General Test constructed-response item data* (RR-91-60). Princeton, NJ: Educational Testing Service.

Bennett, R. E., Ward, W. C., Rock, D. A., & LaHart, C. (1990). *Toward a framework for constructed-response items* (RR-90-7). Princeton, NJ: Educational Testing Service.

Birenbaum, M., & Tatsuoka, K. K. (1987). Open-ended versus multiple-choice response formats—It does make a difference for diagnostic purposes. *Applied Psychological Measurement, 11*, 385–395.

Braun, H. I. (1988). Understanding scoring reliability: Experiments in calibrating essay readers. *Journal of Educational Statistics, 13*, 1–18.

Braun, H. I., Bennett, R. E., Frye, D., & Soloway, E. (1990). Scoring constructed responses using expert systems. *Journal of Educational Measurement, 27*, 93–108.

Breland, H. M., Camp, R., Jones, R. J., Morris, M. M., & Rock, D. A. (1987). *Assessing writing skill*. New York: College Entrance Examination Board.

Bunderson, C. V., Inouye, D. K., & Olsen, J. O. (1989). The four generations of computerized educational measurement. In R. L. Linn (Ed.), *Educational measurement* (3rd ed., pp. 367–407). New York: American Council on Education/Macmillan.

Educational Testing Service (1989). Research plan designed to create a new generation of Graduate Record Examinations. *Examiner, 18*(26).

Fiske, E. B. (1990, January 31) But is the child learning? Schools trying new tests. *The New York Times*, pp. A1, B6.

Frederiksen, J. R., & Collins, A. (1989). A systems approach to educational testing. *Educational Researcher, 18*(9), 27–32.

Frederiksen, J. R., & White, B. Y. (1988). Implicit testing within an intelligent tutoring system. *Machine-Mediated Learning, 2*, 351–372.

Frederiksen, N. (1984). The real test bias: Influences of testing on teaching and learning. *American Psychologist, 39*, 193–202.

Frederiksen, N., & Ward, W. C. (1978). Measures for the study of creativity in scientific problem solving. *Applied Psychological Measurement, 2*, 1–24.

Freedle, R. (1988). A semi-automatic procedure for scoring protocols resulting from a free-response sentence-combining writing task. *Machine-Mediated Learning, 2*, 309–319.

Gitomer, D. H., & Yamamoto, K. (1991). Performance modeling that integrates latent trait and latent class theory. *Journal of Educational Measurement, 28*, 173–189.

Johnson, W. L. (1986). *Intention-based diagnosis of novice programming errors.* Los Altos, CA: Morgan Kaufmann.

Johnson, W. L., & Soloway, E. (1985). PROUST: An automatic debugger for Pascal programs. *Byte, 10*(4), 179–190.

Joreskog, K., & Sorbom, D. (1988). *LISREL 7: A guide to the program and applications.* Chicago, IL: SPSS Inc.

Lazarsfeld, P. F. (1960). Latent structure analysis and test theory. In H. Gulliksen & S. Messick (Eds.), *Psychological scaling: Theory and applications* (pp. 83–86). New York: Wiley.

Lord, F. M. (1980). *Applications of item response theory to practical testing problems.* Hillsdale, NJ: Lawrence Erlbaum Associates.

Matz, M. (1982). Towards a process model for high school algebra. In D. H. Sleeman & J. S. Brown (Eds.), *Intelligent tutoring systems* (pp. 25–50). London: Academic Press.

Millman, J., & Greene, J. (1989). The specification and development of tests of achievement and ability. In R. L. Linn (Ed.), *Educational measurement* (3rd ed., pp. 335–366). New York: American Council on Education/Macmillan.

Rock, D. A., & Pollack, J. (1987). *Measurement gains—A new look at an old problem.* Paper presented at the ETS/DoD Conference, San Diego, CA.

Sebrechts, M. M., Bennett, R. E., & Rock, D. A. (1991). Agreement between expert-system and human raters' scores on complex constructed-response quantitative items. *Journal of Applied Psychology, 76*, 856–862.

Sebrechts, M. M., LaClaire, L., Schooler, L. J., & Soloway, E. (1986). Towards generalized intention-based diagnosis: GIDE. In W. C. Ryan, (Ed.), *Proceedings of the 7th National Educational Computing Conference* (pp. 237–242). Eugene, OR: International Council on Computers in Education.

Sebrechts, M. M., & Schooler, L. J. (1987, July). Diagnosing errors in statistical problem-solving: Associative problem recognition and plan-based error detection. In E. Hunt (Ed.), *Proceedings of the Ninth Annual Cognitive Science Meeting* (pp. 691–703). Hillsdale, NJ: Lawrence Erlbaum Associates.

Sleeman, D. H., & Brown, J. S. (Eds.). (1982). *Intelligent tutoring systems.* London: Academic Press.

Soloway, E., & Ehrlich, K. (1984). Empirical investigations of programming knowledge. *IEEE Transactions on Software Engineering, 10*, 595–609.

Soloway, E., & Iyengar, S. (Eds.). (1986). *Empirical studies of programmers.* Norwood, NJ: Ablex.

Traub, R. E., & Fisher, C. W. (1977). On the equivalence of constructed-response and multiple-choice tests. *Applied Psychological Measurement, 1*, 355–369.

Traub, R. E., & MacRury, K. (1990). Multiple-choice vs. free-response in the testing of scholastic achievement. In K. Ingenkamp & R. S. Jager (Eds.), *Tests und trends 8: Jahrbuch der padagogischen diagnostik* [Yearbook on educational measurement] (pp. 128–159). Weinheim, Germany: Beltz.

Wainer, H., Dorans, N. J., Green, B. F., Flaugher, R., Mislevy, R. J., Steinberg, L., & Thissen, D. (1990). *Computerized adaptive testing: A primer.* Hillsdale, NJ: Lawrence Erlbaum Associates.

Wainer, H., & Kiely, G. L. (1987). Item clusters and computerized adaptive testing: A case for testlets. *Journal of Educational Measurement, 24,* 185–201.

Ward, W. C. (1982). A comparison of free-response and multiple-choice forms of verbal aptitude tests. *Applied Psychological Measurement, 6,* 1–11.

Ward, W. C., Frederiksen, N., & Carlson, S. B. (1980). Construct validity of free-response and machine-scorable forms of a test. *Journal of Educational Measurement, 17,* 11–29.

Wenger, E. (1987). *Artificial intelligence and tutoring systems.* Los Altos, CA: Morgan Kaufmann.

Yamamoto, K. (1987). *A model that combines IRT and latent class models.* Unpublished doctoral dissertation, University of Illinois, Champaign-Urbana.

6

Psychometric Models for Learning and Cognitive Processes

Susan Embretson
University of Kansas

Cognitive psychology has had major impact on our understanding of complex cognitive skills, such as problem solving, thinking, and inference. Increasingly, cognitive psychology is providing a substantive foundation for both instruction and aptitude theory (e.g., Glaser, 1985). Cognitive tasks can be characterized by the component processes, strategies, and knowledge structures involved in solving the task.

Test developers are definitely interested in cognitive theory as a means of conceptualizing the traits that are measured by current tests, particularly since many types of aptitude items have been studied in the laboratory. However, as yet cognitive theory has had little impact on either actual test content or test scores. Currently, testing practices have been heavily influenced by contemporary test theory (known as item response theory or latent trait modeling), which emphasizes optimal methods to score item responses into an index of ability and to select items that give the most information about the central ability factor on the test. Although the item response theory models that are typically applied have many advantages over earlier testing methods, they have little connection with the concerns of cognitive theory about the processes, strategies, and knowledge structures that underlie item solving.

In fact, cognitive psychology seems so remote from test theory that it is sometimes suggested that the cognitive variables should be considered as "qualitative" information or that a whole new kind of test theory is required. Neither extreme is desirable. Certainly it is difficult even to imagine the nature of a whole new test theory, let alone develop a functioning system. In contrast, regarding cognitive theory as providing only qualitative data for measurement lessens its impact on testing. If cognitive theory provides only qualitative information, item development, item selection and testing procedures will be influenced only peripherally.

Another possibility, which is exemplified by this chapter, is to develop some models that are based on contemporary test theory, but yet permit cognitive processing variables to be incorporated directly into the models. Thus, the impact of the cognitive processing variables on the psychometric properties of the test is quantified. Cognitive theory has a more central role because the various indices provide information that can be used for test design.

This chapter presents some test theory models from the author's research program, which combines psychometrics and cognitive psychology. The models contain parameters to account for the impact of cognitive processing variables on item responses. Applying these models can permit cognitive theory to have direct impact on test content and, consequently, on what is measured by the test. Two aspects of the test can be influenced: (a) the stimulus features of the test items and (b) the context of item presentation (e.g., the amount and nature of instruction, cues, practice, or the occasion). Both item content and context can influence the difficulty level and the dimensionality of the test.

Perhaps the most fundamental impact of cognitive psychology on testing is the conceptualization of the examinee's response to an item. This, in turn, has direct implications for the construct validity of the test and for the appropriate psychometric models. Thus, this chapter begins by presenting a reconceptualization of construct validity. Further details are available in Embretson (1983a).

CONCEPTUAL FRAMEWORK
FOR DEVELOPING MODELS
FOR LEARNING AND COGNITIVE PROCESSES

In Cronbach and Meehl's (1955) classical conceptualization of construct validity, the meaning of a test score is derived from the network of relationships of the test with other measures. Meaning thus increases as successively more studies provide information about the correlates of test scores. Cognitive processing studies can be incorporated into the nomological network as another type of information about score meaning. However, as Bechtoldt (1959) noted, determining the meaning of scores from its empirical relationships with other measures confounds meaning (what psychological construct is measured) with significance (what the construct predicts).

Cognitive theory can have a central role in construct validity by distinguishing between two separate research stages—construct representation and nomothetic span (Embretson, 1983a). Construct representation concerns identifying the theoretical constructs (e.g., components, strategies, and knowledge structures) that are involved in responding to the specific items that appear on the test. These variables, obviously, are central to cognitive psychology, and assessing them requires applying the methods of experimental cognitive psychology to test items. Nomothetic span, in contrast, concerns the utility of the test as a measure of individual differences. Nomothetic span includes the relationship of test scores to other measures and to individual differences in the underlying components, strategies, and knowledge structures. Applying Bechtoldt's distinction, construct representation concerns the meaning of scores, whereas nomothetic span concerns the significance of scores.

The relationship of aptitude to cognitive processing may be conceptualized within a hierarchical structure. Aptitude results from solving complex tasks that require correct outcomes from several stages of the task. On many tasks, more than one combination of components can result in task solution. For example, spatial tasks often may be solved by processing verbally or spatially. In this case, aptitude may arise from the successful application of more than one strategy. At the next level in the hierarchy are the processing components. Processing components must be executed correctly to provide information toward solving the item under a particular strategy. At the deepest level are the stimulus features of the items. The specific stimuli in the item influence the difficulty of the processing in the various components.

The hierarchical conceptualization of the processes underlying item responses can be illustrated by the three items from the Spatial Learning Ability Test (Embretson & Waxman, 1989) in Fig. 6.1. In these items, the task is to select the three-dimensional alternative that represents the stem when folded down. Although all three items contain the same stem to be folded, the items vary in either the minimum number of processes required for task solution or the specific difficulty of the various processes.

Item 1 can be solved without mentally folding the pattern by noticing that three of the options have side markings (i.e., shaded side, dark background, rectangular marking); this leaves only one option (2), whose markings can all be forced on the pattern. Item 2, in contrast, has no distractor that does not match a side of the pattern, and all sides must be mentally folded to understand the relative positions of the markings and to recognize the correct option. Thus, Item 1 can be solved by two different strategies (noticing mismatching sides or mentally folding), whereas Item 2 can be solved only by fully folding the stem. Notice that the Item 2 requires more processing than Item 1.

Furthermore, the difficulty of processing also depends on the stimulus features of the stem and the correct answer. In Item 2 in Fig. 6.1, the mental processes in folding and comparing the stem to the correct alternative (2) are relatively easy, because the mentally folded cube has the same orientation as the target and only two surfaces must be carried. In Item 3 however, comparing the stem to the key (4) requires a 180-degree rotation and three surfaces carried, which is much more difficult.

Spatial Folding Items

1.

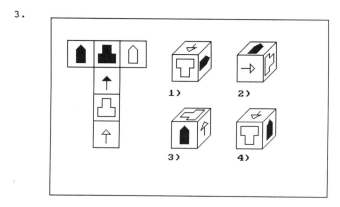

2.

3.

FIG. 6.1. Three items from the Spatial Learning Ability Test. From Embretson (1991). Copyright © 1991 by the Psychometric Society. Adapted by permission.

These examples show how the relative difficulty of an item on the components, or the most successful strategies, will vary between items on a test. Items vary in stimulus content, which in turn influences processing difficulty or strategy feasibility.

The cognitive load of a test item may also vary with the specific testing procedures. Presenting test items with little prior instruction to naive examinees may make adopting a successful strategy the major source of individual differences. After more extensive instruction, such as a dynamic testing procedure, individual differences can depend more heavily on processing skills or knowledge structures. Or, amount of practice alone also can change the cognitive load of the task, as shown by Ackerman (1988).

The conclusion to be drawn from the aforementioned observations is that the cognitive complexity of items varies in meaningful ways. The construct representation of the test can be influenced by selecting items with specified sources of cognitive complexity or by designing the testing procedures.

Nomothetic span is influenced by construct representation. The predictive validity of the test depends on which components of individual differences are represented in the test score. The various components can vary in relative importance in an item set, and to the extent that the components are differentially related to external variables, the predictive validity of the test will be influenced. Thus, tests that are composed of the same item type, but with different relative weighings of the components, will have different patterns of nomothetic span.

For example, the nomothetic span of a spatial folding test depends on which type of item appears on the test. If items like Item 1 appear on the test, the aptitude that is measured represents either successful spatial or successful verbal-analytic processing during encoding. Moderate correlations of test scores with both verbal and spatial measures would be expected. Thus, the span of relationships of the test scores would be high, but the magnitude of correlations would be low, due to the confounding of two strategies in the scores. In turn, the correlations of the spatial folding task with verbal tests also leads to a low expectation for incremental validity (over verbal tests) in predicting various criteria.

If items like Item 2 or Item 3 appear on the test, the aptitude that is measured involves spatial processing. High correlations with spatial measures and low correlations with verbal measures would be expected. Incremental validity over verbal tests, however, for predicting criteria involving spatial skills would be high. Thus, the correlates of aptitude may be expected to differ, depending on the construct representation of the test.

In summary, items can be selected or created, or procedures and training can be designed to influence explicitly the specific cognitive processes that define the major source of individual differences. Consequently, nomothetic span is also influenced. Of course, a means of quantifying cognitive complexity is required, and such quantification would be most useful if specifically related to the psychometric properties of the items. The models to be presented below incorporate cognitive complexity into contemporary test theory models (i.e., latent trait models). A brief introduction to latent trait models will precede the presentation of the cognitive–psychometric models.

LATENT TRAIT MODELS

In the last two decades, test theory has changed substantially. Latent trait models (also known as item response theory models) are rapidly becoming the psychometric standard for measuring abilities. Fortunately, latent trait models interface much better than classical test theory with the methods of cognitive psychology. That is, both test theory and task decomposition employ mathematical modeling of responses to the item task. Thus, a brief introduction to contemporary test theory is needed prior to presenting the psychometric models for cognitive variables.

Unlike classical test theory, the indices used to evaluate test reliability and item reliability do not depend on the variances and covariances of the examinees total scores. Instead, an item response model is a mathematical model of the probability that an examinee passes a specific item. The mathematical model contains parameters to represent the person's ability and parameters to represent the item's properties (e.g., difficulty, discrimination).

Classical test theory was never able to adequately handle the nonlinear relationship of the probability of solving an item to ability. If the probability of solving an item correctly is calculated at each raw score level and plotted, the resulting item characteristics curve is well described as a cumulative normal distribution. Nearly the same item characteristics curve will be produced by a logistic model, which has the advantage of a mathematically simple form. In the Rasch model, the latent response potential, R_{ij}, that item i will be solved by person j is given by the simple difference between ability, θ_j, and item difficulty, b_i, as follows:

$$RP_{ij} = \theta_j - b_i. \tag{1}$$

Thus, if ability exceeds item difficulty, the latent potential for the person solving the item is greater than if ability is less than item difficulty.

Latent response potential, defined as in Equation 1, runs from $-\infty$ to $+\infty$. RP_{ij} may be mapped to the probability that person j will solve item i in the Rasch model as

$$P(X_{ij}=1) = \frac{\exp(\theta_j - b_i)}{1 + \exp(\theta_j - b_i)}. \tag{2}$$

The relationship of item solving to ability in the Rasch model is an S-shaped curve in which the probability of .50 is reached when ability equals item difficulty.

Separating the item parameters from the person parameters in a latent trait model allows cognitive variables to be incorporated into the model. In cognitive psychology, a major method for studying cognitive processes is the mathematical modeling of item difficulty (or response time) by some variables that index the cognitive complexity of the item. The cognitive complexity of the item, in turn, depends on its stimulus properties, which can be manipulated or selected to study effects on processing difficulty. To incorporate cognitive complexity into a latent trait model, for example, item difficulty, b_i, can be replaced by an explanatory model that represents the cognitive complexity of the item. This method and other methods to incorporate cognitive variables into latent trait models are described next.

LATENT TRAIT MODELS
FOR THE COGNITIVE CONTENT OF ITEMS

Several latent trait models to represent cognitive content variables have been proposed (Embretson, 1984; Fischer, 1973; Jannarone, 1986; Mislevy & Verhelst, 1990; Scheiblechner, 1985; Spada & McGaw, 1985; Stegelmann, 1983; Whitely, 1980). Three component latent trait models are described here: the linear logistic latent trait model (LLTM; Fischer, 1973), the multicomponent latent trait model (MLTM; Whitely, 1980), and the general component latent trait model (GLTM; Embretson, 1984). The models operate at different levels of complexity in the impact of cognitive variables on aptitude. The LLTM relates the impact of the stimulus features of the items to component processing difficulty. Applying the LLTM requires that the stimulus features are scored, and then the scores are used to model item difficulty. The MLTM relates the component outcomes to test scores. Applying the MLTM requires both subtask outcome and total item outcome data. The GLTM incorporates both the LLTM and the MLTM, and thus applying the GLTM requires both types of data.

The Linear Logistic Latent Trait Model

The Model. Fischer (1973) proposed the linear logistic latent trait model (LLTM) prior to the current interest in the contribution of cognitive psychology to testing. Thus the linear logistic model had little impact on American psychometrics until the 1980s, although it has been quite influential in European psychometrics (see Fischer, 1973, for a summary of the research).

Prior to using the LLTM, items are scored on M factors that represent the complexity of the items on stimuli that influence processing. However, since only the outcomes to the whole test item are observed, it is assumed that the component difficulties combine additively.

The linear logistic latent trait model is a member of the Rasch model family. The Rasch model (in Equation 2) has a difficulty parameter for each item, b_i, as shown in Equation 2 for the response potential. In the LLTM, the item parameters are constrained so that predicted item difficulty, b_i, is given by a linear combination as follows:

$$b^*_i = \sum_m \eta_m q_{im} + d \tag{3}$$

where q_{im} is the complexity score of item i on factor m, η_m is the difficulty weight of factor m, and d is a normalization constant. Thus, the LLTM is given as

$$P(X_{ij} = 1) = \frac{\exp(\theta_j - \sum_m \eta_m q_{im} + d)}{1 + \exp(\theta_j - \sum_m \eta_m q_{im} + d)} \tag{4}$$

The LLTM may be compared to the Rasch model in Equation 2. Essentially, LLTM replaces the item difficulties, b_i, by a value that is predicted by the complexity factors. That is, the items are scored on m complexity factors, and η_m is the parameter that reflects the weight of complexity factor m on item difficulty. The LLTM is analogous to regressing item difficulties on the complexity factors. The LLTM is applicable to item types that fit the Rasch model. Because the LLTM places additional restrictions on the item parameters, rather than increasing the number of parameters, the LLTM will not fit better than the Rasch model.

Applying the LLTM.   Applications of the LLTM can link aptitude to cognitive process variables in several ways. First, alternative cognitive processing theories may be tested for explanatory power with the LLTM. The theories are operationalized by the cognitive complexity scores. A goodness-of-fit test, based on the likelihood of the data given the LLTM, can compare theories that are hierarchically nested (i.e., the variables of one theory are a subset of the other theory). Incremental fit indices are useful for comparing nonhierarchically nested theories (Embretson, 1983b). Low values for a fit index provide evidence that examinees employ processes and strategies other than those that are operationalized in the LLTM.

Second, applying the LLTM explicates the construct representation of the test from the parameter estimates for the impact of the cognitive variables on item responses. The η_m parameter estimates are analogous to regression weights for the various cognitive variables in explaining task difficulty.

Third, LLTM parameter estimates can be used to develop or select items by their cognitive complexity. Thus, items can be selected from the bank to reflect specific sources of cognitive complexity, which is useful generally for controlling the construct representation of the test. The LLTM parameter estimates also could be used to equate fixed content tests or adaptive tests for sources of cognitive complexity. Furthermore, the LLTM is also useful for item development, as the LLTM parameters may be applied to untried items to anticipate their difficulty. Fourth, abilities can be interpreted with respect to the person's potential for successfully processing the stimuli in the items.

Spatial Aptitude: An Application of LLTM

Spatial folding items, such as presented in Figure 6.1, can illustrate several applications of the LLTM. In general, the spatial folding task has established importance as a measure of spatial aptitude. For example, the Space Relations Test of the Differential Aptitude Test (DAT) contains several variants of the spatial folding task. Supporting data for the Space Relations Test includes correlations with criteria that presumably involve the mental manipulation of objects, such as grades in shop or drawing courses. The DAT Space Relations Test, however, is limited by its too high correlation with verbal tests and its weak incremental validity over verbal tests. A more recent test with spatial folding items is the Spatial Learning Ability Test (SLAT; Embretson & Waxman, 1989). The SLAT items were designed to require more complete spatial processing than the DAT items, because SLAT items contain only directed markings on the sides, such as shown in Item 2 and Item 3 in Fig. 6.1.

Calibrating items by LLTM involves operationalizing a theoretical model of the task. Thus, this section begins by describing a theoretical model for the spatial folding task and then describes how the model can be operationalized in LLTM.

Cognitive Model. Although the spatial folding task has not been studied extensively, several empirically supported theories are relevant. Studies on two-dimensional rotation (Cooper & Shepard, 1973) and three-dimensional rotation (Shepard & Metzler, 1971) of objects, as well as on cube comparison (Just & Carpenter, 1985), indicate that the angle of rotation is linearly related to response time. Further, a study on folding tasks (Shepard & Feng, 1972) suggests that the number of surfaces carried also influences processing difficulty. These findings generally support the theory that spatial processing is the mental analogue of physically manipulating objects.

Recently, Embretson and Waxman (1989) developed an attached folding model for the spatial folding task that is consistent with an analogue theory of spatial rotation. In the attached folding model, four major components are postulated: (a) encoding, (b) attaching, (c) folding, and (d) confirming. Each component is described, in turn.

In encoding, the stem and the distractors are represented in memory. Both the type and orientation of the markings (i.e., the circles, squares, or shading that appears on the sides) are noted. The complexity of the markings presumably influences the difficulty of encoding. The markings could be encoded holistically, and compared perceptually across stimuli, or the markings could be labeled verbally (e.g., "arrows," "shaded sides," etc.) and then compared verbally–analytically.

Attaching and folding are postulated to be the spatial analogue processes in the attached folding model. Fig. 6.2 presents an illustration of the attaching and folding processes. In attaching, two adjacent sides on the unfolded stem are mentally attached to the response option to be evaluated, a two-dimensional representation of a folded cube. The attaching process actually involves three subprocesses, selecting the anchoring sides, mentally rotating the stem (if necessary), and finally mentally attaching the stem to the alternative. In folding, the third side of the cube is mentally placed into position.

Confirming is the last stage. Here the third side of the mentally folded cube is compared to the target view. Confirming is probably also manipulated by the complexity of the marking, particularly if the marking appears differently from different sides, as in the various markings on the items in Fig. 6.1.

The attached folding model is applicable to multiple-choice formats, as in Fig. 6.1, as well as verification formats. It is postulated that falsifying distractors involves the same processes as confirming the key: encoding, attaching, folding, and confirming. However, unlike the key, processing for distractors is self-terminating, as it ceases when a mismatch is identified. Some distractors, for example, can be falsified during encoding, if mismatching markings are detected.

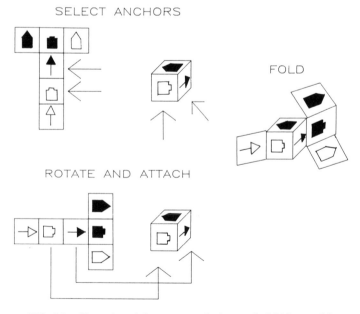

FIG. 6.2.   Illustration of the processes in the attached folding model.

Operationalizing the Cognitive Model for the LLTM. A simplified version of the attached folding model was operationalized for the LLTM by scoring six complexity factors for each item. Encoding was represented by the number of distractors that were falsifiable during the encoding stage. It was scored as the number of distractors with markings that did not match the unfolded stem.

Attaching difficulty was operationalized by the degrees of rotation to anchor the stem to an alternative. To illustrate, Fig. 6.3 shows three keys that vary in the degrees of rotation required for attaching. The stem can be directly overlayed on the first alternative without any rotation, so it would be scored as 0 degrees of rotation. The second and third alternatives, in contrast, require a 90-degree and 180-degree rotation of the stem, respectively.

Folding difficulty was operationalized as the number of surfaces carried in folding. Shown in Fig. 6.4 are one correct alternative and three stems that vary in the number of surfaces that must be carried in folding. The first stem is the easiest because if the shaded circle and shaded square are attached, only one surface needs to be carried to complete the folding. However, if the sides that contain these two markings are attached for the second stem, two surfaces must be carried mentally to bring the third side into place. The last stem requires that three surfaces are carried. Finally, confirming difficulty was operationalized by the existence of directed markings (e.g., arrows, half-shadings, asymmetrical markings, etc.) on the sides of the cube.

The DAT items varied on all six factors, but SLAT items varied only on four factors; degrees of rotation and surfaces carried for both the key and the maximum distractor. The other two factors did not vary on SLAT items, because all items had only directed markings on the sides and had no unanchorable distractors.

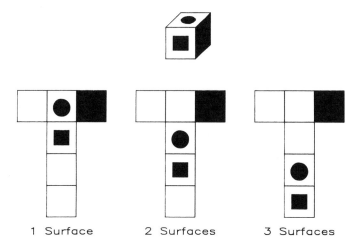

1 Surface   2 Surfaces   3 Surfaces

FIG. 6.3. Illustration of these (correct) response options that involve varying levels of number of surfaces carried.

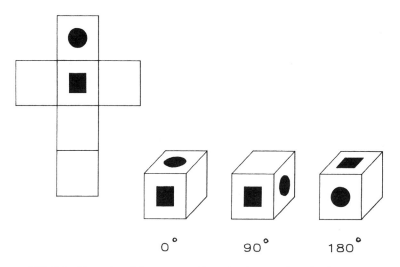

$0°$ $90°$ $180°$

FIG. 6.4.   Illustration of three stems with varying degrees of rotation for attachment to a response option.

Comparing Models by LLTM.   Different cognitive models may be compared with LLTM on the same items by a log likelihood chi-square test, if the models are hierarchically nested (i.e., the variables in the smaller model are a subset of the larger model). The fit of LLTM also may be compared across item sets by fit indices, based likelihood ratios (Embretson, 1984), or correlations between LLTM item difficulties with the Rasch model item difficulties for both nested and nonnested models.

Two different cognitive models were fit for each test with LLTM: (a) a full model that included all six complexity factors and (b) a reduced model that included only the two variables for the stem-to-key relationships (i.e., degrees of rotation and number of surfaces). Lower levels of prediction could be expected a priori for the SLAT, because the items varied on only four factors in the full model. However, the correlations of LLTM estimates from the full model with the Rasch model item difficulties indicated better prediction for SLAT item difficulty ($R = .81$) than for DAT item difficulties ($R = .70$). Furthermore, the pattern of prediction varied between the DAT items and the new items. When only the stem-to-key relationships were included, prediction dropped substantially for the DAT items ($R = .25$) but not for the new items ($R = .80$). Thus, the distractor characteristics have the greatest influence on DAT item difficulty, while the stem-to-key relationships have the greatest influence on SLAT item difficulty.

Table 6.1 presents the LLTM weights for the most complete models for both the DAT and the SLAT. The contrasting role of the stem-to-key relationships versus the distractor relationships is clearly shown in Table 6.1 by the signifi-

TABLE 6.1
Comparison of LLTM Parameter Estimates and Standard Errors
for Cognitive Models on Partial Tests

	DAT (R = .70)	SE	SLAT (R = .81)	SE
Stem-to-key variables				
Surfaces carried	−.01	.04	.81**	.07
Degrees rotation (/100)	−.09	.08	.17**	.03
Distractor variables				
Maximum surfaces carried	.16**	.04	.01	.06
Maximum degrees rotation (/100)	.68**	.06	−.13**	.03
Unanchorable distractor	−.29**	.05	—	—
Director markings	.33**	.10	—	—

cant weights for the models of item difficulty in each test. The cognitive complexity factors for the key have significant weights in the SLAT, but not in the DAT. In contrast, all the factors for the distractors have significant weights in the DAT, but only one distractor factor, degrees of rotation, has a significant negative weight in the SLAT. Although degrees of rotation generally is expected to increase item difficulty, the negative weight observed for the maximum distractor in the SLAT results from a correlation between the degrees of rotation for the key and maximum distractor. In general, the results in Table 6.1 suggest that the processing demands of the items on the two tests are not the same, which indicates that they do not measure quite the same construct.

Explicating Construct Representation. The relative contribution of the processes to the difficulty of a specific item may be evaluated by examining the LLTM equation for the item. For the SLAT, the following equation for item difficulty was calibrated:

$$b_i^* = 0.81q_1 + 0.17q_2 - 0.13q_3 + 0.01q_4 - 1.56 \qquad (5)$$

where q_1 is the surfaces carried to key, q_2 the degrees rotation to key (/100), q_3 the degrees rotation to maximum distractor (/100), and q_4 the surfaces carried to the maximum distractor. Thus, the relative contribution of processes to item difficulty are given by the weights in Equation 5. Here, the number of surfaces carried to the key has the largest weight, so folding is the major contributor to SLAT item difficulty.

The specific sources of cognitive complexity can be given for each item. For example, the difficulty of Item 2 in Fig. 6.1 can be explained by Equation 5. The correct answer (2) involves 0 degrees rotation and two surfaces carried. The maximum distractor (3) involves a 180-degree rotation, and the number of surfaces carried (two) is equal to the key. Therefore, item difficulty is predicted as follows:

$$b^*_i = 0.81(2) + 0.17(0) - 0.13(1.80) - 0.008(2) - 1.56$$
$$= -0.19. \tag{6}$$

For Item 3, computing the item difficulty from the complexity factor values gives the following:

$$b^*_i = 0.81(3) + 0.17(1.80) - 0.13(1.80) - 0.008(3) - 1.56$$
$$= 0.918. \tag{7}$$

Developing and Selecting Items. The several applications of the LLTM in test construction can be illustrated with the SLAT. First, the difficulty of new items can be anticipated from the stimulus features of the item. That is, item difficulties may be anticipated from the model parameter estimates (i.e., Equation 5). An important check on the completeness of the theory for predicting item difficulty can be obtained by regressing the difficulties obtained from an empirical try-out on the anticipated values from the model. Although empirical try-out is still necessary, anticipating item difficulties in advance may be an efficient method in guiding the development of items with specified difficulty levels.

Second, SLAT items can be selected for inclusion in the final item bank by their explainability from the attached folding model. Selecting SLAT items by LLTM fit would minimize the role of processes that are not included in the cognitive model.

Third, SLAT items can be selected to represent specific sources of cognitive complexity. That is, spatial folding tests could be developed to have a uniform or mixed pattern of cognitive complexity. For example, the attaching process could be eliminated as a source of item complexity on SLAT items by specifying no contribution of degrees of rotation to the key (i.e., 0 degrees of rotation). Folding could become the major source of item differences by then specifying a mixed pattern of surfaces carried (i.e., counterbalancing 1, 2, and 3 surfaces).

Item specifications, as just described, are useful for controlling the process that are reflected in items. However, the specifications could also be used for test equating, for either fixed content or adaptive tests. Such specifications help assure that the various tests reflect the same aspects of cognitive processing.

Interpreting Ability. An individual ability score can be interpreted as potential to solve items with specified sources of cognitive complexity if the cognitive model fits well. Suppose that an individual has a high ability of 1.7. The potential to solve items like Item 2 in Fig. 6.1 is given by the additive combination of ability and the sources of cognitive complexity as follows:

$$P(X_{ij}=1) = \frac{\exp[1.7 - (-0.19)]}{1 + \exp[1.7 - (-0.19)]} = .869. \tag{8}$$

In contrast, this same person would have a lower probability of successfully processing more complex stimuli as in Item 3, which requires a 180-degree rotation and three surfaces carried (p = .687).

Influencing Nomothetic Span. Selecting items to represent specified processes in the cognitive model can influence the correlations of the test score with other measures. For example, the too high correlations of the DAT Space Relations test with verbal tests could result from including spatial folding items that are solvable by verbal-analytic processing, such as falsification during encoding or application of effective strategies for the distractors. In contrast, the correlations of the SLAT with verbal tests could be expected to be lower since the items minimize verbal-analytic processing of the distractors, as shown in Table 6.1.

To examine nomothetic span, SLAT scores were correlated with verbal and nonverbal measures from the Cognitive Abilities Test and the Primary Mental Abilities Space Relations Test in a sample of 66 college undergraduates. Table 6.2 shows that the SLAT correlates much more highly with the nonverbal tests than with the verbal tests.

Also shown on Table 6.2 are the loadings from confirmatory factor analysis of the covariances between the tests. The SLAT was the most highly loading variable on the spatial factor, and the spatial factor was not highly correlated with the verbal factor (r = .34). The two-factor model presented in Table 6.2 fit the data (χ^2_9 = 6.68, p = .670). The χ^2 test is not sufficient support, however, since applying the Satorra and Saris (1985) procedure yielded a power estimate of only .47, given an alternative model in which the SLAT split loadings equally on the factors. However, when the alternative model was actually estimated, unconstrained for magnitude of the split loadings, a negligible decrease in χ^2 (.03) was observed, and furthermore, the estimated loading of the SLAT on the verbal factor was also small, and in the wrong direction (λ = −.02). Because the Bentler–Bonnet fit index of .94 for the model in Table 6.2 was high, in combination with the negligible loading on the verbal factor, the data support the relative independence of the SLAT from the verbal tests.

TABLE 6.2
Correlations and Factor Loadings for Six Tests

Variable	(1)	(2)	(3)	(4)	(5)	(6)	FI	FII
Vocabulary (CAT)	1.00						.87	—
Verbal Analogies (CAT)	.72	1.00					.82	—
Figure Analogies (CAT)	.24	.25	1.00				—	.57
Figure Synthesis (CAT)	.14	.26	.27	1.00			—	.54
Space Relations (PMA)	.05	.18	.38	.32	1.00		—	.61
Spatial Learning Ability Test (SLAT)	.14	.27	.41	.43	.47	1.00	—	.75

Multicomponent Latent Trait Model

The multicomponent latent trait model (MLTM) estimates both abilities and item difficulties on each underlying component in the model. For the spatial folding example, abilities and item difficulties would be estimated for each processing stage (i.e., attaching, folding, etc.). In contrast, in LLTM processing complexity is estimated from the stimulus features of items that were postulated to influence processing difficulty. Applications of the LLTM require strong a priori empirical support for a theory of how stimulus complexity influences processing. For the MLTM, however, processing difficulty is estimated directly from task outcomes. A theory about the processing components is required, but the theory need not specify the relationship of stimulus features to processing complexity.

MLTM requires two types of data to estimate the parameters and to test the fit of the model: (a) responses to the standard item and (b) responses to subtasks that are constructed from the item to represent the components. In the spatial folding example, the various processing components are sequentially dependent, as each provides a needed outcome for the next component. Subtasks can be constructed to separate the components, by requiring only the response required of the component and by supplying the correct outcomes from the preceding components. For example, two subtasks could be constructed to separate encoding and attaching from folding and confirming. That is, a subtask that required only selecting an alternative that showed a correct attachment of the stem would measure only the prerequisite outcomes of encoding and attaching. A subtask that required selecting among the four alternatives of the standard task, but given the correct attachment (i.e., overlaying the stem, as in Fig. 6.2), would measure the remaining processes of folding and confirming.

The MLTM is given as follows:

$$P(X_{ijT} = 1) = \prod_k P(X_{ijk} = 1) \tag{9}$$

where $P(X_{ijT} = 1)$ is the probability that person j solves total item i and $P(X_{ijk} = 1)$ is the probability that person j solves component k on item i. In turn, the probabilities for the components are given by the one-parameter logistic latent trait model, as follows:

$$P(X_{ijk} = 1) = \frac{\exp(\theta_{jk} - b_{ik})}{1 + \exp(\theta_{jk} - b_{ik})} \tag{10}$$

where θ_{jk} is the ability of person j on component k and b_{ik} the difficulty of item i on component k.

The MLTM can be used to influence the components that are reflected in the aptitude that is measured by the test. In the MLTM, the pattern of component difficulties may be used to select items such that specified components have the major contribution to individual differences. Selecting items that are extremely easy on a component, so that nearly every one can solve it, will lead to the component contributing little to individual differences. In contrast, selecting items with a range of difficulty on a component will lead to the component contributing to individual differences in aptitude. A full presentation of item selection with the MLTM is beyond the scope of this chapter, but an illustrative example of how component difficulties may be selected is given in Embretson (1983a). The influence of components on nomothetic span is given in Embretson, Schneider, and Roth (1986).

The General Component Latent Trait Model

Embretson (1984) presented a more general model that includes both the LLTM and MLTM as special cases. Basically, the model has a multiplicative relationship between subtask outcomes, as in the MLTM, but also postulates a linear relationship between complexity factors and the component difficulty parameters, as in the LLTM. The general component latent trait model (GLTM) is given as follows:

$$P(X_{ijT} = 1) = (a - g)_k \frac{\exp(\theta_{jk} - (\sum_m \eta_{km}q_{imk} + d_k)}{1 + \exp(\theta_{jk} - (\sum_m \eta_{km}q_{imk} + d_k)} + g \quad (11)$$

where θ_{jk} is the ability of person n on component k, q_{ikm} the complexity of item i on factor m in component k, η_{km} the weight for complexity factor k on component m, d_k the normalization constant for component k, a the probability that an item is solved when the component information is available, and g the probability that an item is solved when at least one component is not available.

This model assesses two types of cognitive variables. First, it assesses the relationship of the components to the total item. Second, it assesses the relationship of the stimulus features of items to the component outcomes.

The general component latent trait model has the same advantages as the multicomponent latent trait model, with the addition of diagnosing how the stimulus features control the component difficulties. Thus, the model offers a more complete diagnostic tool for test design than the multicomponent latent trait model.

Latent Trait Models for the Cognitive Context of the Test

A recent direction in measurement research is examining the effects of changing the cognitive context within a testing session. In dynamic testing, for example, the effects of supplying cues or instruction on ability levels are observed (e.g., Babad & Budoff, 1974; Carlson & Weidl, 1979; Feuerstein, 1979; Campione, Brown, Ferrara, Jones & Steinberg, 1985). A major goal of dynamic testing is to separate current ability level from potential level or modifiability. Vygotsky's (1979) thesis about measuring the zone of proximal development has been particularly influential for dynamic testing. Vygotsky hypothesizes that the sensitivity of an examinee's performance to external aids and cues is theoretically revealing of learning potential.

The cognitive context within a testing session also could include conditions of adversity (conditions that interfere with performance), although little research has yet been generated. For example, individual differences in performance changes under conditions of competing task demands or irrelevant stimuli could provide theoretically interesting measures of resistance to interference.

Another more classical testing issue that could be considered as cognitive context research is age-related changes in ability (e.g., Schaie & Strothers, 1968). In this case, age provides a naturally occurring context over which scores are compared. One issue is the distribution of scores (e.g., growth curves, norms), but measuring individual differences in changes is another important issue in studying how factors associated with age influence ability changes.

An essential aspect of cognitive context research is the hypothesis that ability levels are changing differentially and that individual differences in change have significant relationships to other measures. For example, some support for increased validity in predicting learning has been found for dynamic testing (Carlson & Weidl, 1979; Embretson, 1987; Feuerstein, 1979).

However, even if current research supports measuring individual differences in change as viable substantively, some seemingly insurmountable psychometric problems remain. Bereiter (1963) noted three unresolved psychometric problems in measuring change: (a) the reliability of change is inversely related to the reliability of the tests, (b) change is not measured on the same scale for persons at different initial score levels, and (c) change scores have a spurious negative relationship to initial scores. For the latter, Lord (1963) showed how the negative correlation of the pretest with change arises from the regression effect, even when no real change occurs.

Bereiter's seemingly irresolvable issues in measuring change occurred in the context of classical test theory. Fortunately, contemporary test theory permits a reconceptualization of the issues. Specifically, some problems in measuring change can be resolved by conceptualizing change as a latent variable in the context of a multidimensional item response model. In the following section, a multidimensional Rasch model of learning and change (MRMLC; Embretson, in press) is described. Advantages for measuring change over classical methods are discussed, and an illustrative example from spatial aptitude is presented.

Multidimensional Rasch Model for Learning and Change. Applying the MRMLC requires two or more ability measurements. Conceptually, initial ability can be distinguished from modifiability. The traditional ability measurement is the initial ability on the first occasion, whereas modifiability is the change between two successive measurements.

Assume that items are presented under K conditions, which are administered successively. The first measurement is the standard test condition, while the remaining measurements follow K-1 conditions (e.g., targeted cues, stress, instruction, practice, or just time). Preferably, the multiple measurements are equated tests, rather than the same test administered repeatedly, so that local independence is not violated. Item difficulties are assumed to remain constant over the conditions, so that any increase in item performance is attributed to modifiability, rather than to changes in item difficulty. Furthermore, it is assumed that all items within a condition have equal discriminations, fixed to a unit weight of 1.0 in the MRMLC.

Underlying performance is item difficulty, b_i, and M abilities, θ_{jm} for each person j, so that θ_{j1} is the initial ability and θ_{j2} to θ_{jm} are the modifiabilities that accompany the K-1 conditions. Performance for any item that is administered under condition k is governed by a composite of initial ability and the appropriate modifiabilities for condition k.

Because conditions are administered sequentially, modifiabilities cannot be involved in item performance prior to the condition k that is associated with dimension m. Thus, with the assumption that all nonzero item discriminations are unity, a matrix of item discriminations, A_{KXM}, for K conditions and M abilities is structured as follows:

$$A_{KXM} = \begin{matrix} 1 & 0 & 0 & \cdots & 0 \\ 1 & 1 & 0 & \cdots & 0 \\ 1 & 1 & 1 & \cdots & 0 \\ & \cdot & \cdot & \cdots & 0 \\ 1 & 1 & 1 & \cdots & 1 \end{matrix} \tag{12}$$

According to this formulation, increasingly more abilities are involved in performance at each successive condition k. Thus for example, the first condition involves only initial ability, θ_{j1}, whereas the second condition involves one modifiability, θ_{j2}, as well as initial ability.

Models like Equation 12 have often been proposed for repeated measurement data. For example, Wiener-process simplex models for covariance matrices involve the same structure as Equation 12 for fixed factor loadings to relate the latent variables to the observed variables (see Joreskog, 1970). However, the importance here is that the Wiener-process structure is proposed as a measurement model to define the involvement of abilities at a specific measurement occasion. Thus, Equation 12 specifies a dynamic, rather than a static, concept of ability because at each measurement occasion performance is changing in both dimensionality and level, due to individual differences in modifiability.

Since A_{KXM} shows that for any condition of measurement only learning abilities up to condition k (combined with unit weights), are involved, such a sum of abilities, $\sum_{m=1}^{k} \theta_{jm}$, governs performance. The MRMLC, incorporating a constraint of constant item difficulties across conditions and item discriminations of unity, can be given as

$$P(X_{ij} = 1) = \frac{\exp(\sum_{m=1}^{k} \theta_{jm} - b_i)}{1 + \exp(\sum_{m=1}^{k} \theta_{jm} - b_i)} \qquad (13)$$

where θ_{j1} is the initial ability at $k = 1$, $\theta_{j2}, \ldots, \theta_{jM}$ the learning abilities that correspond to $k > 1$, and b_i the item difficulty.

A counterbalanced design is required to estimate the item parameters of MRMLC, such that each item is observed under each condition. Thus, K groups are required, with some items that are always administered under the initial condition to link the groups. For conditional maximum likelihood estimation, the ability distributions are unconstrained. Indeterminacies of scale are resolved by setting the mean item difficulty to zero. Overall performance increases or decreases are reflected by the means of the k-1 modifiabilities. Maximum likelihood estimators for the items and the abilities are presented by Embretson (1991).

It should be noted that even though the nonzero item discriminations are postulated to be unity, MRMLC is applicable to situations in which initial ability and the modifiabilities have different impacts on performance. Analogous to confirmatory factor analysis, unequal saturations of the variables (items) on the latent dimensions may be reflected in either the loadings (i.e., the discriminations) or in the ability variances. If the item discriminations are set to unity, then the differing impact on performance will be reflected instead in the variance of the abilities.

MRMLC and Bereiter's Issues in Measuring Change

The Reliability Paradox. As the reliability of change increases, the correlation of the pretest with the posttest decreases (see Lord, 1963, for classic formula). This is paradoxical, as suggested by Bereiter (1963), because a low pretest to posttest correlation undermines the interpretability of change in a particular dimension, if the pretest and posttest do not measure the same dimension.

This paradox results from conceptualizing the multiple measurements as influenced by only one dimension. In classical test theory, the focus was on defining an index from observed abilities to represent change. Although many refinements have been proposed, the prototypic concept of a change score, z_{j2}, is a simple difference between a pretest, z_{j1}^*, and a posttest, z_{j2}^*, as follows:

$$z_{j2} = z_{j2}^* - z_{j1}^*. \qquad (14)$$

Although not typical in classical test theory developments, it is instructive to write the desired scores, gain, and initial ability, in terms of the pretest and posttest, as follows:

$$
\begin{bmatrix} z_{j1} \\ z_{j2} \end{bmatrix} = \begin{bmatrix} 1 & 0 \\ -1 & 1 \end{bmatrix} \begin{bmatrix} z_{j1}^* \\ z_{j2}^* \end{bmatrix}. \qquad (15)
$$

Equation 15 may be rearranged as

$$
\begin{bmatrix} z_{j1}^* \\ z_{j2}^* \end{bmatrix} = \begin{bmatrix} 1 & 0 \\ 1 & 1 \end{bmatrix} \begin{bmatrix} z_{j1} \\ z_{j2} \end{bmatrix}. \qquad (16)
$$

The classical definition of change as embodied in Equation 16 can be compared directly to MRMLC abilities in Equation 12 by noting that $\underline{z}_j$ corresponds to initial ability and modifiability, $\underline{\theta}_j$. Thus, the relationship between underlying abilities (initial ability and modifiability) to pretest and posttest abilities is identical in the two models. That is, the posttest is influenced by two separate abilities, initial ability and modifiability, while the pretest is influenced only by the initial ability.

The focus on calculating change scores in classical test theory, rather than modeling the pretest and posttest from underlying abilities as in MRMLC, obscured the inherently multidimensional nature of the change concept. Because the structures in Equations 16 and 12 produce a simplex form for the covariance matrix, the assumption of parallel pretest and posttest measures directly conflicts with the simplex model that produces increasing variances and systematically varying test intercorrelations.

The unidimensional conceptualization of change is also unable to accommodate situations in which changes in performance result from qualitative changes in psychological processes, as noted by Cronbach and Furby (1970). However, a multidimensional model for change, such as the MRMLC, allows changes in processes to be represented as separate dimensions (i.e., modifiabilities).

Change Scores at Different Initial Ability Levels. Bereiter (1963) was concerned that performance changes did not have the same meaning at all levels of the ability scale. For example, a small change in performance may have more meaning if initial ability is high than if it is low. Classical test theory did not provide a means for formalizing Bereiter's concern because performance changes are linearly related to estimated change.

In item response theory, of course, the relationship of ability to performance is nonlinear, and furthermore, the exact change in probability between any two abilities depends on their relative location on the item response curve. Thus, the same change in response probability can have greater meaning for an ability change from a high ability than from a low ability. However, the reverse also can be true, depending on which initial ability level the item is most appropriate (see Embretson, in press, for an illustration).

The expected change score can be calculated from the MRMLC for a particular initial ability and modifiability as the difference in expected raw scores (see Lord, 1980, p. 46 for formula) between the pretest and the posttest, given the item difficulties for each test. Fig. 6.5 presents the expected change scores between a pretest and posttest, with matched item difficulties for various levels of modifiability. Three levels of initial ability are plotted. For the particular items on these tests, Fig. 6.5 shows that expected performance change (i.e., loss) for low negative modifiabilities is greater when initial ability is high, but expected performance change (i.e., gain) for high positive modifiabilities is greater when initial ability is low. These results reflect the insufficient ceiling for the high-ability scores and insufficient floor for the low-ability scores as variables that influence the magnitude of observed performance changes.

The Spurious Negative Correlation of Change and Initial Ability.   In the context of classical test theory, it was noted that the correlation of initial ability and gain has a spurious negative bias, due to the sharing of error variance. Lord (1963), for example, shows that the negative bias in the correlation results from the measurement error for the initial ability being involved also in the change score, but with a change of sign. However, Lord's demonstration did not consider how the type of measurement error may influence this relationship.

Conditions that influence measurement throughout the whole test should be distinguished from conditions within the test, as in classical categorizations of measurement error. Conditions that influence the whole test cause the effective ability to differ from the "true ability." The expected negative bias in the correlations of initial score and change will be realized for this measurement error. More optimal scaling of change, without regard to substantive information on score consistency across some control condition, will not correct for this bias.

However, conditions within the test create another type of measurement error that also can bias the correlation between initial ability and change. The influence of item difficulty levels on the correlation between initial ability and change could not be considered within classical test theory. However, because the MRMLC

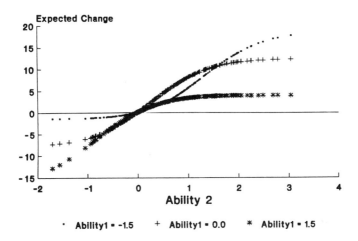

FIG. 6.5. The relationship of expected true change scores to modifiability at three levels of initial ability. From "A Multidimensional Latent Trait Model for Measuring Learning and Change" by S. E. Ebretson, in press, *Psychometrika*. Copyright © 1991 by the Psychometric Society. Reprinted by permission.

is an item response theory model, the impact of item difficulty on the correlation of change and initial ability can be anticipated. A negative correlation between initial ability and change can be expected for observed scores if a test has too little ceiling and floor to observe gains at high ability levels and losses to low ability levels. Thus, change would be underestimated at these extremes, which would create a negative bias in the correlation of initial ability and change. The MRMLC modifiabilities, however, for a given observed change will depend on the initial ability level and so the negative bias will be partially removed. Furthermore, because the MRMLC is an item response theory model, further precision at the extreme abilities is possible with adaptive testing procedures to minimize estimation error, which would further eliminate floor and ceiling effects that produce negative bias.

Spatial Learning Ability: An Example. A recent study with the Spatial Learning Ability Test illustrates a dynamic testing design for which the MRMLC is appropriate (see Embretson & Waxman, 1989, for more details). In this study, spatial ability was measured three times on a sample of Air Force recruits, as follows: (a) a pretest that was preceded by standard test instructions, (b) a first posttest, which was preceded by a short practice period with the physical analogue of the mental folding task, and (c) a second posttest, which was preceded by strategy training in applying the attached folding model (the model was previously described). Subjects with perfect scores on any measures were eliminated from the study due to the unavailability of ability estimates for these scores.

TABLE 6.3
Descriptive Statistics for Effective Abilities
and Test Scores on the SLAT (N = 504)

| | $\bar{X}$ | SD | Correlations | | |
			(1)	(2)	(3)
(1) Pretest	99.74	14.51	1.00		
(2) Posttest 1	106.49	18.23	.76	1.00	
(3) Posttest 2	110.02	19.26	.69	.79	1.00

Note. From Embretson, 1991. Copyright © 1991 by the Psychometric Society. Reprinted by permission.

As in a previous study (Embretson, 1987), spatial ability was highly modifiable by the intervention. Table 6.3 presents descriptive statistics on SLAT standard scores, which are set for a mean and standard deviation of 100 and 15, respectively. Table 6.3 shows that SLAT standard scores are increasing substantially over time ($F_{2,500}$ = 140.17, p < .001). Furthermore, the correlations of the three tests show a simplex pattern in which consistency is increasing.

Table 6.4 presents descriptive statistics for the MRMLC ability estimates, as well as the pretest standard scores and gains. The mean MRMLC initial ability estimate is quite close to the item difficulty mean of zero, which indicates that the test is appropriate for the sample. Further, as for unidimensional Rasch models, the pretest score is highly correlated with the MRMLC initial ability. The positive means of the two modifiabilities shown in Table 6.4 indicate increasing composite ability, particularly on the first posttest. However, although modifiabilities are highly correlated with gain scores, the correlations are lower than the initial ability to pretest correlation. It is also interesting to observe in Table 6.4 that the sign of the (low) correlation between the initial measure and the first change reverses from negative for standard scores to positive for MRMLC estimates, which suggests correction for a negative bias.

SUMMARY

This chapter presented several test theory models that have the potential to incorporate cognitive variables or procedures into the prediction of response probabilities. A major advantage of the models is that they have potential to incorporate cognitive theory directly into the design of tests. Both the construct representation and the nomothetic span aspect of construct validity potentially can be influenced. That is, manipulating the cognitive variables or procedures influences the constructs that are involved in performance and, in turn, the ex-

TABLE 6.4
Descriptive Statistics for MRMLC Abilities,
Pretest Score, and Gain Scores on the SLAT (N = 504)

Variable	$\bar{X}$	SD	(1)	(2)	(3)	(4)	(5)	(6)
(1) Initial Ability	−.16	.90	1.00					
(2) Modifiability 1	.50	.91	.05	1.00				
(3) Modifiability 2	.25	.98	.04	−.30	1.00			
(4) Pretest	99.74	14.51	.99	.07	.03	1.00		
(5) Gain 1	6.75	11.88	−.05	.95	−.24	−.04	1.00	
(6) Gain 2	3.53	12.29	−.02	−.32	.95	−.03	−.31	1.00

Note. From Embretson (1991). Copyright © 1991 by the Psychometric Society. Adapted by permission.

ternal correlates of the test score are also influenced. The actual impact of these models in guiding testing awaits future applications. However, the continuing success of cognitive psychology to understand performance on the complex tasks that measure aptitude, such as paragraph comprehension, analogical reasoning, and spatial folding, is prognostic of success.

REFERENCES

Ackerman, P. L. (1988). Determinants of individual differences during skill acquisition: Cognitive abilities and information processing. *Journal of Experimental Psychology: General, 117,* 288–318.

Babad, E. Y., & Budoff, M. (1974). Sensitivity and validity of training—Potential measurement in three levels of ability. *Journal of Educational Psychology, 66,* 439–447.

Bechtold, H. (1959). Construct validity: A critique. *American Psychologist, 14,* 619–629.

Bereiter, C. (1963). Some persisting dilemmas in the measurement of change. In C. W. Harris (Ed.). *Problems in measuring change* (pp. 3–20). Madison: University of Wisconsin Press.

Campione, J. C., Brown, A. L., Ferrara, R. A., Jones, R. S., & Steinberg, E. (1985). Breakdown in flexible use of information: Intelligence-related differences in transfer following equivalent learning performance. *Intelligence, 9,* 297–315.

Carlson, J. S., & Weidl, K. H. (1979). Toward a differential testing approach: Testing-the-limits employing the Raven's matrices. *Intelligence, 3,* 323–344.

Cooper, L. A., & Shepard, R. N. (1973). Chronometric studies of the rotation of mental images. In W. G. Chase (Ed.), *Visual information processing* (pp. 219–239). New York: Academic Press.

Cronbach, L. J., & Furby, L. (1970). How should we measure change—Or should we? *Psychological Bulletin, 74,* 68–80.

Cronbach, L. J., & Meehl, P. E. (1955). Construct validity in psychological tests. *Psychological Bulletin, 52,* 281–302.

Embretson, S. E. (1983a). Construct validity: Construct representation versus nomothetic span. *Psychological Bulletin, 93,* 179–197.

Embretson, S. E. (1983b, June). *An incremental fit index for the linear logistic latent trait model.* Paper presented at the annual meeting of the Psychometric Society, Los Angeles, CA.

Embretson, S. E. (1984). A general latent trait model for response processes. *Psychometrika, 49,* 175–186.

Embretson, S. E. (1987). Improving the measurement of spatial ability by a dynamic testing procedure. *Intelligence, 11*, 333–358.

Embretson, S. E., Schneider, L., & Roth, D. L. (1986). Multiple processing strategies and the construct validity of verbal reasoning tests. *Journal of Educational Measurement, 23*, 13–32.

Embretson, S. E., & Waxman, M. (1989). *Models for processing and individual differences in spatial folding.* Unpublished manuscript.

Embretson, S. E. (1991). A multidimensional item response model for learning processes. *Psychometrika, 56*, 495–515.

Feuerstein, R. (1979). *The dynamic assessment of retarded performers: The learning potential assessment device, theory, instruments and techniques.* Baltimore: University Park Press.

Fischer, G. (1973). Linear logistic test model as an instrument in educational research. *Acta Psychologica, 37*, 359–374.

Glaser, R. (1985, October). *The integration of instruction and testing.* Paper presented at the ETS Invitational Conference on the Redesign of Testing for the 21st Century, New York.

Jannarone, R. J. (1986). Conjunctive item response theory kernels. *Psychometrika, 51*, 357–373.

Joreskog, K. G. (1970). Estimation and testing of simple models. *British Journal of Mathematical and Statistical Psychology, 23*, 121–145.

Just, M., & Carpenter, P. (1985). Cognitive coordinate systems: Accounts of mental rotation and individual differences in spatial ability. *Psychological Review, 92*, 137–172.

Lord, F. M. (1963). Elementary models for measuring change. In C. W. Harris (Ed.). *Problems in measuring change* (pp. 21–38). Madison: University of Wisconsin Press.

Lord, F. M. (1980). *Applications of item response theory to practical testing problems.* Hillsdale, NJ: Lawrence Erlbaum Associates.

Mislevy, R., & Verhelst, N. (1990). Modeling item responses when different subjects employ different solution strategies. *Psychometrika, 55*, 195–215.

Satorra, A., & Saris, W. E. (1985). Power of the likelihood ratio test in covariance analysis. *Psychometrika, 50*, 83–90.

Schaie, K. W. & Strothers, C. R. (1968). A cross-sequential study of age changes in cognitive behavior. *Psychological Bulletin, 70*, 671–680.

Scheibelchner, H. (1985). Psychometric models for speed-test construction: The linear exponential model. In S. Embretson (Ed.), *Test design: Developments in psychology and psychometrics* (pp. 219–244). New York: Academic Press.

Shepard, R. N., & Feng, C. (1972). A chronometric study of mental paper folding. *Cognitive Psychology, 3*, 228–243.

Shepard, R. N., & Metzler, J. (1971). Mental rotation of three dimensional objects. *Science, 171*, 701–703.

Spada, H., & McGaw, B. (1985). The assessment of learning effects with linear logistic test models. In S. Embretson (Ed.), *Test design: New directions in psychology and psychometrics* (pp. 169–193). New York: Academic Press.

Stegelmann, W. (1983). Expanding the Rasch model to a general model having more than one dimension. *Psychometrika, 48*, 259–267.

Vygotsky, L. S. (1978). *Mind in society: The development of higher psychological processes.* Cambridge, MA: Harvard University Press.

Whitely, S. E. (1980). Multicomponent latent trait models for ability tests. *Psychometrika, 45*, 479–494.

Comments on Chapters 4-6

Bert F. Green
The Johns Hopkins University

Classical test theory has been in place for nearly a century and has been very serviceable. However, it is not much of a theory; $x = t + e$ is about as simple as a theory could be. Yet its simplicity permits easy extension and amplification. Item response theory (IRT), which has been a serious contender for only about two decades, is much stronger, but with its strength comes constraint. Item response theory applies to dichotomously scored items; extending it to more complicated situations takes work.

The chapters by Thissen, Bennett, and Embretson all offer glimpses of extensions to the IRT model, as well as other elaborations of the general problem of designing, scoring, and using tests of individual differences. Several models are presented in general outline, although not in enough detail for the reader to go forth and use any of the models. Interesting examples exemplify the general features of the model and incidentally demonstrate that each of the models is in fact a living, breathing method that could be used effectively.

Whereas it seems appropriate to omit the details, because few readers will want them, there is also no attempt to compare the various alternatives. Each works, but for many situations more than one procedure is available, and there is no guidance as to the relative merits of the alternatives.

Thissen (chapter 4) describes a kind of modification that is needed when different item response alternatives imply different levels of the underlying ability. He discusses two situations, one in which the response alternatives can be ordered, and one in which responses can only be considered to yield nominal classes. With ordered responses, a graded-response model works well; with responses that are not naturally ordered, Bock's nominal model applies.

151

In the attitude and preference arenas, it has long been recognized that the relation of item responses to scale values could be very different from ogives. Bock's nominal model, described by Thissen, serves to include such item responses in the general theory. In principle, more general item characteristic curves could be explored in any application. This model has some commonality with other nonparametric IRT models that are useful when some of the items do not fit the standard mold. What is not said is that if all the items have unusual item characteristic curves, then there is no basis for establishing the underlying scale of measurement (theta), usually called ability. In the extreme, if all the items merely provide latent classes with no inherent order, then there can be no scale at all, at least not without some extra assumptions. Although the model can be written down mathematically, and possibly even computed, the underlying dimension will not be adequately defined unless a substantial number of items follow some version of the standard IRT model. There is no reason to suppose that most of the items need do so, or even that over half need do so. Nevertheless, it is not clear just how much is needed to specify the ability dimension adequately. This deserves further study.

Some other issues need attention. Thissen mentions using an EAP scale score with items from a scale on eating disorders. An EAP score is an expected a posteriori score, obtained as the expected value—that is to say, the mean—of the a posteriori distribution of the underlying variable, which in this instance might be called eating tendency. The Bayesian approach to ability measurement seems wise in general, but what prior distribution of eating tendency is appropriate, and how can it be justified? Psychometricians are comfortable using a normal prior distribution of cognitive ability; are health psychologists equally comfortable with a normal distribution for eating tendency?

This is not to say that maximum likelihood scoring would have been preferable, because there will probably not be very many items contributing to a scale of this sort, and with peculiar item "trace lines," maximum-likelihood scoring can yield inconsistencies. The Bayesian procedure is always computationally preferable, provided a reasonable prior can be justified.

In his application of the nominal model, Thissen also shows how to put two items together to get important diagnostic information, as well as to combine two or more items into useful new "items" fitting the graded-response model. One combined multicategory item is more revealing than viewing the items as two independent dichotomies.

The graded-response model is useful for Likert-type items with ordered response categories, such as "strongly disagree," "disagree," "unsure," "agree," and "strongly agree." The same model is also in great demand for dealing with open-ended cognitive items, as Bennett describes (chapter 5). In this instance a grader assigns a grade from 1 to 4, or A to D, or uses some similar scale for grading the response. The graded-response model is one of several that have generally been called partial-credit models, in which the item responses indicate an ordered range of potential performance, with "higher" responses indicating higher levels of the underlying ability.

Once the scores are assigned by the expert graders, the IRT partial credit models can be used and test scores can be computed. Precisely how to do this cannot be discerned from the Bennett chapter, nor did Thissen provide all the needed details. What one gets from the chapters is a clear understanding of what is possible and where to find out more, if the possibility seems useful.

Bennett goes further, offering the tantalizing possibility of automatic, objective scoring by means of an artificially intelligent computer program. In the realm of mathematics, many of the answers are essentially quantitative, so there is some reason to hope for success in that arena. MicroPROUST attempts to evaluate computer algorithms offered as answers to problems in computer science. GIDE is focused on algebra problems, with the same aim. Both are still experimental, but both are quite promising. These subject matters would seem the ideal guinea pigs for such difficult work, before addressing the even murkier waters of evaluating prose answers to questions in history, political science, and the like.

Of course the issues in creating an artificially intelligent grader are quite apart from IRT, or partial-credit models. Once the grades have been assigned, the IRT partial-credit models can take over, but the big first step of an automatic grader is formidable. Intriguingly, it appears not to be out of reach. PROUST is based on what has become the standard artificial intelligence mode of attempting to mimic good, living, breathing expert scorers. Such systems are often called expert systems, but they have a strong flavor of empirical, regression-like approaches to the problem. That is, substantive theory is conspicuously absent.

GIDE has a bit more generality than is customary. Certain classes of error or "bug" that might infect the responses are identified. These errors, or bugs, can be expected in answers to a whole class of algebra problems. This provides a level of insight better than simple partial credit. The same procedure could assign the partial credit and tell the student why he or she went wrong. This kind of procedure is ideal in situations where the test may appropriately be used as a vehicle of instruction as well as in an evaluative mode.

Thissen and Bennett provide extensions of IRT to open-ended questions, graded responses, and surveys; Embretson provides extensions reaching toward modern theories of cognitive processing, the common paradigm of cognitive psychology today. In doing so, she shows how the assessment of individual differences can take advantage of the analytical approach to behavior that is characteristic of cognitive theorists. By suggesting how to model multicomponent items, she provides connections to partial-credit models on the one hand, and to cognitive psychology on the other. The common ground is a model of sequentially organized item-response processes. This general idea has been pursued sporadically over the past decade, by a few students adept in both cognition and psychometrics, but the fields have seldom been joined. Embretson shows how the joining might happen.

Three models are presented that involve multiple components. In the linear logistic latent trait model (LLTM), the complexity is in the item design. That is, the theory is an explanation of item difficulty. To test the theory, items can be coded for the presumed characteristics that lead to various levels of difficulty. No additional information is needed from the test taker; the extra information comes from the item designers.

In the LLTM the test taker is viewed as having only a single relevant ability—the items vary in difficulty along this ability continuum in accordance with their characteristics. In Embretson's extension (chapter 6), the MLTM, the different components of item difficulty are viewed as dimensions of individual differences. Applying this model requires additional information from the test takers. Almost certainly, it also requires a test individually administered, perhaps by computer, so that responses to each aspect of each item can be separately identified, although the experimental conditions are not discussed in the chapter.

The third model is a combination: GLTM has item difficulty components within each dimension of individual difference. The same kind of experimental data are required, as well as additional analyses of the item component difficulties. Whether many data sets would need this level of complexity is questionable, but the importance of being able to extend the models to meet possible cognitive demands is noteworthy.

As an indication of the kind of power in the multicomponent models, Embretson shows how multiple components can explain some paradoxes of change in learning—the idea being that only some of the components are susceptible to change through learning. This is a traditional psychometric analysis that makes contact with other work in individual differences.

However, the main message from Embretson's work is that we should be ready to collect additional data, and to design careful experiments when extending our psychometric models into the realm of cognitive psychology.

7

Assessing Schema Knowledge

Sandra P. Marshall
San Diego State University

This chapter focuses on tests that measure the knowledge acquired from class-room instruction. The tests are based on the theory of schemas, which underlies much recent research in cognitive psychology. The tests reflect the nature of the subject domain, the instruction about it, and the desired structure of the learner's knowledge about that domain. They are related to the domain and the student through a model of cognition that depicts the essential characteristics of the subject domain and the student's knowledge of it. Their structure and contents are designed to utilize aspects of the structure of long-term memory that are usually ignored. To show how this is applicable, I begin by developing the schema theory that underlies the model. Next, I describe how the theory guides test development and interpretation. Finally, I provide an example from the domain of arithmetic word problems, in which students receive schema-based instruction and are assessed through schema-based tests.

The basic premise is that meaningful learning requires the development of well-formed schemas. Assessment of learning can thus be redefined as the as-sessment of schema formation and use. The central issues of assessment are whether certain schemas have developed and whether key constituents of these schemas are present or absent.

THE NATURE OF A SCHEMA

The *schema* as a psychological construct is widely used but poorly defined in cognitive psychology. It is an underlying structure in many researches (e.g., Anderson, Boyle, Corbitt, & Lewis, 1986; Just & Carpenter, 1987; Kintsch &

155

Greeno, 1985; Rumelhart, 1980). Although some researchers provide explicit examples of schemas, they fail to describe the construct operationally. Most derive their use of schemas either from Bartlett's (1932) research about ghost stories or Minsky's (1975) formulation of frames with slots, although neither Bartlett nor Minsky provided a sufficiently precise definition for experimental verification. Without such a definition, schema theory is of limited value. One objective of the work described here is the formulation of a testable schema construct.

There are two fundamental viewpoints on schemas. The first is the architectural point of view. The schema is viewed as a structural feature of long-term memory, usually as a set of nodes and arcs connecting those nodes. It holds information at its nodes, but the nature of the information contained in the nodes is relatively unimportant. The architectural perspective has prevailed in much of the artificial intelligence literature (e.g., Smolensky, 1986). The second point of view emphasizes the knowledge contained in the schema without examining how it is structured. The schema is just a collection of information. This perspective is particularly evident in research on problem solving (e.g., Gick & Holyoak, 1983). For testing, neither viewpoint is adequate by itself.

To assess schema knowledge fully, one needs to use both perspectives. The assessment ought to take into account how knowledge is linked (i.e., the structural properties) as well as what knowledge is stored in the schema (i.e., the content properties). It ought to estimate both the structure and the contents. These estimates are not easy to make, and we are far from having a complete theory of schema development. Nonetheless, progress on the assessment of schema knowledge can start with a working definition of a schema. The components and their relations will be gauged later by appropriate tests.

Speaking generally, the schema uses a common theme or situation as a means of organizing knowledge stored in memory. It is constructed by each individual as the result of his or her experiences, with common elements of these experiences eventually linking to one another. Its value to the individual lies primarily in problem solving. When the individual accesses the schema, it provides a template against which to evaluate a current problem and points to appropriate responses.

A problem in this sense does not necessarily mean a textbook problem. Consider the problem of negotiating one's way through an unfamiliar airport. The goal is to board the right airplane on time with all of one's accompanying paraphernalia. Depending on the circumstances, this may involve purchasing a ticket, checking luggage, receiving a seat assignment, passing through a safety check, and so on. The individual with a well-developed schema for such situations will have little difficulty. She uses knowledge gained through experiences at other airports to obtain the goal in the unfamiliar one. Subgoals will have to be created and achieved (e.g., finding the ticket counter and locating the gate). Various actions will be taken as needed (e.g., change terminals, rent a luggage cart). By recognizing the relevant circumstances of the problem and accessing the schema appropriate to them, the individual utilizes previously stored knowledge from long-term memory.

When faced with an unfamiliar situation (e.g., a problem), the individual searches memory to retrieve the best schema available for making sense of the situation and for determining possible actions. Not all situations will have a nicely defined schema (as did the airport one described above). In such cases the individual typically must access several schemas and attempt to find the best match between a schema and the current circumstances. It may happen that the individual begins problem solving with one schema only to abandon it and select a second. This is a familiar occurrence in problem solving. The psychological literature on problem solving contains interviews with experts in which they first attempt to solve a problem in one way and then switch to a second approach. Their performance may be explained in terms of schema application. They first tried to implement one schema only to find that it was inappropriate. They then retrieved another schema, which subsequently led to different actions being taken. Ability to select the right schema—at least, eventually—is a salient characteristic of the expert problem solver.

Schema Definition: Content

What constitutes a schema? It has structure and content. The contents, as studied here, consist of four distinct types of knowledge: feature recognition, constraint, planning/goal-setting, and execution. These four components may be described as follows.

1. The *feature recognition* component contains declarative knowledge about the schema. All pertinent features describing the content of the schema reside here. Also found here are specific examples of situations for which the schema is appropriate. Broad abstractions about the situation are located in this component, as are analogies.

2. The *constraint* component houses the set of rules that govern the instantiation of the schema. These conditions must be met if the schema is to be used. The feature recognition component just described deals with recognition of the basic features, but the constraint component tests whether or not a sufficient set of these features are present. This constraint component links the current situation directly with the template of the schema, matching similar elements and flagging unmatched parts. If necessary, it substitutes default characteristics (obtained from the feature recognition knowledge) for missing elements to complete the match.

3. The *planning/goal-setting* component allows planning for implementation of the schema, making estimates about its outcome, and drawing appropriate inferences related to its use. The mechanisms for setting goals and subgoals reside here.

4. Finally, the *execution* component contains information about actions that can be taken or procedures that can be followed to satisfy goals and carry out plans. Typically, a subgoal is created by the planning component and is achieved by calling elements of execution knowledge.

Schema Definition: Architecture

The existence of the four components is not sufficient. They must also be interconnected. A successful call to a particular schema means that the individual recognizes a situation (feature recognition), determines if critical circumstances are present (constraint), formulates appropriate plans for using the schema (planning/goal-setting), and carries out those plans (execution).

For the schema to be a useful knowledge structure, the connections among the four parts are indispensable. They are characterized as a network of networks. Each type of knowledge forms a network. A network as a whole may or may not be connected to the networks of other types of knowledge. This will depend on how fully the schema is developed in the individual's memory. A fully developed schema would have links among component networks as well as links within them. The linkages and the information linked together comprise the network of schema knowledge. Traditional testing models have not addressed this structure. There are substantial advantages in incorporating both structural and content features within the same model.

As an illustration of different types of connectivity, consider the simple case represented in Fig. 7.1. Here there are only two components, X and Y. Nodes A, B, and C are elements in one component; nodes E, F, and G are elements of the second. In Fig. 7.1a, the two components, X and Y, are unconnected, although each component itself is fully linked internally. Given a stimulus prompt to node A, an individual having this knowledge structure would be able to retrieve all the information contained in component X but would be unable to access the nodes of Y (without an additional stimulus prompt to one of the nodes in Y). Similarly, a call to E would result in activation of Y while leaving X untouched.

In Fig. 7.1b the two components are linked through nodes A and E. Now a call to X would result in access to the nodes in both components. There are many ways that X and Y could be linked, ranging from a single connection as in Fig. 7.1b to all possible connections, as shown in Fig. 7.1c. If all the elements in one component are linked together, if all the elements in a second component are linked as well, and if there exists one or more paths between the components, the full components are considered to be connected and can be represented as in Fig. 7.1d. The single arc between X and Y carries a weight indicating whether the link between the components is weak (as in Fig. 7.1b) or strong (as in Fig. 7.1c). Estimating the strength of this link will be an important task for those who wish to assess schema knowledge. This

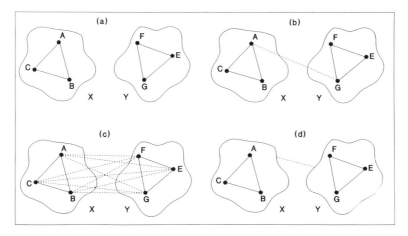

FIG. 7.1.   Two hypothetical components and possible linkages.

aspect of schema assessment takes into account the architectural structure of the schema.

Schema Identification

To determine the primary schemas for a domain, one asks what would be expected of a student who has mastery of the domain. What should the student be able to do? What skills should he or she demonstrate to exhibit competence? Suppose the area of interest is how individuals learn to understand and solve arithmetic word problems. For this case it is not enough that the students have mastery of arithmetic operations. Also expected of them are (a) the ability to understand the situation expressed as a story or word problem and (b) the skills to extract the necessary information from the situation. These together with the means to carry out the computations indicate mastery. The schemas for story problems should therefore focus on these areas. (Examples of specific schemas for this domain are given later in this chapter.)

In addition to identifying the foci of the schemas, we must also specify for each one the elements in the four components already described: feature recognition, constraints, planning/goal-setting, and execution. In so doing, we construct an ideal representation of the schema as an individual might develop it, and we specify the necessary links that should exist among elements and between components. One can think of an individual's knowledge of an entire domain as a very large network or graph. Within this large network are smaller networks corresponding to the individual schemas. Within these schema networks there are finer-grained networks corresponding to the components of the schemas. Finally, within the component networks are still finer-grained networks consisting of the elements that form a single schema component. Fig. 7.2 is an example of a knowledge network of a very simple domain having only three schemas.

As shown in Fig. 7.2, several levels of connectivity will exist. First, the schemas themselves ought to be linked together to form a cohesive knowledge structure about the domain. There will almost certainly be common elements within two or more schemas, and one expects that the larger networks would be linked together. Second, within each schema the four components should be connected. For a schema to be successfully instantiated, all four parts of schema knowledge are necessary. The components cannot function optimally in isolation. Finally, within any component one expects to have a well-connected subgraph or network of nodes. The nodes at this level have the most similarity one to another and have the most direct association. Many paths among nodes would be expected, rather than a single one. Similarly, one expects to have a path from any node in the component to all other nodes, but not necessarily a direct link from each node to all others. The component level of the network is not shown in Fig. 7.2. Each of the nodes labeled F, C, P, and E corresponds to a subgraph of individual elements linked together to form the component (feature, constraint, planning, or execution).

Schema Assessment

How are we to measure the quality of a particular schema possessed by an individual? One way is to examine its *connectivity*, the extent to which its constituent pieces are connected to each other. Each element of information has the potential to activate other information with which it is linked. If an individual retrieves one particular piece of information, how many other pieces are also automatically retrieved and available for processing? The greater the connectivity of the schema, the greater is the amount of information activated. Thus, connectivity is closely related to the determination of spreading activation, a central phenomenon in cognitive psychology. One can measure either the degree of activation as in ACT* (Anderson, 1983) or in harmony theory (Smolensky, 1986), or one can estimate the number of links of the graph that denotes the network (Marshall, 1990a).

Estimating the number and strength of connecting links in a network is one aspect of the assessment of schema knowledge. A second and equally important aspect is examining the types of knowledge that are linked together. Knowing only the number of links does not tell us all we want to know about the connectivity. The links may be connections among several different kinds of knowledge, or they may be pointers instead to many instances of a single kind. Fig. 7.3 contains two graphs illustrating different kinds of linkages. In part (a), node A has six arcs leading to six different nodes. Each of these is a terminal

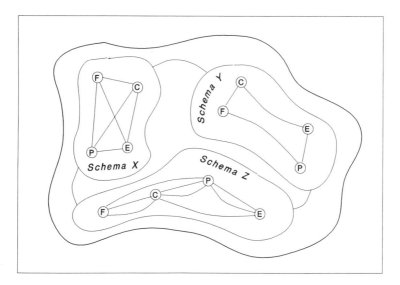

FIG. 7.2.   Hypothetical mapping of a simple domain.

node, having no other connections. Typically, this configuration corresponds
to a graph of a concept with various defining features linked to it (e.g., a bird
has feathers, eats seeds, makes a chirping sound). The features are not themselves linked directly together but can be reached through paths to the common concept. All of the nodes in Fig. 7.3a represent the same type of knowledge.
A different configuration is shown in Fig. 7.3b. Here, node A has four links,
three within the component and one to a node in another component. This pattern suggests a better integration because it encompasses two types of
knowledge.

The test of schema knowledge reflects the network expected of the domain.
It takes into account the specific nodes that are required of a schema and the
ways in which those nodes are related to each other. Its items supply assessments at many levels of the network. An item can test an individual node within
a component of a particular schema by asking a question that calls for knowledge
only of that piece of information. The student's response to the item is the basis for an estimate of the absence or presence of the corresponding node in
the network. One test item per element may be sufficient, or we may wish to
use multiple items. Similarly, an item can evaluate whether the student has two
elements of knowledge within the same component by constructing a test item
that requires both. In most cases, where the student responds correctly to the
item, we can infer connectivity between the corresponding nodes in the knowledge network.

An entire component may be the target of an assessment item. For example, if we are assessing the descriptive elements of a particular schema, we

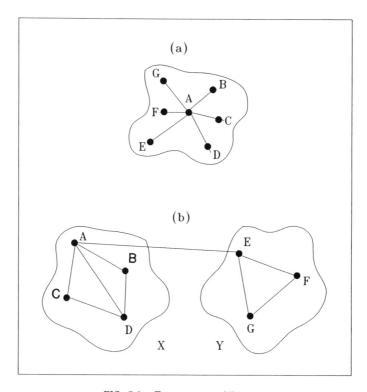

FIG. 7.3.   Two patterns of linkages.

might ask a student to provide a general description of the situation or theme for which the schema has been constructed. Each distinct feature given in the student's response can be treated as a node of the feature recognition network and can be considered to be linked to all other features (i.e., nodes) in the response. Features not mentioned are presumed to be missing nodes.[1] The depth and breadth of this component are estimated from the number of different appropriate elements contained in the student's response and from the way in which they co-occur.

When we move up a level of complexity to look at components and their degree of connection, we have greater difficulty in constructing test items. The difficulty is that the test items must represent two different dimensions of schema knowledge. For example, suppose we desire to assess whether an individual has linked the components of constraint and planning knowledge. The test item must give evidence that the constraint component and planning knowledge are

---

[1]Obviously, this assumption needs to be modified once we have sufficient information to estimate node strength and probability of retrieval. In these initial interviews, we had no prior knowledge of which nodes were likely to be present and unmentioned and which were genuinely absent.

present and that they are jointly applied. Further, if the student answers the item incorrectly, we want to be able to ascertain from the response whether the error arose in the constraint component, in the planning component, or in the link between the two. Such items need to be very carefully constructed, but early experience with them shows that they can be constructed and that the responses are highly informative.

The purpose of cognitive assessment is to estimate how fully developed and how completely related are the components of schema knowledge for an individual. Each test item contributes to the estimate of the contents of the schema and/or to its connectivity. Not all test items will provide the same amount of information about the individual. Some items test many distinct parts of the schema model and hence provide multiple estimates. Some test only a single element or a single link. Consequently, if scores from several items are to be aggregated into a total score, the items will need to be treated differentially to reflect the amount and type of information they yield.

In the following section, I present a system of assessment and its items and I describe the nature of the diagnostic information one may gather from them. Empirical results from a group of students are given, and profiles are developed for a small number of students to demonstrate how the information can be aggregated.

AN EXAMPLE OF SCHEMA-BASED INSTRUCTION AND ITS ASSESSMENT[2]

My associates and I have recently developed a computer-based instructional system designed in part to help students to understand the relationships and situations expressed in arithmetic story problems. The system is called the *Story Problem Solver* (SPS). SPS was developed for use by students in remedial-college and community-college mathematics classes. It assumes that students have already had a great deal of instruction about arithmetic operations and have had exposure to many story problems. Available evidence from large-scale assessments such as the National Assessment of Educational Progress and the California Assessment Program indicates that high school students have difficulty solving story problems, not because they cannot carry out the arithmetic operations, but because they do not know how to determine which operations to implement or which information from the problem to use. They are especially weak in solving multistep problems. SPS addresses these difficulties.

---

[2]The examples given below are based on instruction about story problems that typically spans 8 h. The assessment items given here are removed from their instructional context, and their content may not be readily understood. They are presented in order to show the general format of assessment used here, not to convey information about the particular instructional content of SPS.

SPS focuses on the types of situations found in story problems and provides instruction that is designed to facilitate the development of five specific schemas about story problem situations.[3] The important elements of the four knowledge components of these schemas are embedded in the computerized instruction, and SPS uses a number of diagnostic tasks that are intended to evaluate whether or not students have encoded and linked together the necessary pieces of knowledge.[4]

SPS assesses whether or not a student has acquired requisite knowledge at a particular time. Each segment of instruction is accompanied by a set of assessment tasks. These tasks are not traditional problem-solving exercises in which the student responds with a single numerical answer for each problem. Such an approach is of little value in schema assessment, for reasons already given. Very different items are required for schema evaluation. The evaluation questions of SPS focus instead on structural aspects of the problems.

The assessment tasks are dependent on the specific machine environment of SPS. The tasks are interactive and require the student to make responses via a three-button optical mouse. For most tasks, a set of connected windows appears on the screen (see Figs. 7.4–7.7). The top window is reserved for SPS communication with the student. Instructions and feedback appear here. The middle window contains the problem to be addressed during the exercise. The student's response to the problem is made in the bottom window. Examples given here are of necessity static and cannot capture the screen changes that occur during mouse responses.

SPS instruction is briefly described next with respect to the four knowledge components, followed by examples of the questions asked about the instruction. First, however, it may be useful to elaborate the details of one target schema and to give examples of its components.

The Change Schema

Each schema centers on a general situation that may be expressed in a story problem. One of these is named *Change*. A Change situation is characterized as an alteration in one amount. The change takes place over time and is permanent. Typically, there is a starting amount, some action that increases or decreases the amount, and the resulting or ending amount. All of this information would be stored in long-term memory as feature recognition knowledge.

---

[3]SPS's emphasis on schema development is completely invisible to the student. The instruction focuses directly on *situations*: how to recognize them and use relevant information about them. The term "schema" never appears in instruction, and students are not informed that schema development is the objective.

[4]Details about the five relations taught by SPS and about the system itself may be found elsewhere (Marshall, Barthuli, Brewer, & Rose, 1989; Marshall, Pribe, & Smith, 1987).

INSTRUCTIONS: Identify the parts of the problem that belong in the diagram. Move the arrow over each part. Click and release the mouse button. Drag the dotted rectangle into the diagram, and click the mouse button again when you have positioned the rectangle correctly in the diagram. If you make a mistake, return to the problem and repeat the process. When you are finished, move the arrow into the OKAY box and click the mouse button.

Harry the computer programmer accidentally erased some of his computer programs while he was hurrying to finish work one Friday afternoon. Much to his dismay, when he returned to work on Monday, he discovered that only 24 programs of his original 92 programs had survived. How many computer programs had been destroyed?

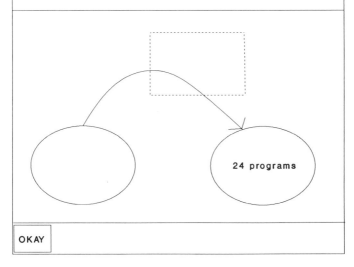

24 programs

OKAY

FIG. 7.4.   Feature recognition task from SPS.

Also in this component might be an example. The initial example used in SPS describes the particular case in which an individual has some money, gets some more, and has a larger amount at the end of the story. We have observed from interviews with our students that many of them encoded specific details of this example as part of their feature recognition knowledge of Change.

Constraint knowledge centers mainly on the presence of the requisite number of problem elements (starting amount, amount of change, ending amount), on the passage of time (past to present, present to future), and on the identifi-

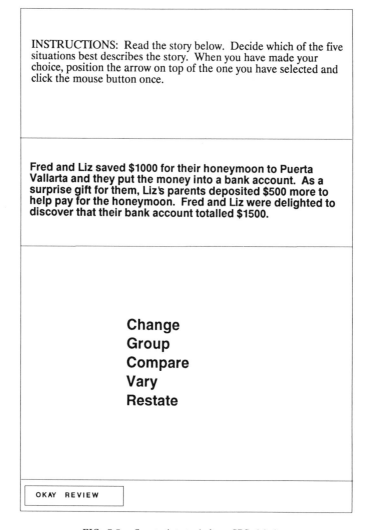

FIG. 7.5.   Constraints task from SPS: labels.

cation of the object being changed (if we start with cookies we must conclude with cookies). For example, a simple problem might be:

Joe has 5 apples. If he eats two of them, how many will be left?

The constraint knowledge would determine that there is the initial starting amount of five apples, that the change comes through eating, and that some unknown number of apples will be left. Moreover, the objects of interest as the starting

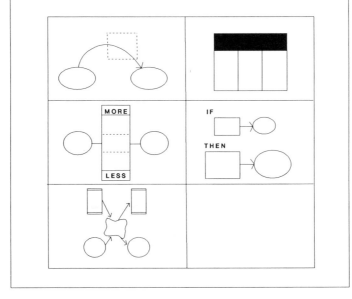

INSTRUCTIONS: Choose the one diagram below that fits this story problem. Move the arrow into the diagram you have selected and click the mouse button.

Dan Robinson recently drove 215 miles from San Diego to Santa Barbara to see his parents. When he arrived at his parents', he noticed that the odometer of his car registered 45631 miles. What was the odometer reading before he made the trip?

FIG. 7.6. Constraints task from SPS: diagrams.

and ending amounts are the same (e.g., apples). The importance of this constraint is evident from the following problem:

Joe has 5 apples. If he eats two of them, how many oranges does he have left?

Planning knowledge for a simple Change situation contains information about how to identify which part of the change is unknown and about how to carry out the correct arithmetic operation to find the unknown value. For example, if the starting amount is unknown and the change is a decrease, then the cor-

INSTRUCTIONS: Read the problem below and study the diagram. For each part of the diagram, decide whether the necessary information is already GIVEN in the problem, whether you can find it by first getting a PARTIAL ANSWER, or whether you can find it as the FINAL ANSWER to the problem. Fill each part of the diagram with one of the three choices. Click in the OKAY box when you have filled the diagram.

Joe won $100 in the state lottery. He spent some of it on toys for his two children. He bought a doll for Sue that cost $25 and he bought a stuffed bear for Ellen that cost $28. How much of his lottery winnings did he have after he bought the toys?

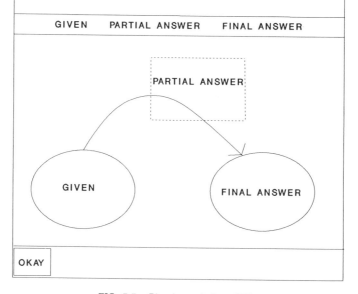

FIG. 7.7.   Planning task from SPS.

rect plan involves the addition of the amount of change and the end amount, as in:

Joe had some apples. He ate 2 of them, and now he has 3 left. How many did he start with?

Finally, execution knowledge is primarily knowledge of arithmetic operations. Knowing that a problem requires subtraction for solution is not equivalent to having the skills of carrying out the operation. In the execution knowledge for the first example given, the individual would need to apply the subtraction algorithm correctly, including using numbers from the problem appropriately in the algorithm. Both planning and execution knowledge become more complicated with multistep problems containing several embedded situations.

The remaining schemas of SPS are group, Compare, Restate, and Vary. For simplicity, in the following description of SPS assessment, only Change situations are depicted. Table 7.1 gives brief descriptions of the other four situations.

Feature Recognition. The feature recognition component of a schema contains elements about the general structure of a story problem appropriate to that schema. Our primary concern here is not the assessment of each element within the subgraph "feature recognition" but rather the assessment of the entire subgraph. Consequently, the tasks for students focus on their ability to identify how the five basic schemas apply to situations expressed in story problems.

As part of the feature recognition or declarative portion of schema knowledge we expect a student to encode information about the relevant parts of the situation depicted in the story. In SPS these parts are introduced and evaluated by means of icons or diagrams that SPS uses to represent the situation.

Feature recognition knowledge in SPS has to do with the number of different parts required by a situation and the ways in which they fit together. Each of the icons has from three to five distinct parts, which are to be filled with information from the story problem. If too many of them are unfilled or if there are more features of the problem than parts to the icon, its corresponding schema is an inappropriate match for the story problem.

TABLE 7.1
Descriptions and Examples of Remaining Situations in SPS

GROUP	*Description:* Class inclusion. Group situation requires two or more groups that can be logically combined into a larger group, usually having a new name. The situation is static. *Example:* The Sociology Department has a large faculty: 15 Professors, 10 Associate Professors, and 8 Assistant Professors.
COMPARE	*Description:* Contrast of size. Compare situation contrasts values associated with two objects with the objective of selecting the object with the higher (or lower) value. No computation is required. *Example:* The best typist in the pool can type 65 words per minute on the typewriter and 80 words per minute on the word processor. She is quicker on the word processor.
RESTATE	*Description:* Verbal and numerical relationships. Restate situations contain two statements about a relationship. One statement relates verbal descriptions of two objects. The second restates the relationship using mathematical values associated with the objects. *Example:* In our office, the new copier produces copies 2.5 times faster than the old copier. The old copier produced 50 pages every minute.
VARY	*Description:* Direct or indirect variation. The situation is conditional: if one object bears a particular mathematical relationship to a second object, then any other object identical to the first also has that mathematical relationship. *Example:* Each of the 5 lawyers in a local firm employed 4 legal secretaries. There were 20 secretaries.

For assessment purposes SPS evaluates a student's ability to place specific numbers, words, or phrases from a story problem within the appropriate parts of a selected icon (see Fig. 7.4). In this exercise, the problem is given in the middle window on the screen. The student may select any part of the problem by positioning the mouse cursor over the selected word or number and pressing the mouse button. A dotted rectangle appears around the chosen text. When the student moves the mouse cursor into one part of the icon in the bottom window and presses the mouse button again (for example, into the lower left oval of Fig. 7.4), the selected text is deposited and the dotted rectangle disappears.[5] Fig. 7.4 demonstrates the partial response of a student who has mapped only one of the three parts of the problem into the icon.

The intention here is for the students to associate the features of the situation with the appropriate figure. Thus, for the Change icon, there are three parts, and the student learns to associate the lower left oval with the starting amount, the rectangle with the change that occurs, and the lower right oval with the ending amount.

Two tasks of varying difficulty are used in this assessment. For each of the five basic situations, the student is first instructed about the important feature knowledge associated with the situation and then given an exercise to test his or her understanding of the situation. For each item in the exercise, the student is shown a story problem and asked to place phrases of the problem in the correct positions on the icon. Each problem presented is an example of the particular situation under current instruction. The number of items in the exercise depends upon the student's success in mapping the story problems onto the icons. This task assesses the student's understanding of the important features of each situation and how they may be expressed in story problems.

The second task evaluates the student's performance over all five situations. Each student responds to a series of problems for which the situations are randomly ordered. As in the first feature-recognition task, the student does not select the icon or the situation. The icon appropriate for the situation depicted in the problem is shown to the student. The student's task is to fill in the icon with the correct elements from the problem. This task differs from the first in that the student does not know in advance which situation will appear in a problem.

Constraints. The constraint instruction centers on conditions that must exist for the schema to be appropriately implemented. An example of a constraint is the role of time in a Change relation. The change takes place over

---

[5]It would be tedious for a student to select only one word or one number at a time for this task. Each problem is coded so that if a student selects one member of a phrase, the entire phrase is highlighted and may be placed in the icon in one move. This practice has two merits. First, it keeps the task from being tedious for the student. Second, it reinforces the instruction by forcing the student to be aware of the importance of the story units and relationships.

time. If the story problem does not develop over two different periods of time, it cannot reflect the change situation.

Students indicate their acquisition of constraint knowledge in two ways. Both require the student to apply constraint knowledge in order to judge whether the conditions necessary for a particular situation have been met. For one task, the student's response is the selection of the name of the situation from a menu of all five names. For example, in Fig. 7.5, the student would read the instructions in the top window, evaluate the story in the problem presented in the middle window, and make a mouse selection of one of the five choices given in the bottom window.

For the second task, the student's response is the selection of the appropriate icon that corresponds to the situation. The general form of this task matches that of the first constraint task. That is, again there are three windows and the student makes a choice from a menu of five items in the bottom window. However, in this case, the menu choices are the five icons. Figure 7.6 contains an example of this task.

Other tasks explicitly link feature recognition and constraint knowledge. In these tasks, SPS presents a series of story problems to the student. For each story problem the student must select the appropriate icon and must also demonstrate how the story problem maps into it. The tasks require multiple responses of the student. First the student identifies the appropriate icon as in Fig. 7.6. If the response is incorrect, relevant feedback is provided to the student by the computer. Next the student is shown a larger version of the appropriate icon and asked to map the story problem (as in Fig. 7.4). These tasks require the students to use their schema knowledge to determine whether one situation is more appropriate for a given story problem than another. Further, they force the student to test for himself or herself whether the constraints of the schema are met by the particular problem.

Planning/Goal-Setting.   One of our objectives in SPS is to help the student understand the problem and to make plans about solving it. We actually do not assess planning alone. Our tasks are designed to look at planning and goal-setting with respect to feature recognition and constraints.

Two levels of planning are possible. First, the student has to anticipate where the unknown of the problem fits into the general situation. For example, the change situation has three parts: the beginning, the amount of change, and the result. In a story problem, any one of these three parts may be unknown. Choice of arithmetic operation depends upon which part of the situation is unknown. We focus on this issue by having the student first examine a story problem and its appropriate icon and then place the word UNKNOWN in the appropriate part of the figure. (Later tasks relate the operation to the location of the unknown.)

Other tasks about planning are relevant for story problems with multiple steps. Students learn to recognize which situation governs the problem and which subproblems must be solved before the top-level situation can be addressed. SPS uses several tasks here. One task calls for the student to identify in an icon which parts are given in the problem, which are partially known but immediately solvable, and which are the true unknowns. Fig. 7.7 contains an example of this task. In this example, FINAL ANSWER represents the icon part that must be found to solve the entire problem. GIVEN represents any known information that can be used without additional computation. PARTIAL ANSWER indicates that a subgoal needs to be set and solved before the value of its component is known. The example in Fig. 7.7 shows the correct mapping by a student for this item.

SPS also has the students identify the situation that corresponds to the primary question asked in the problem. It then works with them to identify secondary questions and their associated situations. The task that assesses their understanding requires two menu choices, one for the overall situation and one for the embedded or secondary one.

Execution. In this group of tasks SPS comes close to asking the students to solve the problems. However, as already stated, the interest is not in whether or not they have mastered arithmetic algorithms. We are concerned with their ability to formulate the appropriate arithmetic expressions to reflect the problem situation. For example, students have a tendency to associate a particular operation with a type of problem. Take a Change situation such as:

Joe had 3 apples and bought 4 more. Now he has 7 apples.

Most students confronted with problems about this situation want to perform an addition. This is not necessarily the appropriate operation. If the problem contains information about the starting amount (*has 3 apples*) and the change (*bought 4 more*), and the change is an increase, then addition indeed is warranted. If, however, the student is given the amount of change (*bought 4*) and the final amount (*7 apples*), and the objective is to determine the number with which he started, addition will not solve the problem. Subtraction is required.

SPS tasks that assess execution skills ask students to identify arithmetic expressions and verbal expressions about arithmetic operations. Feedback on these tasks stresses the importance of identifying the situation correctly and then observing which part of the problem is unknown.

The execution portion of SPS is the briefest. Current emphasis is primarily upon the recognition features, the constraints, and the planning components. Consequently, assessment of the execution component of schema knowledge is not as strong as the assessment of the other three components.

Performance Data

Summary of the **Story Problem Solver.**   I have described the questions used in the computer-based instructional system and given examples to point out how they differ from traditional questions assessing ability to solve arithmetic story problems. A primary asset of these tasks is that they allow estimation of which aspects of schema knowledge have been encoded in memory and which remain to be formed. From the series of tasks presented by SPS, we have traced the schema development for each of a group of students, using the students' responses to SPS tasks together with cognitive analyses of short interviews carried out several times during the course of instruction. These are described next.

Student Profiles. Over a period of 2 weeks, 28 students engaged in 5 sessions each with SPS. The students were college freshmen. Preliminary testing of these students indicated that most had poor problem-solving skills. On a test of 10 multistep story problems administered prior to SPS instruction, the 28 students averaged 6.2 items correct, ranging from 4 to 9, with 50% of them answering only 5 or 6 correctly. The instruction covered all five situations but excluded the final tasks related to Execution. Consequently, the data reported below pertain only to the first three components of schema knowledge: feature recognition, constraint, and planning. Moreover, for consistency with the above emphasis on one schema, Change, only the data from Change assessment are reported here.

A few of the students responded correctly to every or almost every Change item presented by SPS. Others responded correctly to relatively few. One would like to infer from student performance that individuals who are more successful in solving problems have greater understanding of the domain than students who are less successful. From the overall performance percentages, we can only conclude that some students answered more items correctly. With this information alone it is impossible to tell whether or not their schema knowledge differs.

Table 7.2 shows the performance of three pairs of students whose overall performance in SPS appears quite similar. In this table, the performance on the different SPS tasks is broken out according to schema knowledge components. It is clear that these students have differing knowledge about Change.

Consider the first pair of students. Student 03 began slowly, having several errors related to feature recognition knowledge. This student's constraint knowledge appears to be well developed, and his ability to perform well on the linked feature/constraint items suggests that the difficulties from the earlier feature tasks have been remedied. Finally, his responses to the planning tasks (P-F and P-C) indicate that he is also able to put together his knowledge of the three components. On the other hand, Student 12 (who answered exactly the same number of items correctly as Student 03) has a different profile of knowledge. This student found the feature recognition and constraint items relatively easy but had much difficulty with those involving planning. In outlining future instruction for these two students, one would likely implement different strategies. Student 03 seems to be doing well and probably is ready to move

TABLE 7.2
Comparison of Three Pairs of Students
Having Comparable Overall Performance on Change Items

Student	Percent Correct					Total Number Attempted	Number Correct
	F	C	F-C	P-F	P-C		
Pair 1: 03	71	83	100	100	67	22	18
12	83	83	100	50	75	22	18
Pair 2: 05	86	100	100	100	50	23	20
21	100	71	100	100	75	23	20
Pair 3: 22	83	57	50	100	67	22	15
27	67	75	100	50	25	20	13

Note. F, Feature recognition tasks; C, constraint tasks; F-C, tasks requiring both feature recognition and constraint knowledge; P-F, tasks requiring both feature recognition and planning knowledge; P-C, tasks requiring both planning and constraint knowledge.

to the next unit of instruction. However, Student 12 should probably have additional instruction and practice in using planning knowledge.

The second pair of students also had similar overall performance but different success rates according to schema knowledge components. Student 05 initially had some difficulty with the feature recognition items, whereas Student 21 had trouble answering the constraint questions. Both students found the items linking planning knowledge and constraint knowledge to be difficult. Their profiles suggest that this difficulty may be of differing origins. For Student 21, it is likely that the student has not completely mastered the constraints and therefore cannot put planning and constraint knowledge together. This student may benefit from additional instruction on the constraints. In contrast, there is no obvious weakness for Student 05 other than the planning/constraint tasks. Repetition of the instruction leading to this assessment might suffice to improve her improvement.

Finally, the third pair of students are some of the weaker problem solvers in the study. In general, their success rates are below the others in Table 7.2 on all categories. However, important patterns emerge here as well. For example, Student 22 is extremely weak on all three assessments involving constraints. Clearly, this student needs additional help in understanding and encoding this knowledge. In this respect, Student 22 and Student 21 are similar. Student 27 was relatively weak on all areas. The success on the combined feature recognition/constraint assessment following rather low performance on each of these separately may indicate that this student simply needs more time and more practice than other students. Apparently, the repetition for the combined F/C task was sufficient to boost this student's understanding. One might allow the student to practice additional P-F and P-C tasks and then reassess her.

Clearly the students differ in their abilities to solve the different types of assessment items presented by SPS. One wishes to know if these are important differences in problem solving. After all, these are nonstandard questions about topics in arithmetic they have never studied before. Perhaps they are not related to actual problem solving as measured more traditionally. This can be examined by comparing the students' performance on the schema-related tasks to a traditional problem-solving test administered after SPS instruction was concluded.

The items on the traditional test were multistep problems typical of difficult ones found in eighth-grade arithmetic. Students were asked to find a single numerical answer for each one. For scoring, each item was subdivided into the appropriate number of situations, and each situation was scored correct or incorrect. Thus, a problem involving a change, a group, and a vary would have several possible scores. A student might answer all three correctly, might miss any one of the three, might err on any two, or might be incorrect on all three. Furthermore, there are different types of errors that may occur. Some are more serious than others (in terms of the present study). For example, students might understand the problem correctly but make a mistake in carrying out one of the arithmetic operations. These were not counted as errors here because the students demonstrated conceptual understanding of the situations and the operations required to reach solution. On the other hand, choice of an incorrect operation, use of incorrect numbers in the operation, or failure to carry out a step altogether were critical errors that showed lack of understanding. These were always scored as wrong answers.

Scores from all change situations on the test were aggregated for each student and regressed on the scores on the schema-based assessment tasks. This is not an especially robust analysis because of the small number of subjects, but it provides an initial clue about the relationship between traditional problem solving and the more detailed schema analysis. The regression analysis yielded a multiple correlation of .78 (adjusted R^2 = .50), (F = 5.23, p < .004, df = 5, 17). In this regression model, significant coefficients were obtained for the variables of performance on constraint tasks, planning/feature tasks, planning/ constraint tasks, and joint performance on feature and planning/constraint tasks and joint performance on feature and planning/feature tasks. One may conclude tentatively that the schema assessment does indeed predict problem-solving performance. Moreover, it gives more precise information about what is missing in the student's performance because it breaks the performance down into several identifiable components.

Not all items on the 10-item problem solving test provided useful information. A few items were answered correctly by every student, and a few elicited identical incorrect responses from virtually every student. Others, however, revealed several differences in problem-solving success. Each of these was examined with respect to its constituent situations. For example, one problem contained both a change and a vary situation. For each student, the item was given an overall score of 0 or 1 (incorrect or correct), and the score was regressed on the linked schema components for change and vary (e.g., the types of tasks described in Table 7.2). The most satisfactory regression model yielded a multiple R of .77 (adjusted R^2 = .40), (F = 3.07, p < .04, df = 6, 13).[6]

Similar analyses were held on four other questions and yielded comparable results. The adjusted R^2 values were .81, .50, .39, and .18, indicating that performance on the individual items could be predicted from the schema assessment provided by SPS. Again, these analyses must be evaluated with caution because of the small number of subjects.

These analyses provide some estimate of the validity and reliability of the schema assessment used here. Of greater importance is the check on whether the schema assessment really reflects the student's knowledge. As part of the instructional evaluation, we interviewed the students following each instructional session. In the interviews students were asked to describe each situation and to provide as much information as they could about them. They were also asked to demonstrate how they planned to solve particular problems and to justify their plans. Their responses were then used as the basis for developing cognitive maps for each student.

The cognitive maps for Change of the three pairs of students in Table 7.2 are given in Fig. 7.8. Each node in a map corresponds to a particular piece of information the student gave in the interview. Nodes are connected in the cognitive maps if students connected their respective information in the oral responses. The spatial arrangement and length of links are unimportant here. Nodes having the same number and located in the same place on the different student maps refer to the same bit of information. As expected, many of the students said very similar things, reflecting that they had encoded similar parts of the instruction. However, just as the task analyses demonstrated differences in these three pairs of students, so too do the cognitive maps. Comparisons of the two maps for each pair show quite different knowledge. For example, Students S03 and S12 differ not only in the particular nodes they have but also in the connections that occur among nodes they have in common. As pointed out previously, Students S21 and S22 had similar profiles despite having different percentages correct. They also have many similarities in their cognitive maps. Finally, Student S27, one of the weakest in the group, has a corresponding sparse map.

The characteristics in the cognitive maps appear to correspond to the differences observed in the four types of schema knowledge as tested by SPS (see Table 7.2). The construction and analyses of these maps are very difficult and time-consuming. Much has already been done, but a great deal remains to be done. The work is ongoing.

---

[6]The degrees of freedom differ from the first analysis due to missing or incomplete data for some subjects.

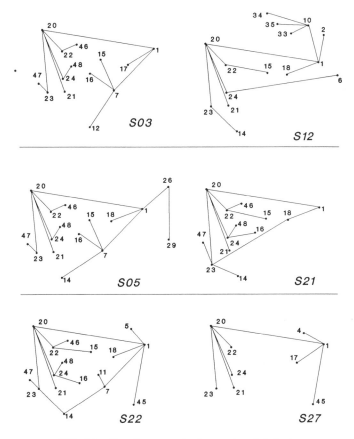

FIG. 7.8. Cognitive maps for three pairs of students.

SUMMARY AND CONCLUSIONS

This chapter described how schema knowledge may be assessed in individuals, and it has outlined an approach for making the assessment. The results obtained thus far using schema theory are encouraging. Test items can be successfully parsed by using the components of schema knowledge. Student profiles of schema knowledge can be developed on the basis of their performance on collections of these items. Validity of the schema approach is demonstrated by comparing test performance with interview data.

The schema perspective developed in this chapter differs from a traditional testing approach in several ways. First, schema knowledge has many dimensions, each of which should be measured. Items may measure single or multiple dimensions and are not necessarily parallel in structure or significance.

Second, the test is not a sample from a universe of items. The items are well chosen to examine schema development, but they do not necessarily reflect the entire domain. Third, fewer items are used in a test of schema knowledge, because in general, responses to these items take more time than responses to conventional items. Fourth, assessment of different individuals may involve different items. Once a particular linkage is demonstrated by the student response to a test item, we may not need to assess the link again. Failure to show the link, however, might lead to a set of probing questions to determine whether it is the link itself that is missing or the nodes that were to be connected. Thus, schema assessment is an example of adaptive testing. Finally, much of what is tested involves intermediate processing. The final numerical answer given by a student to a problem may be less interesting than the steps the individual took to obtain the answer. As a consequence of these differences, new kinds of inferences can be made, based on the results of the assessment. One forms estimates of how the individual's knowledge of a domain is organized and how well the individual can use the knowledge he or she has acquired.

For wider application of schema assessment it is necessary to extend the concepts of validity and reliability. At present, we lack the alternative tests for measuring schema acquisition that could supply validity estimates. At this point, validation comes from the comparison of responses to items with interview responses given by the students at the end of each instructional session. Reliability also needs further study. We assume that use of schema knowledge is a reliable gauge of the individual's network. However, the individual may access elements of a schema on one occasion but fail to do so on another. We need to examine what is meant by reliability in schema access and to develop ways to estimate it.

It may be valuable to look at the amount of time an individual takes to respond to items such as those described in this chapter. Would reaction times be good measures of access or retrieval? Could the items be modified to use reaction-time measures? One can anticipate that it would be valuable to examine a student's retrieval time for the identification of situations and the identification of icons. It would also be important to determine how long it takes a student to retrieve particular constraints associated with a given situation and to put together a multischema plan for solving a complex problem. These and other related questions have yet to be studied.

Additional cognitive issues are currently being explored in SPS, including whether different instructional conditions lead to different problem-solving knowledge. For example, the verbal/visual encoding of knowledge is important. We have looked at the impact of the visual icons on schema development and found their use to improve significantly the students' retention over time (Marshall & Brewer, 1989). We have distinguished learning that accompanies the presentation of example details versus learning that results from presentation of abstract characterizations (Marshall, 1990b).

Many other issues remain to be resolved in future research. One is whether test item scores should be combined, and if so, how this should be done. As shown in the aggregation of the change situations of the problem-solving test, the aggregation is not simply the sum of item scores. The natural output of schema assessment is a profile of knowledge. Can the profile reflect the aggregation of schema knowledge? How would the contributions of each item be weighted? What advantages or disadvantages would aggregation have relative to the profile? Similarly, one needs to decide whether to develop a quantitative measure for each item or whether to accept qualitative scoring on some. Again, the advantages and disadvantages need to be studied.

ACKNOWLEDGMENT

The research reported in this chapter was supported by the Office of Naval Research under contract no. N00014-85-K-0661.

REFERENCES

Anderson, J. R. (1983). *The architecture of cognition.* Cambridge: Harvard University Press.
Anderson, J. R., Boyle, C. F., Corbett, A., & Lewis, M. (1986). *Cognitive modelling and intelligent tutoring* (Tech. Rep. No. ONR-86-1, Contract N00014-84-K-0064). Pittsburgh: Carnegie-Mellon University.
Bartlett, F. C. (1932). *Remembering: A study in experimental and social psychology.* Cambridge: The University Press.
Gick, M. L., & Holyoak, K. J. (1983). Schema induction and analogical transfer. *Cognitive Psychology, 15,* 1–38.
Just, M. A. & Carpenter, P. A. (1987). *The psychology of reading and language comprehension.* Boston: Allyn & Bacon.
Kintsch, W. & Greeno, J. G. (1985). Understanding and solving word arithmetic problems. *Psychological Review, 92,* 109–129.
Marshall, S. P. (1990a). Selecting good diagnostic items. In N. Frederiksen, R. Glaser, A. Lesgold, & M. Shafto (Eds.), *Diagnostic monitoring of skill and knowledge acquisition* (pp. 433–452). Hillsdale, NJ: Lawrence Erlbaum Associates.
Marshall, S. P. (1990b, April). What students learn (and remember) from word problem instruction. In S. Chipman (Chair), *Penetrating to the mathematics structure of word problems.* Symposium presented at the Annual Meeting of the American Educational Research Association, Boston.
Marshall, S. P. & Brewer, M. A. (1989). *Learning from icons: What you see is what you get, or is it?* Unpublished manuscript, San Diego State University, Center for Research in Mathematics and Science Education.
Marshall, S. P., Barthuli, K. E., Brewer, M. A. & Rose, F. E. (1989). *STORY PROBLEM SOLVER: A schema-based system of instruction* (Tech. Rep. 89-01). Center for Research in Mathematics and Science Education, San Diego, CA.
Marshall, S. P., Pribe, C. A., & Smith, J. D. (1986). *Schema knowledge structures for representing and understanding arithmetic story problems.* (Tech. Rep. 86-01). Center for Research in Mathematics and Science Education, San Diego, CA.

Minsky, M. (1975). A framework for representing knowledge. In P. H. Winston (Ed.), *The psychology of computer vision* (pp. 211–277). New York: McGraw-Hill.

Rumelhart, D. A. (1980). Schemata: The building blocks of cognition. In R. Spiro, B. Bruce & W. Brewer (Eds.), *Theoretical issues in reading comprehension* (pp. 33–58). Hillsdale, NJ: Lawrence Erlbaum Associates.

Smolensky, P. (1986). Information processing in dynamical systems: Foundations of harmony theory. In J. McClelland & D. Rumelhart (Eds.), *Parallel distributed processing* (Vol. 2, pp. 194–281). Cambridge: MIT Press.

8

Learning, Teaching, and Testing for Complex Conceptual Understanding

Paul J. Feltovich
School of Medicine, Southern Illinois University

Rand J. Spiro
University of Illinois at Urbana-Champaign

Richard L. Coulson
School of Medicine, Southern Illinois University

INTRODUCTION

Deficiencies in education and in the capabilities of students are gaining increased attention at all levels of the American educational system—from elementary schools to schools of professional education (GPEP, 1984; National Commission on Excellence in Education, 1983; National Science Foundation, 1982; Porter, 1989). Failures among students in the achievement of sound and useful learning of complex subject matter have also been identified in laboratories of cognitive science concerned with education, and the nature of these shortcomings, as well as their causes and possible remedies for them, is coming under increased investigation (e.g., Feltovich, Spiro, & Coulson, 1989; McCloskey, 1983; Spiro, Vispoel, Schmitz, Samarapungavan, & Boerger, 1987; White, in press). Deficiencies in the learning of complex material that are widespread and widely recognized include three major types: misconceptions and incorrect knowledge (*wrong* knowledge), the inability to flexibly apply knowledge in new situations (what was characterized long ago by Whitehead, 1929, as a problem of *inert* knowledge), and the lack of retention of knowledge that was acquired at an earlier time (*lost* knowledge).

Acquiring and retaining a network of concepts and principles about some domain that accurately represents key phenomena and their interrelationships and that can be engaged flexibly when pertinent to accomplish diverse, sometimes novel objectives, is a reasonable definition of understanding in that domain (cf. Bruner, 1963; Greeno, 1977; Gelman & Greeno, 1989; Feltovich et al., 1989).

181

Even in educational settings where understanding, in this sense, is a goal, it appears that this is often not accomplished (Coulson, Feltovich, & Spiro, 1989; Feltovich et al., 1989; Perkins & Simmons, 1988). Deep and useful understanding of complex educational subject matter is not commonplace and comes at a high price, if at all. This may be because conventional educational practices and methods of testing achievement, while sufficient perhaps for uncomplicated material and for low levels of cognitive processing, are inadequate for difficult material when flexible understanding is a goal. Educating and testing for understanding of complicated material may require special, directed effort that is so resource-consuming that it cannot be applied widely across the many concepts of a curriculum. However, if it is important that some hard topics be learned well, then it would seem that these efforts will have to be made for a subset of the most important conceptual clusters. (In the latter part of the chapter, we propose that one answer to the demanding resource investment apparently required for fostering understanding involves selectivity and the establishment of priorities in curricula—where effort and depth in both teaching and testing are tied to the importance and difficulty of concepts to be taught, as well as to the cognitive objectives desired for the learner.)

Drawing on our work, which has revealed limitations among advanced students in their achievement of understanding of complex material, in this chapter we propose that new visions of instruction and assessment are required if education is to promote deep understanding of complex, difficult subject matter (see also Nickerson, 1989). We advance some guidelines for the forms instruction and testing should take when the achievement of flexible understanding is a goal. In the main, we argue that instruction and testing should be congruent with the cognitive goals for students that are desired (a recommendation, which may seem obvious, but not routinely honored)—that if what is desired is that students obtain accurate understanding, instruction and testing should focus on this; that if what is desired is that students be able to apply knowledge, instruction and testing should focus on knowledge application; that if what is desired is that students acquire a structure of knowledge that they will not easily forget, education concentrate on building and assessing this kind of knowledge. Tied to this, we suggest that educational goals for understanding can be aided by knowing how understanding is likely to break down.

The chapter has four main parts. Advanced knowledge acquisition, education where the goals are mastery of complexity and the ability to transfer knowledge to new situations, is discussed in the first part of the chapter. Such learning is different from "introductory" learning, and it is argued that the objectives and practices of introductory learning are often at odds with, and may actually interfere with, those of advanced learning. With reference to research we have conducted on students' learning and understanding of biomedical concepts, the difficulty of achieving understanding of complex material is also discussed, along with characteristics of subject matter that contribute to complexity and proneness to faulty learning. Principles for the design of instruction to promote the goals of advanced knowledge acquisition are presented in the second main section. If testing is to be congruent with this kind of instruction, encouraging and reinforcing the same kinds of goals, it will have to have new foci and characteristics. These are outlined in the third section of the chapter. This is followed, in the fourth section, by a brief discussion of the need for selectivity in curricula, so that the most important and difficult concepts can be given special attention in instruction and testing.

While the chapter may appear at times to focus on instructional practices, this is because instruction, learning, and testing are, effectively, so highly intertwined. Forms of testing that are utilized drive much of learning and instruction, no matter what form the "official" curriculum takes (Frederiksen, 1984). Furthermore, our recommendations for new approaches to learning and instruction will suggest new forms of testing. Given all this, it is necessary to implement systems of testing that are consistent with goals for learning and that, in particular, require for successful performance the kinds of cognitive activities and outcomes valued in the instructional process (cf. Frederiksen & Collins, 1989). Hence, points made about desirable instructional practice are also points about desirable characteristics of assessment, and vice versa. These correspondences are addressed throughout the chapter, but especially in the section which focuses directly on assessment. Thus the sequence the paper follows is cumulative: A section on what goes wrong in learning leads into a section that discusses remedies for the observed patterns of learning failure; the last main section, on testing, is a culminating response to the issues raised earlier.

THE GOALS AND LIMITATIONS OF ADVANCED KNOWLEDGE ACQUISITION

In our work, we have been interested in "advanced knowledge acquisition" (e.g., Spiro et al., 1987; Spiro, Coulson, Feltovich, & Anderson, 1988). This is learning that occurs beyond the introductory stage but before the attainment of expertise (that appears to require long years of practice and experience; Hayes, 1985). This phase of learning has special goals, characteristics, and challenges associated with the attainment of accurate and useful understanding of complex subject matter. As we argue throughout the chapter, these goals make unique demands on the design of effective instruction and testing. The nature of advanced knowledge acquisition and some of the challenges it provides for learning are discussed in this section.

Advanced Knowledge Acquisition and Its Relationship to "Introductory" Learning

Advanced learning and common forms of introductory learning differ in both the instructional goals for students and the forms of assessment used to determine whether these goals have been achieved. In introductory learning the primary educational goal is often exposure to large areas of curricular content ("coverage" of content), without much emphasis on conceptual mastery of knowledge (e.g., Porter, 1989; Spiro et al., 1987, 1988). In particular, students may not be expected to understand concepts deeply or be able to apply them because it is presumed that following exposure heightened understanding and knowledge applicability will be incrementally achieved sometime "later." The demands of assessment, in turn, are often confined to the simple effects of exposure, that is, recognition and recall of information in roughly the way it was presented in instruction. There is much less attention to testing higher-order skills of thought and knowledge application (Fleming & Chambers, 1983; Morgenstern & Renner, 1984). At some point in the educational process the restrictive goals of introductory learning must be superceded; at some point students must be expected to "get it right." That is, students should be expected to attain an accurate and deeper understanding of content material, be able to reason with it, and be able to apply it flexibly in diverse, ill-structured, and sometimes novel contexts (Spiro et al., 1987, 1988). This is the stage of *advanced knowledge acquisition*. The requirements of flexible knowledge *use*, in particular, place heavy demands on conceptual understanding because of the *ill-structured nature* of many domains of real-world knowledge application (e.g., Feltovich, Coulson, Spiro, & Dawson-Saunders, in press). By this we mean that numerous concepts are likely to be pertinent in any case of knowledge application within the domain and that the pattern of relevant concepts may differ across instances of application that are classified as being the same. (For example, clinical cases of "hypertension" are individually complex in that they involve multiple biomedical concepts, and the pattern of concept combination can vary substantially across cases.)

In addition to being different, the methods of education and assessment in introductory and advanced learning would seem, in some important ways, to be opposed to each other. For example, common strategies of simplification in introductory learning such as teaching topics in isolation from related ones (compartmentalizing knowledge), presenting only clear instances (and not the many pertinent exceptions), and requiring only reproductive memory in assessment are often in conflict with the realities of advanced learning—where components of knowledge are fundamentally interrelated, where context-dependent exceptions pervade, and where the ability to respond flexibly to "messy" application situations is required. We have found that these discrepancies between introductory and advanced learning often result in situations where the groundwork set down in introductory learning actually interferes with successful advanced learning (Feltovich et al., 1989; Spiro et al., 1987, 1988; Spiro, Feltovich, Coulson, & Anderson, 1989).

How have we arrived at these contentions about the possible inhibitory relationship between the goals and tactics of introductory learning and the requirements of successful advanced knowledge acquisition? In our laboratory, we have been studying medical students' learning, understanding, and application of biomedical science concepts that are centrally important, by consensus of medical school teaching faculty across the North American continent that we surveyed (Dawson-Saunders, Feltovich, Coulson, & Steward, 1990). Medical school (as well as other schools of professional education) would seem to be a prototype of an advanced knowledge acquisition setting. Students have generally had some prior exposure to what they are learning, and the expectations for advanced mastery are high. Nonetheless, our studies have revealed a substantial incidence of misconception of central concepts. These misconceptions often involve oversimplification, and many have an impact upon knowledge application (Coulson, Feltovich, & Spiro, 1989; Feltovich et al., 1989; Myers, Feltovich, Coulson, Adami, & Spiro, 1990; Spiro et al., 1989). The development of these misconceptions seems at least partially traceable to cognitive and instructional strategies of the sort found in introductory learning. Yet they often persist despite students' having eventually been exposed in some fashion to appropriate information. (The existence of strongly held misconceptions, despite usual classroom efforts at instruction, has been found for difficult concepts in other subject matter areas as well, e.g., physics [cf. White, 1984].) Besides the persistence of specific oversimplifications, it appears that simplificational "habits" of thought and learning acquired in introductory learning are carried over to advanced learning—a tendency that is reinforced by instruction that likewise continues to oversimplify.

The Problem of Oversimplification: Misconceptions Resulting from Reductions of Complexity

It is instructive to examine the nature of misconceptions students acquire, because these are seen to have a direct bearing on our recommendations for testing and instruction. Previewing the kinds of claims that will be made later in this chapter, a detailed understanding of the ways learning can go wrong should provide a guide for how instruction should be done (to avoid those problems) and for what should be tested and how. Likewise, knowing what it is about the nature of subject matter that causes difficulty for students can provide focus for instruction—both for what should receive emphasis and for how this should be taught if students are to be successful.

As noted earlier, many of the deficiencies in understanding we have observed in students appear to result from a cognitive inclination (a disposition in thinking) to simplify complex material—an inclination that is sometimes supported by similar simplificational practices of education (including, as we discuss later, testing). We have termed the general tendency towards oversimplification in learning and understanding the *reductive bias,* and individual instances *reductive biases.* Numerous forms of the bias have been identified (for more detailed treatments, see Coulson et al., 1989; Feltovich et al., 1989; Myers et al., 1990; Spiro et al., 1989). Examples of reductive biases and associated misconceptions are given next. (Note: In each entry, a reductive bias is described first, followed by an example misconception from one of the areas of biomedical science and medicine that has been investigated in our laboratory. Each reductive bias is characterized using a few descriptive statements. These descriptive statements are intended to represent variations on a theme that runs through each reductive bias. This list is only a subset of the reductive biases that we have identified in our studies of conceptual understanding.)

• In general, this first bias is a disposition toward seeing entities as more similar than they actually are (*similarity bias*): treating new examples as exact replicas of prototype examples that have been presented; treating partial analogies between concepts as exact correspondences (analogy treated as isomorphism); failures to discriminate among similar but subtly different concepts.
  Example: The physical density of blood (its mass property) is frequently treated erroneously by students as being the same as and as having the same hemodynamic effects as the viscosity of blood (its "thickness" or "stickiness").
  Example: A superficial similarity in the qualitative relationship between force production in an individual muscle fiber (which involves the length to which a fiber is stretched and the contractile force it can generate at that length) and force production in an intact ventricle of the heart (which involves the volume to which a ventricle is filled with blood and the force of ejection it can then produce) is overly reified, leading to the erroneous belief that the same fundamental mechanisms of force production are operative in the two situations.

• Treating dynamic, changing processes more statically; assuming that a "snapshot" or temporal slice of a dynamic process is representative of its nature; treating rates and derivatives as though they were equivalent to their mathematical integrations (*static bias*).
  Example: Changes in *cardiac output,* which is a rate of blood flow (change of position of volume/minute), are often treated by students as though they were changes of blood volume, leading students to believe, for example, that increases in cardiac output would propagate increases of blood volume, and consequently blood pressure, to the veins (when, in fact, increases in cardiac output lead to decreases in venous pressure).

- Assuming that a schema or general principle accounts for all of a phenomenon when, in fact, it accounts only for a small part; the whole of a system is like some known part of a system; a functional relationship has a single causal basis throughout its range (*uniformity of explanation*).

  Example: The *length-tension relationship*, a function that describes the relationship between the length to which a muscle fiber is stretched and the force it can generate at that length, is assumed by students to have the same causal basis across all the lengths a fiber can achieve. In fact, the causal mechanisms responsible for this function are different at different parts of the possible range of lengths.

- Treating multidimensional phenomena as unidimensional or according to only a small subset of their dimensions (*reduction of simultaneously considered dimensions*).

  Example: The degree of contractile force that a muscle can generate is a product of several factors, including both physical structural factors and others associated with the degree with which the muscle is metabolically activated. In a widely held misunderstanding of the underlying causal basis of congestive heart failure, students reflect their earlier instructional emphases by attending to the structural factors affecting contraction, to the detriment of appropriate consideration of the activational influences.

- Understanding phenomena from the point of view of a single theory, schema, or conceptual perspective, when multiple sources of explanation are actually required (*restricted perspective*).

  Example: Opposition to blood flow in the cardiovascular system (cardiovascular impedance) is interpreted by students from the perspective of obstruction—that is, in terms of factors that provide physical hindrance to the movement of blood through the vessels. This is a perspective that gives prominence to the hemodynamic concept of resistance. A richer understanding of cardiovascular impedance can be gained by adopting a perspective on impedance that focuses on energy production and depletion in the cardiovascular system. From this perspective, factors other than resistance, which are not obstructional, can be recognized as contributing opposition to blood flow by depleting energy produced by the heart, and thus making less of it available to produce flow forward through the circulation. These added factors include the need to accelerate and decelerate the blood mass (because the heart produces pulses of pressure) and the need to move blood into and out of the bulging of stretchy blood vessel walls.

- Treating continuous attributes and processes as though they were discrete (*discreteness bias*): bifurcation of continuous attribute dimensions to their poles (bipolarization); segmentation of continuous processes into discrete steps, with associated agents and acts (step-wise bias).

  Example: When considering the maintenance of acid–base balance in the human body, acid states and base states are treated inappropriately as polar opposites, rather than as reflecting a single continuum regulated by multiple factors.

Example: Continuous blood flow in the cardiovascular system is decomposed in thinking to a set of sequences and steps, causing students, for instance, to misunderstand relationships between output from and input to the heart.

- Treating concepts separately (and as separable) that are, in fact, highly interconnected (*compartmentalization*).

  Example: Pressure-volume relationships in blood vessels—relationships between the size of vessels and the pressure they contain—and *pressure-flow relationships*—relationships between blood pressure and the blood flow through vessels—are often addressed separately in instruction (for example, in different chapters in textbooks) to emphasize different pedagogical points: for instance, differences in blood "storage" capacity between arteries and veins in the case of pressure-volume relationships, and the circulation of blood in the case of pressure-flow relationships. This lack of integration carries over to students' (mis)understanding of the physical opposition to blood flow (cardiovascular impedance), where understanding requires conceptual integration of the two kinds of relationships.

- Assuming that the same elements of knowledge combine in the same routinizable way for all instances of conceptual application that are of the same nominal type when, in fact, the pattern of pertinence and combination changes in different situations (*precompiled schema retrieval*).

  Example: Medical conditions that are all instances of "hypertension," high blood pressure, can vary in their etiologies, contributing factors, and, most importantly for the present discussion, in the concepts from the biomedical sciences necessary for their understanding. Depending on particular circumstances, pertinent concepts can range over those associated with physical resistance to blood flow, the stretchability of blood vessels, the physical mass associated with blood, the volume of blood in the cardiovascular system, and various kinds of mechanisms of hormonal balance and imbalance (and their effects on such things as heart rate). Students' understanding of hypertension suffers from an overly restricted view of the variability of concepts and principles germane across instances of hypertension and, correspondingly, an overly homogeneous perception of the factors relevant across different instances (largely overemphasizing the applicability and uniformity of application of the concept of physical resistance).

- Assuming that a concept always applies in the same way when, in fact, its uses are often linked by only a general family resemblance (*uniformity of application*).

  Example: The relationships that describe the (interlocking) regulation of heart function by the vasculature and the regulation of vascular function by the action of the heart (the so-called *Starling/Guyton relationships*) do not apply in any universal manner; they differ in their application, depending on numerous conditions, including the operative blood volume in the cardiovascular system, the contractility (strength of pumping) of the heart, and the degree of stiffness of the vasculature. Students have difficulty accounting for this variability of application, and this contributes to their difficulties in understanding the relationships between outflow from and inflow to the heart.

* Assuming that if a concept is applicable in idealized conditions, separated from its natural situation of occurrence, it will be applicable in more natural and realistic contexts (*extirpation*). Treating different aspects of a topic of understanding as independent, as able to be treated separately and then "additively" reassembled (thereby, in actuality, missing conceptual interactions). The conceptual whole is equal to the sum of its component parts (*atomization/insulation from synergism*).

    Example: Many of the concepts that apply to the activation and contraction of a single muscle fiber when it is isolated in the laboratory from its natural context as part of a complex of fibers in the heart are erroneously extended by students to apply in the same way to the function of the intact heart. This kind of thinking is fundamental in supporting a widely held misconception of the basis of congestive heart failure.

* Ignoring causal dynamics: comprehension as description rather than explanation; causal mechanisms underlying the covariation of phenomena are glossed over (*superficiality/insufficiency of causal-explanatory understanding*).

    Example: Because the heart becomes enlarged in congestive heart failure, this reinforces the commonly held misconception that the heart fails because individual muscle fibers within the heart become stretched to lengths at which they cannot generate adequate contractile force—when, in fact, the heart enlarges as a function of a complex set of *consequences* of its failing.

Patterns of Incidence and Acquisition of Oversimplification-Based Misconceptions

We have just described some examples of ways that students respond to complexity in subject matter and some of the ways this results in conceptual deficiency. However, it would be misleading to suggest that the consequences of the reductive bias amount simply to an isolated misunderstanding here and there. In fact, the reductive bias appears to participate in a larger scheme that makes the nature of what is acquired in learning more complicated and the task for education and testing more challenging.

Levels of Misconception. First, the misconceptions that students acquire are of different types, which, in aggregate, affect all aspects of cognition. Misconceptions that have been identified exist at several levels of knowledge representation and reasoning, including the treatment of subject matter *content*, the *mental representation* of knowledge for use in thinking, and epistemological presuppositions about the structure and function of physical systems (*world views*). We have found examples at all three levels. Contentive errors often involve overgeneralization (or sometimes overdiscrimination). Areas of subject matter are seen as being more similar or more different than they really are (e.g., the *similarity bias*—as when the effects of blood density and blood viscosity in the cardiovascular system are treated as the same). Errors in mental representation of subject matter also occur. For example, dynamic (constantly changing) processes are often represented more statically (*static bias*—as when changes in blood *flow,* which is the rate of change of position of blood volume, are treated as changes in the simple magnitude of blood volume). Prefigurative *world views,* the assumptions a learner makes about the nature of understanding in general (Feltovich et al., 1989; Pepper, 1942), also cause problems. An example is the common presupposition that parts of systems "add up" to wholes or that components of systems can be isolated from their naturally occurring contexts and still retain their essential characteristics (e.g., *atomization* and *extirpation*).

Networks of Reciprocally Supportive Interactions. Second, misconceptions at all these levels may interact in reciprocally supportive ways (e.g., misconstruing one idea makes it easier to misconstrue another, and vice versa). Beyond this, sets of misconceptions can combine to produce yet other, *higher order misconceptions.* An example of this mutual bolstering of component misconceptions is the widely held misconception regarding the ultimate causal basis for congestive heat failure, which has been used in this section as one source for examples of reductive biases. The primary misconception is that in heart failure the heart loses its capacity to pump an adequate supply of blood because individual muscle fibers of the heart become stretched to lengths at which they have a decreased ability to generate contractile force. This primary misconception can be seen to be a composite of four different, but related, component misconceptions that bolster each other and, in addition, provide multiple ostensibly reasonable paths to the same erroneous conclusion (Coulson et al., 1989).

Misconceptions Have Multiple Sources. Third, multiple sources of influence appear to contribute to the development and maintenance of simplification-based misconception. In particular, cognitive biases toward simplification of complexity on the part of the learner seem to be reinforced by various instructional practices involving simplification (in textbooks, lectures, and so on) that extend beyond introductory learning into more advanced stages of learning, and also by some similar orientations and practices of biomedical science research. For instance, it is not uncommon instructional practice to use simpler (because they ignore the pulsatile pressure produced by the heart) constant-pressure hemodynamic systems to introduce basic properties of the cardiovascular system. This kind of focus neglects properties of the cardiovascular system that are due to the constantly changing pressure produced by the heart and thus contributes to misunderstanding of the concept of opposition to blood flow (where change in pressure and flow are particularly important). In another example, it is common to teach the topic of cardiac muscle function by focusing (at least initially) on skeletal muscle, which is more familiar to students and less complex than cardiac muscle. However, skeletal muscle is different from cardiac muscle on some of the very dimensions of muscle function that are important in the cause of congestive heart failure, the difference being such that an orientation toward skeletal muscle contributes to the misunderstanding of heart failure (Coulson et al., 1989; Feltovich et al., 1989). Simplification in instruction is sometimes mirrored in practices of biomedical science research (cf. Wimsatt, 1980), as when, for reasons having largely to do with experimental tractability, a particular form of cardiac muscle (cardiac papillary muscle) that is most like skeletal muscle is used in studies of cardiac muscle function, contributing to the perception of similarity of skeletal and cardiac muscle (and, hence, to the misconception of heart failure we have observed). Observation of ostensibly defensible reduction of complexity in the practices of authorities, such as teachers and researchers, probably lends justification and credence to simplification as a means for students to achieve understanding and to the understandings thus acquired.

Misconception Affects Knowledge Application. Finally, in addition to their effects on fundamental accuracy of understanding, reductive biases of the sort we have described can carry over to inadequacies in the application of knowledge. This is illustrated in the following protocol excerpt from a student who, in one of our studies, is addressing a clinical case and demonstrates a form of the bipolarization bias with regard to acid–base balance. The bipolarization leads to a most inappropriate clinical interpretation (Myers et al., 1990):

Well, first of all, [the patient has] severe vomiting and diarrhea. Vomiting you lose stomach acid; you're losing acid and that can cause alkalosis. However, severe diarrhea, you're losing bicarbonate, which can cause acidosis. So, if you're going to vomit or have diarrhea, it's better to do both of them at the same time, because you keep your pH balance in the middle. (p. 157)

Among other flaws, this inappropriate "prescription" results from viewing acid and base as bipolar opposites and from the mental extirpation of acid–base balance from its complex context of regulation, including the interaction of acid–base regulation with fluid regulation (e.g., the inappropriate prescription would almost surely add to problems of dehydration, which are already likely to exist in the patient).

In this section we have presented examples of the ways students simplify complex subject matter and of the kinds of misconceptions that can result. We have also discussed some of the ramifications and extensions of this type of approach to learning, including its multilayered influence on cognition, the multifaceted reinforcement of such thinking from various practices of instruction and laboratory science, and the repercussions of oversimplification for knowledge application. What has been proposed is a complex system of knowledge acquisition, error, and cognitive limitation emanating from the artificial simplification of the real complexity of subject matter. In the next section, we address what makes concepts difficult and complex, so that they are likely to induce the reductive orientations to learning that we have discussed.

Notes on the Nature of Conceptual Difficulty: Structure and Process Issues

So far, we have been discussing reductions of complexity and the potential cognitive consequences of this kind of simplification. In this section we address characteristics of concepts that make them complex and difficult, so that they are liable to induce simplification and error, and so that misconceptions, once they develop, may be particularly stable (i.e., strongly held and difficult to emend). This can serve as a guide for the kinds of topics that are likely to require special handling in testing and instruction. A framework for conceptual difficulty and the stability of misconceptions is outlined below. The framework focuses on characteristics of the appropriate understanding to be achieved (e.g., the nature of cognitive processes required for understanding), characteristics of misconceptions associated with the correct idea, differences between the right and wrong ideas, and various kinds of external (outside the individual) sources of support that might exist for a misconception. The broad categories of the framework are given first, followed by examples and illustrations:

Characteristics of the Concept as Correctly Understood and of Its Related Network of Component Concepts. Because any complex concept is likely to be related to others in a conceptual network, this aspect of the framework pertains to the nature of the correct concepts to be attained, such as to their individual difficulty, and to the structure of relations among them. The internal structure of some concepts is intrinsically more difficult than others (e.g., some concepts must be differentiated into more components than others). Similarly, some patterns of relationship among concepts pose more difficulty (e.g., recursive embedding).

Characteristics of the Network of Component Misconceptions That Make up an Overall Misconception. These are characteristics of the faulty mental representation of the correct idea. This has to do with the nature of the component misconceptions that make up a misconception and, again, with the relationships among them. For example, the degree of reciprocal support among the misconceived components—the extent to which belief in one component eases belief in others (and vice versa)—will influence the stability of a misconcention. Also pertinent is the relationship between the erroneous mental representation and the correct ideas. For instance, because of the disposition we have observed for individuals to adopt simple mental models, it would seem that simple misrepresentations of complex correct ideas will tend to be easily adopted and difficult to change (cf. Dember, 1991). In other words, if aspects of the correct idea to be acquired are quite difficult, and if their corresponding elements in the misconception are cognitively easier to handle, this should add greatly to the adoptability and stability of the misconception (because what is "understood" is satisfying and not cognitively strenuous, compared to the correct alternative).

Characteristics of the Concept's Typical Treatment by Authorities. This involves the extent to which popular media, scientific literature, and people who are presumed to know (e.g., teachers) promote the misconception or aspects of it: If important people are saying it, it must be true.

We propose in this scheme that a conception derives its relative propensity to be adopted and maintained partly from *internal, cognitive supports*—having to do with such things as the nature of the cognitive processes required for understanding and the characteristics of related knowledge structures—and from *external supports*, such as the way the concept is treated by textbooks and other authorities. Among other things, *internal support* depends on where a represented misconception stands on various dimensions of *cognitive processing complexity*, in comparison to where the correct conception falls on these same dimensions. A misconception will be more readily adopted and stable to the extent that it falls on the simpler ends of these dimensions of complexity, relative to the correct idea to be attained—for example, linear relationships in the misconception, versus nonlinear ones in the correct idea. Some pertinent dimensions of difficulty and complexity are listed below:

- *Concreteness/abstractness.* Are processes concrete and visualizable or abstract?
- *Discreteness/continuity.* Are attributes and processes discrete or continuous?
- *Static/dynamic.* Do properties or processes depend on fixed entities or values, or do they depend on change? Are characteristics of a process well represented by a fixed "snapshot," or are characteristics of the process inherently entwined with change in the process from snapshot to snapshot?

- *Sequentiality/simultaneity.* Do processes occur in a sequential, stepwise fashion, or are there aspects of simultaneity?
- *Mechanism/organicism.* Are effects tractably traceable to the actions of agents (mechanistic), or are they the product of more holistic, organic functions?
- *Separability/interactiveness.* Do different processes run independently of each other (or with only weak interaction), or are processes strongly interactive?
- *Universality/conditionality.* Are there principles of function or relationships among entities that are universal in their application or validity, or are regularities much more local and context-dependent?
- *Linearity/nonlinearity.* Are functional relationships among processes or entities linear or nonlinear?

Three additional sources of internal support involve the structure of existing or prior knowledge in its relationship to the correct and incorrect ideas. The first might be termed *p-prim congruence,* after the construct of "p-prim" proposed by diSessa (1983). A p-prim is a fundamental belief about how the world works and is similar to what we, in our own work, have called a "prefigurative" conceptual scheme (Feltovich et al., 1989). To the extent that components of a misconception are congruent with such p-prims and those of the correct interpretation are not, the misconception will be more readily adopted and more stably held; the misconception will seem intuitively right, while the correct idea will not. In addition, there will be a kind of "mind-twister" characteristic to the correct notion because it will require a way of thinking that is discrepant with existing interpretive schemes. A second additional source of internal support is the existence of salient examples or analogies that appear to conform to the misconception. The more instances there are in memory of seemingly related kinds of phenomena that appear to be in concert with the misconception (or to its components), the more readily adopted and stable the misconception will be. The third knowledge-related source of support involves internal consistency or congruence among the components of the misconception. Important in this regard is the degree of reciprocation among components, the degree to which belief in some components makes belief in others easier.

In addition to the internal sources of support, another set of supports for a belief is "external" to the individual, involving credence provided by authorities. Is a misconception commonly taught or suggested in textbooks, or implied by various aspects of biomedical science research? For example, one of the factors that contributes to the widely held belief in the misconception of heart failure we have used as an example in earlier parts of the chapter is that it is often proferred in medical textbooks and in clinical teaching.

A brief sketch of our framework for the analysis of conceptual difficulty and likely misconception stability has been presented in this section. The analysis, when applied to a set of concepts (those in a curriculum, for instance), can be used to help identify which among them are likely to need special attention in instruction and testing because they are difficult, likely to be misunderstood, and apt to be hard to change in students. However, for such areas of a curriculum, what is required of instructional practice if accurate, and, in addition, usable understanding is to be achieved? What is required of testing, if the soundness of understanding of complex subject matter is to be assessed? A proposal for the nature of the necessary instruction is taken up next. The instructional principles that are developed within the next section provide dual service, forming the basis not only for instruction but also for the kind of testing proposed in the section which follows the treatment of instruction.

PRINCIPLES FOR INSTRUCTION IN ADVANCED KNOWLEDGE ACQUISITION

Taking into account deficiencies of understanding of complex material that we have observed in advanced students, we outline in this section principles for the design of instruction to achieve the goals of advanced knowledge acquisition, that is, the attainment of accurate, useful, and well-retained understanding of complex material (cf. Cognitive Flexibility Theory—Spiro et al., 1988; Spiro, Feltovich, Jacobson, & Coulson, 1991). Desirable outcomes of learning and the common failures associated with each are taken up next, along with characteristics of cognition, educational practice, and subject matter that appear to contribute to the deficiencies and hence are to be avoided or surmounted in instruction and testing when sound and useful understanding is an objective.

Promoting Accurate Understanding and Overcoming Misunderstanding

As has been discussed, in learning complex and difficult subject matter students frequently acquire misconceptions that can be difficult to dislodge. In addition to our own work in biomedical understanding, such misconceptions on the part of learners have been found in subjects as diverse as arithmetic (Brown & Burton, 1978), physics (Caramazza, McCloskey, & Green, 1981), electricity (Gentner & Gentner, 1983), and climatology (Collins & Gentner, 1983). Often these misconceptions exist despite students' having been exposed in some fashion to accurate materials in instruction (although, as we have noted, some common practices of instruction appear to aid in the development of misunderstanding). Methods of addressing the important sources contributing to the development of misconception are presented next.

Discordant Prior Knowledge and Belief

Among sources of misconception are the prior models and beliefs related to a concept that students bring to the learning situation. New learning does not occur in a vacuum; it is tailored and influenced by what has been learned before—either in formal schooling or in ordinary experience. Such prior knowledge schemes can clash with those necessary for understanding new ideas, such that, for example, existing knowledge accentuates only a subset of facets of a concept to be learned, causing certain dimensions to be missed; or the new material is inappropriately subsumed to the prior knowledge; or prior knowledge causes new concepts to be seen as counterintuitive.

Counterintuitiveness is a major source of misconception. For example, many concepts from formal physics are difficult because they clash with ordinary experience. Many students erroneously believe that for an object to be moving, an applied force must be acting on it at all times because in a frictional world the need for such force is often accentuated. In an example from the cardiovascular domain we have studied, one of the things that makes it so difficult for students to gain a sound understanding of opposition to blood flow (the concept of cardiovascular impedance) is that it is very difficult for them to conceive that making blood vessels more easily stretchable (more compliant) could ever lead to greater opposition to the flow of blood by the vessels (which it can). To reiterate an earlier discussion, dysfunctional prior mental models and beliefs can exist at many levels of cognition, from beliefs about low-level subject matter content, to models of phenomena, to fundamental epistemological models about how the world works and is structured (diSessa, 1983; Feltovich et al., 1989).

Compounding the potential obstructive effects of prior wrong beliefs is the fact that they can be relatively opaque to challenge. By this we mean, first, that these beliefs can be implicit and tacit even to the student, hence hard to detect, and, second, that it is sometimes difficult to create circumstances that constitute challenge to them in such a precise way that the challenge feeds back to the appropriate sources of error. An instance of the latter was alluded to in the physics example given above, where much of the common feedback of everyday experience does not impinge directly enough on the misconception to be effective.

Instruction that assumes accurate, passive reception on the part of the student—that assumes, for example, that because the right information is presented to the student, correct ideas will be developed—is vulnerable to the effects of ingrained prior belief. Ideally, instruction should have a diagnostic component, in which students' preconceptions are made clear, as well as a more prescriptive component, providing directed and interpretable challenges to areas of knowledge that are potential hindrances to the achievement of appropriate understanding (cf. Green, McCloskey, & Caramazza, 1985; White, 1984).

Such considerations lead to the first of a set of design principles for effective instruction:

Principle 1. Know what beliefs and interpretive models, germane to the concepts to be learned, students are likely to hold and the kinds of misconceptions they are likely to develop as a result.

Principle 2. Provide directed challenges to misconceptions likely to be held or acquired.

Conceptual Isolation

Probably in any domain of rich complexity, but certainly in the biomedical sciences, concepts are highly intertwined and interdependent, such that the nature of any one depends on its interactions with many others. For example, the concept of cardiovascular impedance, opposition to blood flow, cannot be understood in isolation from concepts associated with cardiac muscle activation and contraction, regulation of cardiovascular flow, energetic metabolism, and several others. Furthermore, in a situation where concepts are in reality highly interdependent, students' misconceptions can likewise take on interdependencies, so that inadequate or overly compartmentalized understanding in one part of a cluster of pertinent concepts can have repercussions for the understanding of others (Coulson et al., 1989; Feltovich et al., 1989, on "spreading misconception").

Instruction that focuses on concepts in isolation promotes the idea that concepts are more independent and regular (i.e., less subject to variation in the context of other concepts) than they really are. In addition, because the true dependencies are not appreciated, isolated treatments restrict the richer understanding of related concepts and can even undermine their understanding more directly.

Principle 3. Focus on clusters of related concepts, not individual concepts.

Principle 4. Employ anticompartmentalization measures. Emphasize connection and combination, conceptual dependency, and conceptual variation across contexts.

Singular Conceptual Aids

Various kinds of devices are used in instruction in an attempt to aid conceptual understanding. Common among these is the use of analogy. Employing an analogy in instruction allows the learner to import an intact cognitive structure to help in interpreting a new concept, rather than having to construct one more fundamentally. Analogies have been shown to have a powerful effect on learning (e.g., Collins & Gentner, 1983). However, when any single analogy is used to convey a complex, multifaceted concept, it is likely that the analogy will not cover all aspects of the concept (i.e., it will miss some aspects) and may actually be misleading with regard to others (Halasz & Moran, 1982). In fact, we have shown that analogies that help learners achieve the modest goals of introductory learning interfere with the later mastery of more complete treatments (Spiro et al., 1989).

Instruction that utilizes singular adjunct representations as an aid to conceptual understanding runs the risk of restricting understanding of a new concept to only those aspects emphasized in the representation. Furthermore, the representation itself may induce some misunderstandings.

The use of multiple analogies and mental representations has been proposed as a means for alleviating the potential hazards to learning produced by single representations and as a means for enhancing understanding (Burstein, 1985; Burstein & Adelson, 1990; Spiro et al., 1989). Representations can be linked and meshed, such that conceptual aspects missed by one are addressed by others and so that misleading aspects are emended by others (Spiro et al., 1989). Similar approaches using multiple representations could be used to counter the maladaptively reductive effects of a single schema, prototype example, line of argument, and so on.

Principle 5. Multiple representations should be used for complex concepts.

The Reductive Bias

We have already discussed what appears to be a pervasive cognitive tendency on the part of students (and others) toward oversimplification of complex conceptual material. A number of particular cognitive processes involving simplification of complexity have been described, along with some of the kinds of misconceptions that can result (see section, "The problem of oversimplification: Misconceptions resulting from reductions of complexity"). This tendency toward simplification extends from the understanding of subject matter content itself, to the cognitive representational processes by which subject matter is coded for use in thought, to basic presuppositions of epistemology. It appears to be a powerful source of misconception.

Similar cognitive tendencies toward oversimplification have been established in the domain of probabilistic reasoning, where there, too, they often lead to error (e.g., Kahneman, Slovic, & Tversky, 1982). Our research has extended such findings into the domain of complex conceptual processing. It appears that human cognitive processing is such that there is a natural tendency to try to understand things in fundamentally simple ways (cf. Dember, 1991; Smolensky, 1986). This may be adequate when what is being learned is well structured and well defined. It can lead to error and misconception when, in fact, material is complex and complexly structured, as it often is in the biomedical sciences and medicine, and in many other domains (especially those that involve real-world knowledge application).

The bias toward oversimplification also appears to extend to many educational, instructional practices (and even, as we have noted, to some practices of biomedical science research and reporting). For instance, it is fairly common educational practice to simplify complex material, at least in introductory learning, with the hope that complexity can later be introduced incrementally. Our investigations suggest that this strategy often backfires, that initial, simplistic, and cognitively satisfying conceptualizations form obstacles to the progress of students. The basic reductive disposition on the part of the learner, when it interacts with simplificational strategies from instruction, can result in a powerful potion for misconception.

Principle 6. Do not oversimplify. Instead, utilize means to help students deal with the real complexity of things more tractably.

The reductive bias is an important influence that appears to pervade the learning process. It has a part in many of the other factors that contribute to ineffective learning and misconception, for example, the reductive use of analogy discussed above, in which a topic of instruction is overly identified with just those features accentuated by a powerful instructional analogy. It also appears to play a role in the development of knowledge that cannot be adaptively used. This topic is taken up next.

Promoting Flexibly Useful Knowledge in Contrast to Inert Knowledge

One of the goals of advanced knowledge acquisition is the development of knowledge that students can use in novel ways to address substantive problems and tasks. All too often, however, students may in some sense possess knowledge but not be able to use it in any way other than that in which it was originally learned. This problem of "inert" knowledge is generally seen as one of the inadequacies of the educational process (e.g., GPEP, 1984; National Commission on Excellence in Education, 1983). This problem of inert knowledge is addressed here, along with design principles for instruction aimed at combatting this problem.

Passive Versus Active Learning

Good learning is not a passive process of reception of information; rather, it is an active process, on the part of the learner, of constructing new knowledge and incorporating it into what is already known (e.g., Bartlett, 1932; Bransford & Franks, 1972; Chiesi, Spilich, & Voss, 1979; Spiro, 1980). The more actively students process material, the more they embellish it with their own ideas, and the more that they question their own understanding, the more they learn and the more they retain from what they learn (e.g., Anderson, & Reder, 1979; Farr, 1987; Gates, 1917; Markman, 1981). Studies of good and poor learners (e.g., those who are able to solve problems vs. those who are not) reinforce the efficacy of activeness in learning: Better students extend what they learn, fill in gaps in what is presented, challenge what is presented, and question and test their own understanding of what they are learning (Bransford, Stein, Shelton, & Owings, 1982; Chi, Bassok, Lewis, Reimann, & Glaser, 1989).

Instruction that engages students in a passive manner is less likely to engender sound learning and knowledge that will be usable by the students than instruction that engages students actively.

Principle 7. Engage students in an active way. Students should be encouraged to manipulate and use the knowledge they are acquiring.

Purely Abstracted Knowledge Versus the Centrality of Cases

A major goal of the kind of instruction we propose is to promote understanding of important conceptual knowledge in such a way that it can be used in analyzing and working with realistic problems, for example, medical patient cases in the domain of biomedicine. It has been claimed that knowledge and skills of reasoning are highly intertwined. Reasoning is not a process separate from knowledge; instead, it is highly dependent on and intertwined with knowledge. Students' development of reasoning skills in a domain is most successful when these skills are tightly coupled with the manipulation and use of subject-matter content from that domain (Anderson, 1982; Barrows, 1983; Glaser, 1984; Wason & Johnson-Laird, 1972). In addition, there is a growing body of evidence that knowledge is in many ways bound to the contexts in which it is learned; that is, knowledge is more readily available for later use if the settings, cognitive processes, and goals active at the time knowledge needs to be used resemble those that were active when knowledge was acquired (e.g., Anderson, Farrell, & Sauers, 1984; Baddeley, 1982; Lave, 1988; Ross, 1987, 1989; Tulving & Thomson, 1973). Considerations such as these argue that conceptual knowledge should be acquired in close coupling with application and use, in the kinds of situations (cases of application) that will ultimately demand attention (cf. Barrows, 1983; Brown, Collins, & Duguid, 1989). This issue goes to the heart of what knowledge is—whether knowledge is something external from and engaged in use or whether it is something most appropriately thought of as a tool, constructed in the interaction between a mind and situations calling for action (Brown et al., 1989).

However, beyond such considerations, there is another reason why the use of cases should be central in learning complex material when the goal is knowledge application. This has to do with the ill-structuredness of conceptual knowledge in its relationship to instances of realistic application (Feltovich et al., in press; Spiro et al., 1988). As discussed earlier, an ill-structured domain is one in which many concepts, in interaction, are pertinent to an instance or case of knowledge application, and different patterns of concepts might be relevant across cases that appear to be alike or that are categorized as being alike (as in cases of, for instance, hypertension—see section, "The problem of over-simplification: Misconceptions resulting from reductions of complexity"). In an ill-structured domain, the guidance that abstractions and principles can provide for facilitating understanding and determining appropriate action is reduced. This is partly because there is likely to be great variability from case to case in the conceptual elements that will be relevant and in the patterns of combination among these. Single, general principles or concepts will not be sufficient to capture the workings of a case, and there will be variability across cases in the ways that any concept will be used and applied. Concepts whose uses vary greatly across contexts must be tailored to the particulars of application environments. Furthermore, it will be difficult to recognize from the apparent features of a case which elements of conceptual knowledge will be germane, because cases that appear similar may embody different elements of conceptual knowledge, and cases that appear different may embody common conceptual elements. When applications of a concept have such a complex and irregular distribution, it becomes impossible to specify, a priori, case features that should trigger the use of that concept. In such a situation, greater weight must be placed on examining the *family resemblance* (Wittgenstein, 1953) between a new case that is encountered and past cases that embody various sets of concepts.

This discussion is not intended to suggest that conceptual, abstracted knowledge is unimportant in ill-structured domains. Rather, it is to emphasize that when the linkage between conceptual knowledge and cases of application is complex and irregular, the role of abstract knowledge must be increasingly supplemented with and intertwined with elements of case-centered reasoning. The need for embedding conceptual learning within cases of application, while always important, is accentuated.

Principle 8. Couple cases of knowledge application to the learning of conceptual knowledge. Accentuate patterns of concepts involved in cases and their interactions, the variability of cases involving similar concepts, the similarity of cases embodying different concepts, and so forth.

Precompiled Schemas Versus Knowledge Assembly and the Noncompartmentalization of Knowledge

The irregularity of conceptual patterns across cases in an ill-structured domain makes it less likely that large-scale, preassembled structures of knowledge can be usefully imported for understanding and working with cases. Such intact structures assume routinizability in the domains where they apply. By definition, there is no routine in an ill-structured domain. Therefore, prepackaged "common denominator" structures will miss too much of the variability across cases. Ill-structuredness implies kinds of complexity and irregularity that are

not compatible with gross prepackaging of knowledge and interpretive structures. Large, rigid structures are less useful than the ability to assemble and
flexibly recombine smaller units of knowledge. In understanding a new case,
many previous cases, parts of these cases (a new case may be "kind of like
this old one, kind of like that old one"), and diverse pieces of conceptual
knowledge may be helpful.

To support this ability for flexible and adaptive assembly, both conceptual
knowledge and cases should not be compartmentalized. Concepts should be interrelated in diverse ways and not isolated in separate "chapters," and cases
(as well as parts of cases) should be addressed in relation to other cases. When
it cannot be clear in advance what knowledge will be needed or helpful—and
in what patterns of combination—flexibility in response is aided by multiple systems of connections among cases and concepts, cast along multiple conceptual
and clinical dimensions (Spiro et al., 1988). The larger the repertoire of this
kind of connected case and conceptual knowledge available, the greater the support for adaptive knowledge assembly it should provide.

Principle 9. Utilize numerous cases in instruction, including small cases and
parts of cases that convey important lessons.

Principle 10. Emphasize relationships among cases and between cases and
concepts. Model for students the ways that conceptual knowledge is assembled from different sources to *fit* the needs of a new case. Contrast this with
the inappropriate retrieval of prepackaged conceptual prescriptions for thought
and action.

Surface Versus Rich Structural Indexing and Categorization: The Role of Multipurposing and Multiple Perspectives

Having to use knowledge to accomplish goals, to carry out tasks, appears
to elicit and accentuate structural relationships and lead to indexing and categorization schemes characteristic of expertise. In this regard, a phenomenon has
been observed in such diverse areas as maturation (Carey, 1985), the use of
analogy (Gentner, 1988), *reminding,* that is, the circumstance in which one thing
reminds a person of something else (Ross, 1989), problem solving (Chi, Feltovich, & Glaser, 1981), and medical diagnosis (Feltovich, Johnson, Moller, &
Swanson, 1984). What has been observed is that people with little experience
working within a content domain notice, classify by, and have their actions driven
by apparent and superficial ("surface") features of situations. In contrast, with
greater experience, noticing, categorization, and the basis for action come
progressively to be driven by more covert, relational characteristics of situations ("deep" structures), including operative principles and concepts. For example, novice physics problem solvers see and solve problems alike that contain
the same kind of objects (e.g., pulleys), while experts classify and solve problems

alike that embody the same principles of physics (e.g., principles of energy), even though the problems may appear very different on the surface (Chi et al., 1981). This change from overt, surface feature orientations to a focus on complex embedded relational structures has been termed the *relational shift* (Gentner, 1988, 1989). A growing interpretation of the relational shift is that surface features are in some sense easier to "see" in a situation (e.g., a problem) than relational structure, and that it is in working with material to achieve purposes, to do something with it, that relations and relational structure are made more salient and important; in addition, different perspectives and purposes accentuate different aspects of situations as germane (cf. Anderson & Pichert, 1978; Brown, 1989; Bransford, Franks, Vye, & Sherwood, 1989).

Rich, relational indexing schemes (for accessing knowledge), categorization schemes, and patterns of action are constructed from a perspective, in the course of use, tailored to purposes (e.g., the need to accomplish a task, or to evaluate a situation, or to teach). In ill-structured domains, and especially in biomedicine, where the linkage between surface features of cases and applicable concepts is irregular and rich, relational indexing and categorizations are not only particularly important, but also particularly difficult for the learner to construct. Surface orientations will often fail not only because, for example, cases that appear similar may involve different patterns of concepts and concepts applied in different ways, but also because many concepts are likely to be pertinent to any case of application. This is different from a more well-structured domain like physics (at least classroom physics), where indexing of relevant knowledge, classification of problems, and problem solutions can, for the expert, all be organized usefully around a handful of concepts (Chi et al., 1981).

Biomedicine, as an ill-structured domain, is particularly sensitive to changes in perspective and goal. The concepts that are relevant and the uses of these concepts may change, for instance, depending on whether a medical case is being addressed to understand its current state or to project its future course. The adaptability of indexing and categorization necessary in biomedicine is reflected in the indexing systems and categorical structures used by medical experts. These are characterized by multiple, redundant, and nonhierarchical (overlapping, latticelike) systems of knowledge organization, tailored to situations of use (e.g., Clancey, 1989; Feltovich et al., 1984).

Instruction that emphasizes limited perspectives on material and that encourages students to represent, classify, and use materials in only a small number of ways will not prepare them for the flexible application of knowledge across diverse and irregular new situations. "Knowledge that will be used in many ways has to be learned, represented, and *tried out* (in application) in many ways" (Spiro et al., 1988).

Principle 11. Encourage the adoption of multiple perspectives, and the use and representation of knowledge in multiple ways. "Revisit" cases and concepts, from different useful points of view, and for the purpose of achieving different useful kinds of goals.

Promoting Robust Knowledge and Overcoming Lack of Retention

The problem of forgetting or lack of retention of knowledge, if not more serious in biomedicine and medical education than in other fields, has probably had more attention directed to it in these areas than it has had elsewhere. This is because medical education has traditionally had separated "basic science" and clinical parts, with the basic-science, conceptual part occurring in the early years of the curriculum before clinical training begins. The question of what from the basic sciences is retained by students for use in clinical training, and, in fact, what of it is useful and how, has been a continuing concern of medical education. More often than not, studies of the retention of basic science material by students in the later years of medical school have shown rather dismal results (e.g., Levine & Forman, 1973).

This issue of retention is not a simple one, as it involves consideration of the different ways in which having retained knowledge is measured, differences in the kinds of knowledge under consideration in different studies, how long after acquisition (learning) retention is measured, and fundamental notions about what the nature of learning is (for example, whether it makes any sense to say that at some point a body of knowledge was acquired, as though this were some kind of discrete and finalized event, and that this acquired body of knowledge is at some later time retained, or recollectable). Issues such as these involved in thinking about long-term retention are not addressed in detail in this chapter. Instead, we point to the conclusions of a major study of the long-term retention of knowledge and skills, generalizing somewhat over the qualifications and conditionalities expressed there (Farr, 1987).

Knowledge and skills, especially complex knowledge and skills, appear to be better retained when conditions of the following sort hold (Farr, 1987);

1. When material at the time of acquisition is processed deeply, embellished, and connected to and integrated with other knowledge—in general, when knowledge is not compartmentalized, but is richly structured and indexed.
2. When complex material is "understood," rather than learned by rote: "When concepts, principles, and rules complement or supplement teaching of rote knowledge or facts" (Farr, 1987).
3. When, and to the extent that, conditions of training and learning resemble those in which the learned knowledge and skill will be applied. (Notice that this condition for retention is made more complicated in ill-structured domains, where there are special demands for knowledge transfer that

result from the likely variability between conditions of initial learning and later use. This accentuates the need for using multiple cases, multiple perspectives, and multiple goals for knowledge use in the course of learning in ill-structured domains. This will help to promote both retention and transfer.)

Considerations such as those just listed can be recognized as being interwoven throughout the design principles discussed earlier in regard to promoting correct and usable knowledge. Hence, in addition to the functions of facilitating correct and usable knowledge, we would expect instruction that is in conformance with our principles of design to lead also to respectable retention of complex knowledge and skills.

GENERAL GUIDELINES FOR TESTING WHEN DEEP CONCEPTUAL UNDERSTANDING AND KNOWLEDGE APPLICATION ARE GOALS

So far, we have discussed a paradigm for conceptual understanding that: (a) embodies a reconceptualization of the goals of understanding for advanced students; (b) recognizes that those goals are often not accomplished; and (c) suggests that their attainment requires ways of thinking that are in large measure antithetical to cognitive approaches that are appropriate for the earlier, less demanding educational goals. Drawing upon the kinds of deficiencies in understanding that we have observed among advanced students, we have proposed a set of guidelines for instruction when sound and flexibly useful understanding of complex material is a goal. Given the acknowledged influence of the testing process on instructional practices and on students' approaches to learning, the goals and practices of instruction and testing must be in conformance if educational objectives are to be attained (Frederiksen, 1984).

In this section we outline some principles for testing in support of the goals of advanced knowledge acquisition. What we propose for testing has two major motivations. The first stems from the goals of advanced knowledge acquisition themselves—that students should understand complex material accurately and deeply, including the ability to use this understanding in the accomplishment of substantial tasks. If we want students to understand deeply, we must test for deep understanding. If we want students to be able to apply knowledge, we must test for substantial knowledge application. The second motivation comes from the deficiencies in understanding and knowledge application we have observed in advanced students. Testing for understanding of complex material will benefit from knowing where understanding is likely to break down. In addition to outlining the kind of testing we believe is needed, we also give some examples of the kinds of forms such assessment might take.

Testing That Is Focused Both Toward Failures of Understanding and the Desired Goals of Advanced Knowledge Acquisition

Tests of understanding should have a substantial focus on likely points of comprehension failure, of the sort we have discussed earlier in the chapter (see section on "The problem of oversimplification: Misconceptions resulting from reductions of complexity"). Tests should be constructed that specifically target elements of complexity and concomitant potential failure, in the same way that these provide focus for instruction. At the same time, testing should promote desired cognitive goals for students, that is, sound and useful understanding. Analogues in testing of the principles of instruction discussed in the last section include the following:

- *Misconception undermining* (instructional principles 1 and 2): Test items should be crafted to address known misconceptions with regard to a body of subject matter. This pertains not only to subject matter content itself but also to known reductive ways of thinking related to subject matter— for example, treating continuous attributes and processes as discrete. Such items can have both diagnostic value, eliciting the existence of misconceptions, and pedagogical value for correcting them.

  Example: Requiring students to discuss or predict the mechanisms of action of beta-blocking drugs, drugs that actually raise vascular resistance but are used therapeutically to reduce blood pressure, can serve both to diagnose and emend the widely held misconception that opposition to blood flow (cardiovascular impedance) is entirely resistance based.

- *Noticing differences* (instructional principle 1): Items should allow for detection of comprehension failures that result from presuming too much similarity among entities (e.g., recognizing the limitations of analogies and prototype examples).

  Example: Since blood viscosity and blood density are different and contribute differently to opposition to blood flow (but are treated by some students as being the same), items that require students to predict or discuss the effects on blood pressure of changes to density and/or viscosity can test for lack of discrimination and can force the desired discrimination.

- *Conceptual and instructional integration* (instructional principles 3 and 4): Test items should have answers that require the integration of several component concepts or theories, especially when they are likely to have been treated separately in acquisition. Test items should have answers that require the integration of information on the same concept or theory that was likely to have been presented in distantly nonadjacent sections or "chapters" of instruction at the time of learning.

Example: The processes of hypertrophic adaptation, by which muscle responds to abnormal levels of stress, and the processes of diminished pumping ability characteristic of congestive heart failure are often treated separately in instruction and are not well integrated by students, partly contributing to a widely held misconception about the fundamental basis of heart failure (Coulson et al., 1989). Test items that focused on the time-course development of heart failure and its stages (rather than, say, any particular state of it)—items that involve changes in the disease, hypertrophic adaptations to these, further changes, further adaptations, and so forth—would require conceptual integration of the two kinds of processes for successful completion and could assess the extent of this integration in students.

• *Integration of analogies, conceptual aids, and prototype examples* (instructional principle 5): Test items should require assembling from acquisition materials an appropriate subset of presented analogies, examples, or conceptual aids that are relevant to a test question, and further should require using only the relevant parts of those analogies and examples.

Example: A group of analogies relevant to muscle cell operation, such as oarsmen in a scull (related to the "cross bridge theory" of muscle fiber function, which describes the means by which contractile force is produced in a fiber), a turnbuckle (related to the "sliding filament theory," which describes the movement of structures of the fiber in relation to each other), or fingercuffs (which relates to the action of collagen in providing resistance to stretch of muscle fibers and which, because of a set of anatomical and functional differences between skeletal and cardiac muscle, is more pertinent in cardiac muscle), could be presented and the student asked to choose which of two examples, such as a cardiac papillary muscle and a skeletal sartorius muscle, is best represented by the set and to explain why.

• *Reorganization* (instructional principles 5 and 11): Information that was presented in one way should be able to be appropriately reassembled in other ways. For instance, the same example may fit into different organizational compartments (multiple sortings of examples). Information that was grouped together for purposes of exposition in acquisition should be able to be regrouped by the student for newly prescribed purposes.

Example: The following four case descriptions are all instances where implications involving the Law of LaPlace are important but where each represents a problem of an entirely different origin and course of development:

1. A relatively benign mitral valve prolapse (partial failure of the input valve of the left ventricle) in a young woman.

2. A pediatric case of ventricular septal defect (an abnormal hole connecting the lower ventricular chambers of the heart).

3. A ventricular aneurysm (a bulging of the heart wall due to weakened or diseased heart muscle) in a postinfarction (after a "heart attack") old man.

4. A disecting aortic aneurysm (a bulging of the wall of the body's main artery rather like a bicycle innertube bulging through a split in the tire) in a middle-aged man.

A test item could require students to detect the unifying principle of the Law of LaPlace in the group of different cardiac pathologies, when the principle itself was probably learned in the context of the physiology of the lung (or, perhaps, in the context of volume overload hypertrophy and heart failure, contexts rather different from those addressed by the test item). This would require the student to decontextualize the principle from its original acquisition setting and to reconstrue it for new purposes.

- *Multiple perspectives and context sensitivity* (instructional principle 11): Tests should allow for different correct "main idea" answers depending on different perspectives (where the student is required to adopt different perspectives from which to answer).

    Example: The same (medical) clinical case, when addressed from different perspectives such as diagnosis (determination of what is wrong), treatment (trying to ameliorate the condition), prognosis (predicting how the medical condition will progress—untreated and under different courses of treatment), or the monitoring of intermediate efficacy of treatment (determination of whether treatment is on course toward the desired end) can implicate different combinations of biomedical concepts as important for each purpose, or the same concepts used in a somewhat different way. Students can be required to address a case from different points of view such as these, identifying the biomedical concepts relevant in each instance, and describing how they are applicable and what they imply.

- *Underlying causal mechanisms* (instructional principles 7 and 11): Besides being able to answer questions about what is happening in a presented situation, the student should also be able to determine why it is happening. For instance, for natural science phenomena, students who have comprehended material well should be able to go beyond mere description to answer questions involving prediction (what would happen next), postdiction (specifying what came before), determination of inconsistencies in descriptions (critique), experimentation (determining what information is missing and how conditions might be arranged to acquire it), and, especially, causal reasoning about the mechanisms by which a part of a situation is affecting other parts (Forbus, 1985).

    Example: Two patients in heart failure could be described with identical current hemodynamics, that is, the same blood pressures, the same cardiac outputs, the same peripheral pulses, and so forth. One is an instance of old heart failure, reemerging, where the patient had previously been controlled with digitalis and diuretics. The other is an instance of new heart failure appearing in a hypertensive patient whose condition had been managed previously with the drug propranalol (a beta blocker). The student would be required to compare and contrast the current physiological states of the patients, the likely natural histories that eventuated in these states, and the projections of future course (prognoses), giving causal justifications based on the physiological, pharmacological, and pathological concepts and principles pertinent to these situations.

- *Problem solving, decision making, and educated guessing* (instructional principles 7, 8, and 9): Test the ability to apply conceptual knowledge to actual cases or examples that are relevant to the concept or set of concepts being tested (knowledge into practice).

    Example: A set of clinical cases of "hypertension," embodying different ultimate physiological sources for the hypertension and hence engaging different patterns of concepts related to cardiovascular impedance (e.g., heart rate, blood volume, and inertial reactance in one case; hormonal constriction of the vasculature and resistance in another) can test students' ability to recognize the applicability of and to apply concepts associated with impedance. Attention is paid to students' prescriptions for treatment in the different cases, since for individuals with correct understanding of impedance treatments should be differentially sensitive to the different patterns of applicable concepts across the cases.

- *Scaffolding for subsequent comprehension and transfer* (instructional principles 7 and 11): Examine the extent to which current understanding provides a scaffolding for comprehension of new material on the same topic ("new" knowledge as "prior" knowledge for new learning—see the last subsection of this section). Examine the extent to which current understanding supports the analysis of situations and the solution of problems not addressed in instruction.

    Example: Students' understanding of the principles governing the cardiovascular system can be assessed by requiring them to construct a critique of a journal article advancing a new theory of the pumping action of the heart in the propulsion of blood. Attention is directed at the accuracy and creativity of students' use of cardiovascular principles and concepts in this critique.

    Example: Understanding of the principles of cardiovascular impedance can be tested by requiring students to apply them to airflow in the lungs, where they are directly applicable (but where the pattern of importance of concepts is somewhat different), or to any system in which anything flows, for example, information flow in an electronic mail system.

Some General Characteristics of Tests
of Complex Conceptual Understanding

The implementation of these principles of testing requires that test instruments have certain general characteristics and be used and interpreted certain ways. Some of these are discussed in this section.

First, assessing comprehension of complex material will require long enough "stems" to build the requisite dimensions of complexity (in congruence with instructional principle 6). Tests that will allow for targeted assessments of the kind just discussed (e.g., integration across nonadjacent sections/chapters of instructional material; interaction of multiple concepts relevant to the same topic; and so on) will unavoidably have to be much longer than is typical of common tests. (In medical education, for example, test "stems" might take the form of simulations of entire medical patient cases [Norman, Muzzin, Williams, & Swanson, 1985], and students may be required to deal appropriately with such cases in order to become physicians [Barrows, Williams, & Moy, 1987].) Complexity takes time to develop in a test "item." The price of shorter test items is an absence of just those properties in tests that are most likely to cause (and hence reveal) comprehension failure and that may, therefore, be most diagnostic of success in advanced knowledge acquisition.

Second, testing for understanding should be viewed as a montage of partially overlapping "snapshots." An important implication of the view of the goals of understanding as complex, multiply interconnected, multiperspectival, and so on is that testing must involve multiple approaches—a single pass of evaluation will elicit only a subset of the facets of understanding that are to be demonstrated. Thus, with a limited testing scope, it is possible for students who have only partial comprehension to have their understanding greatly overestimated. More importantly, a restricted scope of assessment will miss altogether the complex interrelationships that are at the heart of advanced understanding. Adequacy of understanding must be revealed by assembling a perspicuous montage from a series of partially overlapping assessment snapshots for the same material—no single "picture" (from a single assessment pass) will be comprehensive enough.

It should be restated that singular approaches are also likely to be inadequate, or even misleading, in instruction. For complex material, in both testing and instruction, it seems prudent not to do anything one way. Singular approaches are likely to be detrimental because they: (a) do not provide a wide enough "lens" on the numerous aspects of the material to be taught or understood, (b) are likely to miss the interconnectedness of the target material with other related material, and (c) reinforce a misleading orientation toward complex material, by suggesting that it is simpler than it really is.

Finally, testing for understanding partly requires testing the readiness of current understanding to serve as input to new understanding and to knowledge application. A somewhat paradoxical aspect of the paradigm we are describing is that the adequacy of the outcome of understanding must be determined in part by how well this output can be used subsequently as input (background knowledge) for later comprehension. A student usefully understands a concept or set of concepts when he or she is able to apply that understanding to support comprehension of new material on the same, or perhaps even a distantly related (far transfer) topic. In other words, our earlier points concerning knowledge output (the goals of understanding for advanced learners) and knowledge input (e.g., schema assembly for subsequent comprehension) cannot be fully separated. And testing must reflect this interdependency.

So, to have adequately understood, a learner must have done more than form a coherent representation of the material and reproduce it for a test: The student must have learned from the material in such a manner that what was learned will be flexibly usable in future comprehension situations.

A NOTE ON SELECTIVITY IN INSTRUCTION AND TESTING

It is often said that a typical medical school curriculum includes thousands of concepts (and this is likely true of other substantial curricula as well). The curriculum is dense and the pace is fast. There are, then, considerable pressures on both teachers and learners to move through material quickly, and simplification in both testing and instruction may just be part of a survival strategy. A curricular stance that values "coverage" is prevalent: "What will some future medical residency director think if one of our students has not even heard of (some topic)?" Yet, there are fundamental concepts that should be understood, and from our investigations it appears that achieving this takes considerable time and focused effort. One thing that would be helpful is a method for prioritizing curricular content and for linking educational methods to the cognitive goals held for students. If instruction and testing for deep understanding require intense, directed effort, as appears to be the case, then it is clear that achieving and assessing the achievement of solid and flexibly applicable understanding of thousands of concepts is an impossible goal.

First of all, it should be said that not everything in a curriculum needs to be understood at the same level of depth. In some areas it is sufficient to meet the challenge that "the resident should have at least heard" about some item of curricular content, in which case simple forms of instruction and testing (e.g., overview lectures, hand-out lists, and tests of recall or recognition) should suffice for the purpose. It is also true that not all concepts are difficult to understand. They may, for example, be well structured, relatively self-contained, congruent with intuition, and/or amenable to the reductive tendencies in cognition that we have described. In such cases, standard means of learning and testing are, again, likely to be adequate. But, how is curricular focus to be achieved for those concepts that are truly important, difficult, and hence worthy of substantial investment in testing and instruction?

Our laboratory has employed a method, designed originally to guide us in the selection of topics for our investigations of conceptual understanding, that has also yielded benefit for curricular design and focus. This method has involved three major parts, as follows.

Consultation with People Actively Involved with the Topics. In our case, interviews were conducted with medical school teachers, medical students, and medical practitioners from within our medical school and the local community to gain a first set of ideas about biomedical concepts that are important for practicing medicine and that are also chronically difficult for students to learn, understand, and apply. The key idea was to gain guidance for topics to be studied in laboratory investigation from those who routinely address these topics in their teaching or practice.

Broad Follow-Up Surveying. Based on these interviews, a more formal survey was developed and distributed to a sample of medical teaching faculty at all medical schools in the United States and Canada. The survey addressed the same issues that were addressed in the interviews and yielded a target list of biomedical concepts that medical school teachers (who were in most instances also medical practitioners) considered both important to practicing medicine and difficult for students to learn well (Dawson-Saunders et al., 1990).

Concept Analysis to Identify Sources of Difficulty, and Associated Laboratory Studies. When teachers claim that an idea is difficult to master, this does not necessarily make clear why the material is difficult or what might be done to help students understand better. Furthermore, it may be that concepts teachers perceive to be relatively tractable are, in fact, rather difficult. Our research has involved an ongoing attempt to identify sources of conceptual difficulty and, in addition, to predict the circumstances under which misconceptions will be strongly held. A scheme of analysis for this purpose (called the *Conceptual Stability Scheme,* which shares many of the features of concept analysis outlined earlier in this chapter in the section titled ''Notes on the Nature of Conceptual Difficulty: Structure and Process Issues'') has been under development and is yet another tool for providing curricular focus, by providing greater precision in identifying topics likely to require special attention. Development of this scheme has been a cyclic endeavor, in which the scheme for analyzing and predicting sources of conceptual difficulty is revised, based on the results of empirical studies of students' understanding of selected concepts, and the revised scheme, in turn, is used to guide further laboratory investigation (and so on).

Laboratory work involving medical students, medical practitioners, and using selected concepts from the list obtained from the survey has been conducted to determine why particular concepts are hard, and to determine particular impediments to understanding and the systematic misconceptions individuals acquire. This work involves detailed conceptual screening instruments associated with a target concept (and its set of highly interrelated concepts), as well as directed laboratory tasks used as more precise follow-ups to these initial conceptual probes (Feltovich et al., 1989).

Such an overall program for addressing curricular selectivity, which is sensitive to guidance from practicing professionals in the domain of their everyday work, but which is augmented by laboratory investigation, yields focus for educational effort. It also provides insights into impediments to the understanding of concepts judged to be important.

CONCLUSION

In this chapter we have proposed a set of guidelines for learning and testing in advanced knowledge acquisition, emphasizing particularly those subject matter areas where material is complex and difficult, and deep understanding is valued. The methods we propose are motivated in part by research we have conducted on advanced students' understanding of complex material, which has revealed consistent patterns of deficiency in understanding, and in part by failures of the general educational system that are more widely recognized. We have argued that many of the problems we perceive stem from not adequately addressing the real complexity of material in testing and instruction, or from not instructing and testing in ways commensurate with complex learning goals (e.g., promoting the ability for flexible knowledge use and transfer). Indeed, we have argued that many common practices of education that involve simplification, especially as those interact with a cognitive tendency to simplify, may go beyond not addressing complexity in material to actually undermining the development of the ability to master complicated (difficult, ill-structured, etc.) topics. Hence, the unifying theme for the methods of instruction and testing we propose is that they confront complexity head on—in complicated subject matter and in sophisticated goals for the learner.

In turn, the approaches we advocate are resource intensive and probably cannot be applied uniformly or universally across the many concepts and topics of a curriculum. Hence, we have discussed the need for setting priorities in curricula and have outlined a method for achieving this kind of selectivity.

Even with selective focus, it may be infeasible (or at least impractical) to implement within the day-to-day educational process alone the kind of program for instruction and assessment that we have outlined in this chapter (involving such things as polling to identify likely areas of curricular difficulty, extensive diagnostic evaluation to identify impediments to understanding among these topics, intensive work with students to identify systematic types of error and misconception that they acquire, and so forth). What *is* possible, especially in schools with a relatively restricted and coherent focus (such as schools of professional education), is the development of a system in which pertinent basic cognitive research and the ongoing educational process are tightly coupled. The research program, which can tolerate the resource investment, can carry out the background investigation for instruction and testing, creating information and materials for classroom use. The classroom, in turn, provides direction and feedback for the research endeavor. On another plane, communities of researchers and educators can share the agenda of developing such a system, with different medical education research teams, for instance, addressing the particular problems associated with students' learning and understanding of different biomedical science concepts important to the practice of medicine (e.g., Patel, Kaufman, & Magder, 1991).

ACKNOWLEDGMENTS

The research reported in this chapter was supported in part by the Office of Naval Research, Cognitive Science Division (N00014-88-K-0077), the Basic Research Office of the Army Research Institute (MDA903-86-K-0443), and the Office of Educational Research and Improvement (OEG0087-C1001). The chapter does not necessarily reflect the views of these agencies. Parts of the chapter were presented at the American College Testing Program, January, 1988, and at the Annual Meeting of the American Education Research Association, April, 1988. Joan Feltovich read several drafts of the paper and made many useful suggestions.

REFERENCES

Anderson, J. R. (1982). Acquisition of cognitive skill. *Psychological Review, 18,* 396–406.
Anderson, J. R., Farrell, R., & Sauers, R. (1984). Learning to program in LISP. *Cognitive Science, 8,* 87–129.
Anderson, R. C., & Pichert, J. W. (1978). Recall of previously unrecallable information following a shift in perspective. *Journal of Verbal Learning and Verbal Behavior, 17,* 1–12.
Anderson, J. R., & Reder, L. M. (1979). An elaborative processing explanation of depth of processing. In L. S. Cermak & F. I. M. Craik (Eds.), *Levels of processing in human memory* (pp. 385–403). Hillsdale, NJ: Lawrence Erlbaum Associates.
Baddeley, A. D. (1982). Domains of recollection. *Psychological Review, 89,* 708–729.
Barrows, H. S. (1983). Problem-based, self-directed learning. *Journal of the American Medical Association, 250,* 3077–3080.
Barrows, H. S., Williams, R. G., & Moy, R. H. (1978). A comprehensive performance-based assessment of fourth-year students' clinical skills. *Journal of Medical Education, 62,* 805–809.
Bartlett, F. C. (1932). *Remembering.* Cambridge, UK: Cambridge University Press.

Bransford, J. D., & Franks, J. J. (1972). The abstraction of linguistic ideas. *Cognitive Psychology,* *2,* 331–350.

Bransford, J. D., Franks, J. J., Vye, N. J., & Sherwood, R. D. (1989). New approaches to instruction: Because wisdom can't be told. In S. Vosniadou & A. Ortony (Eds.), *Similarity and analogical reasoning* (pp. 470–497). Cambridge, UK: Cambridge University Press.

Bransford, J. D., Stein, B. S., Shelton, T. S., & Owings, R. A. (1982). Cognition and adaptation: The importance of learning to learn. In J. Harvey (Ed.), *Cognition, social behavior, and the environment* (pp. 93–110). Hillsdale, NJ: Lawrence Erlbaum Associates.

Brown, A. L. (1989). Analogical learning and transfer: What develops? In S. Vosniadou & A. Ortony (Eds.), *Similarity and analogical reasoning* (pp. 369–412). Cambridge, UK: Cambridge University Press.

Brown, J. S., & Burton, R. (1978). Diagnostic models for procedural bugs in basic mathematical skills. *Cognitive Science, 2,* 155–192.

Brown, J. S., Collins, A., & Duguid, P. (1989). Situated cognition and the culture of learning. *Educational Researcher, 18,* 32–42.

Bruner, J. S. (1963). *The process of education.* Cambridge, MA: Harvard University Press.

Burstein, M. H. (1985). *Learning by reasoning from multiple analogies.* Unpublished doctoral dissertation, Yale University, New Haven, CT.

Burstein, M. H., & Adelson, B. (1990). Issues for a theory of analogical learning. In R. Freedle (Ed.), *Artificial intelligence and the future of testing* (pp. 137–172). Hillsdale, NJ: Lawrence Erlbaum Associates.

Caramazza, A., McCloskey, M., & Green, B. F. (1981). Naive beliefs in sophisticated subjects: Misconceptions about trajectories of objects. *Cognition, 9,* 193–215.

Carey, S. (1985). Are children fundamentally different kinds of thinkers than adults? In S. F. Chipman, J. W. Segal, & R. Glaser (Eds.), *Thinking and learning skills: Research and open questions* (Vol. 2, pp. 485–517). Hillsdale, NJ: Lawrence Erlbaum Associates.

Chi, M. T. H., Bassok, M., Lewis, R., Reimann, P., & Glaser, R. (1989). Self-explanation: How students study and use examples in learning to solve problems. *Cognitive Science, 13,* 145–182.

Chi, M. T. H., Feltovich, P. J., & Glaser, R. (1981). Categorization and representation of physics problems by experts and novices. *Cognitive Science, 5,* 121–152.

Chiesi, H. L., Spilich, G. J., & Voss, J. F. (1979). Acquisition of domain-related information in relation to high and low domain knowledge. *Journal of Verbal Learning and Verbal Behavior, 18,* 257–273.

Clancey, W. J. (1989). Acquiring, representing, and evaluating a competence model of diagnostic strategy. In M. T. H. Chi, R. Glaser, & M. Farr (Eds.), *The nature of expertise* (pp. 343–418). Hillsdale, NJ: Lawrence Erlbaum Associates.

Collins, A. M., & Gentner, D. (1983). Multiple models of evaporation processes. In *Proceedings of the Fifth Annual Conference of the Cognitive Science Society,* Rochester, NY.

Coulson, R. L., Feltovich, P. J., & Spiro, R. J. (1989). Foundations of a misunderstanding of the ultrastructural basis of myocardial failure: A reciprocation network of oversimplifications. *Journal of Medicine and Philosophy, 14,* 109–146.

Dawson-Saunders, B., Feltovich, P. J., Coulson, R. L., & Steward, D. (1990). A survey of medical school teachers to identify basic biomedical concepts medical students should understand. *Academic Medicine, 7,* 448–454.

Dember, W. N. (1991). Cognition, motivation, and emotion: Ideology revisited. In R. R. Hoffman & D. Palermo (Eds.), *Cognition and the symbolic processes* (pp. 153–162). Hillsdale, NJ: Lawrence Erlbaum Associates.

diSessa, A. A. (1983). Phenomenology and the evolution of intuition. In D. Gentner & A. L. Stevens (Eds.), *Mental models* (pp. 15–34). Hillsdale, NJ: Lawrence Erlbaum Associates.

Farr, M. J. (1987). *The long-term retention of knowledge and skills.* New York: Springer-Verlag.

Feltovich, P. J., Coulson, R. L., Spiro, R. J., & Dawson-Saunders, B. K. (in press). Knowledge application and transfer for complex tasks in ill-structured domains: Implications for instruction and testing in biomedicine. In D. Evans & V. Patel (Eds.), *Advanced models of cognition for medical training and practice.* New York: Springer-Verlag.

Feltovich, P. J., Spiro, R. J., & Coulson, R. L. (1989). The nature of conceptual understanding in biomedicine: The deep structure of complex ideas and the development of misconceptions. In D. Evans & V. Patel (Eds.), *Cognitive science in medicine: Biomedical modeling* (pp. 111–172). Cambridge, MA: MIT (Bradford) Press.

Feltovich, P. J., Johnson, P. E., Moller, J. H., & Swanson, D. B. (1984). LCS: The role and development of medical knowledge in diagnostic expertise. In W. J. Clancey & E. H. Shortliffe (Eds.), *Readings in medical artificial intelligence: The first decade* (pp. 275–319). Reading, MA: Addison-Wesley.

Fleming, M. & Chambers, B. (1983). Teacher-made tests: Windows on the classroom. In W. F. Hathaway (Ed.), *New directions for testing and measurement* (pp. 29–38). San Francisco, CA: Jossey-Bass.

Forbus, K. D. (1985). Qualitative process theory. In D. J. Bobrow (Ed.), *Qualitative reasoning about physical systems* (pp. 85–168). Cambridge, MA: MIT Press.

Frederiksen, J. R., & Collins, A. (1989). A systems approach to educational testing. *Educational Researcher, 18,* 27–32.

Frederiksen, N. (1984). The real test bias: Influences of testing on teaching and learning. *American Psychologist, 39,* 193–202.

Gates, A. I. (1917). Recitation as a factor in memorizing. *Archives of Psychology, 40,* 104.

Gelman, R., & Greeno, J. G. (1989). On the nature of competence: Principles for understanding in a domain. In L. B. Resnick (Ed.), *Knowing, learning, and instruction: Essays in honor of Robert Glaser* (pp. 125–186). Hillsdale, NJ: Lawrence Erlbaum Associates.

Gentner, D. (1988). Metaphor as structure-mapping: The relational shift. *Child Development, 59,* 47–59.

Gentner, D. (1989). The mechanisms of analogical learning. In S. Vosniadou & A. Ortony (Eds.), *Similarity and analogical reasoning* (pp. 199–241). Cambridge, UK: Cambridge University Press.

Gentner, D., & Gentner, D. R. (1983). Flowing waters and teeming crowds: Mental models of electricity. In D. Gentner & A. L. Stevens (Eds.), *Mental models* (pp. 99–130). Hillsdale, NJ: Lawrence Erlbaum Associates.

Glaser, R. (1984). Education and thinking: The role of knowledge. *American Psychologist, 39,* 93–104.

[GPEP] Panel on the General Professional Education of the Physician. (1984). *Physicians for the twenty-first century: The GPEP report.* Washington, DC: American Association of Medical Colleges.

Greeno, J. G. (1977). Process of understanding in problem solving. In N. J. Castellan, D. B. Pisoni, & G. R. Potts (Eds.), *Cognitive theory* (Vol. 2, pp. 43–83). Hillsdale, NJ: Lawrence Erlbaum Associates.

Halasz, F., & Moran, T. P. (1982). Analogy considered harmful. In *Proceedings of the Human Factors in Computer Systems Conference,* Gathersburg, MD.

Hayes, J. R. (1985). Three problems in teaching general skills. In S. F. Chipman, J. W. Segal, & R. Glaser (Eds.), *Thinking and learning skills: Research and open questions* (Vol. 2, pp. 391–405). Hillsdale, NJ: Lawrence Erlbaum Associates.

Kahneman, D., Slovic, P., & Tversky, A. (Eds.). (1982). *Judgment under uncertainty.* New York: Cambridge University Press.

Lave, J. (1988). *Cognition in practice.* Boston, MA: Cambridge.

Levine, H. G., & Forman, P. M. (1973). A study of retention of knowledge of neurosciences information. *Journal of Medical Education, 48,* 867–869.

Markman, E. M. (1981). Comprehension monitoring. In W. P. Dickson (Ed.), *Childrens' oral communication skills* (pp. 61–84). New York: Academic Press.

McCloskey, M. (1983). Naive theories of motion. In D. Gentner & A. L. Stevens (Eds.), *Mental models* (pp. 299–324). Hillsdale, NJ: Lawrence Erlbaum Associates.

Morgenstern, C. F., & Renner, J. W. (1984). Measuring thinking with standardized tests. *Journal of Research in Science Teaching, 21,* 639–648.

Myers, A. C., Feltovich, P. J., Coulson, R. L., Adami, J. F., & Spiro, R. J. (1990). Reductive biases in the reasoning of medical students: An investigation in the domain of acid-base balance. In B. Bender, R. J. Hiemstra, A. J. J. A. Scherbier, & R. P. Zwierstra (Eds.), *Teaching and assessing clinical competence* (pp. 155–160). Groningen, The Netherlands: BoekWerk Publications.

National Commission on Excellence in Education. (1983). *A nation at risk.* Washington, DC: U.S. Government Printing Office.

National Science Foundation. (1982). *Science and engineering education: Data and information.* Washington, DC: National Science Foundation.

Nickerson, R. S. (1989). New directions in educational assessment. *Educational Researcher, 18,* 3-7.

Norman, G. R., Muzzin, L. J., Williams, R. G., & Swanson, D. B. (1985). Simulations in health sciences education. *Journal of Instructional Development, 8,* 11-17.

Patel, V. L., Kaufman, D. R., & Magder, S. (1991). Causal explanation of complex physiological concepts by medical students. *International Journal of Science Education, 13*(2), 171-185.

Pepper, S. (1942). *World hypotheses.* Berkeley, CA: University of California Press.

Perkins, D. N., & Simmons, R. (1989). Patterns of misunderstanding: An integrative model for science, math, and programming. *Review of Educational Research, 58,* 303-326.

Porter, A. (1989). A curriculum out of balance: The case of elementary school mathematics. *Educational Researcher, 18,* 9-15.

Ross, B. H. (1987). This is like that: The use of earlier problems and the separation of similarity effects. *Journal of Experimental Psychology: Learning, Memory, and Cognition, 13,* 629-639.

Ross, B. H. (1989). Remindings in learning and instruction. In S. Vosniadou & A. Ortony (Eds.), *Similarity and analogical reasoning* (pp. 438-469). Cambridge, UK: Cambridge University Press.

Smolensky, P. (1986). Information processing in dynamical systems: Foundations of harmony theory. In J. L. McClelland, D. E. Rumelhart, & the PDP Research Group (Eds.), *Parallel distributed processing* (Vol. 2, pp. 194-281). Cambridge, MA: MIT (Bradford) Press.

Spiro, R. J. (1980). Constructive processes in prose comprehension and recall. In R. J. Spiro, B. C. Bruce, & W. F. Brewer (Eds.), *Theoretical issues in reading comprehension* (pp. 245-278). Hillsdale, NJ: Lawrence Erlbaum Associates.

Spiro, R. J., Coulson, R. L., Feltovich, P. J., & Anderson, D. K. (1988). Cognitive flexibility theory: Advanced knowledge acquisition in ill-structured domains. In *The tenth annual conference of the cognitive science society* (pp. 375-383). Hillsdale, NJ: Lawrence Erlbaum Associates.

Spiro, R. J., Feltovich, P. J., Coulson, R. L., & Anderson, D. K. (1989). Multiple analogies for complex concepts: Antidotes for analogy-induced misconception in advanced knowledge acquisition. In S. Vosniadou & A. Ortony (Eds.), *Similarity and analogical reasoning* (pp. 498-531). Cambridge, MA: Cambridge University Press.

Spiro, R. J., Feltovich, P. J., Jacobson, M., & Coulson, R. L. (1991). Cognitive flexibility, constructivism, and hypertext: Advanced knowledge acquisition in ill-structured domains. *Educational Technology, 31*(9), 22-25.

Spiro, R. J., Vispoel, W., Schmitz, J., Samarapungavan, A., & Boerger, A. (1987). Knowledge acquisition for application: Cognitive flexibility and transfer in complex content domains. In B. C. Britton (Ed.), *Executive control processes* (pp. 177-200). Hillsdale, NJ: Lawrence Erlbaum Associates.

Tulving, E., & Thomson, D. M. (1973). Encoding specificity and retrieval processes in episodic memory. *Psychological Review, 80,* 352-373.

Wason, P. C., & Johnson-Laird, P. N. (1972). *The psychology of deductive reasoning: Structure and content.* Cambridge, MA: Harvard University Press.

White, B. Y. (1984). Designing computer activities to help physics students understand Newton's laws of motion. *Cognition and Instruction, 1,* 69-108.

White, B. Y. (in press). ThinkerTools: Causal models, conceptual change, and science education. *Cognition and Instruction.*

Whitehead, A. N. (1929). *The aims of education.* New York: Macmillan.

Wimsatt, W. C. (1980). Reductionistic research strategies and their biases in the units of selection controversy. In T. Nickles (Ed.), *Scientific discovery: Case studies* (pp. 213-259). Dordrecht, Holland: D. Reidel.

Wittgenstein, L. (1953). *Philosophical investigations.* New York: Macmillan.

9

New Views of Student Learning: Implications for Educational Measurement

Geofferey N. Masters
Australian Council for Educational Research

Robert J. Mislevy
Educational Testing Service

Recent research in cognitive psychology has drawn attention to the important role that students' personal understandings and representations of subject matter play in the learning process. This chapter briefly reviews some of this research, and contrasts the kind of learning that results in an individual's changed conception or view of a phenomenon with the more passive, additive kind of learning assessed by most traditional achievement tests. To be consistent with a view of learning as an active, constructive process, educational tests are required that focus on key concepts in an area of learning, and that take into account the variety of types and levels of understanding that students have of those concepts. In these tests, scoring responses right and wrong is likely to be less appropriate than using students' answers to infer their levels of understanding. This will require not only imaginative new types of test items, but statistical models that permit inferences about students' understandings once their responses have been observed. Psychometric approaches are sketched to construct measures of achievement from such tests.

INTRODUCTION

Implicit in much of our current measurement theory and practice is a view of learners as passive absorbers of provided wisdom. Most items on standard achievement tests assess students' abilities to recall and apply facts and routines presented during instruction. Some require only the memorization of

detail; they seek evidence that students have absorbed factual details presented in class and are able to reproduce these on command. Other achievement
test items, although supposed to assess higher-level learning outcomes like
"comprehension" and "application," often require little more than the ability
to recall a formula (e.g., $s = v_0 t + \frac{1}{2} at^2$) and to make appropriate substitutions to arrive at a correct answer.

Test items of this type are consistent with a view of learning as a passive,
receptive process through which new facts and skills are added to a learner's
repertoire in much the same way as bricks might progressively be added to
a wall. The process is additive and incremental: Students with the highest levels of achievement in an area are those who have absorbed and can reproduce
the greatest numbers of facts and formulas. The practice of scoring answers
to items of this type either "right" or "wrong" is consistent with the view
that individual units of knowledge or skill are either present or absent in a learner at the time of testing. Under this approach, diagnosis is a simple matter of
identifying unexpected holes or gaps in a student's store of knowledge. These
are subareas of learning in which knowledge is "missing" and in which there
is a need for remedial teaching to fill a deficit.

This approach to the measurement of achievement may be appropriate for
some forms of learning—as when the learner's task is in fact to master a body
of factual material. In recent decades, however, significant advances have occurred in our understanding of the ways in which students learn. In particular,
there has been an increased awareness of the active, constructive nature of
most forms of human learning and of the important role that students' personal
conceptions and representations of subject matter play in the learning process.
Rather than being a passive process of absorbing new material as it is encountered, meaningful learning is increasingly being recognized as an active process
through which students construct their own interpretations, approaches, and
ways of viewing phenomena, and through which learners relate new information to their existing knowledge and understandings. Under this view of learning, the difference between beginning and advanced learners is seen not so much
as a difference in amount of factual knowledge (although this is usually an important aspect of competent performance), as a difference in the types of conceptions and understandings that students bring to a problem, and in the
strategies and approaches that they use.

Support for this view of learning can be found in recent studies in a number
of areas of investigation. In cognitive science, comparisons of novices and experts in various fields of learning show that expertise typically involves much
more than mastery of a body of facts: experts and novices usually have very
different ways of viewing phenomena and of representing and approaching
problems in a field (e.g., Chi, Feltovich, & Glaser, 1981, in physics; Chase &
Simon, 1973, in chess; Lesgold, Feltovich, Glaser, & Wang, 1981, in radiology; Voss, Greene, Post, & Penner, 1983, in social science). Expert–novice

studies suggest that the performances of beginning learners often can be understood in terms of the inappropriate or inefficient models that these learners have constructed for themselves.

Similar observations have been made in the field of science education (see Driver & Easley, 1978; Osborne & Wittrock, 1983; Posner, Strike, Hewson, & Gertzog, 1982). Research into students' science learning has drawn attention to the frequent mismatch between intuitive understandings that students bring to the classroom and the conceptual frameworks assumed by teachers. Caramazza, McCloskey, and Green (1981) observed that the scientific "principles" that students abstract from everyday experience are often strikingly at variance with the most fundamental physical laws. These misunderstandings can go undetected by teachers if correct answers to test questions depend only on superficial knowledge of formulas and formula manipulation techniques (Clement, 1982). There is evidence that students can succeed in high school and even college science courses while still maintaining many of their misconceptions and without acquiring an understanding of underlying principles (White & Horwitz, 1987).

Related work in Sweden (Dahlgren, 1984; Marton, 1981; Marton & Säljö, 1976) has used clinical interviews to explore the different understandings that students have of key principles and phenomena in a number of fields of learning. These interviews have revealed a range of student conceptions of each of the phenomena that the studies have explored, and have illustrated the importance of forms of learning that produce "a qualitative change in a person's conception of a phenomenon" from a lower-level, more naive conception to a more expert understanding of that phenomenon (Johansson, Marton, & Svensson, 1985, p. 235).

Under this view of learning, a student is rarely considered to have no understanding or no strategy when addressing a problem. Even beginning learners are considered to be engaged in an active search for meaning, constructing and using naive representations or models of subject matter. Rather than being "wrong," these representations frequently display partial understanding and are applied rationally and consistently by the individuals who use them. In arithmetic, for example, "it has been demonstrated repeatedly that novices who make mistakes do not make them at random, but rather operate in terms of meaning systems that they hold at a given time" (Nesher, 1986; also see Brown & Burton, 1978).

An implication of this view of learning for the assessment and monitoring of student learning is that much greater cognizance must be taken of the understandings and models that individual students construct for themselves during the learning process. In many areas of learning, levels of achievement might be better defined and measured not in terms of the number of facts and procedures that a student can reproduce, but in terms of his or her levels of understanding of the key concepts and principles that underlie a learning area (Glaser, 1981; Glaser, Lesgold, & Lajoie, 1987; Greeno, 1976).

An example of a study that has investigated students' levels of understanding is Carpenter and Moser's (1984) study of children's arithmetic skills. Carpenter and Moser found that most children in the first to third grades of school are able to provide correct answers to single-digit addition questions like 6 + 8 = ?. But children have a variety of methods of answering questions of this kind (see Table 9.1). These different methods indicate different levels of understanding and proficiency in single-digit addition. Some children solve 6 + 8 = ? by counting out six objects and another eight objects, and then counting all 14 (category 1). Later, children reach an understanding that counting does not have to begin at the number one. They "count on," although not necessarily from the larger number (e.g., "6; 7, 8, . . . , 14"; category 2). Later still, children understand the commutative property of addition (6 + 8 = 8 + 6) and consistently count on from the larger number ("8; 9, 10, . . . , 14"; category 3). Finally, by third grade, many children can solve 6 + 8 = ? using number facts, without counting objects (category 4). To monitor developing competence in single-digit addition, it is not sufficient to record only whether or not a child can provide the correct answer to a question like 6 + 8 = ?. By keeping track of the strategy that a child uses, it is possible to infer the kinds of understanding that she or he has developed.

This chapter considers the problem of constructing measures of achievement that are based not on tests of learners' abilities to recall facts and apply memorized routines, but on inferences about students' levels of understanding of key concepts in an area of learning. Particular attention is given to the requirements of an achievement testing methodology if it is to be consistent with a view of learning as an active, constructive process.

CONVENTIONAL ACHIEVEMENT TESTING

Techniques for constructing achievement tests have been developed and refined over many decades. Most achievement tests begin with a statement of

TABLE 9.1
Outcome Categories for Single-Digit Addition
(e.g., 6 + 8 = ?)

Category	Description
4	Does not need to count objects, but uses number facts to solve 6 + 8 = 14.
3	Always counts on from the larger number ("8; 9, 10, . . . , 14").
2	Counts on, but not consistently from the larger number ("6; 7, 8, . . . , 14").
1	Counts out 6 objects and 8 objects and then counts them all ("1, 2, . . . , 14").
0	Unable to solve.

the instructional objectives to be assessed by each test. According to Bloom, Hastings, and Madaus (1971, p. 28), these objectives should be stated as directly observable student behaviors that can be reliably recorded as either present or absent. They should be "stated in terms which are operational, involving reliable observation and allowing no leeway in interpretation." To achieve this degree of reliability, test constructors are encouraged to write items to assess students' abilities to perform unambiguous, observable tasks such as "stating," "listing," "naming," "selecting," "recognizing," "matching," and "calculating" (Bloom et al., 1971, p. 34).

This emphasis on specifying and testing precise student behaviors has led to the construction of achievement tests composed of discrete items, each relating to a particular behavioral objective, and each scorable as either right or wrong. Multiple-choice items have become especially popular in achievement tests because they can be scored quickly, unambiguously, and even by machine. In some areas of education, machine-scored multiple-choice tests have become the principal mode of evaluating student learning. A disadvantage of conventional achievement tests is that, through their emphasis on precisely defined student behaviors, they can encourage students to focus their efforts on relatively superficial forms of learning (Frederiksen, 1984).

In parallel with these developments in the practice of educational measurement, psychometric methods have been developed for the analysis of students' performances on test items of this kind. These methods have been introduced to transform records of right and wrong answers into measures of achievement, and to evaluate the reliability and validity of these measures. The more complex analytical methods, based on item response theory (IRT), take into account not only differences in the difficulties of individual test items, but also differences in their discriminating powers and, in the case of multiple-choice items, differences in their probabilities of being guessed correctly (Lord, 1980). Under IRT as well as under classical test theory, however, examinees' scores are essentially summaries of their tendencies to make correct rather than incorrect answers.

The alternative to conventional achievement testing discussed in this chapter begins with a consideration of the key concepts, principles, and phenomena that underlie a course of instruction and around which factual learning can be organized. Rather than recording students' understandings of these concepts as simply "right" or "wrong," this alternative approach recognizes that learners have a variety of understandings of phenomena, and that some of these understandings are less complete than others. The purpose of assessment is not to establish the presence or absence of specific behaviors, but to infer the nature of students' understandings of particular phenomena. Consequently, systems of observation very different from collections of distinct and conceptually isolated multiple choice test items are required.

BUILDING ACHIEVEMENT TESTS
AROUND KEY CONCEPTS

The construction of an achievement test usually begins with a table of specifications with subject matter on one axis and types of learning outcomes on the other. Items are written to cover outcomes like "knowledge of terminology," "knowledge of specific facts," and "principles and generalizations." In the use of such a table, these outcomes are treated as different but equivalent: the aim is to write items to cover each. However, because of the requirement that items be based on observable behaviors that can be scored right or wrong, and because it is easier to write items to assess students' knowledge of facts and procedures than to assess their understandings of principles and generalizations, achievement tests tend to be tests of students' abilities to recall and apply factual knowledge.

The method being proposed here begins by identifying key concepts in an area of instruction and building assessment procedures around these. These are fundamental principles, understandings, and approaches that a course of instruction aims to develop. The difference between this approach and the conventional practice of treating "knowledge of principles" as an instructional objective of much the same status as "knowledge of facts" or "knowledge of terms" is that this approach makes the assessment of conceptual understanding the primary focus of the testing procedure.

A second fundamental difference between this approach and the usual approach to achievement testing is the emphasis placed on understanding how students view and think about key concepts. Rather than comparing students' responses with a "correct" answer, the emphasis is on inferring the nature or level of understanding reflected in each student's response.

One area in which a great deal of work has been done to understand how students think about and approach phenomena is that of physics education. Studies in several countries have explored students' understandings of such concepts as acceleration (Trowbridge & McDermott, 1981), electric charge, enthalpy and entropy, force and motion (Viennot, 1979), gravitation (Champagne, Klopfer, & Anderson, 1980; Gunstone & White, 1981), light and the transmission of heat, momentum, potential difference, proportionality, torque, and such principles and models as Newton's laws, conservation laws, the atomic model, and electron flow models for circuits.

A common technique in these studies has been to ask students to describe what is happening in drawings of simple physical systems (e.g., to predict what will happen to an object, to describe the forces acting on a body, or to draw the trajectory that an object will follow). During these interviews, students are asked to explain their responses and their explanations are tape recorded (Johansson, Marton, & Svensson, 1985; McCloskey, 1983). In other studies, students have been asked to manipulate an apparatus in a laboratory to achieve particular effects (e.g., to apply a force to make a body move in a particular direction), while their explanations and comments are tape recorded and later transcribed (McDermott, 1984). Still other researchers (e.g., diSessa, 1982; White, 1983) have developed interactive software for this purpose. In these studies, students are asked to apply "forces" to simulated objects on a screen to make them move to specified positions, to speed up, to slow down, and so on.

An example of the kind of question posed in these studies, taken from the work of McDermott (1984), is shown in Fig. 9.1. In this study, students were presented with a drawing of a pendulum and asked to draw the trajectory that the weight would follow if the string of the pendulum broke when it was midway through its swing (i.e., in the vertical position). Four of the trajectories commonly drawn by students are shown in Fig. 9.1.

Drawings B, C, and D are all incorrect, but they reflect different levels of understanding. Drawings B and C show some understanding that the object will continue moving to the right after the string breaks (Newton's first law). Students who draw trajectory D show no understanding of this and recognize gravity as the only influence on the object's trajectory. Drawing B is almost correct:

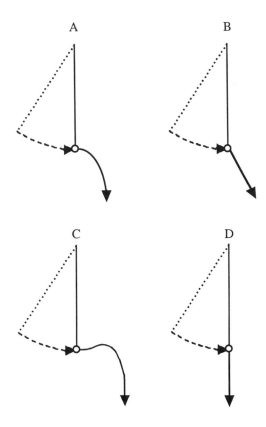

FIG. 9.1. Common responses to a physics task.

these students do not understand that the combination of a constant horizontal velocity and a vertical acceleration will be a parabolic trajectory. Drawing C shows the object continuing in the upward path that it would have followed had the string not been cut, and then falling under the influence of gravity. This drawing suggests a naive "impetus" theory of motion, a commonly held belief that an object will continue in its path (even a curved path) after the removal of the force that kept it moving in that path, until the object's "impetus" dissipates.

The observations made in these studies suggest that students do not simply make "random errors" but operate in terms of naive theories about physical phenomena. In the area of force and motion, these theories can be "remarkably well-articulated, . . . quite consistent across individuals, . . . and strikingly inconsistent with the fundamental principles of classical mechanics" (McCloskey, 1983, p. 299). In his studies of students' attempts to control a simulated object on a screen, diSessa (1982, p. 38) found a "surprising structure of discrete and definite theories" about how forces influence motion. And, through their interviews with Swedish students about aspects of science learning, Johansson et al. (1985) arrived at a similar conclusion:

In our case, a discovery of decisive importance was that for each phenomenon, principle, or aspect of reality, the understanding of which we studied, there seemed to exist a limited number of qualitatively different conceptions of that phenomenon, principle, or aspect of reality. (pp. 235–236)

A number of researchers have observed that the same naive conceptions can be found among students of different ages and with different educational backgrounds. McCloskey (1983), for example, found the same types of naive physical theories among students who had never taken physics, high-school physics students, and college physics students. The only different was in the frequencies of occurrence of these different understandings. McDermott (1984) reported an identical observation in a Norwegian study of high-school physics students, future high-school science teachers, and physics graduates.

A significant finding of these studies is that some students can succeed on traditional achievement tests and graduate from high school and even college physics courses with their naive conceptions of physical principles largely unchanged. Through their physics courses students are able to "master certain methods of calculation without having adopted the conceptualization underlying them" (Johansson et al., 1985, p. 235). Indeed, a misconception "may go undetected because a student's superficial knowledge of formulas and formula manipulation techniques can mask his or her misunderstanding of an underlying concept" (Clement, 1982, p. 66). The result is that "many students emerge from their study of physics and physical science without a functional understanding of some elementary but fundamental concepts" (McDermott, 1984, p. 31).

These findings invite a reconsideration of the way in which we think about and attempt to measure science learning. Clearly, many students are succeeding on precise, operationally defined objectives without developing an understanding of the material that they are learning. For many science educators, the answer is to place greater emphasis not on the learning of scientific facts and formulas, but on changing students' ways of thinking about scientific phenomena: "The formal learning of science can be viewed as involving, at least in part, a shift from one set of beliefs about the physical world to another, one set of conceptions to another" (Osborne & Wittrock, 1985, p. 81), and "In our view, learning (or the kind of learning we are primarily interested in) is a qualitative change in a person's conception of a certain phenomenon or of a certain aspect of reality" (Johansson et al., 1985, p. 235).

CONSTRUCTING ORDERED OUTCOME CATEGORIES

Having identified key concepts in an area of learning and devised contexts (items) through which students' understandings of these concepts can be investigated, the next task is to delineate a set of categories for each item, through which a student's observed responses are related to unobservable states of understanding. In this section and the two following, we address applications in which the most prevalent states of understanding can be ordered. This notion of order is basic to a view of learning as a "shift" in a student's understanding, with a shift constituting the desired "learning" when the change is from a lower-level, more naive understanding to a higher-level, more expert conception of a phenomenon.

This is not to say that all conceptions that students might bring to an item can be ordered from best to worst. We return later in the chapter to consider some ways to model conceptions that differ but are not obviously more or less sophisticated. We begin here, however, by assuming the existence of a set of ordered categories for any given item (as will be illustrated later). For some items this set of categories might be constructed by grouping similarly sophisticated understandings. These constructed categories provide a conceptual framework for recording an individual's response, and introduce the possibility of basing measures of achievement on inferences about students' levels of understanding.

Grouping students' responses to construct a set of categories of understanding is part of the method used by Marton (1981) and his colleagues at the University of Gothenburg. These researchers interview students to explore their understandings of particular concepts and principles, transcribe tape recordings of these interviews, and then carry out detailed analyses of transcripts. "The aim of the analysis is to yield descriptive categories representing qualitatively distinct conceptions of a phenomenon." These categories form an "outcome space" which provides "a kind of analytic map" of students' understandings of each phenomenon. Learning is thought of as "a shift from one conception to another" on this map (Dahlgren, 1984, pp. 24-31).

Carpenter and Moser (1984) provided a picture of such a map. From their analysis of students' performances on single-digit addition tasks, they constructed the five ordered outcome categories shown in Table 9.1. Children in Category 0 are unable to solve 6 + 8 = ?. Children in Category 1 understand that 6 + 8 = ? can be solved by counting the total number of objects in two groups of sizes 6 and 8. Children in Category 2 also understand that the counting of objects does not have to begin at the number one, and so "count on." Children in Category 3 understand the commutative property and count on from the larger number. Children in Category 4 have a level of understanding that enables them to use number facts to solve 6 + 8 = ? without counting.

Fig. 9.2 shows the proportion of a group of Wisconsin children in each of the five outcome categories at each of eight time points during their first 3 years of school. At the beginning of first grade (bottom of the map), about 15% of these children could not solve problems like 6 + 8 = ?, even with blocks (Category 0). Among those children who could solve such a problem, by far

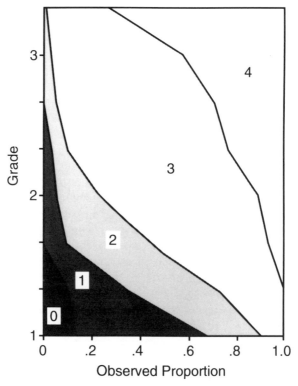

FIG. 9.2.   Observed proportions of children in each of five ordered outcome categories on a single-digit addition item.

the most common strategy was to count out six objects and another eight objects and then to count all fourteen (Category 1). By the beginning of the second grade, almost all these children understood that counting does not have to begin at the number one and were counting on (Categories 2 and 3), although some still did not understand the commutative property and were not counting consistently from the larger number. By the eighth round of observations (top of the map), more than 70% of this group of children could solve single-digit addition problems without having to count objects. Carpenter and Moser (1984) provided similar outcome maps for other aspects of addition and subtraction learning.

COLLECTING OBSERVATIONS

While conversations with students are probably essential for identifying the variety of understandings that learners have of phenomena and for constructing sets of outcome categories, interviews are not practicable as a basis for achievement testing. Alternative observation methods must be found that will permit inferences to be made about students' levels of understanding. These procedures must go deeper than identifying incorrect answers: They must attempt to identify the nature of the understandings and models that individual students are employing. In general, this will require imaginative new approaches to achievement testing.

One possible approach is the "rule assessment" procedure developed by Siegler (1981). This approach uses a carefully constructed set of questions designed to expose different levels of understanding of a concept. While each individual question might be scored as right or wrong, neither the response to any one item nor total score on a set of items are sufficient to differentiate students using different rules. Rather, it is a student's pattern of right and wrong answers that constitutes a basis for inferring his or her level of understanding.

Another approach is to use computer-administered tasks as the testing medium. This approach introduces the possibility of matching each student's response to a library of common responses rather than to a single "correct" answer. In the pendulum task in Fig. 9.1, for example, students might be asked to draw a trajectory on a screen and each student's drawing might then be referred to a library of common student responses. In this way, a student's response might automatically be assigned to one of several ordered outcome categories for that task, and a record made of the student's apparent conception or theory concerning that phenomenon.

A decision about a student's assignment to an outcome category might be based on the students' responses to several related questions, looking for, in Brown and Burton's (1978) terminology, consistent "bugs" in their solutions. The automatic generation of hypotheses about students' understandings might be followed by further questions aimed at confirming those hypotheses. Does a student who draws trajectory C in Fig. 9.1 also believe that an object fired out of a curved tube will continue in a curved path for a short time after leaving the tube? Through carefully designed hints and subquestions it may be possible to emulate in a crude way the type of exploration that can be done through an interview to trace a student's misunderstanding to its source. Ordered outcome categories, for example, might then be defined in terms of responses to a set of related questions or tasks.

In an achievement test of this type, tasks may bear little resemblance to traditional achievement test questions. As diSessa (1982) and White (1983) showed, a great deal of information can be collected about individuals' naive theories of force and motion by asking them to move simulated objects on a screen. A computer can be used to keep detailed records of when students apply forces, in which directions they apply those forces, and how they respond to the motion that they produce. Automatic analyses of student records might be used to infer students' levels of understanding. Simulations of this kind could be used in a wide variety of learning areas—for example, the use of simulated patient management problems to explore students' levels of understanding of medical principles and to expose inappropriate or potentially misleading ways of thinking about particular phenomena (of course, the analysis of these data would be far more complex than the simple examples given here).

CONSTRUCTING MEASURES OF ACHIEVEMENT

If the types of observations that result from these testing procedures are to provide a basis for achievement measurement and are to be a viable alternative to conventional achievement tests, then models and methods analogous to those that have been developed for right/wrong test questions are required to supervise the construction of the new measures.

The starting point in the development of a method for ordered outcome categories is a matrix of observations like the matrix shown in Table 9.2. This hypothetical data matrix shows the responses of 32 students to 8 items (e.g., Carpenter & Moser's single-digit addition items, 1984). Responses to each item are recorded in one of five ordered categories (labeled 0 to 4). Students' scores on each item have been arranged in this matrix in an orderly way with abrupt transitions between adjacent categories. (This can be seen by reading down each column.) The consequence of ordering scores on each item in this way is that it is possible to infer from the full data matrix in Table 9.2 an unambiguous order for these 32 students on the single achievement dimension defined by these eight items.

It is unlikely that a perfectly orderly pattern of scores on an item will occur in practice. The transition from category $x - 1$ to category x of an item is not likely to be sharp, as depicted in Table 9.2, but to be gradual. Rather than expecting a person above a particular level of ability in an area of learning to

TABLE 9.2
Hypothetical Data Matrix for Single-Digit Addition

				Items				
Students	1	2	3	4	5	6	7	8
1	4	4	4	4	4	4	4	4
2	4	4	4	4	4	4	3	4
3	4	4	4	4	4	3	3	3
4	4	4	4	4	4	3	3	3
5	4	4	4	4	4	3	3	2
6	4	4	4	3	4	3	3	2
7	4	4	4	3	4	3	2	2
8	4	4	4	3	3	3	2	2
9	4	4	4	3	3	3	2	1
10	4	4	4	3	3	2	2	1
11	4	4	3	3	3	2	2	1
12	4	3	3	3	3	2	2	1
13	4	3	3	2	3	2	2	1
14	4	3	3	2	3	2	2	0
15	3	3	3	2	3	2	2	0
16	3	3	3	2	3	2	1	0
17	3	3	3	2	2	2	1	0
18	3	3	2	2	2	2	1	0
19	2	3	2	2	2	2	1	0
20	2	3	2	1	2	2	1	0
21	2	2	2	1	2	2	1	0
22	2	2	2	1	2	1	1	0
23	2	2	1	1	2	1	1	0
24	2	2	1	1	1	1	1	0
25	2	2	1	1	1	1	0	0
26	2	2	1	1	0	1	0	0
27	2	2	1	1	0	0	0	0
28	2	1	1	1	0	0	0	0
29	1	1	1	1	0	0	0	0
30	1	1	0	0	0	0	0	0
31	1	0	0	0	0	0	0	0
32	0	0	0	0	0	0	0	0

Note: Table entries are observed outcome categories, coded from 0 to 4.

definitely score x rather than $x - 1$ on an item, it is more realistic to imagine a score of x becoming more likely than a score of $x - 1$ at higher levels of ability. In other words, a probabilistic formulation will in general be more appropriate than a deterministic representation (see Wilson, 1989a).

The psychometric method described here, the partial-credit model (PCM; Masters, 1982; Wright & Masters, 1982), proposes that the probability of a person scoring x rather than $x - 1$ on a particular item i will increase steadily with ability in an area of learning such that

$$\frac{\pi_{nix}}{\pi_{nix-1} + \pi_{nix}} = \frac{\exp(\theta_n - \delta_{ix})}{1 + \exp(\theta_n - \delta_{ix})}, \qquad (1)$$

where π_{nix} is the probability of person n responding in category x ($x = 1, 2,$ . . . , m_i) of item i, θ_n is person n's level of proficiency in the area of learning measured by this set of items, and δ_{ix} is a parameter associated with the transition between outcome categories $x - 1$ and x of item i.

The consequence of applying the simple logistic expression (1) to the transition between each pair of adjacent outcome categories for each item is that a connection is formed between the ordered categories for that item and the underlying variable that the set of items is used to measure. It is this connection that enables performances on each item to be used to estimate students' locations on the underlying variable. The nature of this probabilistic connection is illustrated in Fig. 9.3, in terms of response probabilities for a hypothetical single-digit addition problem.

Fig. 9.3 shows how, under the PCM, the probability of a response in each category of an item changes with increasing student proficiency. It has been

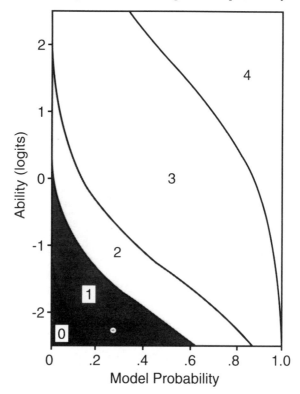

FIG. 9.3.   Modeled probabilities of responding in each of five ordered outcome categories on a single-digit addition item.

drawn to resemble Fig. 9.2. The difference is that Fig. 9.3 does not show observed proportions of students in each category, but modeled proportions. For any given level of θ, one looks across the graph to determine the probabilities of a response in category at this level of proficiency. The basic shapes of the five zones in Fig. 9.3 are fixed by the PCM and are the consequence of using the simple logistic expression (1) to model the transition between adjacent categories of each item. The widths and locations of the zones for each item are estimated from students' responses to that item and are expressed through the δ parameters.

The probabilistic partial-credit model depicted in Fig. 9.3 enables measures of achievement to be constructed from inferences of students' levels of understanding of each of a number of concepts or phenomena in an area of learning. A student's θ parameter indicates not simply a tendency to make correct responses, but tendencies to provide answers reflecting the various levels of understanding on a collection of tasks probing that understanding. The model serves the same function in the analysis of responses recorded in ordered outcome categories as the item response models that have been developed for dichotomously scored responses (Rasch, 1960; Lord & Novick, 1968; Lord, 1980), summarizing, in terms of the task and person parameters, the patterns in the data that are consonant with a conception of student proficiency. Estimation procedures and tests of model–data fit for the PCM were described by Wright and Masters (1982). Tests of item fit (which can be thought of as comparisons of the observed and modeled maps for an item as shown in Figs. 9.2 and 9.3) provide internal consistency indices analogous to traditional item statistics like biserial correlations. Tests of person-fit flag occurrences of unusual response patterns, as might occur when a student's state of understanding is atypical and requires special attention.

PARTIALLY ORDERED STATES

The psychometric model just described can be used when a set of ordered categories is defined for each item. However, attempting to order all conceptions of a phenomenon from "worst" to "best" may not always be fruitful. In some cases, two or more ways of visualizing a problem can be identified, none better or worse than another. If these different conceptions have different implications for instruction, then maintaining a distinction among them can be useful.

Gentner and Gentner's (1983) studies of students' models for electrical circuits provide an example. These studies suggest that many students visualize electric circuits in terms of more familiar physical systems. Some, for example, see electric current as analogous to water flow. Batteries are visualized as reservoirs, and resistors correspond to constrictions in water flow. This analogy facilitates the solution of problems about power sources in parallel and series, but impedes solutions to problems about parallel and series resistors. Other students see an electrical power source as analogous to a crowd entering a stadium, with resistors as turnstiles through which they must pass. This "teeming crowd" analogy facilitates problems about combinations of resistors, but offers little insight into battery combinations.

Each of these models captures some aspects of electrical systems. Students using either model have a better understanding than students with no model at all. On the other hand, neither of these physical models provides a complete understanding of current flow or of the operation of circuits. A higher level of understanding requires an appreciation of the limitations of the physical analogies as models for circuits. In this sense, students who operate with either one of the two models can be thought of as being at similarly intermediate levels of understanding.

From the point of view of traditional test theory and the maximization of test reliability, it is difficult to justify distinguishing among students who use the water flow analogy and those who use the teeming crowds analogy. Items that distinguish between these two groups are likely to contribute little to reliability, as their discriminating power is among people at similar levels of overall proficiency. However, further instruction might well differ for the two groups—first explicating the model that a student's responses suggest he or she may be using (perhaps intuitively), exploring its uses and limitations, then introducing the complementary model and its sphere of usefulness.

To develop a model for these situations, let us suppose that we can identify K states of understanding in a learning area, subsets of which may be ordered, but others of which may not be. Items are characterized by identifiable features that determine their difficulties within these states. In the electrical circuits example, for instance, resistor problems are relatively easier than battery problems for students using the teeming crowds analogy, while the battery problems are relatively easier for those using the water flow analogy. From each student's responses, we wish to infer his or her state of understanding (ϕ_n, which ranges from 1 to K) and degree of proficiency within that state (θ_n).

The essence of this approach is that while a single proficiency summary of performance fails to characterize important differences among learners, it may suffice in some applications to use a single proficiency to characterize differences among learners in the same type of understanding, while further distinguishing among these qualitative states. The fact that these variables can never be known with certainty is reflected by the nature of the inferences that are drawn about students: probabilities that the student is in the possible states, and an estimate of proficiency corresponding to each possibility.

The details of such models are given by Mislevy and Verhelst (1990). In the case of items scored right or wrong, the probability of a correct response to

Item i from Person n, who is in state k of understanding ($\phi_n = k$) and has proficiency θ_n, is given as

$$P(x_{ni} = 1|\theta_n, \phi_n = k, \beta_{ik}) = f_k(\theta_n, \beta_{ik}),\qquad (2)$$

where β_{ik} characterizes such features of Item i as its difficulty and f_k is a function relating examinee and item parameters to probabilities of correct response—both as pertain to persons in level k only. When persons from only one level are under consideration, Equation 2 is a standard IRT model. The item parameters β_{ik} can be expected to vary from one level of understanding to the next, however—and indeed they must vary if the model is to be practically useful for distinguishing students at one level from those at another qualitatively different level.

To illustrate the approach, we present highlights of one of many aspects of an analysis carried out by Wilson (1984), using Robert Siegler's (1981) data and rule-acquisition perspective. For additional examples, the reader is referred to Mislevy and Verhelst (1990), Mislevy, Wingersky, Irvine, and Dann (1991), and Wilson (1989b).

Fig. 9.4 shows two of Siegler's six balance-beam problem prototypes. In E (Equal) items, both the weights and distances are the same on the two sides

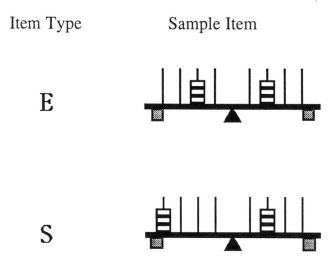

Will the beam tip left, tip right, or stay flat
when the gray blocks are taken away?

Item Type   Sample Item

E

S

FIG. 9.4.   Prototypical balance-beam items.

TABLE 9.3
Hierarchy of Rule Acquisition

Rule	Description
Rule 0	Salience of neither weight nor distance recognized; answers depend on personal factors.
Rule I	If the weights on both sides are equal, it will balance. If they are not equal, the side with the heavier weight will go down. (Weight is the "dominant dimension," because children are generally aware that weight is important in the problem earlier than they realize that distance from the fulcrum, the "subordinate dimension," also matters.)
Rule II	If the weights and distances on both sides are equal, then the beam will balance. If the weights are equal but the distances are not, the side with the longer distance will go down. Otherwise, the side with the heavier weight will go down. (A child using this rule uses the subordinate dimension only when information from the dominant dimension is equivocal.)
Rule III	Same as Rule II, except that if the values of both weight and length are unequal on both sides, the child will "muddle through" (Siegler, 1981, p. 6). (A child using this rule now knows that both dimensions matter, but doesn't know just how they combine. Responses may be based on a strategy such as guessing.)
Rule IV	Combine weights and lengths correctly (i.e., compare torques, or products of weights and distances).

of the scale, and the correct answer is that the beam will balance. In S (Subordinate) items, the same numbers of weights are on both sides, but on one side they are further from the fulcrum. That side will tip down. Following Piaget (Inhelder & Piaget, 1958; Piaget, 1960), Siegler posited that children typically exhibit distinct stages as they acquire competence in proportional reasoning, adding to their repertoire the increasingly sophisticated rules listed in Table 9.3. Children can thus differ as to their stage of understanding, or their proficiency in using the rules they currently command. In particular, a qualitative shift occurs when a child apprehends the salience of distance in balance-beam problems. Before this realization, children see no systematic, relevant, differences between E and S items, and tend to predict the beam will balance in both situations.

Among other analyses, Wilson (1984) analyzed responses to four E and four S items from two perspectives. The first was based on the Rasch IRT model for right/wrong items. Under the Rasch model, the probability that Person n will respond correctly to Item i is a function of the person's proficiency parameter, θ_n, and the item's difficult parameter, β_i:

$$P(x_{ni} = 1 | \theta_n, \beta_i) = \frac{\exp(\theta_n - \beta_i)}{1 + \exp(\theta_n - \beta_i)} \tag{3}$$

(Note the similarity of Equation 3 to 1; the Rasch model for right/wrong items is a special case of the PCM.) Fig. 9.5 illustrates the results. The relative positions of an item and a person on the scale ($\theta_n - \beta_i$) determine the probability of a correct response through Equation 3. Not surprisingly, S items are seen

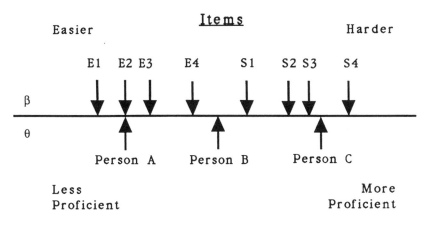

FIG. 9.5. Rasch model representation of balance beam items.

to be harder than E items. If the Rasch model were correct, increasing competence would be reflected in similar increases in the chances of correct response to both E and S items. However, analyses of person fit to the Rasch model revealed relatively fewer correct answers to S items from many children who did well on E items, and relatively fewer incorrect answers to E items from children who did well on S items, than would be expected under the Rasch model.

Wilson resolved these anomalies in the second analysis, based on his *Saltus* (Latin for *leap*) model for development that occurs in stages. Saltus extends the Rasch model by incorporating stage membership parameters for persons and *Saltus parameters* that allow for discontinuities such as the transition from Rule I to Rule II. In this analysis, children who had not experienced the transition were modeled in accordance with Equation 3; those who had were modeled by a model of the same form, but with the Saltus parameter τ subtracted from the difficulty parameters of S items. In terms of Equation 2, f_I and f_{II} both have the functional form given in Equation 3, $\beta_{iII} = \beta_{iI}$ for E items, and $\beta_{iII} = \beta_{iI} - \tau$ for S items. Fig. 9.6 illustrates the effect. In effect, τ measures the quantitative effect on performance associated with a qualitative change in understanding.

OTHER APPROACHES

The psychometric literature has begun to offer models that might be used to guide the construction and analysis of achievement tests of the kind proposed here. Some are mentioned in this section.

Items

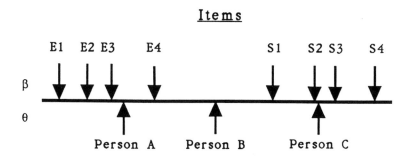

Persons--Stage I or lower

Items

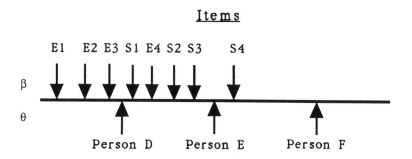

Persons--Stage II or higher

FIG. 9.6. Saltus model representation of balance beam items.

Wilson's (1984, 1989b) Saltus model for hierarchical stages of development (illustrated earlier) provides a stochastic framework for psychological models such as Piaget's (1960) and Siegler's (1981) that posit predictable discontinuities in proficiencies as development occurs, and educational models such as Gagné's (1968) and Riley's (Riley, 1981; Riley, Greeno, & Heller, 1983) that posit detectable patterns of task difficulties as students progress through successive levels of competence.

Latent class models (e.g., Haertel, 1984, 1989; Haertel & Wiley, chap. 14, this volume; Macready and Dayton, 1980) accommodate nonordered states of competence and reconfigurations of proficiencies, without further differentiating students within a state. Computational limitations to less than about 10 items per student have all but precluded their use for measuring individual achievement. Recent developments by Paulson (1985) and Yamamoto (1987) enable the use of these models with up to 60 items, opening the door to precise estimation for individual students and even potentially adaptive testing (Macready & Dayton, 1989).

Yamamoto (Yamamoto, 1987; Yamamoto & Gitomer, chap. 11, this volume) has also introduced a *hybrid* model for a mixture of latent classes and an IRT class. No claim is made that such a mixture accurately reflects the psychological reality of students' behavior, but a practical advantage is emphasized: Explicit classes can be defined to correspond to available instructional options, and an amorphous IRT class accounts for potentially large numbers of remaining classes, distinctions among which are irrelevant to the decision that must be made.

Another approach that leans on IRT to handle bookkeeping tasks in complex problems is Kikumi Tatsuoka's (Tatsuoka, 1983, 1990; Tatsuoka & Tatsuoka, 1987) "rule space" procedure. A standard IRT model is first fit to item responses. If the IRT model were correct, estimates of persons' proficiency would account for all systematic patterns within the data. But Tatsuoka then calculates an index of lack of fit from the IRT model, and studies the joint distribution of proficiency estimates under the IRT model and indices of lack of fit from that model. The ordered pairs of proficiency estimates and fit indices often suffice to identify systematic patterns of response that correspond to particular solution strategies, thereby identifying users of particular erroneous rules as well as correct rules.

Embretson's (1985, chap. 6, this volume) model for multiple strategies requires identifying different sequences of component subtasks that can be used to solve problems. This approach can be applied when it is possible to observe the results of subtask operations as well as a global result, and, as such, is amenable to procedures described earlier that enable the definition of levels of understanding for identified composite tasks. If levels of understanding are ordered, the results of microanalyses using Embretson's model could serve as input to achievement measurement via the partial credit model.

Our discussions and examples have addressed relatively simple situations, with a single developing concept with just a few stages. As such, however, they constitute building blocks for characterizing students' knowledge with respect to larger systems of interconnected concepts. The interested reader is referred to Mislevy, Yamamoto, and Anacker (in press) on the possibility of constructing Bayesian inference networks for this purpose.

CONCLUSION

Recent developments in cognitive and educational psychology reveal that most meaningful learning contrasts markedly to the type of learning implied by standard psychometric procedures—those based on item response theory as well as those using classical true-score test theory. The difference is characterized by the discontinuities of real-world learning, as learners reconfigure their knowledge, combine existing skills in new ways, and develop alternative strategies for solving problems.

It is possible to build achievement tests that measure learning of this kind. It is not possible to do so with traditional item writing rules, test construction procedures, and scoring formulas. To operationalize the new approach, the structure of learning is integral at each step along the way, from writing items through reporting achievement. In return for this greater investment in the psychology of the learning area, one can expect a greater utility: a measure of achievement that, by reflecting the nature of competence as attained thus far, sets the stage for further learning.

REFERENCES

Bloom, B. S., Hastings, J. T., & Madaus, G. F. (1971). *Handbook on formative and summative evaluation of student learning.* New York: McGraw-Hill.

Brown, J. S., & Burton, R. R. (1978). Diagnostic models for procedural errors in basic mathematical skills. *Cognitive Science, 2,* 155–192.

Caramazza, A., McCloskey, M., & Green, B. (1981). Naive beliefs in "sophisticated" subjects: Misconceptions about trajectories of objects. *Cognition, 9,* 117–123.

Carpenter, T. P., & Moser, J. M. (1984). The acquisition of addition and subtraction concepts in grades one through three. *Journal for Research in Mathematics Education, 15,* 179–202.

Champagne, A. B., Klopfer, L. E., & Anderson, J. H. (1980). Factors influencing the learning of classical mechanics. *American Journal of Physics, 48,* 1074–1079.

Chase, W. G., & Simon, H. A. (1973). Perception in chess. *Cognitive Psychology, 4,* 55–81.

Chi, M. T. H., Feltovich, P. J., & Glaser, R. (1981). Categorization and representation of physics problems by experts and novices. *Cognitive Science, 5,* 121–152.

Clement, J. (1982). Students' preconceptions of introductory mechanics. *American Journal of Physics, 50,* 66–71.

Dahlgren, L.-O. (1984). Outcomes of learning. In F. Marton, D. Hounsell, & N. Entwistle (Eds.), *The experience of learning* (pp. 19–35). Edinburgh: Scottish Academic Press.

diSessa, A. (1982). Unlearning Aristotelian physics: A study of knowledge-based learning. *Cognitive Science, 5,* 37–75.

Driver, R., & Easley, J. (1978). Pupils and paradigms: A review of literature related to concept development in adolescent science students. *Studies in Science Education, 5,* 61–84.

Embretson, S. E. (1985). Multicomponent latent trait models for test design. In S. E. Embretson (Ed.), *Test design: Developments in psychology and psychometrics.* Orlando, FL: Academic Press.

Frederiksen, N. (1984). The real test bias: Influences of testing on teaching and learning. *American Psychologist, 39,* 193–202.

Gagné, R. M. (1968). Learning hierarchies. *Educational Psychologist, 6,* 1–9.

Gentner, D., & Gentner, D. R. (1983). Flowing waters or teeming crowds: Mental models of electricity. In D. Gentner & A. Stevens (Eds.), *Mental models* (pp. 99–129). Hillsdale, NJ: Lawrence Erlbaum Associates.

Glaser, R. (1981). The future of testing: A research agenda for cognitive psychology and psychometrics. *American Psychologist, 36,* 923–936.

Glaser, R., Lesgold, A., & Lajoie, S. (1987). Toward a cognitive theory for the measurement of achievement. In R. Ronning, J. Glover, J. C. Conoley, & J. Witt (Eds.), *The influence of cognitive psychology on testing and measurement: The Buros-Nebraska Symposium on measurement and testing* (Vol. 3, pp. 41–85). Hillsdale, NJ: Lawrence Erlbaum Associates.

Greeno, J. G. (1976). Cognitive objectives of instruction: Theory of knowledge for solving problems and answering questions. In D. Klahr (Ed.), *Cognition and instruction* (pp. 123–159). Hillsdale, NJ: Lawrence Erlbaum Associates.

Gunstone, R., & White, R. (1981). Understanding of gravity. *Science Education, 65,* 291–299.

Haertel, E. H. (1984). An application of latent class models to assessment data. *Applied Psychological Measurement, 8,* 333–346.

Haertel, E. H. (1989). Using restricted latent class models to map the skill structure of achievement test items. *Journal of Educational Measurement, 26,* 301–321.

Inhelder, B., & Piaget, J. (1958). *The growth of logical thinking from childhood to adolescence.* New York: Basic Books.

Johansson, B., Marton, F., & Svensson, L. (1985). An approach to describing learning as change between qualitatively different conceptions. In L. H. West & L. A. Pines (Eds.), *Cognitive structure and conceptual change* (pp. 233–257). Orlando, FL: Academic Press.

Lesgold, A. M., Feltovich, P. J., Glaser, R., & Wang, Y. (1981). *The acquisition of perceptual diagnostic skill in radiology* (Tech. Rep. No. PDS-1). Pittsburgh: Learning Research and Development Center, University of Pittsburgh.

Lord, F. M. (1980). *Applications of item response theory to practical testing problems.* Hillsdale, NJ: Lawrence Erlbaum Associates.

Lord, F. M., & Novick, M. R. (1968). *Statistical theories of mental test scores.* Reading, MA: Addison-Wesley.

Macready, G. B., & Dayton, C. M. (1980). The nature and use of state mastery models. *Applied Psychological Measurement, 4,* 493–516.

Macready, G. B., & Dayton, C. M. (1989, March). *Adaptive testing with latent class models.* Paper presented at the annual meeting of the American Educational Research Association, San Francisco, CA.

Marton, F. (1981). Phenomenography—Describing conceptions of the world around us. *Instructional Science, 10,* 177–200.

Marton, F., & Säljö, R. (1976). On qualitative differences in learning: I—Outcome and process. *British Journal of Educational Psychology, 46,* 4–11.

Masters, G. N. (1982). A Rasch model for partial credit scoring. *Psychometrika, 47,* 149–174.

McCloskey, M. (1983). Naive theories of motion. In D. Gentner & A. Stevens (Eds.), *Mental models* (pp. 299–324). Hillsdale, NJ: Lawrence Erlbaum Associates.

McDermott, L. C. (1984). Research on conceptual understanding in mechanics. *Physics Today, 37,* 1–10.

Mislevy, R. J., & Verhelst, N. (1990). Modeling item responses when different subjects employ different solution strategies. *Psychometrika, 55,* 195–215.

Mislevy, R. J., Wingersky, M. S., Irvine, S. H., & Dann, P. L. (1991). Resolving mixtures of strategies in spatial visualization tasks. *British Journal of Mathematical and Statistical Psychology, 44,* 265–288.

Mislevy, R. J., Yamamoto, K., & Anacker, S. (in press). Toward a test theory for assessing student understanding. In R. A. Lesh & S. Lamon (Eds.), *Assessments of authentic performance in elementary mathematics.* Washington, DC: American Association for the Advancement of Science.

Nesher, P. (1986). Learning mathematics: A cognitive perspective. *American Psychologist, 41,* 1114–1122.

Osborne, R. J., & Wittrock, M. D. (1983). Learning science: A generative process. *Science Education, 67,* 489–508.

Osborne, R. J., & Wittrock, M. C. (1985). The generative learning model and its implications for science education. *Studies in Science Education, 12,* 59–87.

Paulson, J. (1985). *Latent class representations of systematic patterns in test responses* (ONR Tech. Rep.). Portland, OR: Portland State University.

Piaget, J. (1960). The general problems of the psychological development of the child. In J. M. Tanner & B. Inhelder (Eds.), *Discussions on child development: Vol. 4. The fourth meeting of the World Health Organization Study Group on the Psychological Development of the Child, Geneva, 1956* (pp. 3–27). Geneva: World Health Organization.

Posner, G. J., Strike, K. A., Hewson, P. W., & Gertzog, W. A. (1982). Accommodation of a scientific conception: Toward a theory of conceptual change. *Science Education, 66,* 211–227.

Rasch, G. (1960). *Probabilistic models for some intelligence and attainment tests.* Copenhagen: Danish Institute for Educational Research.

Riley, M. S. (1981). *Conceptual and procedural knowledge in development.* Unpublished master's thesis, University of Pittsburgh.

Riley, M. S., Greeno, J. G., & Heller, J. I. (1983). Development of children's problem-solving ability in arithmetic. In H. P. Ginsburg (Ed.), *The development of mathematical thinking* (pp. 153–196). New York: Academic Press.

Siegler, R. S. (1981). Developmental sequences within and between concepts. *Monograph of the Society for Research in Child Development, 46.*

Tatsuoka, K. K. (1983). Rule space: An approach for dealing with misconceptions based on item response theory. *Journal of Educational Measurement, 20,* 345–354.

Tatsuoka, K. K. (1990). Toward an integration of item response theory and cognitive error diagnosis. In N. Frederiksen, R. Glaser, A. Lesgold, & M. G. Shafto (Eds.), *Diagnostic monitoring of skill and knowledge acquisition* (pp. 453–488). Hillsdale, NJ: Lawrence Erlbaum Associates.

Tatsuoka, K. K., & Tatsuoka, M. M. (1987). Bug distribution and statistical pattern classification. *Psychometrika, 52,* 193–206.

Trowbridge, D. E., & McDermott, L. C. (1981). Investigation of student understanding of the concept of acceleration in one dimension. *American Journal of Physics, 49,* 242–253.

Viennot, L. (1979). Spontaneous reasoning in elementary dynamics. *European Journal of Science Education, 1,* 205–221.

Voss, J. F., Greene, T. R., Post, T. A., & Penner, B. C. (1983). Problem-solving skill in the social sciences. In G. H. Bower (Ed.), *The psychology of learning and motivation: Advances in research and theory* (Vol. 17, pp. 165–213). New York: Academic Press.

White, B. Y. (1983). Sources of difficulty in understanding Newtonian dynamics. *Cognitive Science, 7,* 41–65.

White, B. Y., & Horwitz, P. (1987). *ThinkerTools: Enabling children to understand physical laws* (Rep. No. 6470). Cambridge, MA: Bolt, Beranek, and Newman.

Wilson, M. R. (1984). *A psychometric model of hierarchical development.* Doctoral dissertation, University of Chicago.

Wilson, M. R. (1989a). A comparison of deterministic and probabilistic approaches to measuring learning structures. *Australian Journal of Education, 33,* 125–138.

Wilson, M. R. (1989b). Saltus: A psychometric model of discontinuity in cognitive development. *Psychological Bulletin, 105,* 276–289.

Wright, B. D., & Masters, G. N. (1982). *Rating scale analysis.* Chicago: MESA.

Yamamoto, K. (1987). *A hybrid model for item responses.* Unpublished doctoral dissertation, University of Illinois.

10

Addressing Process Variables in Test Analysis

Drew H. Gitomer
Don Rock
Educational Testing Service

INTRODUCTION

The probability of making informed educational decisions increases with improved understanding of student cognitive processing within a domain. Regardless of the domain, decision making benefits when problem demands and individual characteristics are well specified. Contrast the educational implications drawn from the statement "John did poorly on the difficult problems" with the more informative "John did poorly on all the problems that required him to make inferences from a piece of text." The second interpretation is more useful because an intermediate analysis of the contribution to difficulty has been done. In this chapter, we present intermediate analyses of mathematical problems as a forum for developing alternative techniques of test analysis. The purpose of the present work is to examine how advances in the understanding of mathematical problem-solving processes, together with new measurement models, can improve the quality of information that can be derived from standardized test items. Despite the many constraints imposed by using existing test items, there is a great deal of information surrounding these items that can be brought to bear on any interpretation of problem-solving performance.

In mathematics problem solving, the need for emphasizing student processes, not simply their products, is clear (Kilpatrick, 1978). Excellent examples of detailed models of student problem-solving processes abound in the literature (e.g., Briars & Larkin, 1984; Riley, Greeno, & Heller, 1983; Schoenfeld, 1985). The process research has taken several forms. One approach has been to collect protocols of students engaged in actual problem solving (Briars & Larkin, 1984). A second, and often complementary, approach has been to develop very detailed models of a circumscribed set of problems and infer cognitive processing on the basis of answers to a set of problems (e.g., Brown & Burton, 1978; Riley & Greeno, 1988).

We begin by specifying the characteristics of standardized test items, including test design, intended uses, analyses, interpretations, and limitations. We then present two alternative analytic models that can expand the usefulness and interpretation of test results within the constraints of current test instruments. The final section contains a discussion of the relative merits of the two models, including suggestions for future directions.

Standardized Testing of Mathematics

This discussion is limited to testing of students in secondary school and focuses on items that would be subsumed under the rubric of algebraic problem solving. It includes problems that require the solving of equations and algebraic word problems, and some knowledge of plane geometry. Specifically, the analyses are based on items that come from an administration of the SAT-M.

Intended Uses.   The SAT is one of a large class of tests that is designed to serve institutional needs by helping to make global judgments about the developed mathematical ability of an individual or of a group of students. Thus, decisions are made as to whether an individual has a mathematics background that yields a high probability of success within a college program. Other uses of this type of test are to make general statements about the level of performance of groups of students. The SAT is not intended to provide any diagnostic information about individuals, either alone or as part of a larger group.

Test Design.   Given the intended uses, items are included in tests because they provide certain types of information. Specifically, items are developed that have certain psychometric characteristics. Desirable items are those that discriminate between individuals displaying intermediate levels of performance. There is less concern with finer discriminations of individuals at the two extremes of performance. Also, items are included that support the idea of unidimensionality: that all items are tapping the same underlying ability. Thus, items are included to the extent that high test scorers do well on the item and low test scorers do less well. Items that do not meet this standard are eliminated from the test.

Analyses.   Traditional analyses require a set of assumptions that are in direct conflict with what is known about the complexity of human cognition. Of paramount importance is the idea that performance on a test, or some related subset of items, is a function of a single theoretical construct. Thus, math scores are interpreted as an index of a construct known as mathematical ability. This leads to other limitations. First, any statistical deviation from this unidimensional theory is treated as *noise* or error variance. A person's observed score represents a true score plus error. What is seldom considered is that the error may, in fact, reflect the inadequacy of the unidimensional model. A second curiosity is that one is then left with the tautology that math ability is defined by one's score on the math test.

Interpretations. The test score is then interpreted as a reflection of where on this continuous dimension a person is located. This suggests a model of learning that is linear and continuous, when in fact we know that human learning is not that simple. There are qualitative differences in understanding and performance that separate individuals that are often not adequately modeled by traditional conceptions.

Conventional norm-referenced interpretations actually provide little information about student understanding. Typically these standardized tests provide an index of correct responding relative to other individuals. No information is provided about what concepts or skills a person has learned and which ones still need development. In fact, two individuals can have the same total score (and same normative rank), but answer different problems correctly. Though they may have very different understandings of a domain, they are considered to be of similar "ability." The work of Siegler (1983) nicely illustrates this point.

Desiderata for Increasingly Informative Tests

Recognizing the inadequacy of traditional approaches for making informed, or diagnostic, decisions about a student (e.g., Cole, 1988), we propose alternative analytic methods that provide a more qualitative understanding of what a test score means in terms of the types of cognitive processes required to solve problems within a test. Central to these approaches is an understanding of the item independent of the statistical characteristics of the item. An independent understanding of item demands permits interpretation that is not subject to the same tautological reasoning noted previously.

The interpretations from these analyses are more qualitative in nature than that detailed already. Although the alternative models also are essentially continuous, the interpretations represent qualitatively different understanding of the targeted domain. Attention is given to response accuracy over subsets of items hypothesized to be addressing similar skills. Thus, alternative interpretations of skill may be useful even for individuals answering the same total number of problems correctly.

Two Alternative Approaches

The following analyses are performed within the context of existing standardized tests. This means that any approach must account for the breadth of item types found on such an instrument. Any given item draws on a complex of skills and knowledge and these skills are not varied systematically within the test. Thus, many of the detailed cognitive models that thoroughly examine the complexity of a relatively narrow domain (e.g., Briars & Larkin, 1984; Riley & Greeno, 1988) are not quite appropriate for the current purpose. What is desired instead are models that attempt to build on the understanding derived from such detailed studies, while at the same time adopting and adapting those concepts for instruments that require more general decisions about a student.

The first approach employs the use of testlets in a hierarchically overlapping skills test (HOST). Testlets are groups of items that are grouped together because of similar item demands. There are certain conditions under which the total score may reflect more than just a rank ordering of examinees. For example, if a test is constructed to reflect a "perfect" Guttman scale, then the total score implies a particular response pattern. Unfortunately, even if items are constructed to form a Guttman scale, they are too unreliable when taken singly to consistently reproduce the response pattern underlying the Guttman scale.

It is suggested that while single items are not reproducible in the Guttman sense, blocks of items that are internally consistent with respect to selected cognitive processing demands may form a special case of a Guttman scale. These blocks of items that are internally homogeneous with respect to their cognitive-processing demands will be referred to as testlets. We are interested in a set of testlets that reflect a particular hierarchical ordering of cognitive skills. That is, this testlet-based approach begins with a notion of a hierarchical knowledge or cognitive-processing structure and then assigns items to testlets that appear to define the various levels in the hierarchy. The testlet should include all the cognitive skills being measured by lower level testlets plus one new more complex skill. Tests so constructed will be referred to as HOST measures, that is, measures that consist of hierarchically overlapping skills testlets. The hierarchical model may reflect a cognitive complexity model in a problem solving test or may simply reflect a curriculum sequencing model in a straight achievement test.

The second approach also distinguishes items on the basis of a theory of cognitive performance demands. This cognitive model is then used as the basis for looking at patterns of responses across all problems and applying latent-class theory (Lazarsfeld, 1960) to statistically model the data. The current application of latent-class theory builds on the premise that given a set of problems, one should be able to infer the particular understanding of an individual based on the responses given to those problems. The necessary conditions are that one understands the cognitive skills involved in the solution of each problem, and that some subset of items will discriminate individuals who differ on one or more of those skills. A more detailed discussion of latent-class theory is provided in chapter 11 in this volume by Yamamoto and Gitomer.

HIERARCHICALLY OVERLAPPING
SKILLS TESTS (HOST)

The present formulation of the model-based procedure assumes that while the majority of the SAT-M items may not be strictly consistent with the hierarchically ordered skill model, a subset of items within the test, the so-called core, may well reflect this hierarchical mode. Whole tests or subsets of items that fit this hierarchical model are referred to as HOST tests. HOST tests differ from the typical criterion-referenced test that simply makes a pass/fail decision in that they have a number of criterion-referenced score points along the total score scale. The building of a HOST subtest within the larger SAT-M requires completion of the following steps:

1. Define a hierarchical cognitive demand model.
2. Select testlets consisting of items that reflect levels in the cognitive demand model (anchor testlets).
3. Evaluate whether student performance on the selected anchor testlets is consistent with the assumed hierarchical model.
4. Tie performance on the anchor testlets to SAT-M scale scores.

Item Breakdown

Using three different SAT-M forms and spaced samples of 2,017, 2,759, and 1,968 students, respectively, a hierarchical model based on three skill levels was developed. The cognitive hierarchy posed here assumes that the knowledge or skills necessary for successfully carrying out arithmetical operations on decimals and fractions, as well as being familiar with the appropriate steps involved in solving simple equations, are prerequisite skills for problem-solving tasks that frequently require additional comprehension and/or insights beyond the rote application of simple rules. Thus the lowest level of proficiency (Level 1) was defined by items that measured one's knowledge with respect to the rote application of simple arithmetical and algebraic rules. Two levels of problem-solving items were then tentatively identified that appeared to differ with respect to the depth and/or the number of insights or transformational steps required for successful solution. The highest level of problem-solving (Level 3) item was more often than not characterized by the translation of a logically complex verbal statement into the proper equation(s). Following a successful translation, the complete correct solution required a second step that involved carrying out the type of rote rule-following procedures that were characteristic of the lowest skill level. Items that defined the lower-level problem-solving proficiency level (Level 2) tended to require the rote application of simple computational rules (Level 1 skills) plus an additional insightful or logical step.

In order to reliably define anchor points along the total test score distribution, a cluster or testlet of items was selected that appeared to encompass the skills that were required for each of the three skill levels described previously. Parameters derived from item response theory (IRT) were then used to corroborate these impressions. IRT models the probability that a person will respond correctly to a test item as a function of a parameter for the person's proficiency, typically denoted θ, and one or more parameters that characterize the item. The IRT model employed in this chapter has three parameters for each item: b, its difficulty; a, its reliability; and c, the probability of a chance correct response from persons with very low proficiencies. The computer programs BILOG and LOGIST are used here to estimate these item parameters from examinee responses.

Items assigned to each of the three levels were also inspected to insure that their IRT difficulty (b) parameter was consistent with the task definition. If there were more than four items that met both the cognitive demand and difficulty criteria at a given level, that testlet was reduced to four items by keeping the items that had the highest IRT discrimination (a) parameters. Thus each form had three four-item testlets, each testlet consisting of items that ideally were homogeneous with respect to difficulty as well as the cognitive process being measured. Examples of problems from each of the proficiency levels are presented next.

The following item is an example of the type of item found in the Level 1 simple application of rules testlet:

If $4 + x = 4.01$, then $x =$
(A) 3.99   (B) 3.9   (C) 3.09   (D) 0.1   (E) 0.01

The point here is that students can solve this equation by simply applying basic rules of algebraic manipulation. Of course, one could get this item wrong by simply being careless. One of the reasons that we are using testlets of four items and requiring three out of four correct in defining proficiency at a given level is to minimize the impact of a "one-time" careless mistake.

An example of a Level 2 testlet item is:

If n is a positive integer, then the least odd integer greater than $2n$ is
(A) $2n + 1$ (B) $2(n + 1)$ (C) $2n + 3$ (D) $2(n - 1)$ (E) $2 + n$

This item was classified as a Level 2 item because of the insightful or concept-understanding step involved. Unlike items at Level 1, which simply call for an application of a technique, items at Level 2 require the student to decide on not only what to do but how to do it. In the example just given, the "how to do it" decision becomes clear once the test taker realizes or comprehends that even integers are always followed by odd integers.

An example of the type of item that was selected for Level 3 is:

A cylindrical can 15 centimeters high fits into a rectangular box just touching all sides of the box. If the volume of the box is 6000 cubic centimeters, what is the radius of the can?
(A) 5 cm   (B) 10 cm   (C) 20 cm   (D) 30 cm   (E) 40 cm

The fact that the test taker may know the rules for estimating the volume of a rectangular cube is not sufficient for solving this problem. At least two logical insights are helpful in the solution. The student must first realize the significance of the cylinder touching all six sides of the rectangular container, and because the cylinder is by definition symmetrical it then follows that four sides of the rectangular box must be equal. Given that "if–then" connection, the student having been given the volume can work backward to find the dimensions of the box and thus the diameter of the cylinder. The last step is of course halving the diameter to arrive at the radius.

The Level 3 problem-solving items typically require an orderly sequence of two or more logical steps. In many cases there is also a "working backward" element. These logical steps are required before one can carry out the final step, which usually consists of the application of simple algebraic rules.

The proposed hierarchical nature of the three levels can be stated succinctly as:

Level 1 = Task recognition + application of simple rules.
Level 2 = Insight + application of simple rules.
Level 3 = Insight + production + application of simple rules.

Mayer, Larkin, and Kadane (1984) presented a similar model based on four knowledge structures. Their four model components are factual/linguistic, schematic, strategic, and algorithmic and were designed to describe cognitive processing in mathematical word problems. A major feature of both the model espoused here and the Mayer et al. model is that the components are assumed to be sequentially dependent during problem solving. That is, to successfully implement a schema the problem solver should have mastered the factual/linguistic knowledge necessary to read the problem. Wheeler and Embretson (1986) have shown substantial error rates in three out of four of the above components in problem-solving items taken from the SAT-M. Wheeler and Embretson found that errors in algorithmic knowledge were rarely present, and thus they were eliminated from all subsequent analysis.

While the Mayer et al. model is similar in its hierarchical structure to the HOST model, it is somewhat different in that the HOST model as presently applied essentially collapses the algorithmic and factual knowledge of Mayer et al. into one component (the lowest-level cognitive demand category). The schematic or understanding phase of the Mayer et al. model parallels the second level of the HOST model, conceptual understanding. The highest level of the HOST model, the application of a strategy, is similar to the Mayer et al. highest-level strategic knowledge.

Validation

Validation of this hierarchical conception took two forms. Empirical support for the hierarchy of testlets just given was gathered through the analysis of the item parameters and the individual response patterns to the selected items. Expert agreement was investigated by comparing the test development experts' classification of the items with that used in assigning items to the three marker testlets.

A *super item* was then defined at each of the three levels for each of the three forms. For example, a student would receive a score on super item A of 1 if she or he got at least three out of the four items correct in the Level 1 testlet. A testlet score of less than three out of four received a super item score of 0. A score of 1 on super item B would indicate that the student got three or more correct of the items in the second level testlet. Thus, a student who had a super item response vector of 110 for the three super items has "passed" both the Level 1 and the Level 2 criteria but not the Level 3 criteria. The validity of diagnostic statements for a given student can be assessed by inspecting the student's super item response pattern. For example, a student with a 101 pattern is not well modeled by the hierarchical model. In short, a diagnostic statement about this student would be tenuous.

Individual probabilities of proficiency at each of the three levels can be obtained from the IRT parameters for each super item and the individual's θ score. That is, given an individual's θ score, one can estimate the probability of that individual passing each of the super items. The θ scale scores can then be put on the SAT scale, and thus the proficiency probabilities can be tied to the SAT scale scores. Tieing SAT-M scale scores to proficiency probabilities, that is, the probability that a student is proficient at each of the three levels defined here, would allow one in theory to make statements about an individual proficiency probability independent of the form he or she was administered.

Fit of the Hierarchical Model. Reversals in the super item response patterns in any one of the three forms indicate a lack of fit of the hierarchical model. For example, if an individual gets three out of four correct on the Level 1 testlet, two out of four correct on the Level 2 testlet, and three out of four correct on the Level 3 testlet, his or her super item response pattern would be 101. This would be counted as a one-step reversal since the individual passed Level 1, failed Level 2, but then passed Level 3. The hierarchical cognitive model underlying the selection of items assumes that if one is proficient at Level 3 then one will also be proficient at Level 2 and Level 1. A two-step reversal would be indicated by a super item response pattern of 001, indicating that the individual is proficient at Level 3 but has not demonstrated proficiency in the prerequisite skills measured in the Level 1 and Level 2 super items. Clearly the hypothesized cognitive model does not fit individuals having this response pattern.

The selection of items comprising the testlets in each form appeared to provide an excellent fit to the data, suggesting that the hierarchical cognitive model is consistent with the data. Only 2%–4% of the sample have any reversals in their super item response pattern. More importantly, only four individuals out of over 6,500 had two-step reversals. That is, while they had at least three items correct in the Level 3 testlet, they got less than three items correct at both the Level 1 and Level 2 testlets. The SAT-M scores of individuals whose super item response pattern shows two-step reversals should be interpreted with considerable caution. Even if the reasons for a reversal are not well understood, the important point here is that the identification of a subset of items that fit a particular cognitive performance model allows the test user, through the examination of individual response patterns, to identify examinees for whom the test scores may not carry the usual meaning.

Expert Agreement on the Item Classifications. The results just given showed empirical support for the validity of the hierarchical scale. The question still remains, however, of whether or not independent experts would classify these items along similar lines as the present researchers. Educational Testing Service (ETS) test-development subject-matter experts classify items in a number of ways, including content area and a quantitative code that is relevant here. Their codes are as follows:

Codes 0–2: Items in these categories require recall of factual knowledge (code 0), perform mathematical operations (code 1), or solve routine problems (code 2).

Code 3: Items in this category require the student to demonstrate comprehension of mathematical ideas and concepts.

Codes 4, 5: Items in these categories require the solving of nonroutine problems requiring ingenuity or insight (code 4) and/or applying higher mental processes to mathematics.

Items often require overlapping skills, and typically problem-solving items are coded 4/5 and the application of rote mathematical operations as 1/2.

If one equates codes 0–2, 3, and 4–5 to the present Level 1, Level 2, and Level 3 classifications, respectively, the agreement on the 36 items forming the testlets across the three forms can be estimated. Using this approach 33 out of the 36 possible classifications are in agreement. Of the three misclassifications, two items were placed at Level 2 by the present researchers while the test development experts assigned them to the code 1/2 category. The remaining item was classified as Level 3 by the present researchers, and the subject-matter experts assigned it to their code 3 category.

Behavioral Anchored Score Points and Proficiency

While there is a total of nine super items across the three forms, all super items are not created equally. For example, the super item based on the testlet defining Level 1 on the first form may have better scaling characteristics than its counterparts in Forms Two and Three. Since all three forms are IRT equated and we have estimated IRT parameters on the nine super items and put them on the same scale as the other test items, it is possible to pool all nine super items and select the one best super item to mark each of the three levels using the information from the IRT parameters. The super-item IRT parameters were estimated using the LOGIST program and a two-step procedure. First the IRT parameters for all the SAT-M items were estimated separately for each form. Student θ scores were also estimated in this step. In the second step the IRT parameters were estimates conditional on the parameters of the original SAT-M items. Thus the super items were put on the same scale as the original SAT-M items. Table 10.1 presents the IRT parameters for each of the three super items in each of the three forms.

Based on the information in Table 10.1 one could use the Level 1 and Level 2 super items from Form One to define the first two levels and the Level 3 super item from Form Three to define the highest level. That is, given the individual's θ score one could estimate his or her probability of proficiency at each of the three levels. The Level 1 and Level 2 super items from Form One clearly had the most desirable scaling parameters. That is, the discrimination parameters were the highest when compared to their counterpart in the other forms, and the guessing parameters were almost exactly zero. In addition, the spreads between the difficulties for Level 1 and Level 2 were quite acceptable. There was very little to go on when making a choice between Forms One and Three

TABLE 10.1
Item Response Theory Parameters for Super Items by Form

Form	Discrimination (a parameter)	Difficulty (b parameter)	Guessing (c parameter)
Form One			
Level 1	2.60	-1.62	.00
Level 2	2.13	-0.12	.02
Level 3	3.00	1.73	.00
Form Two			
Level 1	1.04	-1.67	.00
Level 2	1.69	-0.01	.00
Level 3	2.51	1.60	.01
Form Three			
Level 1	1.00	-1.29	.37
Level 2	1.80	0.02	.01
Level 3	3.00	1.69	.00

with respect to selecting the super item to define Level 3 behavior. Both forms have virtually equivalent item parameters.

The use of four or more items to build a super item tends to make the guessing parameter go away and also yields quite steep slope parameters. The homogeneity within the testlets with respect to cognitive demands, as well as the steep slopes with no guessing, leads to item response functions that have little if any overlap and thus provide anchor points that provide quite good discrimination with respect to the anchor-point behaviors.

Fig. 10.1 presents the criterion-referenced or behavioral-anchored score points in terms of the SAT-M scale. These are the anchor points along the SAT-M scale that define the three levels of cognitive performance. These are based on a maximum likelihood logistic regression procedure that attempts to define cutting scores on the SAT-M scale that reproduce as closely as possible the distribution of people in the four proficiency categories as defined by the actual response pattern to the super items. The dependent variable in the logistic

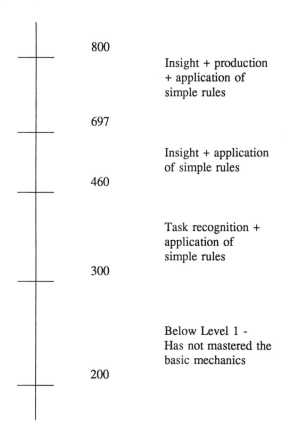

FIG. 10.1. Model-based behavioral-anchored score points on the SAT-M score.

regression is simply a 1 or 0 depending on whether the student got three out of four correct on a particular testlet defining a proficiency level. The independent variable here is the SAT-M scale score. All three samples defined by the separate forms were pooled for this analysis. One could pick thetas that maximized the correspondence with the super item classification, but then the thetas would have to be transformed to the SAT-M scale scores. It was decided to go directly to the SAT scale scores and the logistic regression for the maximization of the correspondence to the super item classifications. Cutting scores on the SAT-M were arrived at by empirically finding the score point that minimized the errors of classification.

Inspection of Fig. 10.1 indicates that students that receive SAT-M scores below 300 typically have not achieved mastery of the simple rote arithmetical and algebraic operations that are the necessary foundation for success at the higher level problem solving skills. Scores at or above 300 but below 460 suggest that the typical student in this range has mastered the basic foundations but he or she has not gained proficiency at the simple problem solving level. Students who score at or above 460 but below 670 are likely to have demonstrated mastery at lower level mathematical problem-solving tasks as well as the subordinate skill level consisting of simple, factually based mathematical operations. Finally, students that score at or above 670 are likely to be proficient in the higher level problem-solving skills as well as the two subordinate skill levels in the hierarchy.

LATENT CLASS MODELING OF SAT ITEMS

The goal of this analysis was to determine whether global process descriptions of the cognitive demands of test items could provide a basis for a deeper understanding of test performance. By examining performance relative to the demands across all items, a more qualitative description of student achievement could be obtained. Students who systematically answered problems requiring certain skills correctly, but answered those requiring additional skills incorrectly, are considered to be at a different qualitative level than those who answered both sets of problems correctly. The distinction from traditional approaches is that required skills are not defined by the nebulous construct of "difficulty," but rather by an independent analysis of problem requirements. Whereas in the previous analysis difficulty was a variable used in the construction of testlets, this approach uses difficulty as an index of the validity of a proposed problem-solving model. Processing characteristics are considered independent of any difficulty information.

Item Breakdown

Twenty-three items from an SAT-M examination that contained 60 mathematics problems were selected. These items were selected because they were mathematical word problems that required the student to create a mathematical representation from a given verbal statement. Thus, problems that only required the solving of an algebraic representation were not included for analysis. Further, quantitative comparison items[1] were not included since they have not been analyzed with the same attention given to more conventional word problems.

The partitioning of items was in accordance with a framework proposed by Days (1984). The framework was selected because it provides a suitable level of generality appropriate for the type of items that appear on the SAT. Days classifies problems according to complexity based on the mathematical representation obtained by translating the problem statement into symbols and then considering the nature of solution steps required to solve the problem based on the representation. The model implicitly attends to a large number of variables identified in the mathematical problem-solving literature (cf. Goldin & McClintock, 1984), such as the transparency of the problem statement (e.g., Lewis & Mayer, 1987) and the types of mathematical transformations required (e.g., Riley & Greeno, 1988).

Complexity was defined as a function of seven different features of the problem. A problem was assigned to one of three levels of complexity on each feature dimension. The complexity levels were then considered across all seven features to determine overall problem complexity. The features were as follows:

1. *Number of symbols.* Symbols representing either numbers or variables. Thus, a problem that stated "There were 2 apples and 5 oranges, how many fruit altogether?" would be considered to have three symbols: the number of apples, the number of oranges, and the number of fruit. This problem dimension was considered complex if the problem contained at least five different symbols, and simple if it contained four or less.

2. *Variables.* Symbols representing unknown quantities. In the example in feature 1, there is only one variable, the number of fruit. This feature was complex if the problem contained at least three variables, simple if it contained only one. Problems with two variables were considered to be of intermediate complexity for this feature.

3. *Explicitness of stated relationships.* An explicit relationship exists when the value of a variable could be obtained by evaluating an expression based solely on explicitly stated relationships. Thus, while the example in feature 1 is explicitly stated "fruit = apples + oranges," a problem that read "There are 3 more oranges than apples. If you were to add 1 of each there would be twice as many oranges as apples. How many fruit to begin

---

[1]These problems present the examinee with two quantities, which can take any of several forms, and asks whether one quantity is greater, whether the two are equal, or whether no determination can be made on the basis of the information given.

with?" is not explicit. The mathematical representation that would be generated requires a translation from the verbal form into a set of equations. This feature was considered complex if the problem contained any implicit relationships, and simple if all relationships were explicit.

4. *Conversions.* Changing one unit of measurement into another. For example, "Jane has two quarts of juice and drinks two cups. How much is left?" requires a conversion between quarts and cups. Complexity was increased if the problem required any conversions.

5. *Operations.* If the problem representation only required simple addition, subtraction, or multiplication for solution then this feature was considered simple. Representations that required combinations of these operations, including multiplication by fractions, were considered to be complex.

6. *Directness of translation.* If the problem required a system of two or more linear equations with two variables, and one of the variables was directly expressed in terms of the other variable, or in terms of some known quantity, then this feature was considered simple. When the representation of one variable in terms of the other variable had to be developed, complexity was increased.

7. *Transformations.* This refers to the number of arithmetic procedures needed to progress from the mathematical representation to the solution. This includes employing the distributive property, arithmetic operations of equality, and other substitutions and combining of terms. Problems requiring more than four transformations were considered complex on this feature.

Overall Complexity. Overall problem complexity was a function of the aggregate of features considered to be complex. If at least five of the features were thought to be complex, then the problem was considered complex. If four of the features were classified as simple or noncomplex, then the problem was coded as having a simple structure. All other problems were classified as having an intermediate complexity structure. Examples of each of the three problem types are presented in Table 10.2. Of course, many mathematics problems can be solved more easily than suggested here by the "normative" model due to the elegance of problem representation. For example, the intermediate problem example becomes very simple once one realizes that the time up the mountain must be twice as long as the time down the mountain. Using that representation, the numbers of symbols and transformations are reduced.

Procedure

Data from an administration of the SAT-M were included from 1,200 test takers. Only the 23 word problems analyzed by the Days framework were included. The data were then analyzed in two different ways. First, traditional test

TABLE 10.2
Sample Problems and Processing Characterization

Sample Problems	Processing Characterization
Low Complexity	
John, working without interruption, finished three different jobs during 7 working hours. If 2 hours and 10 minutes and 1 hour and 30 minutes were spent on the first two jobs, how much time was spent on the third job?	Symbols—4 (Job1, Job2, Job3, Jobtot) Variables—1 (Job3) Explicitness—Explicit Conversions—Yes (hours and minutes) Operations—Simple Directness—Simple Transformations—<4
(A) 3 hr. *(B) 3 hr. and 20 min.* *(C) 3 hr. and 40 min.* *(D) 4 hr.* *(E) 4 hr. and 20 min.*	Only one feature considered complex. Problem classified as *low complexity*.
Intermediate Complexity	
Jane hiked to the top of a mountain at an average rate of 5 kilometers per hour and returned immediately along the same path at an average rate of 10 kilometers per hour. If she started up the path at 2:00 p.m. and returned to her starting place at 8:00 p.m. on the same day, at what time did she reach the top of the mountain?	Symbols—5 (Rateup, Ratedown, Timetot, Timeup, Timedown) Variables—2 (Timeup, Timedown) Explicitness—Implicit Conversions—No Operations—Simple Directness—Simple Transformations—>4
(A) 4:00 p.m. *(B) 5:00 p.m.* *(C) 5:40 p.m.* *(D) 6:00 p.m.* *(E) 6:30 p.m.*	Four features complex, three features simple. Problem classified as *intermediate complexity*.
High Complexity	
At a county fair, the fire company sold pretzels and soda at the same unit price but sold 250 more sodas than pretzels. If soda sales totaled $1400 and pretzel sales totaled $1000, how many sodas were sold?	Symbols—6 (Pretzels, Soda, Price, Sodasales, Pretzelsales, Salesdif) Variables—3 (Pretzels, Soda, Price) Explicitness—Explicit Conversions—No Operations—Complex (decimals) Directness—Complex (number of items arrived at by determining unit price) Transformations—>4
(A) 160 *(B) 600* *(C) 725* *(D) 875* *(E) It cannot be determined from the information given.*	Five variables considered complex. Problem classified as *high complexity*.

analysis programs (IRT) were applied to the data. Second, a latent class analysis using Yamamoto's (1987) program, with classifications based on the problem analysis, was used to analyze the data.

Traditional Test Analysis

Item statistics are presented in Table 10.3. Proportion correct ranges from .143 to .828, with a mean accuracy of .472. Biserials range from .359 to .748 with a mean of .618. Corresponding a, b, and c estimates from a three-parameter BILOG (Mislevy & Bock, 1983) analysis are also presented. The respective means (and standard deviations) for these three parameters are 1.177 (.442), .459 (.902), and .169 (.092).

From such an analysis, several interpretations are typically offered. First, estimates of the difficulty and discriminating capability of any item are obtained. Thus, problems within this sample represent a range of difficulties and are fairly effective in discriminating individuals. The analysis also provides an estimate of each individual's ability or θ, which is a joint function of the individual item estimates, but which is essentially a proxy for number correct (Lord, 1980,

TABLE 10.3
Statistics for SAT-M Items

Item	% Correct	Biserial	a	b	c
14	82.75	.550	0.754	−1.363	.184
2	80.00	.500	0.636	−1.308	.183
1	77.92	.581	0.883	−0.840	.251
15	71.50	.724	1.558	−0.495	.186
4	63.75	.652	1.115	−0.117	.234
17	61.75	.741	1.523	−0.180	.155
3	59.75	.359	0.561	0.909	.402
16	59.25	.620	0.922	0.055	.219
5	58.33	.516	1.096	0.572	.373
18	53.92	.726	1.180	0.033	.114
6	52.83	.733	1.245	0.072	.114
7	51.42	.555	0.614	0.183	.110
19	50.50	.582	1.045	0.554	.250
8	43.33	.581	0.952	0.761	.196
11	31.75	.726	1.122	0.811	.069
10	30.00	.748	1.265	0.879	.078
9	28.42	.494	1.296	1.479	.184
21	28.42	.570	1.877	1.262	.173
20	28.08	.683	1.631	1.079	.125
12	20.92	.545	1.066	1.679	.110
23	19.17	.633	1.006	1.546	.065
22	17.42	.688	2.545	1.355	.076
13	14.25	.703	1.174	1.633	.040

p. 53). Thus, for a given item, we can estimate the probability of an individual correctly responding given the θ estimate for the individual. Also, given the ability estimate of an individual, the probability of answering any given problem correctly is available.

The analysis defines individuals and items on a similar unidimensional scale, θ. Thus, any individual can be characterized in terms of an ability estimate, which in turn is a function of performance on items for which successful performance is also associated with this same construct. Thus, the definition of ability remains circularly tied to how well individuals respond to test items. There is no definition of item demands apart from the observed performance of individuals on those items. Ability remains an elusive construct that has no interpretive meaning beyond ordering individuals and items.

Latent-Class Analysis

The latent-class model was assumed to be hierarchical. That is, problems of less complexity were assumed to be prerequisite to problems of increased complexity. Thus, the classes are ordered into four groups. The first class represents the case in which knowledge is insufficient to solve any problems, beyond guessing. The second class represents individuals who are able to answer only simple problems. The third class represents those who are successful on simple and intermediate problems, and the final class represents understanding of all problems. For each of the latent classes, an ideal response vector is created that represents expected responses given a person's hypothesized level of understanding. It is important to note that the hierarchical nature of this model is a function of the particular theory of problem complexity adopted here, and is not necessary for all latent-class models (Yamamoto & Gitomer, chapter 11, this volume).

A number of conditional probabilities are calculated for this analysis. First, the conditional probabilities of individuals belonging to any class are obtained. In Table 10.4 the proportion of individuals assigned to each class is given along with the ideal response vector for the 23 items. Individuals are well represented in all four classes, though the fewest number of examinees are in the fourth class.

The second set of conditional probabilities refers to the probability of answering a problem correctly given a class. These probabilities are presented in Table 10.5. The first class represents a lack of understanding that would enable successful solution of any problem. The conditional probabilities are quite low, with the mean of .25 being close to chance. In Classes 2 and 3, the expectation is that only a subset of items would be answered correctly. For both classes there are generally sharp distinctions in the conditional probabilities for items hypothesized to be answered correctly or incorrectly for a particular class. The

TABLE 10.4
Ideal Response Vectors for Latent Classes and Proportion of Subjects in Each Class

	Class			
Item	1	2	3	4
1	0	1	1	1
2	0	1	1	1
3	0	1	1	1
4	0	1	1	1
6	0	1	1	1
14	0	1	1	1
15	0	1	1	1
16	0	1	1	1
5	0	0	1	1
7	0	0	1	1
10	0	0	1	1
11	0	0	1	1
17	0	0	1	1
18	0	0	1	1
19	0	0	1	1
8	0	0	0	1
9	0	0	0	1
12	0	0	0	1
13	0	0	0	1
20	0	0	0	1
21	0	0	0	1
22	0	0	0	1
23	0	0	0	1
Proportion/class	.247	.338	.286	.129

Note. 1 = correct, 0 = incorrect.

fourth class consists of relatively high conditional probabilities of answering each item correctly.

It is of particular interest to compare the conditional probability for an item across classes. One would expect the largest discrimination between probabilities to occur between classes that have different expectations of success for a given problem. Thus, for Problem 14, a relatively easy problem, the expectation is that only those individuals in the first class should answer the problem incorrectly. In fact, the first group has moderate success with the problem, but individuals in the other three classes do have a high probability of answering the problem correctly. To be sure, although the model suggests the same pattern for Item 3, no such discontinuity is observed.

Similar patterns can be observed for intermediate complexity items as well. Individuals in Classes 3 and 4 would be expected to answer these problems correctly, but not those in the other two classes. Problem 5 supports such an assumption very nicely. The conditional probabilities for Classes 1 and 2 are virtually

TABLE 10.5
Conditional Probabilities of Correctly Responding to Items for Each Latent Class

	Class							
	1		2		3		4	
Item	PR	P	PR	P	PR	P	PR	P
14	0	.567	1	.880	1	.915	1	.996
2	0	.564	1	.821	1	.910	1	.956
1	0	.538	1	.740	1	.943	1	.984
3	0	.491	1	.550	1	.650	1	.812
5	0	.438	0	.457	1	.705	1	.925
15	0	.307	1	.699	1	.960	1	.999
16	0	.302	1	.527	1	.758	1	.956
4	0	.296	1	.582	1	.841	1	.988
19	0	.294	0	.377	1	.665	1	.892
8	0	.226	0	.334	0	.551	1	.833
17	0	.211	0	.520	1	.916	1	.992
21	0	.200	0	.156	0	.280	1	.792
7	0	.198	0	.497	1	.687	1	.782
18	0	.169	0	.426	1	.810	1	.948
9	0	.168	0	.223	0	.273	1	.693
6	0	.138	1	.428	1	.780	1	.985
20	0	.138	0	.128	0	.331	1	.844
22	0	.119	0	.039	0	.140	1	.712
11	0	.101	0	.123	1	.520	1	.795
12	0	.097	0	.147	0	.219	1	.566
10	0	.095	0	.124	1	.443	1	.839
23	0	.063	0	.099	0	.242	1	.571
13	0	.023	0	.071	0	.152	1	.538
Mean predicted incorrect (PR_0)		.250		.228		.274		—
Mean predicted correct (PR_1)		—		.653		.767		.843

Note. PR: predicted response, 1 = correct, 0 = incorrect. P, Conditional probability of correct answer.

identical and relatively low, while there is a much greater chance of success in the two higher classes. Once again, other items, such as Problem 7, do not support the model quite as nicely. Individuals in the fourth class are the only ones expected to answer the complex problems. Item 21 supports the model nicely, as do most of the items in this category.

Taken together, the data support the qualitatively distinct nature of problem demands that comes out of the task analysis, though with some strong caveats. Nevertheless, the worth of the model can be considered on several dimensions. First, we can compare the statistical fit of the latent class model with the three-parameter BILOG model. The fits, based on the log likelihood function, do not differ. Second, we can examine the discontinuities in the data as a method for determining the practical utility of the present model. One way of doing this is to look at the conditional probabilities for an item over the four classes, comparing those relative to the expected success suggested by the model. For 20 of the 23 items, the largest increase in the conditional probabilities occurs at the predicted step. For example, on Item 2, the model suggests that the largest change in conditional probabilities should occur between Classes 1 and 2. For Item 5, the jump should occur between Classes 2 and 3 and for Item 9 the increase should be found between Classes 3 and 4. Thus, one obtains the same statistical fit as with traditional analysis, yet the interpretation of a given score has more theoretical support than does the unidimensional score.

One of the important points of using latent-class analysis, especially with unordered classes, is that individuals with similar number of correct responses can be assigned to very different classifications as a function of which items are answered correctly. In Table 10.6, response patterns for an individual along with their classification are presented. Both individuals in the first pair of subjects answered six problems correctly, yet the first individual was assigned to the first class and the second was assigned to the second class. The difference in the assignment of the two individuals has to do with the confidence estimate that the person has learned the skills necessary to solve simple problems versus the first individual who is assumed to be guessing. In the second pair, both individuals answer 11 problems correctly, yet one is assigned to the second class, and the other is classified as having the understanding necessary to solve intermediate problems. In these and other cases, different classifications are made on the basis of which items were responded to correctly, and how much information or evidence that response provides for a certain class. For example, if the conditional probability of correctly answering a problem is low for a certain class, and the individual answers the problem correctly, then negative evidence is provided for that individual belonging to that class.

Summary

In independently analyzing problem demands and then modeling individual response patterns relative to that analysis, it has been demonstrated that more meaningful interpretations of test data can be obtained. This information is more consistent with the qualitative nature of student learning and performance. Nevertheless, this demonstration only shows the potential of such an approach. The constraints imposed by using existing items, rather than creating items that systematically vary the types of skills and understanding of interest, necessarily limit the types of interpretations that can be made. Hence, the model of item performance is one that lacks some of the precision of other cognitive models of mathematical problem solving. Yet it was selected because of its appropriateness for the types of items that exist on current standardized tests.

TABLE 10.6
Sample Response Patterns with Equivalent Number Correct
and Different Classifications

Subject	Number Correct	Conditional Probabilities of Class Membership				Response Vector
		1	2	3	4	
A1	6	.871	.129	.000	.000	11001000010000100010000
A2	6	.155	.837	.008	.000	10010000000001101100000
B1	11	.024	.926	.051	.000	11110111000001000110100
B2	11	.004	.220	.775	.000	11110010001000111101000

DISCUSSION

The two analysis frameworks presented here offer the possibility of improving assessment on a number of levels. Additionally, the latent-class and HOST models differ themselves with respect to the following issues.

Reliability

The present approaches have the potential to increase the confidence of making judgments about individuals because more data points (items) are available to make more limited sets of decisions. Rather than having performance of each item contribute to an ability estimate that has a large span, constellations of items are used to place individuals in one of a small set of categories. With both HOST and latent class models, the pattern of responses, rather than the summed estimates of ability across items, is used to model the student. Because the models are built to distinguish individuals among a small set of meaningful categories, and are not interested in making potentially infinite discriminations along a continuum, the probability of stable estimation is also increased.

Processing Demand

To a large extent, both models consider item difficulty in terms of processing demands. While both view difficulty as a metric related to the type of processing demands that are built into the item, only the HOST approach factors in difficulty into the classification structure. The latent-class approach considers processing demands independent from the difficulty of the item. Thus, difficulty need not be controlled for in the traditional test development sense. Rather, difficulty is a potentially important cue about the processing demands of the item.

Both models do not go beyond complexes of item characteristics that determine processing demand by breaking items down more precisely. That does not imply, however, that more detailed processing models could not be developed if such information were deemed useful. For example, the latent-class models might separate the transformation and operations variables from the other processing variables. Then items could be developed that systematically vary transformations while controlling for the other variables. This would double the number of classifications, by considering both problem representation demand variables (i.e., variables, symbols, explicitness, conversions, directness) and algebraic complexity as unique processing demand variables.

Theoretical Validation

One of the most promising assets of these types of approaches is that they provide the opportunity to validate a theoretical model of item performance. The HOST model predicts that certain items make greater processing demands than others and that individuals will have difficulty with items at some level of the hierarchy. However, the model also predicts that they will not experience difficulty with items lower than that level in the hierarchy. Violations of that prediction would count as evidence against the specified model.

In the current example of latent-class modeling, the hypothesized classes are also hierarchically related in terms of processing demand. Processing demand is independently determined from a combination of item characteristics. Weakness of the model would be evident in the statistical fit of the model to the data, and of the patterns of predicted and observed values. In both the HOST and latent-class analyses, the evidence is at least as supportive of categorical modeling as it is of traditional testing assumptions.

While the HOST approach is dependent on hierarchical test construction, the latent class is not bound by such constraints. In fact, one can imagine classes that are qualitatively distinct, yet not hierarchical in nature. To pursue the example just given, there may be individuals who are skilled in representing a problem, but encounter difficulties with complex algebraic transformations. Another group of individuals may be strong algebraically, but weak in representational skills. These two classes obviously are not related hierarchically. However, gathering evidence for these types of classes is dependent on deliberate test item design, addressed later. Existing instruments, because of current design specifications, tend to be more easily interpreted by hierarchical models.

The cognitive demand models that apply here are essentially cognitive operations models where the operations are inferred from and, to a certain extent, limited by the test specifications of the SAT-M. In some sense, however, this can lead to a much broader interpretation because at any given developmental level a student can perform a number of operations successfully. The interpretive task here is to define what the within-level operations have in common and how the between-level operations differ. The usefulness as well as the validity of these interpretations requires the introduction of both external criteria information and additional internal validation through the use of student protocols gathered in a one-on-one situation.

External validation could include the use of classification scores in predicting "unbundled" grades. Other applications might include the measurement of change as a student goes from the PSAT to the SAT-M. Diagnostic interpretations could be made at the group level, for example, school level, and possibly at the individual level if the response pattern approach is used. In a sense the approaches described here might be termed the "unbundling" of the SAT-M. Thus the most relevant criteria would be the unbundled grades.

Interpretation

The interpretations offered by these approaches are more informative than those derived from traditional test analyses. In traditional analysis, individual ability is estimated to fall at some point along an ability dimension. This measure is only meaningful when contrasted with other individuals. Absent such a reference group, the test score is an arbitrary value that describes nothing about what an individual does or does not know.

Interpretations in either of the proposed frameworks are more enlightening primarily because item and test characteristics are described independent of the norm-referenced population. Items are described in terms of the demands that they make on the examinee. Tests are described as complexes of those items. Therefore, a score assignment does not refer to an abstract dimension, but rather to the success an individual has with items that make different processing demands. This sort of interpretation is more informative in terms of diagnostic and instructional decision making.

Again, the interpretations in the current examples are still relatively general. However, these limitations are not inherent in any approach. Instead, they are a result of the very general goals of the testing instrument surveyed and of the current nature of test development that strives for unidimensional measures.

Test Design

HOST and latent-class methodologies both contribute to and benefit from improved test design. Improved test design consists of building items that are constructed on the basis of an underlying theory of problem-solving performance. Theory-based tests make possible theoretically based interpretation of test results. This contrasts markedly with the relatively atheoretical nature of current test development practice.

Given a theoretically based test, the particular features of a model can then be tested. If results are not in accord with the model's predictions, then it is necessary to revise the model, or to understand whether there is a problem in translating from theory to item. An improved theory should then aid in future test design.

Measurement of Change

Current measurement methodologies are not very good at describing change in an individual across time. Change scores tend not to be very meaningful on a standardized, normative scale. What does a 50-point gain mean for a low scorer in contrast with a high scorer? Current practice offers little by way of interpreting these gains.

Both latent class and HOST models present the possibility of describing change in a more informative fashion. People moving from one classification to another in either model demonstrate a describable improvement in processing ability. An example of this type of approach has been attempted within the HOST model.

One use of the proficiency probability scores would be to furnish change scores in longitudinal studies in which one wishes to relate processes to changes in proficiency described on a continuous scale. These proficiency probabilities have particularly desirable characteristics as change measures because they implicitly weight changes that occur on the hard items differently from changes on the easy items. They could prove to be useful in evaluating or relating changes from the PSAT as a junior to the SAT as a senior to educational process measures.

In short, gains over time have a different diagnostic meaning depending on where in the total test score distribution the changes took place. This scoring approach to measuring change explicitly takes into consideration that a student that gets two additional hard items correct upon retesting should get more credit than a student who gets two additional easy items correct. Rock and Pollack (1987) have shown that such diagnostic gain scores are more useful than the raw or residualized gain scores when relating change in tested performance to school processes.

Issues

One criticism that may be leveled at any hierarchical cognitive demand model is that the difficulties associated with the levels are in some sense artificial. That is, one can always construct an extremely hard declarative knowledge item that is at least as hard as any items that would be classified as demanding complex processing. However, in order to do this one must tap specialized content material that only a few students have been exposed to in the normal educational sequence. More importantly, it would be difficult to demonstrate that such proficiency or excessive detailed knowledge is a necessary condition for successful performance in the problem-solving tasks that behaviorally anchor the higher levels.

One other concern that is only partly addressed in this study is the question of reliability. Would a student who is declared proficient at one classification on one form of a test receive the same classification on another form? Because there were not sufficient items to make up two parallel sets of items within one form for either analysis, there is no easy answer to this question. To a certain extent the fact that the observed super-item response patterns provided an excellent fit to the assumed underlying hierarchical model in each of three forms suggests that the hierarchical scale was internally consistent in the HOST model.

A final issue is centered around determining the appropriate level of analytic detail for a given testing purpose. Clearly, the very general models put forth here can be improved through more directed test and item design. However, there is also the potential to have more detailed models that lead to much more specific questions about a student's understanding. No single test can satisfy the needs of specific diagnosis and global institutional claims simultaneously. Guidelines need to be developed that address the conditions under which different levels of analysis are appropriate.

ACKNOWLEDGMENTS

We would like to thank Norman Frederiksen and Bob Mislevy for their constructive comments, Kentaro Yamamoto for important input into the HYBRID analysis, and Judy Pollack for technical programming.

REFERENCES

Briars, D. J., & Larkin, J. H. (1984). An integrated model of skill in solving elementary word problems. *Cognition and Instruction, 1,* 245–296.

Brown, J. S., & Burton, R. R. (1978). Diagnostic models for procedural bugs in basic mathematical skills. *Cognitive Science, 2,* 155–191.

Cole, N. S. (1988). A realist's appraisal of the prospects for unifying instruction and assessment. In *Proceedings of the 1987 ETS Invitational Conference: Assessment in the service of learning* (pp. 103–117). Princeton, NJ: Educational Testing Service.

Days, H. C. (1984). Classifying algebra problems according to the complexity of their mathematical representations. In G. A. Goldin & C. E. McClintock (Eds.), *Task variables in mathematical problem solving* (pp. 297–310). Philadelphia: The Franklin Institute Press.

Goldin, G. A., & McClintock, C. E. (Eds.). (1984). *Task variables in mathematical problem solving.* Philadelphia: The Franklin Institute Press.

Kilpatrick, J. (1978). Variables and methodologies in research on problem solving. In L. L. Hatfield & D. A. Bradbard (Eds.), *Mathematical problem solving* (pp. 7–20). Columbus, OH: ERIC Clearinghouse for Science, Mathematics, and Environmental Education.

Lazarsfeld, P. F. (1960). Latent structure analysis and test theory. In H. Gulliksen & S. Messick (Eds.), *Psychological scaling, theory and applications* (pp. 83–96). New York: Wiley.

Lewis, A. B., & Mayer, R. E. (1987). Students' miscomprehension of relational statements in arithmetic word problems. *Journal of Educational Psychology, 79,* 363–371.

Lord, F. M. (1980). *Applications of item response theory to practical testing problems.* Hillsdale, NJ: Lawrence Erlbaum Associates.

Mayer, R., Larkin, J., & Kadane, P. (1984). A cognitive analysis of mathematical problem solving ability. In R. J. Sternberg (Ed.), *Advances in the psychology of human intelligence* (Vol. 2, pp. 231–273). Hillsdale, NJ: Lawrence Erlbaum Associates.

Mislevy, R. J., & Bock, R. D. (1983). *BILOG: Item analysis and test scoring with binary logistic models.* Mooresville, IN: Scientific Software, Inc.

Riley, M. S., & Greeno, J. G. (1988). Developmental analysis of understanding language about quantities and of solving problems. *Cognition and Instruction, 5,* 49–101.

Riley, M. S., Greeno, J. G., & Heller, J. I. (1983). Development of children's problem-solving ability in arithmetic. In H. P. Ginsburg (Ed.), *The development of mathematical thinking* (pp. 153–196). New York: Academic Press.

Rock, D. A., & Pollack, J. (1987). *Measuring gains—A new look at an old problem.* Paper presented at the ETS/DoD Conference in San Diego, CA.

Siegler, R. S. (1983). Information processing approaches to cognitive development. In W. Kessen (Ed.), *Handbook of child psychology: History, theory, and methods* (Vol. 1, pp. 129–211). New York: Wiley.

Schoenfeld, A. H. (1985). *Mathematical problem solving.* Orlando, FL: Academic Press.

Wheeler, A., & Embretson, S. (1986). *The effects of test anxiety on the cognitive components of mathematical reasoning.* Unpublished manuscript.

Yamamoto, K. (1987). *A model that combines IRT and latent class models.* Unpublished doctoral dissertation, University of Illinois, Champaign-Urbana.

Comments on Chapters 7-10

John B. Carroll
University of North Carolina at Chapel Hill

In one way or another, the four chapters on which I comment here are devoted to making tests meaningfully connected with processes of learning and performance of cognitive tasks—more meaningfully, that is, than may have been the case for earlier generations of tests. Actually, making tests meaningfully connected with learning is hardly a new idea. It was present even in some of the earliest modern discussions of standardized achievement tests, as in a text by Monroe, DeVoss, and Kelly (1917). The idea of testing for understanding was central in the work of Ralph Tyler and his associates in developing the highly innovative educational achievement tests used in the so-called Eight-Year Study of the Progressive Education Association (Smith & Tyler, 1942). The theme of making tests to measure understanding rather than merely factual knowledge occurs every so often in the series of handbooks of educational measurement sponsored by the American Council on Education (Lindquist, 1951; Linn, 1989; Thorndike, 1971), but without great emphasis or a singular focus. The problem, it seems, is that it has been very difficult for test constructors—whether they be full-time professionals at the job, or teachers or professors—to move away from easier approaches and to develop evaluation procedures that will assess students' deep comprehension of concepts in mathematics, science, history, literature, or whatever. Developing such procedures requires much effort, time, and creativity—elements that are often in short supply in educational measurement work.

The basic premise of Sandra Marshall's chapter (chapter 7) is, as she states, that "meaningful learning requires the development of well-formed schemas."

"Assessment of learning," she continues, "can thus be redefined as the assessment of schema formation and use." Schema theory, she says, underlies much recent research in cognitive psychology, but "the schema as a psychological construct is widely used but poorly defined in cognitive psychology." Her initial problem is how to define the term. In this, I think, she is only partly successful, perhaps because her presentation is abstract and highly general. The drawings in Figs. 7.1–7.3 are hard for the reader to connect to examples of schemas in the real world. I found it useful to look up David Rumelhart's (1980) discussion, to which she refers, of what a schema might be. His analogy of a schema to a play, with its plot and characters, was immediately meaningful. The schema or idea of buying something, for example, can be thought of as carrying out a little play that involves a buyer, a seller, some merchandise, and a medium of exchange (money, or even clam shells). Marshall's notion, therefore, could be seen as one of treating arithmetic story problems as little "plays" in which various kinds of quantities are the "actors"; the precise ways in which these quantities are to be related and handled in solving a problem would define *schemas* that are to be recognized and used by the problem solvers.

This, at least, was the idea I arrived at after studying Marshall's text and figures (Figs. 7.4–7.7) that were intended to demonstrate how the idea of schema could be applied to the process of solving arithmetic story problems. I came to understand that her instructional program was designed to teach students to recognize different kinds of schemas underlying simple arithmetic story problems, in terms of a rather idiosyncratic mode of diagramming such schemas (as illustrated in the lower part of Fig. 7.6). I gathered that she proposes that there are five basic schemas—Change, Group, Compare, Vary, and Restate—that could underlie all such problems. Unfortunately, she found it necessary to limit herself to talking only about the Change schema—where the "characters" are usually amounts (of number, money, etc.) that "change" after certain actions. It is not clear to me whether the five schemas she posits are actually necessary or sufficient to cover—singly or in combination, perhaps—all arithmetic story problems that might be devised. Although I probably should not trust my introspections, I sense that I don't tend to think of these kinds of problems in terms of the schemas she offers. What was most surprising to me was that the subjects Marshall used for validating her system were college freshmen, some of whom were having difficulty solving story problems that I imagine most bright fourth or fifth graders would solve without any trouble! Yet the problems she presented are described as "nonstandard questions about topics in arithmetic [these students] have never studied before." How this could be, when most of the questions deal with situations requiring simple arithmetic operations for their solution, escapes me. I fell to wondering whether this seemingly awkward system of classifying story problems was indeed the most appropriate system for helping college freshmen who are disabled in mathematics.

Be that as it may, Marshall's chapter is of interest in that it offers a possible procedure for training students in a certain mode of thought in solving arithmetic story problems and for testing the understandings they derive from this training. There is not much, if any, test theory in this chapter—and only the slightest hint of a research design for evaluating the system of instruction through certain multiple regression analyses. The focus seems to be on whether students acquire the schemas that are taught, not on whether they thereby become more successful in solving arithmetic story problems. Whether acquisition of schemas, in Marshall's terms, could be a causal element in producing greater competence is not yet clear from her research. This research, however, seems to be only in its early stages; one hopes that further work will produce more convincing evidence for the schema scheme!

The chapter by Feltovich, Spiro, and Coulson (chapter 8) is impressive for its thorough discussion of the problems of teaching and testing for complex conceptual understanding in biomedical education. Diagnosing and understanding the multiple causes of heart failure, for example, in terms of basic physical and biological concepts is something that requires much more than rote memory for technical terms and their meanings. It would require precise and discriminating knowledge of the conditions under which the relevant concepts would apply and interact in particular cases. Although the authors focus on problems in biomedical education, it is evident to a careful reader that similar problems of advanced understanding would be encountered in many other disciplines, from nuclear physics to psychology and sociology.

The authors start by focusing on the differences that exist between introductory learning in a field and the acquisition of advanced knowledge. Introductory learning merely presents concepts for simple *memoriter* learning, frequently oversimplifying and glossing over fine nuances and exceptions. Feltovich et al. provide a useful classification of types of oversimplification that occur in introductory learning. Acquiring advanced knowledge, in contrast, implies the ability to "apply it flexibly in diverse, ill-structured and sometimes novel contexts"—with full recognition and discrimination of the ambiguities and multiple possibilities that can be presented by real-world situations. Educational testers are more familiar and, probably, more comfortable with situations in which introductory learning is to be assessed. They are aware that the assessment of advanced understanding is much more difficult and elusive.

Essentially, Feltovich et al. present a theory of conceptual difficulty that has implications not only for how instruction should be designed to promote advanced conceptual understanding but also for how the attainment of this kind of conceptual understanding is to be assessed. They present a series of 11 principles for designing instruction, followed by notes on how these principles can also apply in testing. The general characteristics of the required tests include such things as (a) sufficient length of stems to build up "the requisite dimensions of complexity," (b) multiple approaches to insure testing of complex interrelationships in different circumstances, and (c) evaluation of the student's readiness, at a given stage, for new learning and understanding. The authors recognize that the ideal tests might be too extensive and time-consuming; they have had to develop a strategy for confronting the problem of "selectivity" in the biomedical curriculum.

This chapter by Feltovich et al. has even less than Marshall's of what we usually think of as test theory. It contains only brief suggestions about what tests of advanced understanding might look like, and it has only hints of the authors' degree of success in using and validating such tests. Its value comes, rather, in its detailed proposals about instruction in advanced conceptual understanding and the evaluation of such instruction. These proposals might well be adapted for use in other domains of instruction.

Masters and Mislevy (chapter 9) introduce their chapter on new views of student learning by recounting cases in which students exposed to instruction in various subjects develop incorrect understandings of concepts. They state their aim as being to consider "the problem of constructing measures of achievement that are based, not on tests of learners' abilities to recall facts and apply memorized routines, but on inferences about students' levels of understanding of key concepts in an area of learning." In essence, this aim is similar to that of the other chapters considered here. These authors, however, emphasize that one answer to the problem might be to expand testing procedures to permit scores to reveal fine-grained differences in levels of understanding. This would be done, they say, through (a) the identification of key concepts in an area of learning, (b) constructing tests of such concepts with "ordered outcome categories" through which students' observed responses are related to unobservable states of understanding, and (c) depicting the results in terms of placement of students into the ordered categories. They provide two brief illustrations of such procedures. One concerns the various states of understanding that can be exhibited by children learning to add numbers like 6 + 8—at the simplest level, by counting—and at a more advanced level, by using learned number facts. The other illustration addresses children's solutions to balance-beam problems, for which Siegler (1981) showed that a hierarchy of rules can be established to interpret different stages of understanding.

This chapter introduces a modicum of test theory by showing how a Rasch-like model can be fitted to ordered response data, even when subjects may use different strategies to solve problems. It also suggests that various other psychometric models, for example, Wilson's (1989) Saltus model, can be used for evaluating stages of learning. The impression, however, is that these models can be applied only to relatively simple and very well-defined concept-learning problems. It is not clear, for example, whether these procedures could be used to address the advanced concept understandings discussed by Feltovich et al.

Even greater use of test theory is made in the chapter by Gitomer and Rock (chapter 10), on "addressing process variables in test analysis." Like Sandra Marshall, they are concerned with arithmetic story problems—but this time, with those in the Scholastic Aptitude Test—Mathematics (SAT-M), for which they analyze data extensively. For their purposes, they assume that SAT story problems can be classified in terms of the types and complexity of the processing that these problems require, and that this complexity of processing can be related to the difficulty of such items as indexed by item response theory (IRT).

They present two alternative approaches to analyzing multiple-choice items. One, which they call the HOST (hierarchically overlapping skills test) approach, uses "testlets" composed of small numbers of items that can be shown to represent particular, operationally describable levels of cognitive demand. The other uses a latent-class modeling technique. Essentially, their approaches exemplify procedures for what I have called, in chapter 12 in this volume, the behavioral scaling of test performance, and indeed they present a behavioral scaling interpretation of the SAT-M scale. As they show, the lowest level starts at a value of 300, for "task recognition + application of simple rules," proceeding to a value of 460, where "insight" begins to be added, and then to a value of 670, where "production" begins to become involved in the solution of problems. Through this kind of behavioral scaling with reference to levels of cognitive task demands, ability becomes no longer "an elusive construct that has no interpretive meaning beyond ordering individuals and items." The two approaches appear to yield similar results, even though their logical bases are somewhat different.

Both of these approaches assume that test items for mathematical story problems can be scaled hierarchically, in some general sense, in that the behaviors tapped by the lower-level items are deemed to be prerequisite to the behaviors tapped by the higher-level items. The procedures are of a relatively global character in that they do not assume detailed analyses of processes in performing the item tasks, in contrast to Marshall's approach, in which there is an attempt to specify the schemas involved in a given story problem. Nevertheless, they offer ways of examining the kinds of processes involved in items of various difficulties and of relating those processes to a scale that must almost by definition be assumed to be unidimensional, that is, a scale for measuring the ability to solve mathematical story problems.

We thus have in these chapters a modest sample of the kinds of approaches that are currently being explored, at this stage of the educational measurement enterprise, in order to yield appraisals of students' levels of understanding of concepts involved in several areas of the curriculum, particularly in mathematics but also in applied science. In none of them did I find any discussion of whether "short-answer" or multiple-choice techniques are generally adequate for testing comprehension, or whether more complex testing procedures are called for. In fact, every one of the chapters seemed to sanction multiple-choice formats, along with other formats. Apparently most of the authors feel, as I do, that it is possible for well-designed items in multiple-choice format to test deep comprehension. What is somewhat discouraging is the enormous amount of effort that seems to be demanded by each of these approaches—effort that requires not only careful use of concepts from cognitive psychology but also high creativity in the construction of testing procedures and diligent attention to data management and analysis. Although the general public clamors for tests that better measure conceptual understanding, it needs to recognize what this will take in terms of hard work and dollars.

REFERENCES

Lindquist, E. F. (Ed.) (1951). *Educational measurement*. Washington, DC: American Council on Education.

Linn, R. (Ed.) (1989). *Educational measurement* (3rd ed.). New York: American Council on Education & Macmillan.

Monroe, W. S., DeVoss, J. C., & Kelly, F. J. (1917). *Educational tests and measurements*. Boston: Houghton Mifflin.

Rumelhart, D. A. (1980). Schemata: The building blocks of cognition. In R. Spiro, B. Bruce, & W. Brewer (Eds.), *Theoretical issues in reading comprehension* (pp. 33–58). Hillsdale, NJ: Lawrence Erlbaum Associates.

Siegler, R. S. (1981). Developmental sequences within and between concepts. *Monographs of the Society for Research in Child Development, 46*.

Smith, E. R., & Tyler, R. W. (1942). *Appraising and recording student progress*. New York: Harper.

Thorndike, R. L. (Ed.) (1971). *Educational measurement* (2nd ed.). Washington, DC: American Council on Education.

Wilson, M. R. (1989). Saltus: A psychometric model of discontinuity in cognitive development. *Psychological Bulletin, 105*, 276–289.

11

Application of a HYBRID Model to a Test of Cognitive Skill Representation

Kentaro Yamamoto
Drew H. Gitomer
Educational Testing Service

The aim of this chapter is to introduce a measurement model that directly relates item characteristics to qualitative aspects of performance, with the explicit goal of providing instructionally useful diagnostic information about an examinee. Traditional psychometric models, including in particular logistic item response theory (IRT) models (Lord, 1980; Lord & Novick, 1969), are used to represent individuals on a single continuum of proficiency, an assumption clearly at odds with conceptions of performance derived from recent developments in cognitive psychology and the field of artificial intelligence. While traditional psychometrics may be sufficient and even desirable for some testing decisions, they provide little information relevant to the diagnosis of examinee knowledge or processing skill (Frederiksen, 1986; Glaser, 1972). Quantitative scores are especially misleading when differences in performance are not adequately characterized as being sequentially ordered.

The inadequacy of logistic item response models has led psychometricians to consider new measurement models that are more consistent with contemporary views of human learning and performance. Such models are made more complex by virtue of adding more dimensions (Tatsuoka & Tatsuoka, 1987), adding more parameters (Muthén, 1988, 1989), decomposing the ability construct (Embretson, 1984), adding more ability dimensions (Reckase, 1985), or developing alternate sets of item parameters (Mislevy, 1990). The HYBRID model combines traditional IRT with latent-class approaches, in order to model more qualitative aspects of performance. This chapter covers: (a) a description of the HYBRID model, (b) an outline of parameter estimation procedures, and (c) an application of the model to an actual data set.

AN INTRODUCTION TO THE HYBRID MODEL

The HYBRID model was developed out of the desire to capitalize on the strengths of latent-trait and latent-class models, while overcoming the limitations inherent in each of these approaches. The IRT, characterizing examinees in reference to a single continuum of proficiency, has had great utility in scaling, selection, equating, and management of items, especially in large-scale testing programs. The goals of such tests are consonant with what IRT does best, namely, assigning a single unidimensional continuum scale value to an examinee. However, the construct of proficiency as a unidimensional continuum is largely governed by the intended usage of the test rather than an attempt to describe the qualitative aspects of ability or knowledge of an individual. If a test is to be instructive to examinees and/or teachers, detailed descriptions of knowledge and processing skill are more useful to facilitate further learning than a report of one's relative standing in the population of examinees. Standard IRT is not adequate to describe the qualitative aspects of ability differences that emerge through more detailed analyses of responses. For example, instead of obtaining a total number right score, researchers have looked at patterns of correct and incorrect responses to infer the particular understanding of an individual. Latent-class measurement models build directly on the relationship between response patterns and categorical classification. Patterns are evaluated on the assumption that correct solutions indicate that the student has acquired the cognitive skills necessary to solve a problem, and incorrect solutions indicate some deficit in that set of skills.

Lazarsfeld introduced latent structure analysis, which encompassed both continuous and discrete item response models, in the 1950s. Since then, improvements in modeling latent classes have been made, though the mathematical aspects of the models are fairly consistent among the work of Lazarsfeld and Henry (1968), Goodman (1974), Dayton and Macready (1976), Wilcox (1979), and Paulson (1986). Though latent-class models have been in existence for quite some time, the lack of available parameter estimation programs that could handle more than 10 items in a reasonable time prohibited wide acceptance. Paulson (1986b), using the marginal maximum likelihood estimation method of Bock and Aitkin (1981), was able to estimate parameters of many latent classes efficiently.

Each class in a latent-class model is characterized by a particular response vector (an idealized response pattern), representing hypothesized performance under a particular cognitive state. Examinee responses may not be perfectly consistent with the idealized response pattern of any class. Therefore a vector of probabilities is created that represents the likelihood that an individual in a given class will respond to a problem in a given manner. The supposition is that we can predict with some degree of certainty how an examinee will answer a given set of problems if we know the particular understanding an examinee brings to a task. Conversely, we can infer a particular cognitive state based on the responses given to those problems. Research along these lines has been carried out by Brown and Burton (1978) and Birenbaum and Tatsuoka (1981) in the area of arithmetic, by Siegler (1981) using balance-beam problems, and recently by Gitomer and Van Slyke (1988) in a study of electronic gate problem solving.

In contrast to IRT models, latent-class models are suitably applied to unordered classes of performance. Latent-class models can represent both unordered and ordered cognitive processes, using sets of conditional probability vectors, with each vector representing a unique set of cognitive processes. However, it is difficult to discriminate among ordered classes accurately. Ordered classes, especially if there are many, are more consistent with continuous models.

Although advances have been made in the estimation algorithms of the latent-class model, the major difficulty in identifying the latent-class model still remains namely, to delineate mutually exclusive and together exhaustive classes. That is, a set of classes must be defined that will include all respondents. It may be theoretically possible to represent knowledge domain in its entirety by the exhaustive list of latent classes. However, such a practice leads to a potentially unlimited number of latent classes, or limited only by the number of unique response patterns. Of course, such a model is uninformative and unmanageable. The rule-space methodology was developed by Tatsuoka in response to this problem, in the context of classifying response patterns as to the so-called *rule of operation* that one can use in solving a problem in some well-defined domain, such as arithmetic or algebra (Tatsuoka & Tatsuoka, 1987). Tatsuoka used the IRT model to estimate not only the IRT ability, but also a value for a *caution index* for each response pattern, which is a function of residuals of responses from the IRT model. By mapping all response patterns by their estimated ability values and values of the caution index, it is possible to find clusters of points if they exist, with each cluster representing a group of similar response patterns that are consequences of a particular rule applied to problems. The utilization of the qualitative information about knowledge and rules of operation in the rule-space method occurs after a continuous model has been applied. In contrast, the HYBRID model uses the information, such as rules of operation, from the beginning, in terms of model parameters that are more similar to those of the latent-class model than those of the rule-space method. In the following sections, the HYBRID model and later an application of the model to the data collected by Gitomer and Van Slyke (1988) are described.

HYBRID MODEL OF IRT AND LATENT CLASSES

The HYBRID model (Yamamoto, 1987) was developed to cope with the aforementioned problems, namely, the need for models to represent qualitative aspects of performance, while at the same time recognizing that performance of some individuals may best be captured by continuous models. The HYBRID model is a hybrid of IRT and latent classes. Examinees are characterized either on an IRT scale or as belonging to one of several latent classes that represent key, qualitatively meaningful cognitive states. As with many measurement models, conditional independence is assumed to hold for both IRT and latent-class groups.

There are three sets of parameters for the HYBRID model: (a) IRT parameters (a set of item parameters for each item and an ability parameter for each examinee), (b) the relative proportion of individuals in the IRT and latent classes for the population as a whole, and (c) a set of conditional probabilities for each of the latent classes. Note that the ability parameter is only meaningful to those examinees who can be best characterized by the IRT model rather than the latent class models. The program estimates these parameters using the marginal maximum likelihood method (Bock & Aitkin, 1981; Mislevy, 1983). Every possible option to constrain model parameters that HYBIL (Yamamoto, 1989) is able to do is selected in the input file.

A practical way to understand the parameters of the model is to view the ability domain as being divided into multiple classes. Some classes are ordered, in the sense that the conditional probability of a correct response in one class is always greater for all items than it is for the other class. These ordered classes are represented by the IRT model with one set of parameters. The other classes are not ordered and a set of conditional probabilities characterizes each class uniquely, along with an estimate of the proportion of individuals best described by each class.

ESTIMATION OF MODEL PARAMETERS

This section presents an overview of the estimation method unique to the HYBRID model very briefly. The estimation method is a straightforward extension of Bock and Aitkin's (1981) marginal maximum likelihood (MML) method. There are more detailed descriptions of the MML method in Harwell, Baker, and Zwarts (1988) and in Yamamoto (1989).

The parameterization of the IRT model is conventional, and the following example represents the two-parameter logistic IRT model, where $P(x_i = 1|\theta_j, \xi_i)$ is the conditional probability of a correct response for item i with the parameter values $\xi_i = (a_i, b_i)$ by an examinee with ability θ_j:

$$P(x_i = 1|\theta_j, \xi_i) = \frac{1}{1.0 + \exp[-Da_i(\theta_j - b_i)]} .$$

The propensity of correct responses for a subject j in a latent class k ($k > 1$, i.e., $k = 2, 3, \ldots, K$, if there are $K - 1$ latent classes) can be expressed as follows. Note that $\gamma = 1$ represents the IRT group and $\gamma > 1$ the latent classes:

$$P(x_i = 1|\gamma = k) = P_{ki} .$$

By the assumption of conditional independence in the IRT model as well as for latent-class groups, the conditional probabilities of observing a response vector **x** under the IRT class and the $K-1$ latent classes are as follows.

$$P(\mathbf{x}|\theta,\xi) = \prod_{i=1}^{I} P(x_i = 1|\theta,\xi_i)^{x_i} [1 - P(x_i = 1|\theta,\xi_i)]^{1-x_i} \qquad \text{(IRT)}$$

$$P(\mathbf{x}|\gamma = k) = \prod_{i=1}^{I} P(x_i = 1|\gamma = k)^{x_i} [1 - P(x_i = 1|\gamma = k)]^{1-x_i} \quad \text{(LC)}.$$

Let us suppose that the mixture population is distributed with a density function $f(\theta) \cdot P(\gamma = 1)$ in an IRT subpopulation and in the combined latent-class subpopulation with $P(\gamma > 1)$. Note that the mixture of IRT and latent classes is represented by Γ with the density function $P(\gamma)$. The marginal probability of observing a response pattern **x** given the model parameters ζ and Γ is the summation of conditional probabilities over all classes including the IRT group and the latent classes, which can be expressed as

$$P(\mathbf{x}|\zeta) = \sum_{k=1}^{K} P(\mathbf{x}|\zeta,\gamma = k) P(\gamma = k)$$

$$= \int_{\theta} P(\mathbf{x}|\theta,\xi) f(\theta) \, d\theta \, P(\gamma = 1) + \sum_{k=2}^{K} P(\mathbf{x}|\zeta,\gamma = k) P(\gamma = k).$$

Calculating the integral and succeeding derivatives to identify maxima for this function is cumbersome. Therefore, a method based on Dempster, Laird, and Rubin's (1977) EM algorithm is used for actual parameter estimation. Bock and Aitkin (1981) advanced the idea of using EM with probit-analysis inner cycles in the area of IRT parameter estimation, by replacing the theta continuum with convenient quadrature points for the integration. By following their approach, the idea of discrete theta within IRT is used; latent classes are of course already discrete by definition.

As its name suggests, the EM algorithm is divided into two steps: the expectation step (E-step) and the maximization step (M-step). The E-step entails estimating the proportion of correct responses on each item and the proportion of subjects in the predetermined ability intervals for the IRT group, as well as in given latent classes. The M-step deals with maximizing the log likelihood function to obtain new parameters, using estimated statistics from the E-step as if they were known, observed values.

The E-Step

After approximating the theta distribution, which may be continuous, by a discrete distribution over a finite number of points θ_q for the IRT group q, the posterior distribution over θ of the IRT group given a response vector $\mathbf{x}_j$ is the conditional probability of $\mathbf{x}_j$ given item parameters and ability divided by the marginal probability of $\mathbf{x}_j$ given item parameters, and can be expressed as

$$P(\theta_{q'}|\zeta,\mathbf{x}_j,\gamma = k) = \frac{P(\mathbf{x}_j|\zeta,\theta_{q'},\gamma = k) \, A(\theta_q)}{P(\mathbf{x}_j)} \, P(\gamma = k),$$

where $P(\mathbf{x}_j)$ is the marginal probability of $\mathbf{x}_j$, and is given by

$$P(\mathbf{x}_j) = \left[\sum_q P(\mathbf{x}_j|\theta_q,\zeta,\gamma = 1) \cdot A(\theta_q) \right] \cdot P(\gamma = 1)$$
$$+ \sum_{k=2}^{K} P(\mathbf{x}_j|\zeta,\gamma = k) \cdot P(\gamma = k).$$

The posterior probabilities of the IRT group ($\gamma = 1$), and latent class ($\gamma > 1$) are

$$P(\gamma = 1|\zeta,\mathbf{x}_j) = \frac{\sum_q P(\theta_q|\zeta,\mathbf{x}_j,\gamma = 1) \cdot P(\gamma = 1)}{P(\mathbf{x}_j)}$$

and the posterior latent-class probability for class k is

$$P(\gamma = k|\zeta,\mathbf{x}_j) = \frac{P(\mathbf{x}_j|\zeta,\gamma = k) \cdot P(\gamma = k)}{P(\mathbf{x}_j)}.$$

Then the two sets of estimates needed to derive provisional estimates of propensity of correct response on item i, given a quadrature point or a class, are the number of tries $N_{\gamma iq}$ and the number of correct responses $R_{\gamma iq}$. They are

$$\hat{R}_{liq} = \sum_{j=1}^{J} \frac{x_{ij} \cdot P(\mathbf{x}_j|\theta_q,\zeta,\gamma = 1) \cdot A(\theta_q)}{P(\mathbf{x}_j)} \cdot P(\gamma = 1),$$

$$\hat{N}_{liq} = \sum_{j=1}^{J} \frac{P(\mathbf{x}_j|\theta_q,\zeta,\gamma = 1) \cdot A(\theta_q)}{P(\mathbf{x}_j)} \cdot P(\gamma = 1),$$

$$\hat{R}_{ki} = \sum_{j=1}^{J} \frac{x_{ij} \cdot P(\mathbf{x}_j|\zeta,\gamma = k)}{P(\mathbf{x}_j)} \cdot P(\gamma = k),$$

$$\hat{N}_{ki} = \sum_{j=1}^{J} \frac{P(\mathbf{x}_j|\xi,\gamma = k)}{P(\mathbf{x}_j)} \cdot P(\gamma = k).$$

The M-Step

The maximization step consists of maximizing likelihood equations entailed by the likelihood function. By differentiating the logarithm of the likelihood expression with respect to a generic parameter u, which can be either an item parameter of IRT or a parameter of latent classes, we get

$$\frac{\partial \ln L(\xi|\mathbf{X})}{\partial u} = \sum_{j=1}^{J} \frac{\partial \ln \sum_\gamma P(\mathbf{x}_j|\xi,\gamma) \cdot p(\gamma)}{\partial u}$$

$$= \sum_{j=1}^{J} \frac{1}{\sum_\gamma P(\mathbf{x}_j|\xi,\gamma) \cdot P(\gamma)} \cdot \frac{\partial \ln \sum_\gamma P(\mathbf{x}_j|\xi,\gamma) \cdot P(\gamma)}{\partial u}$$

Notice that the first derivative of the log-likelihood with respect to IRT item parameters reduces to the ordinary MML problem for IRT as addressed by Bock and Aitkin (1981), as summands in the differential for $\gamma = 2, \ldots, k$ become zero. Likewise, differentiating the log-likelihood with respect to latent-class parameters causes the IRT portion to drop out. Thus the M-step maximization for the IRT parameters and the latent-class parameters can be carried out independently. The several methods to estimate ability parameters are described in Bock and Aitkin (1981) and Yamamoto (1989).

Let u_i be a parameter of item i. By applying Bayes' theorem, and Bock and Aitkin's (1981) idea of discrete theta points to approximate integration, the earlier equation for IRT item parameters can be rewritten as follows:

$$\frac{\partial \ln L(\xi|\mathbf{X})}{\partial u_i} \doteq P(\gamma = 1) \cdot \sum_q \frac{\partial P_i(\theta_q)}{\partial u_i} \cdot \frac{[R_{iq} - N_{iq} \cdot P_i(\theta_q)]}{P_i(\theta_q) \cdot Q_i(\theta_q)},$$

where $\partial P_i(\theta_q)/\partial u_i$ for a_i and b_i are $-D(\theta_q - b_i) \cdot P_i(\theta_q) \cdot Q_i(\theta_q)$ and $D \cdot a_i \cdot P_i(\theta_q) \cdot Q_i(\theta_q)$, respectively. Marginal maximum likelihood estimates of item parameters are found as the roots of the expressions obtained by setting the derivatives of the marginal log likelihood equal to zero. In the M-step of the EM algorithm, this expression is solved with the E-step expectations $\hat{R}_{iq}$ and $\hat{N}_{iq}$ replacing R_{iq} and N_{iq}. Let u_k be a parameter of latent class k. The likelihood equation takes the form

$$\frac{\partial \ln L(\xi|\mathbf{X})}{\partial u_k} = \sum_{i=1}^{I} \frac{\partial P_{ki}}{\partial u_k} \cdot \frac{R_{iq} - N_{iq} \cdot P_{ki}}{P_{ki} \cdot (1 - P_{ki})}.$$

Again, in the EM algorithm, each M-step proceeds with the E-step expectation R_{iq} and N_{iq}. The values of latent-class parameters that make this equation zero may be derived algebraically, depending on the type of latent classes. A feature that distinguishes many latent-class models proposed in the past is the type of constraints imposed on the conditional probabilities. Let us demonstrate a solution on one type of latent class; the same constraint will be used to analyze the real data later. Recall that a latent class k is characterized by a response vector $\mathbf{T}$ of I many zeros and ones. The L-type constraints are characterized by one constant α_k representing the conditional probabilities of correct response to items for which $T_i = 1$, and another constant β_k, the probability of correct response to items for which $T_i = 0$. For example, let us suppose $I = 7$ and $T = 1110000$. Then a vector of conditional probabilities given a class k is (α_k, α_k, α_k, β_k, β_k, β_k). Further,

$$\frac{\partial P_{ki}}{\partial \alpha_k} = 1 \quad \text{and} \quad \frac{\partial P_{ki}}{\partial \beta_k} = 0 \quad \text{for items such that } T_i = 1$$

and

$$\frac{\partial P_{ki}}{\partial \alpha_k} = 0 \quad \text{and} \quad \frac{\partial P_{ki}}{\partial \beta_k} = 1 \quad \text{for items such that } T_i = 0.$$

In order to confirm that the converged value is not a local maximum, comparisons should be made on the results obtained by using various starting values. The complete assurance of global maxima is not available at this time.

At present, the fit of the mixture model to a data set cannot be evaluated exactly using existing statistical methods, such as the chi-square test, except in very limited cases. The chi-square test against the general multinomial model can be carried out if the number of subjects is large and the number of items is small, and the distribution of subjects over all possible response patterns is not sparse. However, this chi-square test on data having a sparse response pattern distribution is not warranted. For more general cases, there is not a consensus regarding the appropriate indicator even for an IRT-only measurement model. In light of this, we suggest the usage of several indices to seek convergent evidence, such as chi-square and Akaike's "an information coefficient" (AIC). Although the chi-square distribution may not be exactly appropriate, the likelihood ratio of nested models is available to examine the model fit. For example, comparison of the fit of two models, such as an 1PL IRT versus 2PL IRT model, can be made by examining the improvement in the log-likelihood, taking into account the number of degrees of freedom expended. When the competing models are not nested, the aforementioned log-likelihood test is even less appropriate. In such a case in place of the log-likelihood test, AIC can be used. More recent work by Aitkin (1989) suggests a possibility that his notion of direct likelihood inference can be used as a general index of the model fit. At this time his likelihood hypothesis testing is not available.

Once the model parameters are estimated, the posterior probability distributions can be used to classify the subjects to the IRT group or to the one of latent classes. A heavy concentration of the posterior distribution of each response pattern in one of the classes or in the IRT group makes it easy to classify the examinee. Within the IRT group, posterior probability on one quadrature point would be correlated with the neighboring quadrature points. In addition, in the IRT group, classification to a particular quadrature based on its mode is not qualitatively informative. Instead, a very informative statistic would be the weighted mean across all quadrature points, which provides a summary information.

ANALYSIS OF ELECTRONIC GATES PROBLEMS

Application of the HYBRID model is appropriate when inferences about the cognitive demands of items and of the cognitive skill of individuals are desired. Most sets of standardized test items do not encourage such inferences because the cognitive demands of items are not understood, nor are they varied systematically. Also, in cases where each item requires distinctly unique and inseparable cognitive skills, the HYBRID model offers very little beyond standard IRT. The HYBRID model is most applicable when a part or the whole of the understanding required to answer each question in a particular way is shared with other items. The Gitomer and Van Slyke (1988) data made up an ideal HYBRID application because item demands were explicitly defined, item characteristics were manipulated systematically, and a cognitive error analysis revealed that examinees did make consistent types of errors across subsets of items that shared identifiable characteristics.

Data

The domain is comprised of a subset of common symbols for electronic logic gates that are used in digital electronic circuits. Because the ability to read and interpret logic gate symbols is one of the basic skills for any electronics technicians who troubleshoot equipment, the domain has substantive significance. Inputs and outputs to these mechanisms are binary and are distinguished by differences in voltage levels (high [H] or low [L]). The level of inputs into a gate determines a single output as a function of the particular Boolean logic internal to a gate. For example, a two-input OR gate will have an output value of HIGH when at least one of the inputs is high.

In the present study two types of logic gates are examined: exclusive OR (XOR) and exclusive NOR (XNOR) gate types. Both gate types have exactly two inputs. The XOR gates operate on the following principles: If both inputs are the same (HH or LL), then the output is L. If the inputs are mixed, then the output is H. Operation of the XNOR gate is the inverse. That is, in the mixed condition the output is L, while when inputs are the same the output is H.

Complicating gate interpretation further is that inputs are affected by the presence of negators, which invert the original input. Thus, a high input that is inverted becomes a low input and vice versa. Negators are represented by small circles placed on the input. Illustrations of each of the 10 XOR and 10 XNOR gate symbols are presented in Fig. 11.1.

To correctly interpret any gate symbol, an individual must understand the principle of operation of that gate, as well as the effects of negated inputs. In examining individual performance it was observed that individuals responded systematically and erroneously to items that shared certain characteristics (Gitomer & Van Slyke, 1988). For example, for XOR gates some individuals correctly interpreted mixed inputs as having a HIGH output and LL inputs as

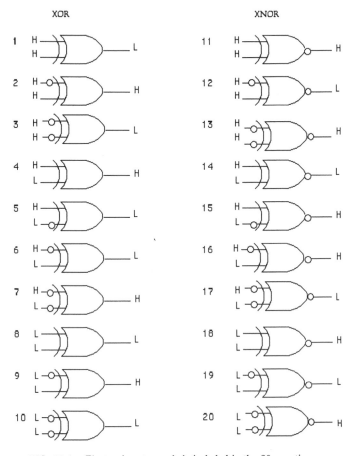

FIG. 11.1. Electronic gate symbols included in the 20 questions.

having a LOW output, but incorrectly thought that HH input gates had HIGH output. Frequently, parallel errors were made for the XNOR gates. That is, the only errors were for the HH input gates, but for the XNOR gates, the output was incorrectly assumed to be LOW.

Because the error patterns were qualitatively different and could be ascribed to specific areas of misunderstanding, a latent-class analysis might seem appropriate. However, for many technicians, systematic errors were not observed. For these individuals, a latent trait model might be most appropriate. Thus, given this sample, the HYBRID model of Yamamoto seemed ideal.

METHOD

Subjects

Two hundred fifty-five avionics technicians in the U.S. Air Force participated in the study. These individuals maintain aircraft electronics equipment, including communications, navigation, instrumentation, and radar systems. The group was primarily male and had aptitude scores that were relatively high (mean overall AFQT [Armed Forces Qualifying Test] scores were approximately in the 75th percentile).

Test Materials and Procedure.   A paper-and-pencil test including 288 logic gate items was comprised of two replications of 144 discrete item types. The test was not timed. Each item consisted of a logic gate type together with a set of inputs. The task was to determine the correct output (H or L).

RESULTS

For this analysis, only the XOR and XNOR gate types were examined. There were two replications of ten XOR gates and ten XNOR gates (see Fig. 11.1). An inspection of the responses suggested that certain error patterns were fairly frequent across subjects. The five most frequent, shown in Table 11.1, were included as ideal classes in the HYBRID model. As a basis for comparison, conventional IRT models were also applied to the data.

Statistical Considerations

Using traditional test analysis procedures provided a mixed message concerning model selection and interpretation. Table 11.2 illustrates that difficulties and biserials are quite respectable. Difficulties are moderate and the biserials sug-

TABLE 11.1
Error Descriptions with Corresponding Response Vectors for 20 Items

Class		Ideal Response Vector (T_{ki})
1	XOR treated with OR logic XNOR treated with NOR logic	01110111100111011110
2	XOR treated with NAND logic XNOR treated with AND logic	11011010111101101011
3	XOR treated with NOR logic XNOR treated with OR logic	10001000011000100001
4	XOR treated with AND logic XNOR treated with NAND logic	00100101000010010100
5	Reversal of XOR–XNOR	00000000000000000000

gest that doing well on one item bodes well for test performance overall. Further, in order to find similarity of two subscales the test is split into subscales of XOR and XNOR items, the correlation between the subscale scores is .808. Internal consistency was assessed as moderately consistent by Cronbach's $\alpha = 0.879$, and average interitem correlation was .266. Therefore, classical test theory affirms the assumption of measuring a single trait with a fairly consistent measurement instrument, exhibiting a reasonable score distribution.

TABLE 11.2
Percentage of Correct Response and Biserial Correlation

Item	% Correct	R_b
1	66.7	.474
2	69.8	.708
3	71.0	.644
4	74.9	.787
5	63.9	.356
6	71.4	.652
7	67.8	.691
8	74.5	.670
9	71.8	.781
10	64.3	.563
11	59.6	.531
12	74.5	.706
13	72.2	.389
14	71.8	.724
15	58.0	.528
16	75.3	.461
17	72.9	.690
18	72.9	.555
19	72.2	.685
20	64.3	.454

However, a factor analysis paints a different picture. Factor analysis can be used to separate pools of items into sets of items that can be considered unidimensional (Bejar, 1980). While the first factor is associated with overall success, the remaining factors are closely associated with the idealized classes derived from the error analysis. It is not the case, though, that the identified classes can be derived clearly from the factor analysis. The second factor has high loadings for items that are correct in Class 3 (see Table 11.1). Thus, an individual high on this factor might be in Class 3 and one low might be in Class 1, for which the model predicts an inverse response pattern. However, the classes represent qualitatively distinct understandings of the domain, not a continuum of some ability. Without supporting error analysis, a very different and misleading interpretation of the factor analysis would be made.

Taken together, the test is sensitive to more than one dimension. However, it is not the case that different items are associated with different dimensions. Rather, it is more accurate to think of the relationship as each item providing information about an individual's weight on all dimensions simultaneously. The factor analysis provides no rationale for breaking the test up into meaningful subscales.

Given the assumptions of IRT, a first question was whether a continuous IRT model could be used to model the data. Three different IRT models, with one, two, and three parameters, respectively, were fit to the data. The χ^2 statistic is not completely appropriate for this data set because of the very sparse response distribution of response patterns relative to all possible patterns. However, the chi-square distribution of the likelihood ratio test may be used with caution to compare models with different parameter restriction. The fit comparison of nonnested models can be performed by using an information coefficient (AIC) (Akaike, 1985). The results are summarized in Table 11.3. The 2pl IRT fits significantly better than the 1pl IRT. The gain in the likelihood ratio in going from the 2pl to 3pl model is not significant when one considers the additional parameters. The AIC indicates that the 3pl model fits poorly compared to the 2pl model. A chi-square fit statistic for item parameters by Bock (1972) indicates that item parameters for five items are not well fit by the 1pl IRT model. All item parameters fit well in the two- and three-parameter models. Thus, the results indicate that the most appropriate IRT model to describe this data is the 2pl model.

An examination of the observed conditional probabilities of correct responding also showed a monotonic increase with ability for all but two items, which can be taken for further confirmation of the appropriateness of using IRT. For both items, the observed conditional probability decreased once by less than 0.05 between the two quadrature points $\theta = -1.33$ and $\theta = -0.44$. Therefore, the available standard indicators indicate that the 2pl IRT model is acceptable for these data. The standard interpretation of theta values would of course be that higher theta values represent increasing mastery of the subject domain.

TABLE 11.3
Comparison of Fit of the Models

Model	$-2 \times$ (log likelihood)	Number of parameters	AIC
1pl-IRT	5383.8	20	5423.8
2pl-IRT	5273.6	40	5353.6
3pl-IRT	5256.1	60	5376.1
3pl-IRT (c fixed) +5LC	4942.7	50	5042.7

Note. AIC = -2 (log-likelihood) + 2 (number of parameters); a smaller value indicates a superior fit of a model to the data.

The fundamental question in this study is whether the application of the HYBRID model, with classes specified from an empirical cognitive analysis, can significantly improve diagnostic assessment in terms of both psychometric and substantive considerations. We contrasted the two-parameter IRT models with a HYBRID model combining IRT with the five latent classes described previously. The constraint used for conditional probabilities of a latent class was $\alpha = 1.0 - \beta$ type. This model assumes consistent model deviation for all items, regardless of whether they are predicted to be answered right or wrong.

The 3pl IRT model was used in the HYBRID model, with the c parameter fixed at .5 for guessing. In effect, then, a two-parameter model was tested. The reason for this was that the REVERSAL class predicts all incorrect responses. If c were not fixed at .5, the responses of individuals in this class would have been picked up by the IRT model, rather than by the latent-class portion of the model. This is due to the fact that all zero responses have ordinal relationship to any response pattern, and hence the lowest ability level can correspond perfectly. Given a dichotomous response format, one would expect random guessing to result in correct responding one-half of the time. Someone in the REVERSAL class would perform significantly worse than chance on these items, even though such an individual must understand a great deal about the domain. A strong argument could be made that greater understanding is evidenced by this individual than by someone who answers half the items correctly by guessing.

The results of the model fit are summarized in Table 11.3. The 3pl (fixed c) + 5LC model fits the data significantly better than any one of the IRT models. Estimated latent class parameters are listed in Table 11.4. The vectors of conditional probabilities strongly resemble the manifest response patterns of the latent classes. This is strong evidence that individuals are responding in a manner highly consistent with the hypothesized classes. Thus, on statistical grounds, the mixed model fits the data better than any of the continuous models.

TABLE 11.4
Conditional Probability of Correct Response for Latent Classes

Class	Conditional Probabilities	
	$\alpha_k, T_{ki} = 1$	$\beta_k, T_{ki} = 0$
1	.84	.16
2	.93	.07
3	.93	.07
4	.92	.08
5		.07

Substantive Considerations

The most important difference between the continuous and discontinuous models emerges upon interpretation of the results. A profoundly different diagnostic picture is evident when the HYBRID model is applied to the data. Based on the cognitive analysis, the five most frequent classes were included as ideal classes in the HYBRID model.

Nearly 25% of the response patterns were modeled by one of the five latent classes. The proportions for each class are presented in Table 11.5. Additionally, over 15% of the subjects answered all items correctly. Thus, for those individuals who made at least one error, almost 30% were modeled by the latent class portion of the program. For almost all individuals modeled by a latent class, the posterior distribution among classes was highly peaked, indicating that the selection between classes was very clear. The rest of the response patterns were best fit to a continuous model.

Besides the fact that the HYBRID model fits the data significantly better than either a two- or three-parameter IRT model, we get a very different interpretation of ability in the IRT group (see Fig. 11.2). The slope is much steeper with individuals assigned to a latent class removed, suggesting a strong demarcation between those who have mastered the domain concepts and those who have not.

The difference in the slopes between the IRT component of the mixed model and the pure IRT model has several causes. First, individuals with the lowest accuracies are placed in a latent class in the mixed model. Belonging to this class suggests the existence of a great deal of domain knowledge that could be remedied by realigning exclusive logic with a particular symbol. In spite of lower accuracy, there is evidence of greater domain understanding for these individuals than for those who are considered to be guessing. Second, much of the gradual increase found in the middle of the regression curves is actually "modeling noise" contributed by individuals who best belong in one of the discrete classes. An examination of the conditional probabilities that an item is answered correctly

TABLE 11.5
Proportions of Individuals Modeled by Each Latent Class

Class		Proportion of Subjects
1	XOR treated with OR logic XNOR treated with NOR logic	.144
2	XOR treated with NAND logic XNOR treated with AND logic	.024
3	XOR treated with NOR logic XNOR treated with OR logic	.028
4	XOR treated with AND logic XNOR treated with NAND logic	.025
5	Reversal of XOR–XNOR	.028

given a class demonstrates that including these individuals on a continuous dimension misrepresents the actual performance (see Fig. 11.3).

Correlations of the estimated conditional probabilities of an individual being assigned to an IRT quadrature point or a latent class are presented in Table 11.6. Each quadrature point represents a potential estimate of ability. The pattern of correlations shows that the probability of belonging to any latent class is unrelated to the probability of belonging to any other class. Similarly, the prob-

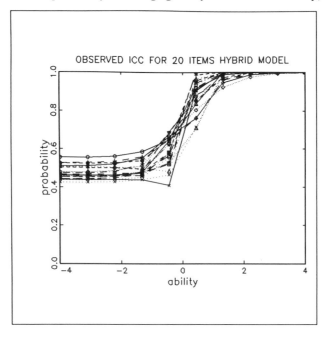

FIG. 11.2.   Observed ICC for 20 items HYBRID model using 3 parameter logistic model (fixed c) and latent classes.

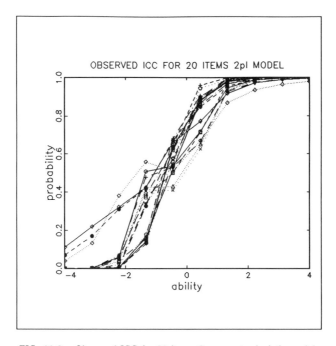

FIG. 11.3. Observed ICC for 20 items 2 parameter logistic model.

ability of belonging to any class is unrelated to overall estimates of ability. Within the IRT model, however, the probability of belonging to neighboring IRT classes is higher than the association between more distant classes. This table once again supports the contention that much of the data are not consistent with a continuous model.

DISCUSSION

Substantively, a number of improvements are offered by adopting a mixed model that characterizes individuals on the basis of their qualitative understanding. First, each of the diagnostic classes is linked to a specified understanding of the domain. A theoretical link to a classification increases the potential for improved instructional decision making. Individuals can be provided adaptive instruction that is targeted to specific needs. There is no need to resort to a generic form of instruction that is not profitable for many individuals. Further, there may be important instruction that could benefit an individual who has a consistent misunderstanding that only affects a small subset of problems. Such an individual would not be given remediation if the total score exceeded a specified cut boundary.

TABLE 11.6
Correlations of Posterior Probabilities

	Ten quadrature points of IRT										Latent classes				
	1	2	3	4	5	6	7	8	9	10	1	2	3	4	5
1	1.00										-.07	-.02	-.02	-.02	.00
2	.52	1.00									-.20	-.09	-.06	-.05	-.08
3	.51	1.00	1.00								-.19	-.09	-.06	-.05	-.08
4	.44	.98	.99	1.00							-.20	-.10	-.07	-.06	-.09
5	.02	.52	.53	.63	1.00						-.20	-.10	-.12	-.11	-.13
6	-.10	-.38	-.39	-.41	-.40	1.00					-.26	-.11	-.12	-.12	-.12
7	-.08	-.32	-.33	-.36	-.41	.01	1.00				-.25	-.09	-.10	-.09	-.09
8	-.07	-.28	-.29	-.31	-.35	-.09	.93	1.00			-.22	-.07	-.08	-.08	-.08
9	-.06	-.26	-.27	-.29	-.33	-.10	.89	1.00	1.00		-.20	-.07	-.08	-.07	-.08
10	-.06	-.26	-.27	-.29	-.33	-.10	.88	.99	1.00	1.00	-.20	-.07	-.08	-.07	-.07
1											1.00				
2											-.07	1.00			
3											-.08	-.03	1.00		
4											-.06	-.03	-.03	1.00	
5											-.08	-.03	-.03	-.03	1.00

Second, learning and performance are, for the most part, not adequately modeled by unidimensional constructs. The latent-class modeling does not require such constraining assumptions. Rather, we can talk about discrete classes of performance that differ qualitatively from one another, much the way cognitive scientists conceptualize individual differences in performance.

Third, the HYBRID model provides a statistically more adequate model for this data. The data clearly are not well represented by unidimensional constructs. Yet the smooth, gradual increase in the IRT only-item characteristic curves belies an incomplete, even inaccurate understanding of the sample. Rather than having a group of individuals whose performance gradually increases with ability, the HYBRID model reveals that there are individuals who understand the domain completely, those who are only guessing, and a large group of individuals with specific partial understanding of the domain. These partial understandings are in no sense hierarchical, and a one-dimensional continuous model is inadequate. Similarly, factor analysis may suppress the qualitative differences of individuals, especially when those differences result in inverse response patterns. Categorical differences can be interpreted incorrectly as continuous phenomena.

Fourth, the nearly unattainable assumption of an exhaustive list of cognitive states can affect estimated parameters adversely if the violation is not small for the standard latent-class model. In addition, as we learn more about the cognitive structure of a particular domain, the list of cognitive states and the relationship among them may change. It is more realistic to accept that we do not know everything but we know something about a particular cognitive structure. Such a partial knowledge can be represented well by latent classes in the HYBRID model, and the IRT portion of the model can capture unknown or ordered classes. It is possible to reduce the contribution of unknowns to parameters of latent classes.

In adopting an IRT framework, multidimensional tests are typically handled in several ways. First, items not fitting a unidimensional model are often eliminated. Another possibility is to break the test up into unidimensional subscales. Latent-class analysis permits the analysis of the full set of items relatively free from the notion of dimensionality.

It is worth reiterating that a primary attribute of this approach is the necessity for specifying the nature of item performance prior to the test analysis. It is also helpful to build in substantial redundancy in the test items. Classification would be more accurate if more than one item provides information about membership within a class. Put another way, any cognitive skill should be requisite in the performance of multiple items (Haertel & Wiley, chapter 14, this volume).

The HYBRID model provides the opportunity to represent some aspects of cognitive structure determined from a separate cognitive analysis in the form of a set of conditional probabilities. It is not possible to model such cognitive structures using traditional IRT techniques. The identification of known structural components, such as salient understandings or misconceptions of materials, is always a good idea, and it results in a model that fits better and is more representative of learning as well. The ability to confirm a model that is derived from a cognitive theory, aside from statistical considerations, represents the greatest potential of models such as HYBRID.

Admittedly, the present work focuses on an especially simple domain that is analyzed relatively easily. Yet detailed cognitive analyses of more complex domains have been developed. This understanding can lead to improved educational assessment that is driven by theories of domain performance rather than the quantitative properties of items, tests, and examinees, modeled by traditional psychometric methods.

Additional examples of application of the HYBRID model can be found in Mislevy and Verhelst (1990) and Yamamoto (1990). The model was applied to a data set with examinees using one of two strategies of responding, especially when a strategy is IRT and the other is randomly guessing. Mislevy and Verhelst found that 1pl IRT and one randomly guessing latent class fit the data nearly as well as 3pl IRT with nearly three times as many number of degree of freedom. Yamamoto extended the model to the multiple-item response models per examinee; that is, a subset of responses of an examinee is best described by a latent class (a guessing class), while IRT is most appropriate for the rest of the responses. Such a model was useful to evaluate speededness of test which was scored number-right. Speededness of test can manifest itself in many ways, for example, when students are running out of time, they may switch from a strategy of thoughtful responses to a strategy of patterned or random responses.

REFERENCES

Akaike, H. (1985). Prediction and entropy. In A. C. Atkinson & S. E. Fienberg (Eds.), *A Celebration of Statistics* (pp. 1–24). New York: Springer-Verlag.

Aitkin, M. (1989). *Direct likelihood inference*. Unpublished paper. Tel Aviv, Israel: Tel Aviv University.

Bejar, I. I. (1980). Biased assessment of program impact due to psychometric artifacts. *Psychological Bulletin, 87,* 513–524.

Birenbaum, M., & Tatsuoka, K. K. (1981). *The effect of different instructional methods on error types and the underlying dimensionality of the test.* (Tech. Rep. 81-3-ONR). Urbana, IL: University of Illinois, Computer-Based Educational Research Laboratory.

Bock, R. D. (1972). Estimating item parameters and latent ability when responses are scores in two or more nominal categories. *Psychometrika, 37,* 29–51.

Bock, R. D., & Aitkin, M. (1981). Marginal maximum likelihood estimation of item parameters: Application of an EM algorithm. *Psychometrika, 46,* 443–459.

Brown, J. S., & Burton, R. R. (1978). Diagnostic models for procedural bugs in basic mathematics skills. *Cognitive Science, 2,* 155–192.

Dayton, C. M., & Macready, G. B. (1976). A probabilistic model for validation of behavioral hierarchies. *Psychometrika, 41,* 189–204.

Dempster, A. P., Laird, N. M., & Rubin, D. B. (1977). Maximum likelihood from incomplete data via the EM algorithm. *Journal of the Royal Statistics Society* (Series B), *39*, 1–38.

Embretson, S. (1984). A general latent trait model for response processes. *Psychometrika, 49*, 175–186.

Frederiksen, N. (1986). Toward a broader conception of human intelligence. *American Psychologist, 41*, 445–452.

Gitomer, D. H., & Van Slyke, D. A. (1988). Error analysis and tutor design. *International Journal of Machine Mediated Learning, 2*, 333–350.

Glaser, R. (1972). Individuals and learning: The new aptitudes. *Educational Researcher, 1*, 5–13.

Goodman, L. A. (1974). The analysis of qualitative variables when some of the variables are unobservable. Part I—A modified latent structure approach. *American Journal of Sociology, 79*, 1179–1259.

Harwell, M. R., Baker, F. B., & Zwarts, M. (1988). Item parameter estimation via marginal maximum likelihood and an EM algorithm: A didactic. *Journal of Educational Statistics, 13-3*, 234–271.

Lazarsfeld, P. F., & Henry, N. W. (1968). *Latent structure analysis*. Boston: Houghton-Mifflin.

Lord, F. M. (1980). *Applications of item response theory to practical testing problems*. Hillsdale, NJ: Lawrence Erlbaum Associates.

Lord, F. M., & Novick, N. R. (1969). *Statistical series of mental test scores*. Reading, MA: Addison-Wesley.

McCutcheon, A. L. (1987). *Latent Class Analysis*. Sage University Paper series on Quantitative Applications in the Social Sciences, 07-064. Beverly Hills: Sage Publications.

Mislevy, R. J. (1983). Item response models for grouped data. *Journal of Educational Statistics, 8*, 271–288.

Mislevy, R. J., & Verhelst, N. (1990). Modeling item response when different subjects employ different solution strategies. *Psychometrika, 55*, 195–215.

Muthén, B. (1988a). Some uses of structural equation modeling in validity studies: Extending IRT to external variables. In H. Wainer & H. Braun (Eds.), *Test validity* (pp. 213–238). Hillsdale, NJ: Lawrence Erlbaum Associates.

Muthén, B. (1989a). Using item specific instructional information in achievement modeling. *Psychometrika, 54*, 385–396.

Paulson, J. A. (1985). *Latent class representation of systematic patterns in test responses* (Research Rep. No. ONR 85-1). Portland, OR: Portland State University.

Paulson, J. A. (1986). *Estimation of parameters in latent class models with constraints on the parameters* (Research Rep. No. ONR 86-1). Portland, OR: Portland State University.

Reckase, M. D. (1985). Multidimensional IRT models. In D. J. Weiss (Ed.), *Proceedings of the 1982 Item Response Theory and Computer Adaptive Testing conference*. Minneapolis, MN: University of Minnesota, Computer Adaptive Testing Laboratory.

Siegler, R. S. (1981). Developmental sequences within and between concepts. With commentary by Sidney Strauss and Iris Levin; with Reply by the author. *Monographs of the Society for Research in Child Development, 46*(2, Serial No. 189).

Tatsuoka, K. K., & Tatsuoka, M. M. (1987). Bug distribution and statistical pattern classification. *Psychometrika, 2*, 193–206.

Wilcox, R. R. (1979). Achievement tests and latent structure models. *British Journal of Mathematical and Statistical Psychology, 32*, 61–72.

Yamamoto, K. (1987). *A model that combines IRT and Latent Class models*. Unpublished doctoral thesis. Urbana, IL: University of Illinois Urbana-Champaign.

Yamamoto, K. (1989). *HYBIL; A computer program to estimate HYBRID model parameters*. Princeton, NJ: Educational Testing Service.

Yamamoto, K. (1990, April). *Modeling the mixture of IRT and patterned responses by a modified HYBRID model*. A paper presented at 1990 American Educational Research Association meeting in Boston.

12

Test Theory and the Behavioral Scaling of Test Performance

John B. Carroll
University of North Carolina at Chapel Hill

Behavioral scaling is proposed as a general term to cover various procedures for making test results directly interpretable in terms of what examinees know or can do. It is more inclusive than what has come to be known as *criterion-referencing*, which applies when tests are deliberately designed to provide behavioral information with reference to specific objectives of school learning. Test theory has an important role in behavioral scaling, but behavioral scaling requires use of a person characteristic function (PCF) rather than the item characteristic function. Problems that have arisen in efforts to scale tests behaviorally are discussed. Inasmuch as behavioral scaling is of particular importance and relevance in the case of cognitive ability tests, illustrations are given of behavioral scaling as applied to three subtests of the Woodcock–Johnson Psycho-Educational Battery—Revised, measuring *Gc*, *Gf*, and *Gv*, respectively. Data came from the norming versions of the tests given to 1,800 subjects ranging in age from 4 to 85. The behavioral scaling of these tests permits meaningful interpretation of differences over age groups.

INTRODUCTION

A perennial problem in psychological and educational measurement has been the interpretation of test results in terms of statements about what an examinee knows or can do, as opposed to statements about where the examinee stands relative to others. Conventional ways of interpreting test results have involved some sort of numerical scale that is to be given what is essentially a normative interpretation. Scales for all kinds of tests have been developed; often they have tended to acquire meanings in their own right. For example, people tend to interpret points on the IQ scale or on the College Board Scholastic Aptitude Test scale in terms of subjectively judged degrees of intelligence or aptitude, but without clear ideas of what kinds of intellectual tasks individuals with given scores are able to perform.

Glaser (1963) introduced a distinction, now well recognized and widely used, between what he called *norm-referenced* and *criterion-referenced* tests. (He noted that such a distinction had been recognized earlier.) In his opinion, traditional test theory had led to the development of tests that might be quite satisfactory as norm-referenced tests for emphasizing differences among individuals, but that could be unsatisfactory for assessing differences between groups or the changes that might result from instruction. Subsequent developments in test theory have yielded some progress in developing domain- or criterion-referenced tests (Millman & Greene, 1989) and assessing their reliability (Feldt & Brennan, 1989, pp. 140–143). Nevertheless, even criterion-referencing of tests seldom addresses very well the problem of making clear what students' scores tell about what they can or cannot perform. There is also a tendency among test specialists to feel that the construction of criterion-referenced tests must follow different guidelines from those governing the construction of norm-referenced tests. Because the concept that underlies criterion-referencing ought to be applicable even to many types of norm-referenced tests, it appears that criterion-referencing is not the term of choice in referring in a general way to the process of relating test scores to behavior.

Instead, I propose the term *behavioral scaling.* This is not a new term. In 1955, I chaired an American Psychological Association symposium entitled "The behavioral scaling of psychological and educational tests." One of the participants was Ledyard Tucker, who reported what he called "some experiments in developing a behaviorally determined scale of vocabulary." I have at hand a copy of Tucker's (1955) paper, which from the standpoint of an early version of item response theory considered the problem of establishing a scale with units such that "an increase of one [unit] anywhere along the scale corresponds to an increase in probability of a correct answer from .5 to .7 for an item of appropriate difficulty and standard discriminating power." It was only in this sense that Tucker's scale would represent measurable differences in persons' "behavior." The nearest that Tucker came to alluding to what I would call behavioral scaling was in the fact that he offered specific multiple-choice vocabulary items to illustrate each of the 10 points of his scale, ranging, as he said, "approximately from the 15th percentile of fourth graders to the 85th percentile of [a] higher college group." For example, scale point 1 was illustrated by an item requiring recognition of the similar meanings of *throw* and *toss,* while scale point 10 was illustrated by an item concerned with the meaning of *imbue.* Presumably, by knowing an individual's score on this scale, one could predict what items the individual would probably get right, and the items that the individual would be likely to fail. However, Tucker did not consider prediction of the item difficulties themselves, or comment on the nature of the items found at given scale points.

The behavioral scaling of tests refers to the process of stating in behavioral terms what test results directly imply with regard to what examinees know or can perform. Behavioral scaling is thus one aspect of construct validity. It does not, or need not, extend to problems of external or predictive validity, although adequate behavioral scaling of tests could be of great assistance in dealing with problems of external validity.

In this chapter I propose to do three things:

1. Discuss the role of test theory in making behavioral scaling of tests possible or more meaningful.
2. Discuss a number of requirements and procedures in the behavioral scaling of tests.
3. Explore the use of certain procedures of behavioral scaling as applied to selected tests of cognitive ability.

THE ROLE OF TEST THEORY

Because behavioral scaling is most meaningfully applied to tests that are "good" or satisfactory in some general sense, test theory can help in the construction and analysis of such tests in terms of dimensionality, reliability, discrimination power, and range of difficulty level.

Behavioral scaling would be most readily applied to tests that approach unidimensionality. The construct intended to be measured should be essentially unidimensional in the sense that a single dimension can account for nearly all the variation in ability that is measured. Studies of the items measuring the National Assessment of Educational Progress (NAEP) Reading Proficiency Scale, for example, found that reading skill is essentially unidimensional (Zwick, 1987a, 1987b), despite the fact that logically, many separate skills can be identified in reading behavior. (For example, knowledge of any particular word or sentence structure could be regarded as a separate skill, but in point of fact, such skills tend to be highly correlated in any wide-ranging population.) Modern test theory has made considerable advances in procedures for assessing test dimensionality; Zwick's articles present an excellent review and application of such procedures. It is noteworthy that while reading comprehension as measured by NAEP procedures was found to be unidimensional, other curricular domains measured by NAEP, such as science (Mullis & Jenkins, 1988), appear to be multidimensional to the extent that separate scales (though substantially cor-related) have had to be established for reporting results.

At the same time, it is possible that behavioral scaling could be applied to tests that measure two or more constructs, that is, tests that would be found to be multidimensional. Results of using the linear logistic model of Fischer (1977, 1983), for example, could be behaviorally scaled if separate attention is devot-ed to each of the two or more constructs identified by such a model. The problem of multidimensionality also arises in connection with hierarchical models of in-telligence, where a test could be found to measure not only a first-order factor but also a second-order factor, or even a third-order factor. It would be desir-able to be able to apply behavioral scaling not only to the first-order factor but also to the higher-order factors.

Given that a test is found to be approximately unidimensional, an appropri-ate test theory model can be applied—for example, the Rasch one-parameter model, or a two- or three-parameter logistic model. (The three-parameter model is generally to be preferred because of its greater flexibility.) Such models or-dinarily yield scales both for item (task) difficulty and for ability, and normally these are in the same metric. The item difficulty metric can take account of variations in item reliability, and procedures are provided for translating raw scores (or transforms such as proportion-correct) into the ability metric. Be-havioral scaling can be applied either to the ability metric or to the item difficulty metric. As applied to the ability metric, statements can be made concerning the tasks that individuals at a given level on the ability metric are able to perform at some specified threshold level (e.g., with a probability of .50, or of .70, follow-ing Tucker's suggestion already mentioned, or of .80, following a suggestion of Bock, Mislevy, & Woodson, 1982). These statements would have to refer to behavioral scaling statements applied to the item difficulty metric—that is, statements concerning the nature of tasks placed at given levels on that metric.

It has been customary in item response theory to consider ability–difficulty relations in terms of the item characteristic curve (ICC)—that is, the function showing the increase of probability of correct response on a given item as abili-ty increases. Such a function is useful in considering the operation of given items, but it fails to depict the overall functioning of a series of items in measuring an ability. For this purpose it seems more useful to use the person characteris-tic function (PCF), the function that shows the *decrease* of proportion correct, over items, as difficulty increases (Carroll, 1985). This function is based on the same mathematical expression as is the ICC, but variation in probability of cor-rect responses is examined over item difficulty rather than over ability. Whereas for the ICC, each item can have a different ICC, for the PCF, each level of ability has a different PCF.

The PCF is necessarily based on aggregation of items; ideally, it would be assumed that all items have the same discrimination power. This assumption is in fact made by the one-parameter Rasch model; in the case of the two- or three-parameter logistic models such an assumption must be made in behavioral scaling.

The PCF has the further advantage over the ICC of depicting the variation over item difficulties in expected proportion correct for a given individual (or group of individuals with closely similar scores). If the item difficulties are behaviorally scaled, it is possible to describe an individual's or group's gradient of success in terms of statements about success at different described levels of difficulty. For example, if an individual were to be indexed as being at 200 on the NAEP Reading Proficiency Scale (implying, presumably, that the individual's success at that point is approximately 80%), a PCF function would also supply information as to expected success rates at 150, 250, or other points on the scale. Smith, Stenner, Horabin, and Smith (1989; see also Stenner, Horabin, Smith, & Smith, 1988) have proposed what they call a Lexile Scale of Reading Comprehension, based on reading difficulty measurements of texts or test items. They give illustrative PCF information for an individual with related lexile ability of 1000 as follows:

Text Difficulty	Sample Titles	Predicted Success Rate
600	(*Old Man and the Sea*—Hemingway)	96%
800	(*The Time Machine*—Wells)	90%
1000	(*Reader's Digest*)	75%
1200	(Encyclopedia)	50%
1400	(*The Washington Post*)	25%
1600	(*New England Journal of Medicine*)	10%

Here, the lexile ratings are linear transforms of Rasch-model item and ability indices; the behavioral scaling is in terms of typical reading material rated at specified levels of difficulty. Values on the lexile difficulty scale are pegged at a 75% success rate for individuals at given points on the scale.

PROCEDURES OF BEHAVIORAL SCALING

Can Behavioral Scaling Be Applied to Any Test?

The proper answer to this question is probably in the negative. A critical requirement is that the test be well constructed, be of adequate length and reliability, and consist of a series of items or tasks, of varying difficulties, that are more-or-less uniformly valid in measuring the construct intended to be measured. The role of test theory in test construction for behavioral scaling has already been discussed. The requirement of varying difficulties is made because behavioral scaling needs reference points at different levels along a difficulty scale. If all items were of similar difficulties, behavioral scaling could refer only to a narrow band of the ability scale. Indeed, behavioral scaling depends on the assumption that an ability is defined in terms of individual differences in the points on a specified scale at which persons are able to perform at threshold levels.

It is often helpful, in producing behaviorally-scaled tests, to make an analysis of the behavioral domain that is to be sampled by the test. This process is illustrated in the "domain tests" constructed by Flanagan and associates (Flanagan et al., 1964, pp. 3–96) for Project TALENT. Domain tests were constructed in each of three areas: vocabulary, spelling, and reading comprehension. Work on the domain vocabulary test has apparently never been formally published, but from a draft manuscript in my possession (M. F. Shaycoft, 1968) it appears that the object was to develop a test that would indicate, for any given student, the absolute size of the student's English vocabulary in terms of number of word *meanings* the student knows. In developing this test, word meanings were systematically sampled from dictionary entries, and test items were drawn up in an effort to ascertain whether the respondent actually knew the specified word meaning, allowing for chance success by guessing in five-choice vocabulary items.

The domain test in spelling consisted of 150 words sampled systematically from the 5,000 words that were highest in frequency in the Thorndike–Lorge word list (Thorndike & Lorge, 1944). It was thus possible to make statements about the probability with which students could correctly spell words in this set of 5,000 words.

The domain for the tests in reading comprehension was defined in terms of the kinds of fiction and magazine nonfiction that students at the high-school level were likely to read.

Systematically defining the content domain is highly desirable for purposes of behavioral scaling, but it would not be necessary or even possible in all instances. Many well-constructed cognitive ability tests would be amenable to behavioral scaling, even though not based on systematic analyses of their content domains.

How Are Behavioral Scaling Statements to Be Framed?

The behavioral scaling statements that are to be attached to points on the item difficulty scale (or to points on the ability scale, with reference to thresholds of ability) can take any of several forms. Exactly what form or forms they may take can depend on the nature of the construct. For example, if the test is based on the sampling of a defined content domain, behavioral scaling can refer to attributes or categories of that domain.

A fourfold classification of types of behavioral scaling statements is proposed:

Type I: Specification of Illustrative Items, Tasks, or Relevant Materials

The simplest type is the specification of illustrative items, tasks, or materials associated with given scale points. This was the method used by Tucker (1955); he gave one illustrative item at each of 10 scale points, stating that an individual at that scale point would be expected to have a 70% chance of passing the item.

This type of behavioral scaling statement is often useful, particularly when it accompanies statements of other types. The main problem with it is that the test user cannot always be expected to have a clear idea about the difficulty of an item or what it presumably measures; furthermore, the behavioral scaling statement is not readily generalizable to other items of similar difficulty. The difficulty of a single item can be affected by many factors—the exact phrasing of the stem and the alternatives, for example. Even if more than one illustrative item is offered for a given scale point, as has been done for anchor points of the NAEP Reading Proficiency Scale (National Assessment of Educational Progress, 1985), it is sometimes left up to the test user or interpreter to form an impression of what behaviors the statement could be generalized to, or what level of ability or competence the scale point represents.

A variant of this is illustrated by the behavioral scaling statements attached to scores on the Project TALENT domain test of reading comprehension, namely, the specification of literary or magazine materials that a student with a given score would be expected to comprehend—a procedure also used by Smith et al. (1989) for their lexile scale of reading comprehension, as noted earlier.

Type II: Verbal Description of Competence Associated with Given Scale Points

A second type of behavioral scaling statement is the verbal description of a level of competence in terms of typical behaviors expected at that level. It is illustrated by the scaling statements attached to the various anchor points of the NAEP Reading Proficiency Scale (Beaton, 1987, pp. 381–390). These statements were drawn up by specialists in the teaching and testing of reading comprehension on the basis of groups of NAEP exercises selected to represent given anchor points.

It is difficult to formulate statements of this kind that are sufficiently meaningful, precise, and unambiguous. In many circumstances this form of description may be the most satisfactory that can be obtained, but the phraseology of such statements needs to be thoroughly thought through, edited, and checked.

A variant of this is illustrated by a procedure that was used to provide behavioral scaling of objective foreign language proficiency tests (Carroll, 1967). For each of several foreign languages, groups of students and teachers widely varying in proficiency were given a standard language proficiency interview and assigned ratings on five-point scales of speaking and reading proficiency that have been widely accepted in the U.S. government for purposes of appraising language proficiency for foreign service. Each point on these scales is defined both in a brief description and with an amplified description; for example, point 3 on the speaking scale is described as "minimum professional proficiency," or in more detail, "able to speak the language with sufficient structural accuracy and vocabulary to satisfy representation requirements and handle professional discussions within a special field." Substantial correlations having been found between these ratings and objective proficiency test scores (r ranging from .63 to .82), the test scores were behaviorally scaled by equating them to the ratings and thus to the verbal descriptions provided for those ratings.

Type III: Use of Task or Content Parameters

A third general type of behavioral scaling uses parameters that describe the item or task content with reference to physical or other attributes (e.g., the difference in musical pitch, measured in hertz, in a pitch discrimination task) or with reference to a behavioral domain. Examples of the latter are the descriptions attached to scores on Project TALENT's domain tests in spelling—where the score indicates the number or percentage of words, in the first 5,000 words of the Thorndike–Lorge list, that the student can spell correctly. A further example is the lexile scale of reading comprehension (Smith et al., 1989) mentioned earlier, which is based on measures of vocabulary difficulty and sentence length in text material.

Such parametric descriptions have the virtue of clarity and objectivity, but test users may not always be able to grasp their meaning without thorough acquaintance with the characteristics of the task, scale, or domain. If, for example, one is told that a person is estimated to know 20,000 word meanings, one might be hard pressed to judge whether this signals a mediocre, average, or large vocabulary. Most test users would prefer to fall back on a normative interpretation. Despite its apparent scientific superiority, the parametric approach to behavioral scaling is beset with certain problems and requires that the test interpreter be adequately informed about the nature of the scale. But then, the problem is perhaps no more serious than that faced by a person familiar with the Fahrenheit scale of temperature who tries to learn the meaning of points on the Celsius scale.

Type IV: Reference to Levels of Cognitive Processing

A fourth type of behavioral scaling statement would make reference to the level of cognitive processing involved in correct response at a given item difficulty level. No illustrations of such statements have come to my attention, but I give such an illustration in connection with a cognitive ability test next.

BEHAVIORAL SCALING OF THREE COGNITIVE ABILITY TESTS

In order to explore procedures and problems in behaviorally scaling cognitive ability tests, a study was made of item data for selected subtests of the Woodcock–Johnson Psycho-Educational Battery—Revised (Woodcock & Johnson, 1989), or actually for the norming versions of those subtests. The data, kindly supplied by R. Woodcock (the chief author of the test), appeared to be particularly suitable for this purpose, for several reasons: (a) The tests are individually administered and require open-ended responses rather than choices among alternatives (as in typical paper-and-pencil tests); thus, the value of the chance success parameter, c, can be assumed to be zero. (b) Complete data were available on a large number of cases selected over a wide range of ages (4–85) and amounts of ability. (c) The test items were carefully devised, selected, revised, and arranged in order of difficulty by the test's authors to measure abilities over a wide range. (d) It is highly likely that each test is essentially unidimensional. (It was beyond the scope of this chapter to investigate the dimensionality of the tests.)

The objective was to illustrate how person characteristic functions can be derived and used, in conjunction with information on item difficulties and other characteristics of items, to assign substantive meanings to test scores in terms of increasing levels of cognitive performance. An effort was made to interpret these levels in terms of the knowledge bases and information-processing requirements necessary to attain them.

The cognitive ability portion of the Woodcock–Johnson Psycho-Educational Battery—Revised contains in all 21 subtests. For present purposes, data from three tests were selected for analysis:

1. *Picture Vocabulary*. According to the authors' manual, this test measures the ability to name familiar and unfamiliar pictured objects, and measures primarily verbal comprehension or crystallized intelligence (Gc). The norming version studied contained 33 items arranged in approximate order of difficulty. (The publication version contains 58 items.) Subjects are presented with these items, in order, in such a way as to determine the level of difficulty that each can attain. That is, a subject is given successive items until the subject can be confidently predicted to fail all or nearly all of the remaining items, after which testing is discontinued. Items are scored 1 for passing and 0 for failing; the total score is the number of passes.

2. *Concept Formation*. This test "measures the ability to identify rules for concepts when given both instances of the concept and non-instances of the concept. . . . This test primarily measures reasoning or fluid intelligence (Gf)." The revised test (identical to the norming version studied here) contains 35 items, administered in order of difficulty until the subject can be predicted to fail the

remainder. The score is the number of passes. The test is a controlled-learning task, and when subjects make errors in the learning phase, they are corrected. Part of the difficulty level of an item in this test is therefore a function of its location in the test.

3. *Visual Closure.* According to the authors, this test "measures the ability to identify a drawing or picture that is obscured in one of several ways. The picture may be distorted, having missing lines or areas, or have a superimposed pattern. This test primarily measures visual processing (Gv)." The norming version of the test contains 37 items arranged and administered in approximate order of difficulty. (The publication version contains 49 items.) The score is the number of passes.

Data on 1,800 individuals given these tests were processed by the program LOGIST (Wingersky, 1983) in order to determine estimates of item and ability parameters as a basis for behavioral scaling. This program uses maximum likelihood procedures to estimate the values of the IRT parameters a, b, and c for each item of a test and the values of θ for each individual in a sample given the test, on the basis of the expression for the expected probability of success on an item:

$$ p = c + \frac{1 - c}{1 + \exp[-1.7a(\theta - b)]} , \tag{1} $$

where a is the item discrimination parameter, b is the item difficulty parameter, and c is the pseudo-guessing parameter. In use of the program with the Woodcock–Johnson tests, the value of c was set equal to zero because there was little reason to believe that any responses arose from chance guessing. For each test, the analysis considered the 1,800 cases as a single sample despite great variation in age. For purposes of behavioral scaling, it was assumed that any given test score had the same meaning and corresponded to the same person characteristic function, regardless of the age of the subject.

The data were also analyzed by a program that determined empirical probabilities of passing selected groups of items for selected score groups.

BEHAVIORAL SCALING
OF THE PICTURE VOCABULARY TEST

Performance on the Picture Vocabulary test involves two abilities: (a) ability to recognize a pictured object as something that has a name or commonly accepted appellation, and (b) ability to give that name from active recall vocabulary. In both cases, retrieval from long-term memory is required. Behavioral scaling thus should make reference to the parameters of the knowledge base (behavioral scaling Type III).

Word frequency in large counts of running words in English text is a variable that has often been used to estimate the familiarity of words in active or passive vocabularies, and hence it was considered as a possible basis for behavior-scaling the items. The total frequency of all acceptable responses for an item was assessed using the *American Heritage Word Frequency Book* (Carroll, Davies, & Richman, 1971). This was easily done for items with one or more single words as responses, but difficulties were encountered in the case of phrases like "movie house" and "panning gold." Also, because the frequency list does not include information about meanings, it was necessary to exclude frequencies of responses like *falls* (item 11) because *falls* could be a verb having little to do with *waterfalls* (another acceptable response). Thus, some judgment was required in assessing word frequencies. In the case of single-word responses (e.g., *padlock*, item 5) frequencies for related words—plurals, capitalizations, etc. (e.g., *PADLOCK, padlocks*, and *padlocked*)—were included. Frequencies for combined entries were computed by the method illustrated on p. 3 of the *Word Frequency Book* and stated in terms of the SFI (Standard Frequency Index) measure used there. The resulting values of SFI are listed in Table 12.1, which also presents various item statistics.

The behavior-scaling analysis was limited to 27 items (items 4–34, exclusive of 4 items considered invalid by the test's authors) because of missing data for the others. The correlation between SFI and b was disappointingly low in absolute magnitude, $-.528$, in contrast to correlations around $-.8$ found in other contexts (Carroll, 1980). The smallness of this correlation is probably due to the inaccuracy of the SFI measure in assessing the familiarity of the objects or activities pictured and the familiarity or recallability of the names. Because of the low correlation, it was decided to lay aside the word-frequency ratings and to use, instead, ratings of word familiarity found in Dale and O'Rourke's (1981) *Living Word Vocabulary*.

For each of some 44,000 English word meanings (often two or more meanings for a given word), the *Living Word Vocabulary* gives two ratings: (a) the grade level at which the word was tested (tests were given only at Grades 4, 6, 8, 10, 12, 13, and 16), and (b) the percent correct responses for students at that grade level (for the computations described below, the percentages were converted to proportions). Dale and O'Rourke's intent was to specify the lowest grade level at which the percent correct responses (in three-choice vocabulary items) would be at least 67%. In the present study, both ratings were tabulated for the most probable response word (and meaning) to each item in the Picture Vocabulary test. The multiple correlation of b (from LOGIST) with the grade rating and the logit of the Dale–O'Rourke proportion correct was computed; the resulting R was .858, both variables having significant contributions (for grade rating, $t = 5.84$, $p < .001$; for logit of proportion correct, $t = -2.66$, $p < .05$). The regression equation was

$$\text{Est}(b) = -1.1013 + .2719(\text{Grade}) - .7815[\text{logit}(P)].$$

TABLE 12.1
Picture Vocabulary Test: Item Statistics (N = 1,800)

Item Number	p	$\zeta(p)$	LOGIST Values a	b	SFI	Grade Rating
4	.9851	-2.17	1.42	-2.69	52.6	3.95
5	.9687	-1.86	1.97	-2.09	38.0	3.06
6	.9578	-1.73	1.53	-2.09	51.7	1.35
7	.9627	-1.78	2.15	-1.97	51.0	2.83
9	.9285	-1.46	1.56	-1.79	46.0	3.44
11	.9040	-1.30	1.90	-1.53	49.2	3.44
12	.8800	-1.17	1.47	-1.48	56.2	4.11
10	.8572	-1.07	1.86	-1.28	44.4	5.61
14	.8278	-0.95	1.76	-1.16	39.1	3.27
15	.7814	-0.78	1.99	-0.96	53.8	5.41
19	.6806	-0.47	2.54	-0.56	52.0	5.93
16	.6734	-0.45	1.87	-0.55	33.6	6.23
17	.6555	-0.40	1.56	-0.51	55.0	5.72
18	.5361	-0.09	1.36	-0.12	47.4	6.99
20	.5376	-0.09	1.88	-0.11	47.9	6.36
21	.5216	-0.05	1.78	-0.06	38.3	9.48
23	.3114	0.49	1.82	0.62	40.5	7.52
25	.2966	0.53	2.18	0.65	41.7	8.62
22	.2695	0.61	2.18	0.74	45.2	8.96
26	.2210	0.77	2.36	0.90	23.8	11.74
27	.1784	0.92	2.36	1.06	44.8	7.39
28	.1429	1.07	2.22	1.22	37.3	9.35
31	.1301	1.13	2.16	1.29	35.6	14.30
30	.0839	1.38	2.51	1.50	37.3	11.29
32	.0760	1.43	2.77	1.53	38.1	14.44
34	.0474	1.67	1.43	2.05	42.7	10.29
33	.0339	1.83	1.60	2.14	41.3	7.92
Mean		-0.15	1.93	-0.19	43.9	7.00
SD		1.17	.37	1.38	7.5	3.39

Note. Items arranged in order of values of b. Items numbered 8, 13, 24, and 29 in the test were considered invalid by the test's authors; hence, data for these items were missing. Data for items 1-3 and 35-37 are not listed because these items were not used in the analysis, due to missing data either for LOGIST values or grade ratings, or both. Raw scores were based on only the 27 items listed.

For ready interpretation, the resulting values of Est(b) were rescaled linearly so that they had a mean (7.0) and standard deviation (3.388) identical to the mean and standard deviation of the grade ratings. The rescaled grade ratings for the items are listed in Table 12.1. For purposes of scaling them against values of b their regression on b was computed as

$$\text{Est(Grade rating)} = 7.4111 + 2.1125b.$$

The next task was to construct a graph showing estimated PCFs for selected raw scores as a function of item difficulties, with the behavioral scalings represented by the rescaled grade ratings aligned with the item difficulties. In constructing such a graph, it was necessary to consider the relation between raw scores (X) and the values of θ reported by the program LOGIST. In the general case this relation can be nonlinear, but in the present case it was clearly linear, with a correlation of .99916. The linear regression of θ on X was

$$\text{Est}(\theta) = -2.5976 + .1792X.$$

The values of $\text{Est}(\theta)$ were substituted into the three-parameter logistic equation 1, giving expected probability of success as a function of the difference between θ and b. Considering that c is assumed to equal zero, this equation becomes one for a two-parameter model:

$$p = \frac{1}{1 + \exp[-1.7a(\theta - b)]} \, . \tag{2}$$

The value of a selected for use in this equation was the mean of the values of LOGIST a for the 27 items used in the analysis, namely, 1.93. (Experimentation with other possible values indicated that this value was likely to produce best fit to the empirical data.)

Fig. 12.1 is the resulting PCF graph showing a series of parallel lines giving, for selected raw scores or score intervals, expected probabilities of success as a function of item difficulty values b, shown on the baseline. Probabilities of success are given in terms of logits, where $\text{logit}(p) = \ln[p/(1-p)]$, because this metric yields straight-line relations with b. Several horizontal lines are shown for logits of particular interest, namely, that for $p = .5$ (at logit $= 0$), the customary threshold level; that for $p = .8$ (at logit $= 1.39$), the mastery threshold suggested by Bock et al. (1982); and that for $p = .90$ (at logit $= 2.20$), a somewhat more stringent mastery threshold that I believe is useful to consider.

A further baseline is given in terms of the rescaled Dale-O'Rourke Grade Ratings, making it possible to predict what grade rating is likely to be attained for a given combination of raw score and probability. For example, for individuals in raw score group 16–17 (mean 16.5), 80% mastery can be predicted for words with grade ratings of 7.3, while 90% mastery can be predicted for words with grade ratings of 6.8. Placed along the grade-rating baseline are sample words drawn from the test, but the presumption would be that the statistics would apply to any words that might be sampled from the Dale-O'Rourke list. In this sense the Picture Vocabulary test can be considered to be behaviorally scaled.

Superimposed on the graph are also points derived from the empirical data for selected score groups and nine sets of items ordered in average value of b. At least by inspection, it can be seen that there is generally a close fit between the predictions of the model and the empirical data. The fit is especially good for logits lying between -3 and $+3$ (corresponding to probabilities between approximately .05 and .95); outside of these bounds, the fit is

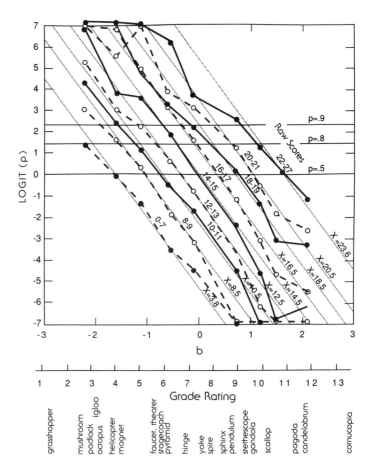

FIG. 12.1. Empirical PCF Curves for Picture Vocabulary Test data. Logit transforms of success probabilities are plotted against mean item difficulties (*b*) for
9 item sets, for each of 9 score-interval groups. Oblique parallel lines show expected logits for given score groups by the 2-parameter IRT model (Equation
2), with *a* = 1.93.

sometimes less good, mainly because of greater random error in probabilities
near 0 or 1.

BEHAVIORAL SCALING
OF THE CONCEPT FORMATION TEST

This appeared to be a test for which it might be possible to obtain a behavioral
scaling criterion that measures the difficulty of the items as a function of
information-processing characteristics (behavior-scaling Type IV). In this test,
the examinee learns how to induce, from instances and noninstances that are

presented, rules by which stimuli are indicated as instances of a concept as opposed to noninstances. Noninstances and instances are presented as rows of stimuli, the noninstances at the left and the instances, each enclosed in squares, at the right. The test begins with a number of nonscored example items illustrating rules such as "[instance is] red" or "[instance is] two" (as opposed to there being only one entity). (Note that in this description I state the rules, in quotes, that are only implicit in the task, but in learning the task, examinees must be able to state such rules.) The first 15 items employ rules with only one term, the terms being selected from the oppositions red/yellow, round/square, big/little, and one/two that describe simple displays of geometric figures. In items 1–6, there is just one noninstance and one instance; in items 7–10, there are two noninstances and two instances; in items 11–15, four of each are given. Items 16–18 introduce two-term rules with the Boolean operator AND: for example, "[an instance must be] red AND square." In these items, there are six noninstances and two instances, a total of 8 stimuli. Items 19–21 introduce two-term rules with the operator OR: for example, "[an instance is either] yellow OR big." In these items there are two noninstances and six instances, a total of 8 stimuli. Items 22–24 introduce three-term OR rules, such as "[an instance must be] yellow OR square OR one." In these three-term items, there is one noninstance and there are seven instances.

From the start of the test up to item 24 the examinee is generally aware of the number of terms in the rule and whether it is an AND or an OR rule; further, wrong responses are corrected. From item 25 to the end at item 35, however, there is a mixture of item types, and wrong responses are not corrected. The examinee must induce, from the materials presented, what kind of rule is involved.

Given the structure of the task, the following characteristics of the items could be considered as elements in a behavioral-scaling criterion:

1. The number of noninstances (1–6).
2. The number of instances (1–7).
3. The total of (1) and (2) = the number of stimuli (2–8).
4. The number of terms (1–3).
5. Presence (1) or absence (0) of AND in the rule.
6. Presence (1) or absence (0) of OR in the rule.
7. Use (1) or nonuse (0) of the opposition *red/yellow*.
8. Use (1) or nonuse (0) of *round/square*.
9. Use (1) or nonuse (0) of *big/little*.
10. Use (1) or nonuse (0) of *one/two*.
11. Presence (1) or absence (0) of the item in the "mixture" part of the test (items 25–35).

The object was to use a linear combination of these variables in predicting item difficulty values, either in terms of LOGIST b or in terms of $\zeta(p)$, as shown in Table 12.2. It was found that predictions were significantly better against $\zeta(p)$, and therefore results are reported here only against this criterion. Because of the structure of the task and the use of dummy variables, however, the intercorrelation matrix of these variables (even excluding variable 3, which is the sum of variables 1 and 2) had such an amount of multicollinearity that it was singular. Investigation of the multiple regression of $\zeta(p)$ on these variables led to the decision to use only variables 3, 4, 5, 6, 7, 8, 10, and 11, whose intercorrelation matrix presented no singularity. The multiple correlation of these variables with $\zeta(p)$ was .9575, with variables 3, 5, 6, and 11 having t values significant with $p < .01$. The multiple correlation for variables 3, 5, 6, and 7 alone was .9464, all t values being significant with $p < .001$. The other variables were included in the final regression equation in order to provide further differentiation among items, and to take advantage of the slightly higher multiple R.

The final regression equation was

$$\text{Est}[\zeta(p)] = -1.47 + 0.1000X(3) + 0.0306X(4) + 0.5696X(5)$$
$$+ 0.8324X(6) - 0.1465X(7) + 0.1288X(8)$$
$$+ 0.0314X(10) + 0.4237X(11). \tag{3}$$

Values of $\text{Est}[\zeta(p)]$ for the 35 items were rescaled to have a mean of 50 and a standard deviation of 10 and are called D-scores (analogous to T-scores). The D-score values for the items are listed in Table 12.2 and constitute readily interpretable measures of item difficulty based on item characteristics.

A PCF graph (Fig. 12.2) was constructed for this test by the same procedures that were used for the Picture Vocabulary Test. The regression of θ on raw scores X was sufficiently nonlinear to suggest that in computing Equation 2, values of θ be inserted corresponding to individual raw score values as given by a fitted curve, and this was done. (The linear correlation was .971.) The value of a was 1.61, the mean of the LOGIST values for individual items. For finding the correspondence between b and the difficulty scores D, the regression of D-scores on b was

$$\text{Est(D)} = 53.9159 + 8.1857b.$$

The graph provides a further baseline depicting the scale of D-scores.

As before, the graph also shows points from the empirical data, for selected item sets and score groups. There is an interesting tendency for the PCF curves to be flatter than expected for high values of logit(p) and the easier items. This is possibly due to the fact that the test involved a learning phase in which individuals were likely to make some errors on easy items even if they eventually

TABLE 12.2
Concept Formation Test: Item Statistics ($N = 1,800$)

Item Number	p	$\zeta(p)$	LOGIST Values		D-Score
			a	b	
5	.9282	-1.46	.83	-2.71	35.9
6	.9360	-1.52	1.12	-2.52	37.8
1	.9210	-1.41	.91	-2.49	33.7
2	.9229	-1.42	.95	-2.46	35.9
4	.8904	-1.23	.72	-2.38	37.8
3	.9061	-1.32	.89	-2.31	36.4
7	.8421	-1.00	1.29	-1.45	40.9
11	.8178	-0.91	1.44	-1.24	42.8
8	.7834	-0.78	.97	-1.20	38.9
9	.7851	-0.79	1.07	-1.16	39.4
15	.7966	-0.83	1.36	-1.13	42.8
10	.7912	-0.81	1.28	-1.12	40.9
12	.7842	-0.79	1.22	-1.10	45.0
14	.7611	-0.71	1.45	-0.91	47.0
13	.7200	-0.58	1.30	-0.73	45.5
16	.5806	-0.20	1.33	-0.15	51.9
25	.6020	-0.26	2.40	-0.13	42.3
26	.5779	-0.20	2.25	-0.06	47.3
33	.5138	-0.03	1.85	0.12	53.4
29	.4639	0.09	2.00	0.27	53.4
18	.4339	0.17	1.28	0.34	56.7
27	.4272	0.18	1.18	0.36	62.5
17	.4144	0.22	1.12	0.41	53.8
34	.4040	0.24	2.26	0.44	62.3
31	.3945	0.27	1.22	0.47	58.3
22	.3744	0.32	2.46	0.51	58.3
21	.3726	0.32	2.16	0.52	57.8
28	.3734	0.32	2.08	0.52	62.8
19	.3695	0.33	2.25	0.53	55.9
23	.3606	0.36	2.43	0.55	58.8
24	.3422	.0.41	2.00	0.60	58.8
20	.3168	0.48	2.20	0.67	60.5
35	.2995	0.53	2.63	0.70	65.2
32	.2850	0.57	2.30	0.75	65.2
30	.2612	0.64	2.26	0.82	64.7
Mean		-0.31	1.61	-0.48	50.0
SD		0.69	0.57	1.14	10.0

Note. Items in order of LOGIST b values.

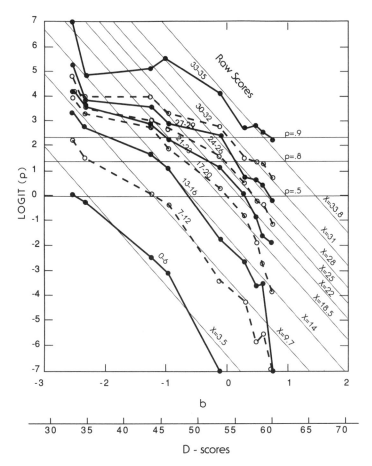

FIG. 12.2. Empirical PCF Curves for Concept Formation Test data. Logit transforms of success probabilities are plotted against mean item difficulties (*b*) for
9 item sets, for each of 9 score-interval groups. Oblique parallel lines show expected logits for given score groups by the 2-parameter IRT model (Equation
2), with *a* = 1.61.

were able to make high or at least above-average scores. Only a PCF analysis
is able to display this phenomenon.

As an aid in interpreting the D-score difficulty values, Table 12.3 has been
prepared to show what elements in the equation for predicting difficulty come
into play for various items and difficulty values. The items are ordered in difficulty,
and the actual values of the elements in Equation 3 are shown. As may be seen,
for difficulty values (D-scores):

33–38. The examinee has to handle only two stimuli, with a one-term rule
that does not involve AND or OR, and is not in the "mixture" part
of the test.

TABLE 12.3
Concept Formation Test: Items Arranged in Order of Assigned Difficulty Values
(D-Scores), with Elements Determining Them

						Variable			
Item Number	D-Score	(3) Number Stimuli	(4) Number Terms	(5) AND	(6) OR	(7) Red/ Yellow	(8) Round/ Square	(10) One/ Two	(11) In Mixture Items
1	33.7	2	1	0	0	1	0	0	0
2	35.9	2	1	0	0	0	0	0	0
5	35.9	2	1	0	0	0	0	0	0
3	36.4	2	1	0	0	0	0	1	0
4	37.8	2	1	0	0	0	1	0	0
6	37.8	2	1	0	0	0	1	0	0
8	38.9	4	1	0	0	0	0	0	0
9	39.4	4	1	0	0	0	0	1	0
7	40.9	4	1	0	0	0	1	0	0
10	40.9	4	1	0	0	0	1	0	0
25	42.3	2	1	0	0	0	0	0	1
11	42.8	8	1	0	0	1	0	0	0
15	42.8	8	1	0	0	1	0	0	0
12	45.0	8	1	0	0	0	0	0	0
13	45.5	8	1	0	0	0	0	1	0
14	47.0	8	1	0	0	0	1	0	0
26	47.3	4	1	0	0	0	1	0	1
16	51.9	8	2	1	0	1	0	0	0
29	53.4	8	1	0	0	0	1	0	1
33	53.4	8	1	0	0	0	1	0	1
17	53.8	8	2	1	0	1	1	0	0
19	55.9	8	2	0	1	1	0	0	0
18	56.7	8	2	1	0	0	1	1	0
21	57.8	8	2	0	1	1	1	0	0
22	58.3	8	3	0	1	1	1	0	0
31	58.3	8	2	1	0	1	0	0	1
23	58.8	8	3	0	1	1	1	0	0
24	58.8	8	3	0	1	1	1	1	0
20	60.5	8	2	0	1	0	1	1	0
34	62.3	8	2	0	1	1	0	0	1
27	62.5	8	2	1	0	0	1	0	1
28	62.8	8	2	0	1	1	0	1	1
30	64.7	8	3	0	1	1	1	0	1
32	65.2	8	3	0	1	1	1	1	1
35	65.2	8	3	0	1	1	1	1	1

39–41. The examinee deals with up to four stimuli, with a one-term rule that does not involve AND or OR, and is not in the "mixture" part of the test.

42–48. The examinee can deal with up to eight stimuli, but still with only a one-term rule that does not involve AND or OR, and is usually not in the "mixture" part of the test.

49–53. Like 42–48, but sometimes in the "mixture" part of the test.

54–57. Like 49–53, but the examinee can start to deal with two-term AND rules, sometimes with OR rules, but not in the "mixture" part of the test.

58–63. The examinee deals with two- and sometimes three-term rules using AND and OR, even in the "mixture" part of the test.

64–65. Like 58–63, but always involving three-term OR rules.

Item difficulty is clearly a function of the complexity of the tasks in terms of the number of stimuli to be inspected and dealt with, the number of terms in the rule, and the type of rule—particularly if it involves OR. The more difficult tasks call on rather complex processes of induction and deductive reasoning.

BEHAVIORAL SCALING
OF THE VISUAL CLOSURE TEST

This test of what the authors call *visual processing* (*Gv*) requires examinees to name objects that are pictorially presented with varying degrees of indistinctness or obscuration. A behavioral scaling of this test could be of Type III in the sense that the scale would refer to attributes of the stimuli—that is, the degree of obscuration.

In most cases, it may be assumed that subjects, even young and inexperienced ones, would be able to name the objects if no obscuration were present. In many items, outline line drawings are presented with some or many parts of the lines omitted. Other items use one of five techniques to obscure the object: a superimposed horizontal grid of stripes (obscuring about 50% of the drawing); a two-way grid (obscuring about 67% of the drawing); a grid consisting of concentric circular bands; blurring by out-of-focus photography; and presenting the object in an unusual perspective. These techniques are not used in any systematic way; for example, there is only one item presenting an object in an unusual perspective, and photographic blurring is used only in two of the more difficult items. It is difficult to measure objectively the amount of obscuration; indeed, the item difficulty becomes the best operational measure of that, but it has an arbitrary unit of measure. Even if it were possible to measure the degree of obscuration, this might not predict difficulty very precisely because there is an interaction between the way an object is obscured and how perceivable the object is. For example, in presenting a drawing of a diamond wedding ring with a superimposed circular grid, perceivability will vary depending on the relative positioning of the ring and the grid. The test is largely a product of the art and skill of the test authors in making pictured objects perceivable to different degrees.

Given the difficulty of objectively measuring the amount of obscuration and its effect, a rather simple and somewhat subjective procedure of behavioral scaling was employed, if only to illustrate what might be done for tests of this type. Items in which line drawings were obscured by omitting lines were judged (by the present author) for the amount (percentage) of lines deleted, on a scale that ranged from 5 to 95, and since these judgments had a correlation of .742 with $\zeta(p)$, the assigned criterion values were found according to the corresponding regression equation. Items using other techniques of obscuration were simply assigned the average of the $\zeta(p)$ values of those items. The resulting assigned difficulty values were rescaled to D-scores with a mean of 50 and a standard deviation of 10, and these D-scores are listed in Table 12.4.

A PCF graph (Fig. 12.3) was constructed for this test by the same procedures that were used for other tests. The scale of D-scores on the baseline is labeled with approximate percentages of obscuration at selected points. In constructing the graph, it was found that the regression of θ on raw scores X was highly linear, with a correlation of .9967; the regression of θ on X was

$$\text{Est}(\theta) = -5.5072 + 0.2463X.$$

In these computations, the data for W-J item 4 were excluded because of an abnormally high value of b, -12.17, for this extremely easy item. The value of a was 1.08, the mean value of LOGIST a for individual items. For finding correspondences between b and D-scores, the regression of D on b was

$$\text{Est}(D) = 53.2523 + 3.0319b.$$

DISCUSSION

Behavioral Scaling of Items

Behavioral scaling of items was most successful in the case of the Concept Formation test, where item difficulty predicted on the basis of objectively codable item characteristics had a correlation of .958 with obtained item difficulty. There was, of course, some capitalization on chance in the computations; it would be possible to cross-validate the predictions in a further study, particularly if item characteristics were more systematically varied. Behavioral scaling was largely successful in the case of the Picture Vocabulary test when appeal was made

TABLE 12.4
Visual Closure Test: Item Statistics (N = 1,800)

Item Number	p	$\xi(p)$	LOGIST Values a	LOGIST Values b	Assigned D-Score
8	.9936	−2.49	0.64	−5.21	48.4
10	.9941	−2.52	0.72	−4.86	36.1
3	.9995	−3.29	1.46	−4.44	35.3
2	.9968	−2.72	1.14	−4.04	47.2
7	.9956	−2.62	1.07	−4.00	35.3
12	.9934	−2.48	0.95	−3.99	51.4
6	.9919	−2.40	0.94	−3.88	35.3
1	.9989	−3.05	1.83	−3.86	35.3
11	.9712	−1.90	0.68	−3.62	48.4
5	.9930	−2.46	1.66	−3.08	23.6
14	.9638	−1.80	0.83	−3.02	35.3
19	.9444	−1.59	1.01	−2.39	51.1
13	.9941	−2.52	1.31	−2.15	51.4
22	.8821	−1.19	0.89	−1.85	51.4
21	.8165	−0.90	0.71	−1.58	51.4
20	.8384	−0.99	0.99	−1.45	51.1
18	.8290	−0.95	1.05	−1.36	47.2
23	.6905	−0.50	1.18	−0.65	55.7
28	.6916	−0.50	1.47	−0.60	55.7
29	.6205	−0.31	1.50	−0.34	55.7
24	.6029	−0.26	1.25	−0.30	51.4
33	.4989	0.00	0.83	0.03	48.4
35	.3872	0.29	0.73	0.50	55.7
31	.3489	0.39	0.81	0.64	60.0
34	.3762	0.32	0.55	0.65	60.0
32	.2160	0.79	1.14	1.07	55.7
44	.1329	1.11	1.31	1.40	51.1
42	.1695	0.96	0.90	1.43	48.4
48	.0972	1.30	1.15	1.71	64.6
37	.1561	1.01	0.71	1.74	47.2
41	.0705	1.47	1.34	1.80	60.0
43	.0822	1.39	0.82	2.20	64.6
52	.0199	2.06	1.75	2.22	62.2
45	.0494	1.65	1.02	2.30	60.0
50	.0054	2.55	1.73	2.74	62.2
47	.0272	1.92	0.91	2.90	62.2
Mean		−0.56	1.08	−0.93	50.4
SD		1.68	.34	2.46	9.8

Note. Items in order of LOGIST b values. Items numbered 9, 15, 16, 17, 25, 26, 27, 30, 36, 38, 39, 40, 46, 49, and 51 in the test were considered invalid by the test's authors; data for these were missing. Data for item 4 were excluded because its value of p was .9995; LOGIST b = −12.17.

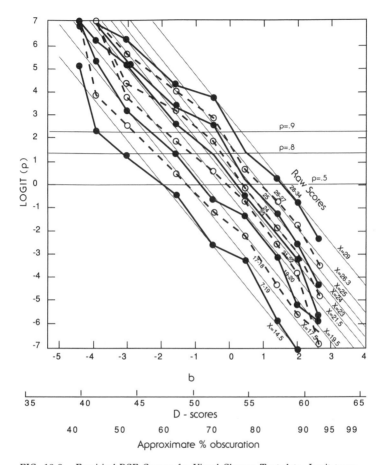

FIG. 12.3. Empirical PCF Curves for Visual Closure Test data. Logit transforms of success probabilities are plotted against mean item difficulties (*b*) for
9 item sets, for each of 9 score-interval groups. Oblique parallel lines show expected logits for given score groups by the 2-parameter IRT model (Equation
2), with *a* = 1.08.

to reasonably valid estimates of word familiarity. A correlation of .858 between
predicted and obtained item difficulty was found. For the Visual Closure test,
this correlation was only .793 and it was to some extent artifactual. It was limited by the fact that it was not possible to obtain objective estimates of the critical aspect of the items, namely, their degree of obscuration. It should be possible,
however, to study the role of visual obscuration in a test of visual closure by
a systematic variation of this variable.

For each of the three tests, the PCF (person characteristic function) procedure made possible the drawing up of graphs relating test scores to item difficulties. It is believed that this procedure permits a true behavioral scaling of test

scores in that it allows one to associate a given test score with a specifiable level of difficulty attained. For example, in the case of the Concept Formation test it is possible to interpret a given score as indicating a 90% chance of attaining a certain level of difficulty in concept formation, described in terms of the kinds of inductive inferences that the examinee is able to make.

Age Trends

Space limitations preclude presenting data on age trends in terms of score distributions for age groups. The behavior scaling of the test makes it possible, however, to interpret age trends in terms of specifiable levels of mastery attained on the average at different ages.

For example, on the Picture Vocabulary test the average child at age 5.5, with a raw score of 7.6 on 27 items, has a 50% chance of knowing words placed at grade 4.7, but a 90% chance of knowing words placed at grade 3.4 ("knowing" being defined in terms of the child's being able to recognize a picture and give an acceptable name for it). By age 19.5, the average person has a raw score of 19.2 on 27 items and a 50% chance of knowing words placed at grade 9.3, but a 90% probability of knowing words placed at grade 7.8.

Results from the Concept Formation test indicate that at age 5.5, the average child has a raw score of 9.6 and a 50% chance of performing tasks placed at a D-score of 42.1 (dealing with up to eight stimuli but only with simple one-term rules), but a 90% chance of performing tasks placed at a D-score of 32.8 (the bottom end of the range of tasks involving one-term rules and dealing with only two stimuli). By age 19.5, the average person has a raw score of 28.5 and a 50% chance of performing tasks at a D-score of about 59 (dealing with two- and sometimes three-term rules involving AND or OR), but a 90% chance of succeeding on tasks at a D-score of 53.6—dealing with one-term rules, sometimes in the "mixture" part of the test, and starting to deal with two-term rules involving AND, but not in the "mixture" part of the test where the examinee is "on his (or her) own."

Most of the age changes on the Visual Closure test occur between the ages of 4 and 16, at least for the average child. At age 5.5, the average child has a raw score of 17.5 and a 50% chance of perceiving objects with about 65% of the stimulus deleted, but a 90% chance of perceiving objects with less than 60% deleted. At age 19.5, the mean raw score is 25.1 and there is a 50% chance of perceiving objects with 80% deleted, but a 90% chance of perceiving objects with about 72% deleted. (These figures on percentages deleted must be taken with caution because they are not based on careful measurements. They are given only to suggest trends.)

It appears, in any case, that the technique of behavioral scaling presented here has great promise in clarifying the nature of different types of cognitive ability and describing given levels of performance. It would be interesting and informative to apply it to a wide range of cognitive ability and achievement tests.

ACKNOWLEDGMENTS

I am grateful to Dr. Richard W. Woodcock of Measurement Learning Consultants, Tolovana Park, OR, for supplying item response data from the norming of certain subtests of the *Woodcock-Johnson Psycho-Educational Battery— Revised*, to DLM Teaching Resources, Allen, TX, for permission to publish certain details about these tests, and to Dr. Albert E. Beaton of Educational Testing Service for arranging to have the item response data analyzed by the IRT program LOGIST.

REFERENCES

Beaton, A. E. (1987). *Implementing the new design: The NAEP 1983-84 technical report* (Report 15-TR-20). Princeton, NJ: National Assessment of Educational Progress, Educational Testing Service.

Bock, R. D., Mislevy, R. J., & Woodson, C. E. (1982). The next stage in educational assessment. *Educational Researcher, 11*(3), 4-11, 16.

Carroll, J. B. (1967). Foreign language proficiency levels attained by language majors near graduation from college. *Foreign Language Annals, 1*, 131-151.

Carroll, J. B. (1980). Measurement of abilities constructs. In A. P. Maslow (Ed.), *Construct validity in psychological measurement: Proceedings of a Colloquium on Theory and Application in Education and Employment* (pp. 23-41). Princeton, NJ: Educational Testing Service.

Carroll, J. B. (1985). Defining abilities through the person characteristic function. In E. E. Roskam (Ed.), *Measurement and personality assessment* (pp. 121-131). Amsterdam: North Holland.

Carroll, J. B., Davies, P., & Richman, B. (1971). *The American heritage word frequency book*. Boston: Houghton Mifflin.

Dale, E., & O'Rourke, J. (1981). *The living word vocabulary: A national vocabulary inventory*. Chicago: World Book-Childcraft International.

Feldt, L. S., & Brennan, R. L. (1989). Reliability. In R. L. Linn (Ed.), *Educational measurement* (3rd ed., pp. 105-146). New York: American Council on Education & Macmillan.

Fischer, G. R. (1977). Linear logistic test models: Theory and application. In H. Spada & W. F. Kempf (Eds.), *Structural models of thinking and learning* (pp. 203-225). Bern, Switzerland: Huber.

Fischer, G. H. (1983). Logistic latent trait models with linear constraints. *Psychometrika, 48*, 3-26.

Flanagan, J. C., Davis, F. B., Dailey, J. T., Shaycoft, M. F., Orr, D. B., Goldberg, I., & Neyman, C. A., Jr. (1964). *The American high school student*. Pittsburgh: University of Pittsburgh.

Glaser, R. (1963). Instructional technology and the measurement of learning outcomes. *American Psychologist, 18*, 519-521.

Millman, J., & Greene, J. (1989). The specification and development of tests of achievement and ability. In R. L. Linn (Ed.), *Educational measurement* (3rd ed., pp. 335-366). New York: American Council on Education & Macmillan.

Mullis, I. V. S., & Jenkins, L. B. (1988). *The science report card: Elements of risk and recovery. Trends and achievement based on the 1986 National Assessment*. Princeton, NJ: Educational Testing Service.

National Assessment of Educational Progress. (1985). *The reading report card: Progress toward excellence in our schools; Trends in reading over four national assessments, 1971–1984*. Princeton, NJ: Educational Testing Service.

Shaycoft, M. F. (1968). *Development and preliminary analysis of a test to estimate size of vocabulary*. Palo Alto, CA: American Institutes for Research.

Smith, D. R., Stenner, A. J., Horabin, I., & Smith, M. (1989, May). *The lexile scale in theory and practice: Final report for NIH Grant HD-19448*. Paper presented at the meeting of the International Reading Association, New Orleans.

Stenner, A. J., Horabin, I., Smith, D. R., & Smith, M. (1988). Most comprehension tests do measure reading comprehension: A response to McLean and Goldstein. *Phi Delta Kappan, 69*, 765–767.

Thorndike, E. L., & Lorge, I. (1944). *The teacher's word book of 30000 words*. New York: Bureau of Publications, Teachers College, Columbia University.

Tucker, L. R. (1955, September). *Some experiments in developing a behaviorally determined scale of vocabulary*. Paper presented at the meeting of the American Psychological Association, San Francisco.

Wingersky, M. (1983). LOGIST: A program for computing maximum likelihood procedures for logistic test models. In R. K. Hambleton (Ed.), *Applications of item response theory* (pp. 45–56). Vancouver, BC: Educational Research Institute of British Columbia.

Woodcock, R. W., & Johnson, M. B. (1989). *Woodcock–Johnson Psycho-Educational Battery— Revised: Tests of Cognitive Ability*. Allen, TX: DLM Teaching Resources.

Zwick, R. (1987a). Assessing the dimensionality of NAEP reading data. *Journal of Educational Measurement, 24*, 293–308.

Zwick, R. (1987b). Assessment of the dimensionality of NAEP Year 15 reading data. In A. E. Beaton, *Implementing the new design: The NAEP 1983–84 technical report* (Report 15-TR-20, pp. 245–284). Princeton, NJ: National Assessment of Educational Progress, Educational Testing Service.

13

A Generative Approach to Psychological and Educational Measurement

Isaac I. Bejar
Educational Testing Service

INTRODUCTION

Response generative modeling (RGM) is an approach to psychological measurement that involves a "grammar" capable of assigning a psychometric description to every item in a universe of items and is also capable of generating all the items in that universe (Bejar & Yocom, 1991). Such an approach to measurement, if feasible, could have at least three important implications. First, the interpretation of scores from a generative instrument would be greatly facilitated because the process for generating the item is explicitly stated. Second, the possibility of generative modeling implies that we have a complete understanding of the underlying response process. Such knowledge might allow us, in turn, to abandon the multiple-choice format in favor of open-ended formats, a longstanding desire of psychometricians (e.g., Frederiksen, 1990), but without the expense associated with scoring open-ended responses. In other words, the same knowledge base that is used to create items can be brought to bear on the scoring of open-ended responses. Third, the ability to assign a psychometric description to an item is the key ingredient in what might be called *intelligent test development aids*. Job aids, in general, are rapidly becoming the key to increased productivity in many fields (e.g., Harmon, 1986). In a testing context, test development job aids might become essential if bills to outlaw pretesting succeed in becoming law (because it is through pretesting that test developers estimate the difficulty of an item before the test is administered in a final form), especially in light of growing statistical theory designed to allow equating tests "with little or no data" (Mislevy and Sheehan, 1990). Some speculations on the future of job aids for test development can be found in Bejar (1989); a discussion of open-ended assessment from a generative perspective, with special emphasis on certification testing, can be found in Bejar (in preparation); see also Baker (1988) and the Summer 1989 issue of the *Journal of Educational Measurement*.

The purpose of this chapter is to: (a) elaborate on the rationale behind RGM; (b) review its roots and how it relates to current thinking on validity; and (c) assess its feasibility in a wide variety of domains.

HISTORICAL BACKGROUND

Although item response theory (IRT) today enjoys unanimous endorsement of test developers and psychometricians, just a few years ago other psychometric frameworks were serious contenders. One contender was Tryon's item sampling model (Tryon, 1957). He distinguished between three theories: the true-and-error-factor theory, which is a primitive IRT model; the theory of equivalent item samples, also known as a classic test theory (Gulliksen, 1950); and a theory based on random sampling from a universe of items, which Tryon endorsed. The tensions that lead to the item sampling model can be surmised from Osburn's (1968) influential paper:

> Few measurement specialists would quarrel with the premise that the fundamental objective of achievement testing is generalization. Yet the fact is that current procedures for the construction of achievement tests do not provide an unambiguous basis for generalization to a well defined universe of content. At worst, achievement tests consist of arbitrary collections of items thrown together in a haphazard manner. At best, such tests consist of items judged by subject matter experts to be relevant to and representative of some incompletely defined universe of content. In neither case can it be said that there is an unambiguous basis for generalization. *This is because the method of generating items and the criteria for the inclusion of items in the test cannot be stated in operational terms* [italics added]. (p. 95)

Whereas local independence is the most critical assumption in IRT, the existence of a universe of items, or the possibility of generating one, was the core of the random sampling approach. And just as lack of local independence could prevent correct modeling of some abilities (e.g., Bock, Gibbon & Muraki, 1988, p. 277), an inability to formulate a universe of items could prevent the correct implementation of the random-sampling model. Loevinger (1965), for example, objected to the item sampling model because the

> term population [universe] implies that in principle one can catalog, or display, or index all possible members even though the population [universe] is infinite

and the catalogue cannot be completed. . . . No system is conceivable by which an index of all possible tests [items] could be drawn up. There is no *generating* [italics added] principle. (p. 147)

If Loevinger is correct, then RGM would be doomed because RGM shares with the random sampling model the assumption that there is a generation principle. However, RGM does not require that the generated items constitute a random sample. Moreover, RGM goes much farther than the random sampling model by proposing that there is not only a generating but also that items be generated with psychometric parameters already estimated, as it were.

Strictly speaking, the random sampling model is a mathematical one, and by itself does not attempt to generate items. That component was to have been provided by an earlier attempt at generative item writing. The attempt that received most attention was that of Bormouth (1970), which was perceived at the time (e.g., Cronbach, 1970) as a potential breakthrough in item writing. However, the genesis of the approach appears to be in instructional psychology (e.g., Hively, 1974; Uttal, Rogers, Hieronymous, & Pasich, 1970). An extensive summary of those efforts can be found in Roid and Haladyna (1982), and a shorter one in Bejar (1983). The reason those efforts have not matured into a viable psychometric framework appears to be due to two factors: following too closely one source of inspiration, namely, Chomskyan linguistics, and clinging to a behavioristic, as opposed to cognitive, orientation—in retrospect, quite paradoxical sources of inspiration.

Chomsky (1965) introduced the distinction between competence and performance to demarcate the purely linguistic phenomena from the psychological reality of language use. Competence refers to the universe of sentences that a user of the language ought to be able to comprehend or utter. In practice, of course, language users fail to comprehend certain sentences and make all kinds of grammatical mistakes when speaking or writing. Chomsky chose to focus on the phenomena of more linguistic relevance or what the language user ought to know, rather than modeling actual language use, or performance. Both Bormouth and Hively also focused exclusively on the competence and not the performance. That is, they aimed to generate the universe of items that students ought to be able to respond to correctly. This meant the generation of items without a concomitant psychometric description that might reflect the underlying response process required to respond to an item thus generated. The problem, as Merwin (1977) pointed out, was that what ought to have been the case often was not. For example, items generated to represent an educational objective were found to differ in their difficulty or in the proportion of students who answered it correctly. There was no possible explanation for this variability in the absence of a performance component.

Interestingly, there were exemplars for the integration of competence and performance early on. Miller (1962), for example, proposed that the syntactic complexity of a given sentence would affect its comprehensibility, and called the theory the Derivational Theory of Complexity. The implicit performance model in the theory is that sentences require more, or less, mental computations depending on their syntactic attributes and therefore are harder, or easier, to comprehend. That this approach was not recognized as a model for generative psychometrics may be in part due to the strong behavioristic trends in psychology and education at the time. It was, according to some historians (Gardner, 1985), Skinner's lack of rebuttal to Chomsky's (1965) critique of Skinner's (1957) *Verbal Behavior* that was the beginning of the end for behaviorism.[1]

In short, RGM shares some of the concerns with earlier attempts at generative modeling but in some respects could not be more different. Specifically, the item sampling model and related item-generation algorithms constitute a psychometric model for classic behaviorists, for whom talk of underlying processes is not admissible. RGM, in contrast, has a cognitive orientation. This means that the postulation of underlying processes and knowledge structures required to respond to an item is not only admissible but at the heart of the approach: It is by incorporating information about the demands a given item imposes on the cognitive apparatus that it becomes possible to "pre-estimate" the parameters of some response model. Moreover, unlike the item sampling model, which rejects the postulation of latent ability and therefore is philosophically at the other extreme of the IRT family of response models, RGM is compatible with IRT.

The scope of RGM is not limited to achievement items, as many of the earlier attempts to generative item writing were. As we demonstrate later, RGM is, in principle, applicable to any domain, including achievement and instructional domains. In fact, a forerunner of RGM can be found in an instructional context. Uttal et al. (1970) used the term generative instruction to describe an alternative to the machine learning efforts of the 1960s, which were based on Skinnerian principles. The purpose of generative instruction is not to strengthen the linkage between a stimulus and a response but rather to diagnose the source of difficulties in learning. This idea was subsequently elaborated by Brown and Burton (1978) in the context of arithmetic instruction. In short, a generative approach cuts across domains and, as we will see, is a natural framework

---

[1]Of course, in psychology we can only speak of rounds. Behaviorism may be on its way back disguised as connectionism. Although behaviorism-as-connectionism opens the black box it might as well be kept closed: inspecting a neural net after it has been trained to emulate some human behavior is not likely to be informative; information is distributed throughout a network of nodes. Even when such a model accounts for verbal behavior (e.g., Rummelhart, McClelland, & the PDR Research Group, 1986; but see Prince & Pinker, 1988) all we have learned, it seems, is that through pairing stimuli and responses learning can take place. The computational attractiveness of these models is undeniable, but it remains to be seen whether they will replace the computer as the metaphor to modeling human cognition. More likely, connectionist ideas will be incorporated into cognitive models to improve the granularity of the account (M. Just, personal communication June 15, 1989).

for the assessment of complex skills, such as troubleshooting, clinical diagnoses, and pedagogical skills.

RGM AS AN APPROACH TO VALIDATION

In addition to integrating the model of content and response, RGM exemplifies an approach to construct validation. Validation has traditionally focused on an accounting of *response consistency* or covariation among items. Indeed, construct validation has been described as implying "a joint convergent and discriminant strategy entailing both substantive coverage and response consistency in concert" (Messick, 1981, p. 575). There has been far less emphasis on an accounting of response difficulty (but see e.g., Campbell, 1961; Carroll, 1980; Davies & Davies, 1965; Egan, 1979; Elithorn, Jones, Kerr, & Lee, 1964; Tate, 1948; Zimmerman, 1954). These two focuses, response consistency and response difficulty, are not antithetical by any means. Embretson (1983) has proposed an approach to validity in which both considerations are integrated. From this validational perspective knowing the latent structure of a test—for example, its factorial structure or its fit to a particular item response model—is clearly essential to an interpretation of test scores but is not the entire story. An accounting of response difficulty would clearly enhance the validational status of a test because to obtain that accounting a model incorporating the mental structures and processes needed to solve the item would be required. If that model has been derived from a theory that has empirical support, then, clearly, the validational status of the test scores derived from such a test have a head start, compared to a test developed following the actuarial model where the characteristics of the items are not known until it is administered to a sample of examinees.

Not only are accountings of response difficulty and consistency not antithetical, they entail parallel considerations. For example, within the response-consistency tradition, the extent to which covariation is accounted for by relevant and irrelevant (e.g., method) variables is often the basic data from which validity is assessed (e.g., Campbell & Fiske, 1959). A similar consideration is equally applicable in an accounting of response difficulty. For example, if it were shown to be the case that the difficulty of analogy items from, say, the SAT or the GRE were purely a function of word difficulty, then we could reasonably conclude that the validity of scores derived from such items would be suspect.[2]

---

[2]Actually, with our increased understanding of the process of vocabulary acquisition (e.g., Curtis, 1987; Sternberg, 1987), good performance on a vocabulary test cannot really be discarded as an indication that the person is merely studious. Research suggests that vocabulary scores are good predictors of academic criteria because the process of vocabulary acquisition is a form of reasoning, which presumably accounts for the correlation of vocabulary tests with other tests.

Psychological theorizing has changed substantially since the original article on construct validity (Cronbach & Meehl, 1955). The current strength of the cognitive perspective has led psychology from functionalistic theories to structuralist theories. More specifically, psychology now emphasizes explaining performance on the basis of the systems and subsystems of underlying processes and structures, rather than identifying antecedent–consequent relationships. Cronbach and Meehl's emphasis on building theory through the nomological network, which contained primarily antecedent (test score) to consequent (other measures) relationships, can be viewed as a functionalistic approach.

Embretson (1983) has proposed a major reformulation of the validation process consisting of two stages: construct representation and nomothetic span. This reformulation can be viewed as the culmination of debates on the role of structure and function in individual differences psychology (e.g., Carroll, 1972; Messick, 1972).[3] In Embretson's reformulation, a construct is a theoretical variable that is a source of individual differences. Construct-representation research seeks to identify the theoretical mechanisms that underlie task performance by cognitive task analysis methods. That is, the component processes, strategies, and knowledge structures that underlie performance identify the construct(s) that is (are) involved in the task. Nomothetic-span research, in contrast, concerns the utility of the test for measuring individual differences. It refers to the span of relationships between the test score and other measures. Nomothetic span is supported by the frequency, magnitude, and pattern of relationships of the test score with other measures.

In Cronbach and Meehl's conceptualization, the correlations of individual differences on the test with other measures both define the construct and determine the quality of the test as a measure of individual differences. In Embretson's integrated conceptualization of construct, validity has qualitatively different types of data to support construct representation and nomothetic span. The former is supported by data on how within-task variation in the items' attributes influences performance, while the latter is supported by between-task covariation, for example, correlation among tests.

In short, RGM capitalizes on the convergence of several trends and can be seen as an approach to implement a structural perspective of validation by integrating item development, response model fitting, and validation. RGM integrates all three processes into a unified framework where item creation is guided by knowledge of psychology of the domain, and concomitantly psychometric

---

[3]Structure and function are ambiguous terms. Messick (1972), for example associates *structure* with the results of factor analysis, and talks about the *functional* links among traits and performance outcomes. Guttman (1971), however, associates *structure* with the system of a priori relations among variables (see Lohman and Ippel, chapter 3, this volume). The term *construct representation* in Embretson's formulation has both structural and functional overtones, whereas *nomological span,* which coincides with the Cronbach and Meehl (1955) nomological network idea, is primarily functional.

descriptions (e.g., parameters on an IRT model) are attached to the item as it is generated. Then every time a test is administered the psychology of the domain is tested, by contrasting the theoretical psychometric description with the performance of examinees, thus perennially assessing the validity of the scores. This approach to validation has much in common with other efforts to develop and validate psychologically inspired tests or batteries (e.g., Frederiksen, 1986; Guttman, 1969, 1980; Kyllonen, 1990).

EVIDENCE FOR THE FEASIBILITY OF RGM

The two major ingredients for a generative approach are (a) a mechanism for generating items and (b) sufficient knowledge about the response process to estimate the psychometric parameters of the generated items. The feasibility of the approach, therefore, can be judged by whether items can, in fact, be generated and whether the predicted parameters are, in fact, observed. In the following sections I present evidence, from my own research and that of others, suggesting that RGM is indeed feasible. At times, however, the discussion turns speculative because in some domains where the approach would seem feasible no attempts to implement generative modeling have been made.

Spatial Ability

Not surprisingly, good examples of the feasibility of RGM can be found in the domain of spatial ability. For one thing, the generation of spatial items seems simpler; for another, spatial ability has been under intense scrutiny of cognitive psychologists. In this section I present evidence for mental rotation items and hidden figure items (see also Irvine, Dunn, & Anderson, 1989).

Mental Rotation. It is seldom the case that sufficient knowledge has accumulated about an ability to make RGM immediately feasible. One exception is mental rotation. Although psychometricians have long used two-dimensional figural rotations in tests, it was experimental psychologists (Shepard & Metzler, 1971) who thoroughly analyzed the mental process. There now exists a large body of literature (cf. Corballis, 1982) establishing that an angular disparity between the two figures largely determines the time to respond.

A generative approach to the measurement of this ability means controlling the difficulty of an item through the angular disparity between two stimuli. Imagine, for example, a test consisting of 20 distinct pairs of figures that can be presented at rotations ranging from 20 to 180 degrees. In an adaptive test every examinee would be presented with the 20 items, but examinees of different levels of ability would be presented with items at a different angle. Clearly, such an adaptive procedure requires a computer. All examinees would perhaps be given the first pair at 100 degrees. A higher-ability examinee would then be presented subsequent items at larger rotations. Although it might be feasible to tailor the test to the examinee and score on the basis of rotation angle alone, in practice there are at least two problems with that idea. First, the difficulty of any given item is a function of not only rotation but also the complexity of the figure. Second, mental rotation is the type of skill where speed of response is an appropriate consideration. Therefore, in order to use all the information we need to calibrate each item separately and record how long it takes the examinee to respond.

To judge the feasibility of RGM for this task requires that we calibrate several pairs of figures on some item response model and that we estimate the difficulty of the pair at several degrees of rotation. The expectation for mental rotation data is that the relationship of difficulty on angular rotation is linear for several elapsed times (Bejar, 1990). The expectation was tested by fitting the simplest possible psychometric model of an 80-item test based on figures such as those in Fig. 13.1. The examinee's task is to determine if the figure on the right is a rotation of the one on the left. There were eight basic items presented at five angles (20, 60, 100, 140, and 180 degrees) in their true-and-false version (in the false version the second figure is the mirror image of the first figure), in order to establish the relationship between angular disparity and difficulty.

Fig. 13.2 shows the result of a calibration for a typical item based on the responses of nearly 200 high school students. As can be seen, there are some departures from the predictions, although, in general, the fit for this item is

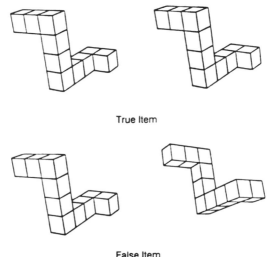

True Item

False Item

FIG. 13.1.   Sample mental rotation item.

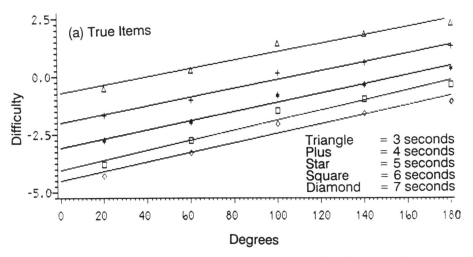

FIG. 13.2.   Relationship of estimated difficulty on angular disparity at several
elapsed times: triangle, 3 s; plus, 4 s; star, 5 s; square, 6 s; diamond, 7 s.

good. The major deviation from linearity occurred at 100 degrees. Also, beyond 5 seconds a tendency toward a quadratic relationship between difficulty
and angular disparity emerges, a situation that suggests that beyond a certain
elapsed time different response strategies may come into play. In principle, such
departures from linearity might be avoided by adapting the test to the examinee,
which was not done with these data. In other words, as long as the item is not
too difficult for an examinee, responses may in fact be just a function of angular
disparity.

The results for the false items are quite different in that angular disparity
does not seem to control response time, as it does for the true items. That
is, the false items seem to tap the decision aspect of performance, while the
true items are tapping the mental rotation aspect. Needless to say, this introduces
a complication. Thus, it may not be practical to use a true–false format in a real
application. A multiple-choice version may eliminate the problem but introduces
the complexity that the attributes of the alternatives would have to be considered in the modeling process.

Hidden Figure Items.   Unlike the mental rotation items, for which the
determinants of performance are understood, very little is known about the determinants of performance on hidden figure items. A theory that addresses performance on tasks of this type has been proposed by Duncan and Humphreys
(1989), and although it was not used as the inspiration for representing hidden
figure items, it is consistent with the representation that was chosen. That
representation needs to capture not only the complexity of the item but also

lend itself to generating items that have the same underlying representation but a different visual realization, that is, items that should have the same difficulty but appear visually different. For convenience, we call the items generated in this fashion *clones*, although they could also be called *isomorphs*, as is done by cognitive researchers interested in the cognitive equivalence of problems (e.g., Kotovsky & Simon, 1988). Fig. 13.3 shows a typical hidden figure item and a corresponding clone. The task for the examinee is to determine if the smaller figure is embedded in the larger one.

The representation chosen to represent items and obtain clones was a matrix consisting of counts indicating how close the target figure appears at each possible position in the larger pattern and was based on the Hough transform (Mayhew & Frisby, 1984), an artificial intelligence technique used in object recognition (see Bejar & Yocom, 1991). We tested the validity of this representation by implementing a computer program capable of generating clones and then comparing their psychometric characteristics on the basis of responses from high school students. In other words, we tested the psychometric equivalence of pairs of isomorphs or clones. This "weakened" version of full generative modeling, where instead of generating items of known difficulty we just generate items that have the same difficulty as the generating item, was necessary because

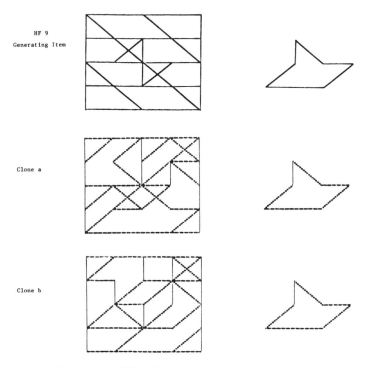

FIG. 13.3. Typical hidden figure item and two corresponding clones.

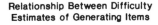

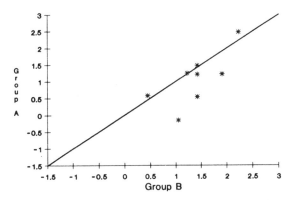

FIG. 13.4.   Regression of logit of proportion correct for pairs of clones administered to two respective random samples.

the lack of theoretical development for performance on this item type. The results demonstrated that the clones behaved as such in terms of their difficulty as well as distribution of response times. Fig. 13.4 shows the relationship between the logit for proportion correct for pairs of clones. Fig. 13.5 shows the cumulative response times for two clones. It can be seen that they are very similar, and this was true for the other items as well.

Reasoning Tests

Reasoning tests, both deductive and inductive, lend themselves to generative modeling. In this section we discuss the impressive evidence for inductive reasoning provided by Butterfield, Nielsen, Tangen, and Richardson (1985) using letter series, preliminary evidence on analogical reasoning, and speculation on the feasibility of generative modeling of deductive and quantitative reasoning items.

Inductive Reasoning.   Butterfield et al. describe a comprehensive approach to describing and generating letter series, as well as a theory of item difficulty, the two ingredients of generative modeling. The items consist of series of letters produced according to a set of rules, and the examinees task is to predict the next element in the series. Arbitrary series can be generated by applying operators to generate the next letter in the series. The operators considered by Butterfield et al. are Next (N), Back (B), and Identical (I). The generic form of an item can then be succinctly described as the rules of construction in terms of these operators.

DISTRIBUTION OF RESPONSE LATENCY FOR ITEM 4M

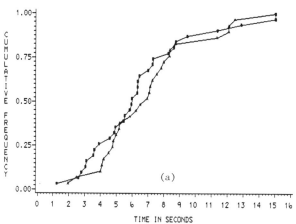

(a)

DISTRIBUTION OF RESPONSE LATENCY FOR ITEM 4C

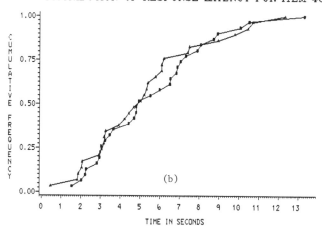

(b)

FIG. 13.5. Cumulative response time for (a) a generating item administered to
two random samples, and (b) two clones administered to respective random
samples.

The following item,

DDQQEEPPFFOO

is described by the form $N_1I_1B_2I_2$ and two starting values, in this case C and
S. The subscripts refer to a position in the starting string. From a starting value
of C we first apply $N_1(C) = D$, yielding a D, and then apply $I_1(D) = D$, yielding another D. We now move to the second element of the string which starts

from S. Applying the B operator yields $B_2(S)$ = Q and applying I yields $I_2(Q)$ = Q. In short, Butterfield et al. are able to characterize series abstractly, as well as generating series that have a given abstract characterization. Although oriented to open-ended series, their methodology can be used with multiple-choice versions as well. The following multiple-choice item from the Factor-Referenced Cognitive Tests Kit (Ekstrom, French, & Harman, 1976) asks the examinee to choose the series that does not belong:

NOPQ   DEFK   ABCD   HIJK   UVWX

The first, third, fourth and fifth can be represented by the rule N_1 with starting points N, A, H, and U, respectively. Thus, to create multiple-choice versions one would use the theory to generate options that have the same generation principle.

In addition to characterizing items abstractly, RGM requires a mapping from that characterization to the parameters of psychometric model, such as difficulty. Butterfield et al., building on earlier research by Simon and Kotovsky (1963), proposed and demonstrated a theory of item difficulty that suggests that the difficulty of a series is indexed by the knowledge required to discover the most-difficult-to-represent string in the series. They also proposed several indices of that representational difficulty. Several experiments demonstrated the validity of the scheme. Moreover, when applied to predict the difficulty of items in the Primary Mental Abilities Test they accounted for 90% of the variance in item difficulty. This is impressive because those items did not enter into the formulation of the theory.

Deductive Reasoning. There is not really a comprehensive demonstration of RGM deductive reasoning. There are, however, several lines of research concerned with, among other things, an accounting of difficulty of several types of deductive reasoning tasks. This accumulation of results and variety of theoretical accounts (see Galotti, 1989) would make it an excellent domain for attempting a generative approach. Moreover, because of the conflicting accounts of deductive reasoning such an investigation may have psychometric value as well as helping to shed some light on the field.

The work of Johnson-Laird, Byrne, and Tabossi (1989) illustrates the potential feasibility based on a mental models approach. A mental model consists of "tokens arranged in a particular structure to represent a state of affairs" (Johnson-Laird, 1983, p. 398). Specifically, Johnson-Laird et al. examine the difficulty of problems with multiply quantified premises, for example:

None of the Princeton letters are in the same place as any of the Cambridge letters. All the Cambridge letters are in the same place as all the Dublin letters. Therefore, none of the Princeton letters are in the same place as any of the Dublin letters.

They show that the difficulty of the problems is a function of the number of mental models that the solver needs to postulate to solve the problem: Problems that required a single model were found to be easier than problems that required two mental models. A theory of difficulty that accounts for only two levels of difficulty has a long way to go for psychometric purposes. On the other hand, the generation of deductive reasoning items would not present serious difficulties because of their structured format. In short, generative modeling of deductive problem solving appears feasible, but further work is needed to fully account for variations in difficulty. A complete accounting will require incorporation of biases that test takers follow when asked to think deductively. An approach that is generative in spirit but incorporates logical biases in item construction has been described by Colberg and Nester (1987).

Analogical Reasoning. Analogical problem solving has a long psychometric tradition, but surprisingly little is known about the formal characteristics of such items. A recent study (Bejar, Chaffin, and Embretson, 1991) has begun to remedy the situation by studying intensely a large number of analogy items from the Graduate Record Examination (GRE) General Test. The study showed that despite the fact that the analogies are in a verbal modality, vocabulary knowledge, as such, is not even remotely the main determinant of performance or item difficulty. (Of course, vocabulary knowledge is required to answer the items, but the more difficult items are not so because they involve infrequent words.)

The generation of analogies has been demonstrated by Chaffin and Hermann (1987). The possibility of generative modeling of analogical reasoning, that is, generating items with known psychometric characteristics, was considered by Bejar et al. (1991). They concluded that given the current state of the art in computational linguistics, working at the word-pair level was more feasible. By using word pairs as the building block, multiple-choice generative modeling could be implemented in this fashion: Prepare a database of word pairs and store along with the word-pair information such as the semantic relational features of the word pair, the frequency of the words making the pair and possibly other information as well. The generation of an item starts by deciding which major semantic class to use. Bejar et al. found 10 major classes in the GRE item pool. Each major class has distinctive features that, in turn, make it possible to classify word pairs into subclasses. Thus, to create an item we chose the stem and the key to be from the same subclass and chose options that are from the same class but different subclasses. Thus, the template for creating analogy items is:

Stem: Word-pair$_{ij}$
    Key: Word-pair$_{ij}$, where $i = j$
    Nonkey: Word-pair$_{ij}$, where $i \neq j$,

where i refers to a major semantic class, such as part-whole, class-inclusion, etc., and j refers to a subclass within the major class. Essentially, the template says that the stem and the key should be from the same class and subclass whereas the nonkeys should be from the same major class but different subclasses. Clearly, this approach assumes that a semantic analysis is available for each word pair in our database, a process that at the moment must be done "by hand" (but see Miller, Fellbaum, Kegl, & Miller, 1988, and Byrd et al., 1987, for advances in computational linguistics that may eventually allow an automated implementation).

Constructing items according to a semantic analysis would qualify as generative were it not for the fact that the semantic class is a potent determinant of difficulty. Bejar et al. studied different factors of difficulty and found that for the GRE pool the semantic class was the strongest determinant and not word frequency as Carroll (1980) had speculated, nor processing demands as we would have expected from recent research (Sternberg, 1977; Pellegrino & Glaser, 1982).

Although the difficulties of generating multiple-choice analogies does not appear insurmountable, it may be easier to do so in an open-ended format. The first idea that comes to mind for an open-ended analogy item is to present the examinee with a word pair and then ask the examinee to produce one or more pairs that exemplify the same relation. This approach, however, is not likely to be adequate because the granularity of a typical multiple-choice item is very fine and therefore requires responses that demand a high level of reasoning. That is, the exact nature of the relation represented by the stem is not certain until the options are examined. For example, a stem like grain:husk obviously calls for a part–whole relationship, but in the context of a GRE or SAT item the options would all be part–whole relationships, which requires the examinee to determine the exact kind of part–whole relationship.

A format that preserves the inductive nature in an open-ended format is the analogical series, where the stem consists of two or more word pairs that specify the nature of intended analogy. We will discuss it briefly to illustrate the claim made earlier, namely, that the knowledge that makes possible generative modeling may make it possible to abandon the multiple-choice format in favor of open-ended items.

Consider the following analogical series where the examinee is asked to provide one or more word pairs consistent with the series:

husk:grain, shell:turtle

The solution is not just any part-whole word pair but one where the part plays a protective function. A possible correct answer is armor:knight or peel:orange. This format is compatible with recent theorizing about the nature of analogical reasoning. Earlier theories focused almost exclusively on processing models and paid no attention to the structure of knowledge. More recent theorizing (e.g., Gentner, 1983) by contrast emphasizes the structural details of the process.

In short, a generative approach to either multiple-choice or open-ended analogical reasoning based on word pairs as the "building blocks" seems feasible
because of advances in our understanding of performance on such tasks, such
as the role of the semantic class on difficulty, improvements in our understanding of the nature of the analogical process itself (e.g., Gentner, 1983), and advances in computational linguistics.

Quantitative and Arithmetic Reasoning.   As one might have suspect-
ed, arithmetic and quantitative items lends themselves well to a generative approach. It is not difficult to think in the case of arithmetic, for example, of means
of generating items (see Roid and Haladyna, 1982). For the same reason, the
factors that might affect difficulty naturally suggest themselves. The most promi-
nent line of research on difficulty factors is called *task variables*. The culmination of this line of research can be found in the volume edited by Goldin and
McClintock (1984).

The work on automated generation of quantitative items, however, has
evolved independently of the work on task variables and for the most part has
concentrated on arithmetic problems (e.g., Hively, Paterson, & Page, 1968).
However, it also ignored psychometric difficulty as an attribute of the generated items (see Merwin, 1977). As a result of this lack of convergence between
research on determinants of difficulty and item generation we cannot point to
an exemplar of generative modeling of arithmetic or quantitative reasoning.
However, implicit in the Brown and Burton (1978) work on diagnosis of arithmetic skills is a problem generation mechanism that aims to generate items that
would be consistent with the current diagnosis (see Burton, 1982) and illustrates that generative modeling need not be associated with a specific measurement framework, such as IRT. In a diagnostic context the questions to be
administered next should be those that are most informative with respect to
the different diagnoses under consideration. Obviously, this purpose of measurement calls for a different representation of the examinee. We discuss some
of these representations later, in a discussion of the assessment of complex skills.

Quantitative skills involve more than arithmetic computations, of course. The
solution of word problems is perhaps a more important component of quantitative reasoning. Much of the early work on word problems focused on surface
variables of the problem, or at least on a characterization of the problem without
necessarily establishing that such characterization in any way was consistent
with the problem as approached by the examinee. An important chapter by Riley,
Greeno, and Heller (1983) may have changed that. They distinguished between
the "specific" and "global factors" that affect problem difficulty. Global factors refer to surface characteristics of the problem. Specific factors refer to the
deep characteristics of the problem, which describe the relationships among the
quantities involved in the problem. The taxonomy of specific factors they proposed consisted of four classifications: Change, Equalize, Combine, and Com-

pare. Each of these types has a schema associated with it that embodies the understanding required for solving problems of that type.

Another approach to classifying quantitative reasoning problems has been provided by S. K. Reed (e.g., Reed, Ackinclose, & Voss, 1990), who categorizes problems into classes, such as Cost, Distance, Fulcrum, Work, etc., and then classifies within each such class by the equation implied by the problem. For example, the following is a Cost problem:

A group of people paid $238 to purchase tickets to a play. How many people were in the group if the tickets cost $14 each? (Reed et al., p. 85)

The equation that characterizes this problem is $14 = \$238/n$. Although the classification has been found useful for tutoring purposes, for generative modeling purposes further detail would be needed. In the problem there are three quantities involved: the number of people, the cost of the ticket, and the total price. Therefore, variants of the problem are possible as follows:

Ten people paid $238 to purchase tickets to a play. How much did they pay for each ticket?

Ten people went to see a play and each paid $14 per ticket. How much did they pay altogether?

In general, given n variables there will be n problem variants, if we limit our attention to considering quantities as given or unknown. In reality, there are more variants because the quantities involved in the problem can enter into different types of relations. For example, in motion problems the entities may be traveling in the same or opposite directions. We refer the reader to the important work of Hall, Kibler, Wenger, and Truxaw (1989) and Mayer (1981), who seem to have provided, so far, the most comprehensive taxonomies of quantitative reasoning items.

With these taxonomies in hand, the generative modeling of quantitative reasoning might proceed by estimating the difficulty of items in cells of a multidimensional taxonomy. The generation of items from a given cell would necessarily be based on templates or well-defined scripts from which specific isomorphs could be generated. The validation of the generation of items from cells in this taxonomy could be assessed by the degree to which the psychometric parameters from a given cell are well predicted and the within-cell residuals are constant across all cells. Unless the latter holds, there are performance factors that are not captured by the taxonomy and the generative modeling is not complete. Stating generative modeling in this form makes it evident that methods derived from generalizability theory have relevance to RGM when we focus on the item as the unit of study, instead of the examinee. Specifically, methods for test constructed from tables of specifications (Jarjoura & Brennan, 1982; Kolen & Harris, 1987) seem relevant.

Verbal Ability

Verbal ability is measured by tasks such as sentence completion, reading comprehension, and vocabulary tests. Vocabulary tests, despite their simplicity, are
one of the best predictors of intelligence (Sternberg, 1987). The high correlation between intelligence and performance on a vocabulary test has been a bit
of a mystery, but as a result of research on the nature of vocabulary acquisition
it is now clear that the reason for the correlation was that performance on vocabulary tests is an indicator of the knowledge acquisition ability of the examinee
(Jensen, 1980, p. 146).

Vocabulary. The generation of multiple-choice vocabulary tests by computer would appear to be trivial. We might choose two synonyms to play the
stem and key roles and then choose other words for the distractors. Examination of vocabulary tests, however, reveals that the distractors are chosen in
such a way that they are not unrelated to the stem. Therefore, difficulty is to
some extent a function of the likelihood that the examinee has encountered the
words included in the item but also how close the distractors are to the stem.
As items get more difficult, the examinee must make finer distinctions. Therefore, in order to generate items of a wide range of difficulty the generation procedure would have to have access to a finely tuned lexical database. Psychologically
motivated lexical databases are not readily available at the moment but may be
in the future (Miller et al., 1988), and at the very least would be useful to assist
the test developer in constructing items.

Interestingly, the measurement of verbal ability through sentence-based items
appears more immediately feasible. Bejar (1988) discussed a system for the assessment of writing ability, which could easily be applied to sentence completion as well. The system relied on a grammar correction engine known as
WordMAP, published by Linguistic Technologies. The system envisioned by
Bejar (1988) is shown in Fig. 13.6. It assumes a database of sentences from
which items would be created. The system does not aim to generate natural
text but rather to generate items based on sentences that have been previously
selected for their suitability to assess specific writing errors. Because performance would be expected to depend on a variety of syntactic and semantic attributes of the sentence (e.g., Bejar, Stabler, & Camp, 1987), that information
would be stored along with the sentence.

The system would generate an item by choosing a sentence from the database and introducing an error, for example, a subject–verb agreement. The sentence with the error is then presented to the examinee, who would rewrite it
to remove the error. Scoring of the corrected sentence is possible through a
"grammar engine." Bejar (1988) showed that WordMAP could handle most
of the constructions and errors in the Test of Standard Written English (TSWE).
More recently, Breland and Lytle (1990) showed that WordMAP could be used

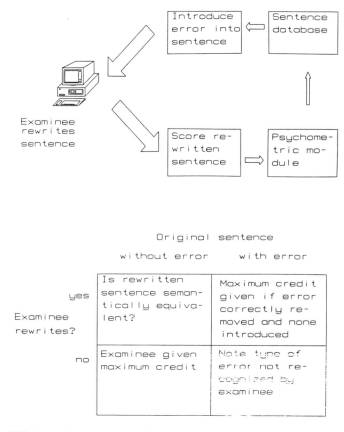

FIG. 13.6.   System for generative assessment with sentence-based items.

to score actual essays. That is, counts obtained from WordMAP regarding errors and style were shown to predict ratings from readers very well. WordMAP has no idea about the meaning of the text it analyzes, but the results from Breland and Lytle suggest that it can be used in lieu of a second rater.

Ackerman and Smith (1988) has shown that measurement of writing ability should include both sentence mechanics and essays. The results presented in this section suggest that generative sentence-based assessment of sentence mechanics could be coupled with computer-scored essays and the score from a single rater into a more valid but less expensive measure of writing ability.

Reading Comprehension.   Reading comprehension, as measured by sentence completion items could be implemented generatively with a system similar to the one in Figure 13.6, except that instead of introducing a grammatical or stylistic flaw into the sentence a word would be omitted. Unfortunately, very little is known about the sentence completion item type, despite the fact that is used by most admissions tests. Examination of a number of these items suggests that not any sentence lends itself to be a stem for a sentence completion item and that a small set of rules would account for the choice of deletion (Fellbaum, 1987).

The assessment of reading comprehension through the reading of longer texts takes two forms. One is based on the cloze procedure, where words are deleted from the text according to a set of rules, and the examinee is supposed to replace the word or choose from a set of possible replacements. The other possibility for measuring reading comprehension, found in most admissions tests, is to present a text and then ask questions about the text. Generative modeling for this item type would seem to be especially challenging. It requires first, an understanding of the effect of text attributes on comprehension and second a procedure to generate questions about the text.

A characteristic of typical items of this type is that performance, as in most reading tasks (Just & Carpenter, 1987), requires background knowledge. That is, reading comprehension is a function of the attributes of the text but also of what the examinee brings to the reading task. In fact, Perfetti (1989) has distinguished between reading *comprehension* and reading *interpretation* to emphasize that what he calls interpretation requires both extracting the meaning from the text and applying world knowledge to it, whereas what he calls comprehension is just extracting the meaning from the text. Generative modeling of interpretation appears especially challenging because in effect the question generation mechanism would have to have world knowledge equivalent to that of potential examinees. On the other hand, generative modeling of what Perfetti calls comprehension requires a mechanism for posing questions based on a given text and a theory of difficulty to anticipate the difficulty of those questions. Katz (1988) has developed a system called START that automatically analyzes English text and automatically transforms it into a propositional representation in such a way that questions based on the text can be generated. Examination of the questions generated by START for a GRE passage show, however, that they are of the factual type and would not be appropriate for the measurement of reading ability of prospective graduate students. Nevertheless, the system might have applications for younger testees and in the assessment of English as a second language, if a theory of difficulty can be developed for it.

In short, generative modeling of reading comprehension appears especially difficult because of the role background knowledge plays on performance and because questions that best tap that comprehension must call on background knowledge as well as the specifics of the text.

Complex Skills

In this section I discuss the assessment of skills that are not well characterized by a total score and call for a richer representation of the tasks and the examinee. First, I discuss achievement testing of the type that takes place in computer-based instruction where the computer would, ideally, guide the student through an optimal path. Next, I discuss the assessment of pedagogic skills. Finally, I discuss generative assessment of trouble shooting and diagnostic assessment skills.

Achievement Testing. A generative approach to achievement testing remains to be developed. Part of the challenge no doubt is due to the elusive nature of the concept of achievement (cf. Green, 1974; Cole, 1990). A generative approach that is consonant with current thinking on the nature of learning (e.g., Glaser, 1988) is likely to be different from the approaches we have discussed for the assessment of generic abilities because ranking individuals would not be the focus of measurement. In achievement testing we are often interested in providing diagnostic information for a student, a teacher, or a computer to formulate an instructional plan. Therefore, the selection of questions would not be based on difficulty, but rather on the degree of information that the answer to a question would provide in updating the several hypotheses under consideration to account for a student state of knowledge. An example of this approach is illustrated by the work on fractions of Brown and Burton (1978). The essence of the approach is to concoct the next item so that it would be maximally informative with respect to a hypothesis about the misconceptions harbored by a student. Although their notion of explaining performance in terms of bugs is not currently widely endorsed by cognitive psychologists, the general approach remains sound (e.g., Bejar, 1984) and has even been cast within an IRT framework (Yamamoto and Gitomer, chapter 11, this volume; Tatsuoka & Tatsuoka, 1987).

In general, achievement testing that is also diagnostic requires that we represent a student not as a point on a scale but rather as a complex data structure, such as a vector of misconceptions or a network, the nodes of which could stand for beliefs, hypothesis, concepts, etc. that describe the student's knowledge state. The purpose of measurement then is to estimate the activation, that is, the degree to which concepts and beliefs, for example, are present, as well as the interconnectedness among the concepts. Traditional measurement models are not oriented to representing the examinee in that form, and therefore a methodology is lacking for estimating achievement for such complex representations of the student. Although such representations are the essence of cognitive models, utilizing them for measurement, rather than description, is not common yet. A description is a declaration or set of assertions about the knowledge state of a student, without inferential power. Measurement, by contrast, entails generalizations, given a description. For example, given an ability estimate based on an IRT model we can make inferences about the probability that someone with that ability will respond to other items measuring the same ability. Thus, for cognitive descriptions to qualify as measures we need to be able to estimate them and demonstrate their inferential power (cf. Mislevy, chapter 2, this volume).

344

The advent of connectionist computational models opens up interesting possibilities because of the flexibility they provide to model a wide variety of phenomena as well as for their computational convenience. As an example, consider the modeling of physics knowledge in terms of beliefs about physical observations (Ranney & Thagard, 1988). In this case the description consists of a network of nodes for a given student. Some of these nodes stand for evidence, world knowledge, hypotheses, and explanations that describe the student's knowledge state. Ranney and Thagard (1988) build the network by transcribing a think-aloud protocol into nodes and connections among nodes. What makes their system suitable as a measurement tool is that they superimpose a set of constraints on the network, based on Thagard's theory of explanatory coherence (Thagard, 1989). For example, among the principles or constraints proposed by the theory are the analogy principle, which states that analogous hypotheses explaining analogous evidence are coherent with each other. These constraints have the effect of controlling the propagation of activations throughout the network. After each piece of new information the network is allowed to "settle." The settled network is then the current estimate of the student's knowledge state. A further characteristic of the approach that makes it suitable for assessment purposes is that the representation of the student as a network is dynamic. That is, as new information becomes available it can be propagated throughout the network. Thus, the network represents the state of knowledge or beliefs on a moment-by-moment basis.

An obstacle to becoming a practical method of assessment is the reliance of think-aloud protocols as a means of computing the initial network. However, it would seem feasible to bootstrap the network from a structured questioning procedure. That is, instead of expecting the student to verbalize observations and hypothesis through a think-aloud protocol, a questioning procedure would extract information from the student. Once the network is bootstrapped, predictions can be made about the student beliefs and tested against questions posed to assess those beliefs. The answer to each such question is further data to be fed to the network. The goal of the entire procedure is to move the student toward some ideal network. Therefore, the questioning procedure would have access not only to the student's network but also to a network representing an ideal student. Marshall (1990) has devised a related procedure for mathematic word problems. She presents a series of problems to a student and, after the student has worked a set of problems, the student responds to a structured questioning procedure about the problems just solved. The result is a network, which, at the moment, is used for descriptive purposes but could easily be used as the basis for dynamic instruction and assessment.

Teaching Skills. Because generative modeling is based on a model of the examinee it has the potential to be used for the assessment of teachers as well. For example, the information used to model the examinee can also be used "in reverse" to generate case studies for a teacher to diagnose. This would correspond with the generation of medical and troubleshooting scenarios to be discussed below. Such an approach to the assessment of teachers would be very much in line with the preoccupation with integrating an "expanding body of knowledge on children's learning and problem solving to classroom instruction" (Carpenter, Fennema, Peterson, Chiang, & Loef, 1989, p. 500).

As with the characterization of expertise in other fields (e.g., Chi, Feltovich, & Glaser, 1981), a cognitive approach has become fashionable (cf. Borko & Livingston, 1989). For example, Borko and Livingston suggest that a characteristic of more experienced teachers is the ability to reason pedagogically, which means the ability of the teacher to adapt content knowledge to the background of a specific group of students (Shulman, 1987). Such reasoning presupposes the ability of the teacher to characterize, in some detail, each student's knowledge state. In other words, more experienced teachers are able "to predict misconceptions students may have and areas of learning these misconceptions are likely to affect" (Borko & Livingston, 1989, p. 491).

In short, the picture that emerges is that teacher expertise requires not only subject-matter knowledge, which can be measured in the usual manner, but also the ability to transform that knowledge in such a way that students varying in their knowledge can benefit most effectively. Measures of the latter remain to be developed. One possibility is an assessment task that requires the candidate to characterize the knowledge state of a group of students. As part of the exercise the teacher would prepare a set of problems and simulate its administration to a group of students. The simulation would then return to the teacher the answers provided by each student. The teacher's task would then be to characterize each student's knowledge state. From there the simulation could continue in a number of directions. For example, as a next step the teacher might be asked to prepare a teaching plan that is suited to the mix of students generated by the simulation.

Troubleshooting. Tasks that require diagnostic expertise, such as equipment troubleshooting and clinical diagnosis, are naturals for generative assessment, especially if approached from a model-based perspective. For example, in a troubleshooting situation a model-based approach would estimate the mental representation of the device under consideration, that is, the structural and functional description of the device as known to the examinee (e.g., Kieras, 1990). This sense of model-based is seen in AI research to distinguish between model-based (deep) and shallow (rule-based) expert systems.

In short, a generative approach to the assessment of troubleshooting skills would be to infer the examinee's conception of the device from responses to short questions that tap knowledge of different aspects of the device. The tasks would be generated from an algorithm that has access to a description of the device and generates troubleshooting tasks that collectively tap all the procedural and device knowledge. An alternative approach is to present open-ended tasks and record all the actions taken by the examinee and infer from those actions their mental model of the device, as well as procedural, declarative, and heuristic knowledge. Both approaches are compatible because knowledge of the domain is required to generate discrete items and interpret open-ended performance. However, assessment based on short questions items may be more efficient without sacrificing information.

For example, consider the generative assessment of troubleshooting of the circuit in Fig. 13.7. The circuit is a full adder after Fulton and Pepe (1990). The circuit has three commands that can be sent to the circuit and five responses (or measurements) that can be obtained from it. Table 13.1 shows the relationship between the eight possible input configurations and the correct outputs. There are, however, 32 possible output vectors (the number of distinct vectors of length n is, in general, 2^n, or 2^5 in this case), which leave 24 possible troubleshooting tasks. Obviously, if the examinee can correctly pinpoint the problem in each of these 24 tasks he or she must have an adequate mental model of the device. The more interesting question is to infer the partial device in the examinee's mind when there is less than perfect performance.

In practice, the assessment of troubleshooting skills is most likely to take place in an instructional context. Lesgold, Ivill-Friel, and Bonar (1989) discuss a system for teaching basic electricity principles, where the system not only needs to know electricity but also must contain instructional expertise to guide instruction and testing.

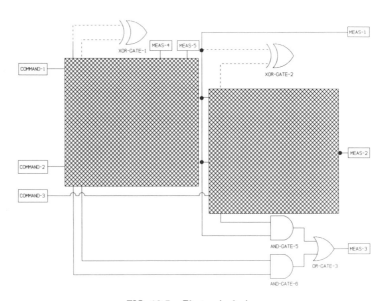

FIG. 13.7.   Electronic device.

TABLE 13.1
Relationship Between the Possible Input and Output Configurations
for the Circuit in Fig. 13.7

			Measure				
Command-1	Command-2	Command-3	1	2	3	4	5
0	0	0	0	0	0	0	1
1	0	0	1	1	0	1	0
0	1	0	1	1	0	0	1
0	0	1	0	1	0	0	1
1	1	0	0	0	1	0	0
0	1	1	1	0	1	0	1
1	0	1	1	0	1	1	0
1	1	1	0	1	1	0	0

Note. The first three columns refer to the possible input arrangements, and the last five columns refer to correct output arrangements

As with device troubleshooting, the representation of medical expertise with "shallow," that is, if–then rules, has been found to be inadequate for many purposes. Causal or model-based representations have now been proposed that have important uses in expert systems and for clinical training. An important by-product of that trend for assessment from a generative perspective is the possibility of generating clinical scenarios or patients (e.g., Parker & Miller, 1988; Pearl, 1987, chapter 4; Miller, 1984). When a clinical scenario is represented as a probabilistic causal network it is possible to update the network as new information becomes available from, say, clinical tests ordered by the examinee, or other simulated clinician–patient interactions. Actions and decisions can then be evaluated with respect to a perfect clinician represented by the network. Some ideas for generative assessment of medical expertise are discussed by Braun, Carlson, and Bejar (1989). A system that lends itself to measurement from that perspective has been discussed by Warner and associates (1988).

CONCLUSIONS

There is a growing concern among some psychometricians (e.g., Goldstein & Wood, 1989) that the kind of theorizing that accompanies item response theory has little to do with what the test it is applied to is supposed to measure. They even suggest that the research performed under the IRT rubric should be relabeled Item Response modeling instead. This chapter is, in a sense, a constructive reaction to the concern and evolves naturally from attempts within the IRT tradition (e.g., Fischer 1973) to incorporate substantive or collateral detail as part of the response modeling process. It also represents an example of what Snow and Lohman (1988) call the link between laboratory and field. RGM not only links laboratory and field but also challenges the item writer and psychometrician to test their knowledge base constantly—indeed, every time a test is administered.

While the foregoing results point to the feasibility of an approach to measurement where response modeling and response theory are integrated under a generative framework, it also raises the question of whether there is a single psychological framework under which such an ambitious undertaking would fit. Even if RGM were successfully implemented in a wide range of domains, chances are that somewhat incompatible procedures and assumptions would be used to model each domain. This is because RGM is not a psychological theory, or even a methodology, but rather a philosophy of test construction and response modeling that calls for their integration. It is more than likely that the application of RGM to specific item types will not yield a coherent picture that encompasses a multitude of domains. A complete picture requires an account of interdomain covariation, that is, the relationship of test performance across different domains, as well as within-domain variation in item parameters. The challenge, therefore, would be to model specific domains through a common set of assumptions in such a way that the within-domain psychometric characteristics can be anticipated as well as interdomain covariation.

Stating the challenge in this form underscores the communality that exists between cognitive psychology and differential psychology. A major objective of cognitive psychology has been an accounting of learning or performance in specific tasks, that is, within-domain phenomena. The results for the most part have been a variety of microtheories, each optimized for the phenomenon at hand, just as different microtheories of item difficulty are likely to emerge from attempts to implement RGM. Even if the microtheories are successful there is another aspect of the data that must be accounted for, namely, interdomain covariation.

An accounting for interdomain covariation is really not different from the "transfer problem" that has persisted in learning and cognitive psychology. Indeed, Messick (1972) has proposed the transfer problem as an arena for incorporating function into individual differences theorizing. Whereas psychometricians have attempted to account for the degree to which test scores covary—and for the most part have failed, according to Carroll (1988)—for the cognitive psychologist the problem is to account for transfer—or more often than not, lack thereof. Psychometricians may have described the covariation among a wide range of tests, but such descriptions do not constitute an accounting. Similarly, cognitive psychologists are often at a loss to explain lack of transfer. According to Larkin (1989, p. 303): "Although attractive, the notion that transferable knowledge is a core of general problem-solving skills has been historically unproductive." She argues that the answer lies in incorporating more detail: "Instruction in skills is most effective if we can understand in detail what we want to teach and focus instruction accordingly. Detailed models of strategies for related domains, methods for setting subgoals, knowledge of task management, and learning skills seem a promising road to this end" (Larkin, 1989, p. 304).

Knowing that cognitive and differential psychology share concerns is reassuring but does not answer the question of whether a single framework can serve as the foundation for RGM across a variety of domains. A similar question has been raised by computational psychologists (Boden, 1988, p. 171), who phrase the questions in terms of a general theory of problem solving, and by intelligence theorists (e.g., Sternberg & Powell, 1982).

One answer, of course, is that such a general theory is not possible, a view taken by modularity psychologists (e.g., Fodor, 1983) and by cognitive anthropologists who argue that the modeling of problem solving must take context and situations into account (Lave, 1988). Others, however, argue that it is indeed possible, and they propose a scheme, or architecture, under which we can subsume a variety of problem-solving behaviors (Newell, 1989). The Newell–Simon (1972) approach to problem solving is especially relevant to psychometrics because of its concern with problem difficulty. As early as 1972 Newell and Simon (1972, p. 93) discussed at length problem difficulty in ways that are totally consistent with the componential approaches to psychometric modeling of Carroll (1976), Sternberg (1977), and Whitely (1980) and even the disjunctive–conjunctive distinction discussed by Jannarone (in preparation). In the Newell–Simon theory, the problem solver is viewed as constructing problem spaces for each problem. The difficulty of a problem is then, in part, a function of the problem space: "The size of the problem space provides one key to the estimation of problem difficulty. The problem space defines the set of possibilities for the solution, *as seen by the problem solver*" (Newell & Simon, 1972, p. 93, italics added).

Clearly, Newell and Simon had an idiographic view of difficulty in mind when they defined problem spaces as being specific to a problem solver, but later in the book they consider nomothetic individual differences and attribute them primarily to the contents of long-term memory and to "basic structure" (p. 865): "it follows that any proposal for communality among problem solvers not attributable to basic structure must be represented as an identity or similarity in the contents of the LTM—in the production system or in other memory structures" (p. 865).

The applicability of the Newell–Simon framework to an accounting of individual differences on a psychometric instrument, the Raven Progressive Matrices, has been demonstrated by Carpenter, Just, and Shell (1990). They account for performance on this test, considered to be one of the purest measures of intelligence, by explicating the differences in level of performance in the form of simulation models that perform at different levels. Briefly, the kinds of models they postulate consist of a set of productions, or condition–action rules, to represent the content of long-term memory. When those productions are activated by the requirements of the problem, they deposit information in short-term memory. The solution to a problem is obtained by operating on the content of short-term memory. Within this framework individual differences can be a function of the content of long-term memory and the working memory capacity, or basic structure as originally formulated by Newell and Simon. But in the case of the Raven, which uses totally novel stimuli, working memory capacity may in fact be more important because there is not much information to be retrieved from long-term memory.

In general, and especially with achievement tests, long-term memory would be expected to play a larger role. However, basic structure, or working memory capacity, would seem to be centrally involved, even in domains that are knowledge dependent, because working memory capacity is involved not only in the solution of the current problem but also in the creation and storing of the knowledge, which is now triggered to solve the current problem. Thus, working memory capacity may be the equivalent of g in differential psychology, postulated by Spearman (1923) to account for the consistent covariation among intellectual tasks. However, we now know that there is more than g. A breakdown of the "factorial pie" in terms of crystallized and fluid intelligences (e.g., Horn, 1970) has received a wide acceptance (e.g., Snow & Lohman, 1989). This breakdown seems to fit with an equating fluid intelligence to working memory capacity, and crystallized intelligence to productions, or knowledge.

The notion that there can be an all-encompassing theory of problem solving has not gone unchallenged (e.g., Boden, 1988, p. 171). One argument is that problem solving is not computationally encapsulated but involves *cognitive penetrable* phenomena, a term originated by Pylyshyn (1984), which means that the problem solver is influenced by his or her desires and beliefs. This view would seem to suggest that the actual difficulty of a problem for a given individual would be a function of that person's ability, the nature of the problem, and his or her beliefs. From a psychometric perspective this need not be a fatal a problem as it might be to a purely psychological theory, because psychometric models can deal with error. Moreover, there is no reason why the penetrability could not itself be modeled by establishing the link of beliefs and desires into a response mechanism (cf. Boden, p. 174). An example of modeling penetrability within a psychometric framework is provided by Colberg and Nester (1987), who are able to anticipate the range of illogical beliefs and incorporate those as part of the prediction of difficulty of deductive reasoning items. In short, penetrability need not be a fatal problem, at least from a psychometric perspective.

The Newell–Simon approach has been characterized as embodying a symbolic paradigm (Smolensky, 1986). A contender to the Newell–Simon framework argues for a subsymbolic approach. Smolensky (1986), for example, illustrates electronic problem solving from a subsymbolic perspective where, instead of representing knowledge as productions, knowledge is distributed in a network, the nodes of which represent bits of knowledge. The states of that network are assumed to correspond to psychological meaningful states.

Both symbolic and subsymbolic approaches to modeling cognition lend themselves to psychometric modeling, and are appealing because of their psychological underpinnings but seem better suited for within-task analyses. The covariation among tasks needs also to be accounted for. Such an accounting could come about from a detailed analysis of studies that describe performance covariation across a variety of tasks. The most obvious source of data for such an analysis is found in the factor-analytic literature. The value of such analyses is demonstrated by two metanalyses. Snow, Kyllonen, and Marshalek (1984) reanalyzed several data sets and concluded that Guttman's (1954) radex theory of intelligence was correct. That is, performance across a variety of cognitive tasks can be described as a circular map. Located at the center of the map we find performance on Raven's Progressive Matrix test, presumably representing g. Moreover, the circle can be divided into three slices, corresponding to verbal, quantitative, and spatial domains. The tests on the periphery are simpler, and as we move toward the center their complexity increases. The rich detail provided by Snow et al. seems to be beyond the scope of the Newell–Simon or mental models frameworks. The second reanalysis of existing data was provided by Carroll (e.g., 1980), who postulates 10 basic information-processing components as the basis for the factors that factor analysts have postulated to account for covariation among test scores.

Clearly, we are not at the point where we decide what is the best approach to a general psychological framework for test construction. Perhaps a variety of perspectives should be encouraged. What RGM does is to provide a Popperian mechanism for psychometric modeling. According to Popper (1959/1968), the scientific status of a theory depends on its falsifiability. Moreover, evidence in favor of a theory is not as convincing unless that evidence was obtained as part of a challenge, that is, in an attempt to falsify the theory. RGM links item construction and response modeling in a single package so that the linkage, that is, the predictions about response behavior, are challenged every time a test is administered. Thus, the administration of a test becomes a psychological experiment, which in turn may lead to the improvement of both theories and tests.

ACKNOWLEDGMENTS

I'm grateful to Irving Sigel, Larry Frase, Norman Frederiksen, Robert Mislevy, and Lawrence Stricker for valuable comments on earlier versions of this manuscript. Those suggestions I did not incorporate into this manuscript will surely improve future ones.

REFERENCES

Ackerman, T. A., & Smith, P. L. (1988). A comparison of the information provided by essay, multiple-choice, and free-response writing tests. *Applied Psychological Measurement, 12,* 117–128.

Baker, F. B. (1988). Computer technology in test construction and processing. In R. L. Linn (Ed.), *Educational Measurement* (pp. 409–428). New York: Macmillan.

Bejar, I. I. (1990). A generative analysis of a three-dimensional spatial task. *Applied Psychological Measurement, 14,* 237–245.

Bejar, I. I. (in preparation). *Leveraging the computer for test delivery by automating the scoring of open-ended items.* Princeton, NJ: Educational Testing Service.

Bejar, I. I. (1983). *Achievement testing: Recent advances.* Beverly Hills, CA: Sage Publications.

Bejar, I. I. (1984). Educational diagnostic assessment. *Journal of Educational Measurement, 21,* 175–189.

Bejar, I. I. (1988). A sentence-based automated approach to the assessment of writing: A feasibility study. *Machine-Mediated Learning, 2,* 321–332.

Bejar, I. I. (1989, August). *Generative response modeling and test development job aids: An approach to improving validity through technology.* Presented in Implications of Measurement Theory for Language Assessment at the ETS TOEFL Invitational Symposium on Language Acquisition and Language Assessment, Princeton, NJ.

Bejar, I. I., Chaffin, R., & Embretson, S. (1991). *Cognitive and psychometric analysis of analogical problem solving.* New York: Springer-Verlag.

Bejar, I. I., Stabler, E. P., & Camp, R. (1987). *Syntactic complexity and psychometric difficulty: A preliminary investigation* (RR-87-25). Princeton, NJ: Educational Testing Service.

Bejar, I. I., & Yocom, P. (1991). A generative approach to the modeling of isomorphic hidden-figure items. *Applied Psychological Measurement, 15,* 129–137.

Bock, R. D., Gibbon, R., & Muraki, E. (1988). Full-information item factor analysis. *Applied Psychological Measurement, 12,* 261–280.

Boden, M. A. (1988). *Computer models of mind: Computational approaches in theoretical psychology.* New York: Cambridge University Press.

Borko, H., & Livingston, C. (1989). Cognition and improvisation: Differences in mathematics instruction by expert and novice teachers. *American Educational Research Journal, 26,* 473–498.

Bormuth, J. R. (1970). *On the theory of achievement test items.* Chicago: University of Chicago Press.

Braun, H., Carlson, S., & Bejar, I. I. (1989). *Psychometric foundations of testing based on patient management problems* (RM-89-2). Princeton, NJ: Educational Testing Service.

Breland, H. M., & Lytle, E. G. (1990, April). *Computer-assisted writing assessment using WordMAP™.* Presented at NCME 1990 Annual Conference, Boston, MA.

Brown, J. S., & Burton, R. R. (1978). Diagnostic models for procedural bugs in basic mathematical skills. *Cognitive Science, 2,* 155–192.

Burton, R. R. (1982). Diagnosing bugs in a simple procedural skill. In D. Sleeman & J. S. Brown (Eds.), *Intelligent tutoring systems* (pp. 157–183). New York: Academic Press.

Butterfield, E. C., Nielsen, D., Tangen, K. L., & Richardson, M. B. (1985). Theoretically based psychometric measures of inductive reasoning. In S. E. Embretson (Ed.), *Test design: Developments in psychology and psychometrics* (pp. 77–147). New York: Academic Press.

Byrd, R. J., Calzolari, N., Chodorow, M. S., Edwards, D., Klavans, J. L., & Neff, M. S. (1987). Tools and methods for computational linguistics. *Computational Linguistics, 13,* 219–240.

Campbell, A. C. (1961). Some determinants of the difficulty of non-verbal classification items. *Educational and Psychological Measurement, 21,* 899–913.

Campbell, D. T., & Fiske, D. W. (1959). Convergent and discriminant validation by the multitrait-multimethod matrix. *Psychological Bulletin, 56,* 81–105.

Carpenter, T. P., Fennema, E., Peterson, P. L., Chiang, C. P., & Loef, M. (1989). Using knowledge of children's mathematics thinking in classroom teaching: An experimental study. *American Educational Research Journal, 26,* 499–531.

Carpenter, P. A., Just, M. A., & Shell, P. (1990). What one intelligence test measures: A theoretical account of the processing in the Raven Progressive Matrices Test. *Psychological Review, 97,* 404–431.

Carroll, J. B. (1972). Stalking the wayward factors. *Contemporary Psychology, 17,* 321–324.

Carroll, J. B. (1976). Psychometric tests as cognitive tasks: A new "Structure of Intellect." In L. Resnick (Ed.), *The nature of intelligence* (pp. 27-56). Hillsdale, NJ: Lawrence Erlbaum Associates.

Carroll, J. B. (1980). Measurement of abilities constructs. In *Construct Validity in Psychological Measurement*. Proceedings of a colloquium on theory and application in education and employment. Princeton, NJ: Educational Testing Service.

Carroll, J. B. (1980). *Individual difference relations in psychometric and experimental cognitive tasks.* L. L. Thurstone Psychometric Laboratory Report No. 163 (ERIC Doc ED-191-891).

Carroll, J. B. (1988, April). *Factor analysis since Spearman: Where do we stand? What do we know?* Presented at a symposium, Learning and Individual Differences: Abilities, Motivation, and Methodology, Department of Psychology, University of Minnesota.

Chaffin, R., & Herrmann, D. J. (1987). Relation element theory: A new account of the representation and processing of semantic relations. In D. Gorfein & R. Hoffman (Eds.), *Memory and learning: The Ebbinghaus centennial conference.* Hillsdale, NJ: Erlbaum.

Chi, M. T. H., Feltovich, P. J., & Glaser, R. (1981). Categorization and representation of physics problems by experts and novices. *Cognitive Science, 5*, 121-152.

Chomsky, N. (1965). *Aspects of the theory of syntax.* Cambridge, MA: MIT Press.

Colberg, M., & Nester, M. (1987, August). *The use of illogical biases in psychometrics.* Paper presented at the 7th International Congress of Logic, Methodology and Philosophy of Science. Moscow, USSR.

Cole, N. S. (1990). Conceptions of educational achievement. *Educational Researcher, 19*, 2-7.

Corballis, M. C. (1982). Mental rotation: Analysis of a paradigm. In M. Potegal (Ed.), *Spatial abilities: Developmental and psychological foundations* (pp. 173-198). New York: Academic Press.

Cronbach, L. J. (1970). Review of On the theory of achievement test items, by J. R. Bormuth. *Psychometrika, 35*, 509-511.

Cronbach, L. J., & Meehl, P. E. (1955). Construct validity in psychological tests. *Psychological Bulletin, 52*, 281-302.

Curtis, M. E. (1987). Vocabulary testing and vocabulary instruction. In M. G. McKeown, & M. E. Curtis (Eds.), *The nature of vocabulary acquisition* (pp. 37-51). Hillsdale, NJ: Lawrence Erlbaum Associates.

Davies, A. D. M., & Davies, M. G. (1965). The difficulty and graded scoring of Elithorn's perceptual maze test. *British Journal of Psychology, 14*, 295-302.

Duncan, J., & Humphreys, G. W. (1989). Visual search and stimulus similarity. *Psychological Review, 96*, 433-458.

Egan, D. E. (1979). Testing based on understanding: Implications from studies of spatial ability. *Intelligence, 3*, 1-15.

Ekstrom, R. B., French, J., & Harman, H. (1976). *Kit of factor-referenced cognitive tests.* Princeton, NJ: Educational Testing Service.

Elithorn, A., Jones, D., Kerr, M., & Lee, D. (1964). The effects of the variation of two physical parameters on empirical difficulty in a perceptual maze test. *British Journal of Psychology, 55*, 31-37.

Embretson, S. E. (1983). Construct validity: Construct representation versus nomothetic span. *Psychological Bulletin, 93*, 175-197.

Fellbaum, C. (1987). A preliminary analysis of cognitive-linguistic aspects of sentence completion tasks. In R. O. Freedle, & R. P. Duran (Eds.), *Cognitive and linguistic analyses of test performance* (pp. 193-207). In R. O. Freedle (Series Ed.), *Vol. XXII: Advances in Discourse Processes.* Norwood, NJ: Ablex.

Fodor, J. (1983). *The modularity of mind.* Cambridge, MA: MIT Press.

Fischer, G. H. (1973). The linear logist test model as an instrument in educational research. *Acta Psychologica, 37*, 359-374.

Frederiksen, N. (1990). Introduction. In N. Frederiksen, R. Glaser, A. Lesgold, & M. G. Shafto (Eds.), *Diagnostic monitoring of skill and knowledge acquisition* (pp. 4-6). Hillsdale, NJ: Lawrence Erlbaum Associates.

Frederiksen, N. (1986). Construct validity and construct similarity: Methods for use in test development and test validation. *Multivariate Behavioral Research, 21,* 3–28.

Fulton, S. L., & Pepe, C. O. (1990, January). An introduction to model-based reasoning. *AI Expert,* 48–55.

Gardner, H. (1985). *The mind's new science: A history of the cognitive revaluation.* New York: Basic Books.

Galotti, K. M. (1989). Approaches to studying formal and everyday reasoning. *Psychological Bulletin, 105,* 331–351.

Gentner, D. (1983). Structure-mapping: A theoretical framework for analogy. *Cognitive Science, 7,* 155–170.

Glaser, R. (1988). Cognitive and environmental perspectives on assessing achievement. In *Assessment in the Service of Learning: Proceedings of the 1987 ETS Invitational Conference* (pp. 37–43). Princeton, NJ: Educational Testing Service.

Goldin, G. A., & McClintock, C. E. (Eds.). (1984). *Task variables in mathematical problem solving.* Philadelphia, PA: Franklin Institute Press.

Goldstein, H., & Wood, R. (1989). Five decades of item response modelling. *British Journal of Mathematical and Statistical Psychology, 42,* 139–167.

Green, D. R. (Ed.). (1974). *The aptitude-achievement distinction: Proceedings of the Second CTB/McGraw-Hill Conference on Issues in Educational Measurement.* Monterey, CA: CTB/McGraw-Hill.

Gulliksen, H. (1950). *Theory of mental tests.* New York: Wiley.

Guttman, L. A. (1971). Measurement as structural theory. *Psychometrika, 26,* 329–347.

Guttman, L. A. (1954). A new approach to factor analysis: The radex. In P. F. Lazarsfeld (Ed.), *Mathematical thinking in the social sciences.* Glencoe, IL: Free Press.

Guttman, L. A. (1969). Integration of test design and analysis. In *Proceedings of the 1969 Invitational Conference on Testing Problems.* Princeton, NJ: Educational Testing Service.

Guttman, L. A. (1980). Integration of test design and analysis: Status in 1979. In W. B. Schrader (Ed.), *Measuring achievement: Progress over a decade.* Proceedings of the 1979 ETS Invitational Conference. San Francisco: Jossey-Bass.

Hall, R., Kibler, D., Wenger, E., & Truxaw, C. (1989). Exploring the episodic structure of algebra story problem solving. *Cognition and Instruction, 6,* 223–283.

Harmon, P. (1986). Intelligent job aids: How AI will change training in the next five years. In G. Kearsley (Ed.), *Artificial intelligence and instruction: Application and methods.* Reading, MA: Addison-Wesley.

Hively, W. (1974). Introduction to domain referenced testing. *Educational Technology, 14,* 5–9.

Hively, W., Paterson, H. L., & Page, S. H. (1968). A universe-defined system of arithmetic tests. *Journal of Educational Measurement, 5,* 275–290.

Horn, J. L. (1970). Organization of data on life span development of human abilities. In L. R. Goulet & P. B. Baltes (Eds.), *Life-span developmental psychology; research and theory* (pp. 423–466). New York: Academic Press.

Irvine, S. H., Dunn, P. L., & Anderson, J. D. (1989). *Towards a theory of algorithm-determined cognitive test construction* (Report). Devon, UK: Polytechnic South West.

Jannarone, R. (in preparation). *Measuring quickness and correctness concurrently: A cognitive IRT approach.* Columbia, SC: Psychology Department, University of South Carolina.

Jarjoura, D., & Brennan, R. L. (1982). A variance components model for measurement procedures associated with a table of specifications. *Applied Psychological Measurement, 6,* 161–171.

Jensen, A. R. (1980). *Bias in mental testing.* New York: Free Press.

Johnson-Laird, P. N. (1983). *Mental models: Towards a cognitive science of language, inference, and consciousness.* Cambridge, MA: Harvard University Press.

Johnson-Laird, P. N., Byrne, R. M. J., & Tabossi, P. (1989). Reasoning by model: The case of multiple quantification. *Psychological Review, 96,* 658–673.

Just, M. A., & Carpenter, P. A. (1987). *The psychology of reading and language comprehension.* Needham, MA: Allyn & Bacon.

Katz, B. (1988). *Using English for indexing and retrieving* (A.I. Memo No. 1096). Cambridge, MA: Massachusetts Institute of Technology.

Kieras, D. E. (1990). The role of cognitive simulation models in the development of advanced training and testing systems. In N. Frederiksen, R. Glaser, A. Lesgold, & M. G. Shafto (Eds.), *Diagnostic monitoring of skill and knowledge acquisition* (pp. 51–73). Hillsdale, NJ: Lawrence Erlbaum Associates.

Kolen, M. J., & Harris, D. J. (1987, April). *A multivariate test theory model based on item response theory and generalizability theory.* Paper presented at the Annual Meeting of the American Educational Research Association, Washington, D.C.

Kotovsky, K., & Simon, H. A. (1988). *What makes some problems really hard: Explorations in the problem space of difficulty* (ONR Report N00014-85-K-0696). Pittsburgh, PA: Community College of Allegheny County.

Kyllonen, P. C. (1990, April). *Taxonomies of cognitive abilities.* Presented at the American Educational Research Association Meeting, Boston, MA.

Larkin, J. H. (1989). What kind of knowledge transfers? In L. R. Resnick (Ed.), *Knowing, learning, and instruction: Essays in honor of Robert Glaser* (pp. 283–305). Hillsdale, NJ: Lawrence Erlbaum Associates.

Lave, J. (1988). *Cognition in practice: Mind, mathematics and culture in everyday life.* New York: Cambridge University Press.

Lesgold, A., Ivill-Friel, J., & Bonar, J. (1989). Toward intelligent systems for testing. In L. R. Resnick (Ed.), *Knowing, learning, and instruction: Essays in honor of Robert Glaser* (pp. 337–360). Hillsdale, NJ: Lawrence Erlbaum Associates.

Loevinger, J. (1965). Person and population as psychometric concepts. *Psychological Review, 72,* 143–155.

Marshall, S. R. (1990, April). *What students learn (and remember) from word problem instruction.* Presented at AERA 1990 Annual Convention in symposium, Penetrating to the Mathematical Structure of Word Problems, chaired by S. F. Chipman, Boston, MA.

Mayer, R. E. (1981). Frequency norms and structural analysis of algebra story problems into families, categories and templates. *Instructional Science, 10,* 135–175.

Mayhew, J., & Frisby, J. (1984). Computer vision. In T. O'Shea and M. Eisenstadt (Ed.), *Artificial intelligence: Tools, techniques, and applications.* New York: Harper & Row.

Merwin, J. C. (1977). Considerations in exploring alternatives to standardized tests. In A. J. Nitko (Ed.), *Exploring alternatives to current standardized tests: Proceedings of the 1976 National Testing Conference* (pp. 5–24). Pittsburgh, PA: University of Pittsburgh.

Messick, S. (1972). Beyond structure: In search of functional models of psychological process. *Psychometrika, 37,* 357–375.

Messick, S. (1981). Constructs and their vicissitudes in educational and psychological measurement. *Psychological Bulletin, 89,* 575–588.

Miller, G. A. (1962). Some psychological studies of grammars. *American Psychologist, 17,* 748–762.

Miller, G. A., Fellbaum, C., Kegl, J., & Miller, K. (1988). *WORDNET: An electronic lexical reference system based on theories of lexical memory* (Rep. No. 29). Princeton, NJ: Cognitive Science Laboratory, Princeton University.

Miller, P. L. (1984). *A critiquing approach to expert computer advice: Attending.* Palo Alto, CA: Kaufmann.

Mislevy, R. J., & Sheehan, K. M. (1990, June). *How to equate tests with little or no data.* Presented at the Psychometric Society Meeting, Princeton, NJ.

Newell, A. (1989). Putting it all together. In D. R. Lahr & K. Kotovsky (Eds.), *Complex information processing: The impact of Herbert A. Simon* (pp. 339–445). Hillsdale, NJ: Lawrence Erlbaum Associates.

Newell, A., & H. A. Simon (1972). *Human problem solving.* Englewood Cliffs, NJ: Prentice-Hall.

Osburn, H. G. (1968). Item sampling for achievement testing. *Educational and Psychological Measurement, 28,* 95–104.

Parker, R. C., & Miller, R. A. (1988). Using causal knowledge to create simulated patient cases: CPCS Project as an extension of INTERNIST-1. In P. L. Miller (Ed.), *Selected topics in medical artificial intelligence* (pp. 99–115). New York: Springer-Verlag.

Pearl, J. (1987). *Probabilistic reasoning in intelligent systems: Networks of plausible inference.* San Mateo, CA: Kaufmann.

Pellegrino, J. W., & Glaser, R. (1982). Analyzing aptitudes for learning: Inductive reasoning. In R. Glaser (Ed.), *Advances in instructional psychology* (Vol. 2, pp. 245–269). Hillsdale, NJ: Lawrence Erlbaum Associates.

Perfetti, C. A. (1989). There are generalized abilities and one of them is reading. In L. R. Resnick (Ed.), *Knowing, learning, and instructions: Essays in honor of Robert Glaser* (pp. 307–335). Hillsdale, NJ: Lawrence Erlbaum Associates.

Popper, Sir K. (1968). *The logic of scientific discovery.* New York: Harper & Row. (Original work published 1959)

Prince, A., & Pinker, S. (1988). On language and connectionism: Analysis of a parallel distributed processing model of language acquisition. *Cognition, 28.*

Pylyshyn, Z. W. (1984). *Computation and cognition: Toward a foundation for cognitive science.* Cambridge, MA: MIT Press.

Ranney, M., & Thagard, P. (1988). *Explanatory coherence and belief revision in naive physics* (Tech. Rep. No. UPITT/LRDC/ONR/APS-17). Pittsburgh, PA: University of Pittsburgh, Learning Research and Development Center.

Reed, S. K., Ackinclose, C. C., & Voss, A. A. (1990). Selecting analogous problems: Similarity versus inclusiveness. *Memory and Cognition, 18,* 83–98.

Riley, M. S., Greeno, J. G., & Heller, J. I. (1983). Development of children's problem-solving ability in arithmetic. In H. P. Ginsburg (Ed.), *The development of mathematical thinking* (pp. 153–196). New York: Academic Press.

Roid, G., & Haladyna, T. (1982). *A technology for test-item writing.* New York: Academic Press.

Rummelhart, D. E., McClelland, J. L., & the PDR Research Group. (1986). *Parallel distributed processing: Explorations in the microstructure of cognition, Volume 1: Foundations.* Cambridge, MA: MIT Press.

Shepard, R. N., & Metzler, J. (1971). Mental rotation of three-dimensional objects. *Science, 171,* 701–703.

Shulman, L. S. (1987). Knowledge and teaching: Foundations of the new reform. *Harvard Educational Review, 57,* 1–22.

Simon, H. A., & Kotovsky, K. (1963). Human acquisition of concepts for sequential patterns. *Psychological Review, 70,* 534–546.

Skinner, B. F. (1957). *Verbal behavior.* New York: Appleton-Century-Crofts.

Smolensky, P. (1986). Information processing in dynamical systems: Foundations of harmony theory. In D. E. Rummelhart, J. L. McClelland, & the PDP Research Group (Eds.), *Parallel distributed processing: Volume 1: Foundations* (pp. 194–281). Cambridge, MA: MIT Press.

Snow, R. E., Kyllonen, P. C., & Marshalek, B. (1984). The topography of ability and learning correlations. In R. J. Sternberg (Ed.), *Advances in the psychology of human intelligence* (Vol. 2). Hillsdale, NJ: Lawrence Erlbaum Associates.

Snow, R. E., & Lohman, D. F. (1989). Implications of cognitive psychology for educational measurement. In R. L. Linn (Ed.), *Educational Measurement* (3rd ed., pp. 263–331). New York: Macmillan.

Spearman, C. (1923). *The nature of "intelligence" and the principles of cognition.* New York: Macmillan.

Sternberg, R. J. (1977). *Intelligence, information processing and analogical reasoning: The componential analysis of human abilities.* New York: Wiley.

Sternberg, R. J. (1987). Most vocabulary is learned from context. In M. G. McKeown & M. E. Curtis (Eds.), *The nature of vocabulary acquisition* (pp. 89–105). Hillsdale, NJ: Lawrence Erlbaum Associates.

Sternberg, R. J., & Powell, J. S. (1982). Theories of intelligence. In R. J. Sternberg (Ed.), *Handbook of human intelligence* (pp. 975–1005). New York: Cambridge University Press.

Tate, M. W. (1948). Individual differences in speed of response in mental test materials of varying degrees of difficulty. *Educational and Psychological Measurement, 8,* 353–374.

Tatsuoka, K. K., & Tatsuoka, M. M. (1987). Bug distribution and statistical pattern classification. *Psychometrika, 52,* 193–206.

Thagard, P. (1989). Explanatory coherence. *Behavioral and Brain Sciences, 12,* 435–502.

Tryon, R. C. (1957). Reliability and behavior domain validity: Reformulation and historical critique. *Psychological Bulletin, 54,* 229–249.

Uttal, W. R., Rogers, M., Hieronymous, R., & Pasich, T. (1970). *Generative computer-assisted instruction in analytic geometry.* Newburyport, MA: Entelek, Inc.

Warner, H. R., Haug, P., Bouhaddou, O., Lincoln, M., Warner, H. Jr., Sorenson, D., Williamson, J. W., & Fan, C. (1988). ILIAD as an expert consultant to teach differential diagnosis. In R. A. Greenes (Ed.), *Proceedings of the Twelfth Annual Symposium on Computer Applications in Medical Care* (pp. 371–376). New York: Computer Society Press.

Whitely, S. E. (1980). Latent trial models in the study of intelligence. *Intelligence, 4,* 97–132.

Yamamoto, K. (1989). *Hybrid model of IRT and latent class models* (RR-89-41). Princeton, NJ: Educational Testing Service.

Zimmerman, W. S. (1954). The influence of item complexity upon the factor composition of a spatial visualization test. *Educational and Psychological Measurement, 14,* 106–119.

14

Representations of Ability Structures: Implications for Testing

Edward H. Haertel
Stanford University

David E. Wiley
Northwestern University

INTRODUCTION

Over the last several years, cognitive psychology and, more generally, cognitive science have undertaken the analysis of cognitive tasks and of learning in a fashion that acknowledges greater psychological complexity than earlier traditions. There has been increasing attention to the fine structure of abilities underlying task performance, and on the processes by which these abilities are acquired. This work has included attention to the kinds of complex learning that take place in schools (e.g., Burton, 1982, and VanLehn, 1990, on the acquisition of skill in subtraction). There has also been a flowering of new, complex tasks intended to assess learning outcomes. These new tasks are, in a direct sense, strong criticisms of the technologies of multiple-choice item response and even of the meaningfulness of dichotomous scoring of open-ended task responses.

A positive result of these emphases may be increased attention to the learning transitions between task performance states. Closer analysis of complex task performance focuses attention on sequences of performance states, which ultimately lead to the end states that have been the primary targets of earlier analyses. A negative result, from our perspective, may be the blurring of distinctions between states of task performance and states of underlying ability. It is, of course, easier to keep the analysis of learning focused on the transition from one performance state to another (e.g., Falmagne, Koppen, Villano, Doignon, & Johannesen, 1990), but this approach tends to make the specification of what is learned task-specific, which in turn makes generalization to future performance of different tasks conceptually unclear.

Evolving frameworks juxtapose the learning experiences of which individuals partake and the states of ability with which they enter those experiences. The interaction of ability patterns with learning experiences results in new learning, that is, transitions to new ability patterns. One of the fundaments of these interactions is the fact that specific new learnings require specific earlier prerequisite learnings. Mapping these prerequisite relations is a major task of both learning psychology and curriculum.

Current test theory seems ill equipped either to characterize the fine structure of these ability patterns or to build on this structure to more clearly represent the acquisition and structure of aggregate abilities. The achievements of latent trait theory (item response theory or IRT) relate more to the adequate treatment of observable dichotomies or polytomies than to contemporary psychological conceptions of underlying abilities or learning. Given that the trait conceptions embodied in all of the commonly used IRT models appear to be variants of Thurstone factor models, even the most elaborated frameworks for assessing ability structures assume that subtests are in some way "homogeneous." That is to say, "structure" exists between, but not within, subsets of items referenced to a common set of (one or more) latent traits or factors. The abilities to be assessed are also commonly assumed continuous in their distribution, which seems at best a poor approximation if one's interest is in the small steps or stages through which learning actually occurs. Latent traits seem to represent ill-defined composites of many abilities whose fine structure is not taken into account. In addition, the relationships among abilities through which factor models and their variants represent "structure" are correlational, not contingent or prerequisite in nature. Perhaps these are some of the reasons why it is so difficult to see most aggregate abilities as anything other than hazy collections with arbitrary boundaries.

Thus, in our view, it is of great importance to broaden and deepen the characterization of ability and its relation to task performance. The complex tasks now emerging as a part of new assessment paradigms cannot be adequately treated without a thorough revision and extension of the underlying conceptual structure. This revision must incorporate clear linkages between ability and task performance, and must allow for the characterization of both status and change in ability (learning). This chapter introduces a framework for thinking about tasks, abilities, learning, and their interrelationships that fits more smoothly with these emerging understandings. The first major section discusses the idea of *tasks*, taking up task performances, task specifications, and task definitions. This is followed by a section that defines *abilities* and introduces the idea of mappings from ability states to task performance states. The following two sections, in turn, take up *ability structures* and *task structures*, showing how both tasks and abilities may be formulated at different levels of complexity, and elucidating their internal structure. These sections also develop the framework's implications for relationships between ability structures and task structures. The last major section lays out some implications of the foregoing discussion for testing.

WHAT IS A TASK?

A *task* is a goal-directed human activity to be pursued in a specified manner, context, or circumstance. Tasks may vary from relatively simple (e.g., responding to a multiple-choice item) to complex (e.g., conducting a symphony).

Task Performance, Specifications, and Definitions

A task *performance* is a particular instance or example of such an activity. As such, it has three characteristics:

1. It has a goal.
2. It has a beginning and an end, and therefore a duration.
3. It can be evaluated with respect to success in attaining its goal.

By goal, we mean the goal toward which the task performance is directed, not the goal that a task formulator might have in setting the task (e.g., to further learning or to make inferences about ability). By specifying a beginning and an end, we do not mean to imply that a task must have a constant or consistent timing, but merely that one can tell when the performance starts and when it ends. Finally, the process and the products of the performance must be characterizable in relation to the performance goal. This might only mean that performance is judged to be either satisfactory or not, or it might imply an elaborate multicriterial evaluation of performance (cf. Wiley, 1990).

A task *specification,* in contrast to a performance, is a setting of the conditions under which a task performance can take place. That is, it allows a task to be defined in such a way that it can be performed more than one time by more than one person or group. For example, an open- and a closed-book examination might have the same goals of successful performance for the individuals taking the examinations, but the specifications of conditions are sufficiently different that the two would commonly be judged as distinct tasks. Typically a task specification would address:

1. The environment or circumstances within which the task performance will take place: physical environment and timing, as well as information, tools, equipment, physical resources, etc. to be made available.
2. The communication directed to the performer of the task, often specify-

ing its goal, evaluative criteria to be applied, the circumstances and conditions within which it is to be performed, and the tools available to perform it.

A task specification sets up an equivalence class of task implementations or realizations. A realization belongs to a particular equivalence class as long as its conditions match those of the specification. It is this framework that allows two different individuals to perform the same task and also permits more than one performance of the same task by a single individual.

A full task *definition* includes (a) the task specification and (b) the task goal, usually elaborated with standards and criteria for judging performance. Thus, the definition both encompasses the criteria for deciding whether a performance does, in fact, correspond to a specific task and provides the basis for its evaluation.

Goals, Goal Aspects, Subgoals, and Subtasks

The goal of a task implies the criteria for success evaluation. At the minimum, such an evaluation could result in two outcomes: success and nonsuccess. However, goals can be expressed in a variety of ways, and evaluations can differentiate among more than two possible outcomes. For example, a goal might have two differentiable outcomes for which success or nonsuccess could be judged separately. If each outcome were judged dichotomously, then four outcome states would be possible: success on both outcomes (i.e., full goal attainment), success on only the first outcome, success on only the second, and success on neither. These success states form a partially ordered set (*poset*).[1]

The assessment of goal attainment need not be dichotomous, and is often quantitative. Athletic events typically represent this kind of evaluation. Golf results in a graded score reflecting the number of times the ball was struck prior to game completion. Some athletic events are judged on the time taken for completion, resulting in a continuous numerical value. Often multiple judgments are made of performance and these are combined into an overall score (e.g., diving).

The fact that goals can vary in character and complexity suggests some important conceptual distinctions. A task can have a single goal with several different aspects or can have several subgoals. These are distinguished by two related characteristics: time order and goal dependence. A *subgoal* can be attained discretely. That is, the activities directed toward it can occupy a distinct time subduration from other parts of the task performance. The performance can result

---

[1]A partially ordered set, also referred to as a *poset*, is one in which some, not necessarily all, pairs of elements are strictly ordered. A partial order relation is defined as reflexive, antisymmetric, and transitive (e.g., Birkhoff, 1967).

in the successful attainment of a subgoal prior to success on other subgoals. Thus, subgoals imply the possibility of partitioning a task performance into sub-task performances.

An example of a task with subgoals might be a round of golf. This activity can be thought of as having a two-level subtask structure: holes within rounds, and strokes within holes. Golf is an interesting example in that the holes are not logically tied together in an order structure. Because of the additive scor-ing, the formal structure of a round does not logically require that the second hole be played immediately following the first. The within-hole structure, on the other hand, is sequentially dependent. The second stroke cannot be under-taken without finishing the first. In this case, the outcome of the first stroke is the initial state for the second, and that second subtask is different in its re-quirements depending on the earlier outcome.

A *goal aspect* is distinct from a subgoal, and does not imply a subtask struc-ture. In this case, successful performance may be complex and may have dis-tinctive features that cannot be broken into subdivisions that can be performed separately. An example is the traditional pursuit rotor task for investigating psy-chomotor learning. In this task, a spinning plate has a spot on it that conducts electricity. The person performing the task has a stylus with which to make electrical contact with the spot. The object is to maximize the time that the stylus is in contact with the spot. Performance can be evaluated with respect to a number of distinct aspects: contact time, average distance of stylus from the spot, "smoothness" of performance, etc. These aspects all reflect the in-dividual's performance capabilities, but they cannot be segmented into "sub-tasks." Attempting the goal entails a performance that may be evaluated with respect to all of the goal's aspects.[2]

The difference between aspects and subgoals (or subtasks) does not imply that particular tasks cannot have both. Tennis performance, for example, has aspects such as backhand and forehand performance, which are integrated into the overall game performance. It would be misrepresenting the game to treat these aspects as subtasks. On the other hand, the "serve" is a game stage taking a determinate time at the beginning of each game, which could be charac-terized a subtask. Depending on the context, some distinctions for some tasks may verge on being arbitrary.

WHAT IS AN ABILITY?

In this chapter, the term *ability* encompasses what is commonly classified as knowledge and skill, both procedural and conceptual. An ability is a human charac-

---

[2]Note that this discussion applies to the task at issue, not to tasks that might be constructed to facilitate performance on it. Thus, in the pursuit rotor task, separate "training" tasks could be designed to improve "smoothness" or contact time, but these would not be subtasks of the origi-nal task.

teristic required for successful task performance. At the simplest level, an ability can be identified with the capacity to perform the class of task performances defined by a single task specification. Because it must enable more than a single task performance, the concept implicitly follows from the formulation of an equivalence class of task implementations or realizations, all of which require the same ability for successful performance. However, in order to be an ability, a human characteristic must not only differentiate successful from unsuccessful task performance, but must also apply to some tasks and not to others. That is, every ability must be defined so that it subdivides tasks into two groups: those to which that ability applies and those to which it does not. A one-to-one correspondence between a set of abilities and a single task specification is only the simplest possible case. Abilities may apply to more than one task, and tasks may require more than one ability. Thus, the subdivision of tasks by abilities also implies a subdivision of abilities by tasks. Each particular task subdivides abilities into two groups: those required to perform that task successfully and those not required.

This further implies that if the abilities required by one task are a subset of those required by another, then the two tasks can be ordered with respect to *difficulty*. If one task, say *B*, requires all of the abilities required by a second task *A* along with at least one additional ability, then task *A* is "easier" than task *B* (and concomitantly, *B* is "more difficult" than *A*). By this definition, task performances or realizations within the same task specification must be equally difficult.[3]

Concatenating Abilities and Tasks

Clearly, several tasks can be conjoined into a larger task. This can be done in several different ways. Just two tasks, say *A* and *B*, can be combined by:

1. Combining goals, defining success on the conjoined task in one of two ways: (a) conjunctively, as success on both task *A* and task *B*, or (b) disjunctively, as success on either task *A* or task *B*.
2. Constructing performance contingencies, making successful performance on one task, say *A*, prerequisite to successful performance on a second task, say *B*. (One way to accomplish this is to make successful perform-

---

[3]The term *difficulty* is used here in a different sense than usual in test theory, to refer to a theory-driven partial ordering derived from tasks' ability requirements. Unlike the conventional "item difficulty" defined as proportion of examinees responding correctly, the difficulty referred to here does not permit comparisons of all pairs of items. Moreover, difficulty as used here pertains to theoretical capability, not actual performance. One could incorporate an error structure relating underlying capabilities to manifest performance in such a way that a given item was more difficult than another in one sense of the term and less difficult in the other.

ance on task A yield information necessary for successful performance on B).

By conjoining two or more tasks, we not only create a new, combined task, we also make the original tasks *subtasks* of the new one. At the same time, in a most direct way, we define a new combined ability. Suppose, for example, that success on a conjoined task C is defined by success on both tasks A and B. This implicitly defines a new ability, c, as that which enables successful performance of task C. Because the combination was conjunctive, the ability requirement for the combined task is the combination of the abilities necessary to successfully perform component tasks A and B separately, say abilities a and b, respectively. (We postpone the elaboration of the task structure until later.)

In the course of studying an ability-task domain, this process is often reversed. The ability to perform a particular task comes to be seen as more complex than a single ability conception allows. Component abilities are then hypothesized, informed by analyses of performance, and new tasks are constructed with the intent of reflecting the separate components more directly. In this way, successful performance on the more complex task is related to combinations of successful performances on the component-specific tasks. Thus, the ability requirement of the original complex task is redefined as a combination of component abilities.

Ability States

The foregoing discussion implies that at the minimum, any ability must have at least two states (including complete lack of an ability as a possible state of an examinee with respect to that ability). In the simplest case, an individual either (a) possesses the ability to successfully perform the task or (b) does not. If we denote these states by 1 and 0, respectively, then the set of ability states corresponding to the above tasks (A, B, C) and abilities (a, b, c) are as shown in Table 14.1.

That is, if an ability (e.g., a) is identified with a single task (A), and if the task is thought of as either being successfully performed or not, then the set of distinct ability states can be conceived as a corresponding dichotomy ($\{0,1\}$).

TABLE 14.1
Abilities and Ability States for Two Dichotomous Tasks and Their Conjunction

Task	Ability	States
A	a	$\{0,1\}$
B	b	$\{0,1\}$
$C = A$ and B	$c = a$ and b	$\{0,1\} = \{\{(0,0), (0,1), (1,0)\}, \{(1,1)\}\}$

When we analyze a complex task according to its component subgoals (and corresponding subtasks) or goals aspects, then the combined ability states for the complex task are all of the possible combinations of the states for the separate abilities entailed by those subtasks or aspects.

In this example, the component abilities (a and b) are each dichotomies, and so there are four possible ability–state combinations. The states of (a,b) are (0,0), (0,1), (1,0), and (1,1). In this case, only one of the four combinations, (1,1), is sufficient to succeed on the combined task C. Thus, the (1,1) ability–state combination maps into the ability state 1 on the combined task, whereas the remaining three ability–state combinations map into 0. This new dichotomy defines ability c.

Abilities with More Than Two States

In the aforementioned example, the fact that four ability states underlie two illustrates that there may be more information in complex task performances than is recorded in a dichotomous judgment of successful versus unsuccessful performance. Rather than merely judging performance on C as satisfactory versus unsatisfactory, it might be possible to make separate judgments about performance on A and B, so that all four combined ability states were distinguishable. Ability C would then have four states, which would be partially ordered:

This example illustrates certain requirements for the states of an ability:

1. The set of all states of an ability, whether it is complex or simple, must contain at least two particular states: complete possession of the ability, which will be denoted I, and complete absence of the ability, which will be denoted O. In this example, these are (1,1) and (0,0), respectively.

2. The set of all states of an ability is partially ordered. In particular, O < I. If the set consists of more than two states, then for every additional state X, O < X < I.

From our perspective, complex abilities should be conceived initially as consisting of all possible combinations of states of their component abilities, even though these state combinations may then be collapsed into a smaller number of states representing classes of the original ability-state combinations.[4] We

---

[4]Note that a partial ordering of the original ability-state combinations constrains the manner in which such classes may be constructed. One could not, for example, map ability-state combinations (0,0,0) and (1,0,1) into the same combined ability state and at the same time map (0,0,1) into a different state. Ability structures are discussed more extensively in the next section.

term this collection of ability states, together with its order relation, an *ability-pattern lattice* or *ability-state lattice.*

ABILITY STRUCTURES

The preceding section addressed the internal structure of a single ability, characterizing it as a partially ordered set of ability states. This section addresses the possible relations among two or more distinct abilities, and develops the notion of an asymmetric, prerequisite relation between abilities, which marks an important departure from prevailing psychometric models. We then relate the structure of a set of abilities to the structure of the set of (combined) states of those abilities, and show how ability-state patterns enable a characterization of possible learning paths.

Prerequisite Relations Among Abilities

The factor-analytic character, including continuity assumption, in most latent ability models has largely limited the assessment of ability interrelations to covariances or correlations, which are fundamentally symmetric with respect to the two abilities involved. A stronger form of ability relationship is sequential dependency. That is, a given state of one ability a (e.g., I_a) must be acquired before it is possible to reach a given state of a second ability b (e.g., I_b). These kinds of relations have not been adequately represented in typical (continuous) ability definitions. Sequential dependency is a distinguishing characteristic of the models of information-processing psychology, as opposed to trait psychology.

We begin by limiting attention to the simplest case, that of two dichotomous abilities. We will say that dichotomous ability a is *prerequisite* to b (alternatively, that b *depends on a*), denoted $a \rightarrow b$, if state I of ability b can only be attained by those who have already attained state I of ability a. This relation is reflexive (an ability is prerequisite to itself), antisymmetric (if two abilities are each prerequisite to the other, they are the same), and transitive (if one ability is prerequisite to a second and the second is prerequisite to a third, then the first is prerequisite to the third). Thus, a set of dichotomous abilities with prerequisite relations forms a partially ordered set. Note that, as in any poset, pairs of abilities are not necessarily ordered. That is, two abilities are not required to be in prerequisite relation to one another. If every ability in a set has an order relation with every other ability (i.e., is either prerequisite to or dependent on each of the others), then the ability set is strictly, linearly ordered (i.e., a chain).

Posets allow particular abilities to be both directly multiply contingent on and directly multiply prerequisite to other abilities. For example, in the following ability set, abilities a, b, and c are not related to each other but are directly prerequisite to ability d. Thus, ability d could not be acquired unless all three abilities a, b, and c had been acquired. Abilities e and f are directly contingent on ability d and indirectly contingent on abilities a, b, and c. Acquisition of either e and f could not occur unless abilities a, b, c, and d had all been acquired.

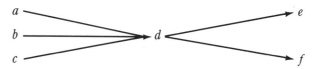

In this notation, the arrows indicate that (state I of) the ability at the tail of the arrow is prerequisite to (state I of) the ability at the head. We use this notation systematically to characterize posets. Arrows are always used to denote immediate prerequisites only. Thus, any two abilities connected by a chain of arrows headed in a consistent direction from one to the other will be in order relation to each other.

There are only two (nonisomorphic) posets of two elements each. One is the unordered set (a independent of b) and the other is the ordered pair (either $a{\rightarrow}b$ or $b{\rightarrow}a$). Note that if the labeling of abilities is taken into consideration, there are, in all, three posets of two elements each. The five nonisomorphic posets of three elements are as follows:

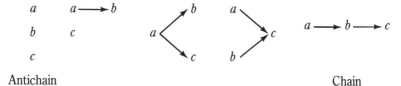

Antichain   Chain

In the literature on posets, completely unordered sets (e.g., the leftmost poset illustrated) are called antichains, and linearly ordered sets (e.g., the rightmost poset) are called chains. There are only five nonisomorphic posets on three dichotomous abilities, but if the labeling of the three abilities is taken into account, there are 19 possible posets in all. For example, these include the six chains corresponding to all possible orderings of a, b, and c. The number of ability posets increases rapidly as more abilities are considered. For four dichotomous abilities, there are 219 posets (16 nonisomorphic); for five abilities, 4231 posets (63 nonisomorphic); and for six abilities, 130,023 posets (318 nonisomorphic) (Birkhoff, 1967).

Ability-State Pattern Lattices

Recall that for the simplest example (two dichotomous abilities), there are three possible cases:

I. a and b unordered   II. $a{\rightarrow}b$ III. $b{\rightarrow}a$

The ability-state patterns *(a, b)* that are possible given each of these cases are:

I.   { (0,0), (1,0) (0,1), (1,1) }
II.   { (0,0), (1,0), (1,1) }
III. { (0,0), (0,1), (1,1) }

Each ability-state pattern represents a distinct combination of abilities mastered. We note that these ability-state patterns are also partially ordered:

I.

$$(0,0)\begin{array}{c} \nearrow (1,0) \searrow \\ \\ \searrow (0,1) \nearrow \end{array}(1,1)$$

II. $(0,0) \longrightarrow (1,0) \longrightarrow (1,1)$

III. $(0,0) \longrightarrow (0,1) \longrightarrow (1,1)$

Here the partial order relations between the combined ability-state patterns are induced by the fact that the states *within* each ability are ordered, that is, that within each ability, $0 \rightarrow I$ (in this case, $0 \rightarrow 1$). The order relation *between* the two abilities, such as $a \rightarrow b$ in case 2 above, has a different consequence.[5] It *eliminates* specific combinations as impossible. In this case, $a \rightarrow b$ eliminates (0,1). [This is because state I of *b* requires state I of *a* to be previously attained, allowing (1,1) but disallowing (0,1).] Thus, a consequence of the prerequisite structure among the abilities, generally, is a reduction in the number of realizable combinations of ability states. It should be emphasized that the poset of ability-state patterns is completely determined by the structure of the separate abilities (in this case, dichotomies) and by the prerequisite relations between abilities.

A theorem of Birkhoff (1967) shows that each (ability) poset induces an ability-pattern lattice and that these lattices constitute a special category of lattices called *distributive*. The theorem demonstrates that for each poset of dichotomous abilities, there is a unique distributive lattice. A second theorem, also by Birkhoff, inverts this proposition, defining a unique poset for each distributive lattice of ability-state patterns.

The specification of an ability-pattern or ability-state lattice for a set of abilities allows the resolution of several important issues. First, it enables a precise description of a broader ability composed of a set of component abilities. This description is just the lattice itself. Since the lattice description specifies all of the states of the composite ability, it also allows an understanding of the potential ''approximations'' to the full lattice, which can be made by collapsing and grouping states. In particular, it gives a clear picture of the consequences of ''scaling'' a broad ability into a strictly ordered, graded scale, and informs the

---

[5]We note that the within-ability relations are relations between ability states. Between-ability relations are distinctive because the sets on which they are defined have elements of a different character. We use arrows to characterize *both* types of relations.

370HAERTELANDWILEY

further reduction of a complex ability to a continuum, as in conventional factor-analytic models.

Learning Transitions and Learning Paths

The characterization of ability states in terms of lattices allows a natural specification of learning transitions. In Case 1 discussed earlier, that of two unordered abilities, the ability-state pattern lattice consisted of four partially ordered combined states: {(0,0), (1,0), (0,1), (1,1)}. The beginning state, (0,0), is connected to the end state, (1,1), by two chains. The first, $(0,0) \rightarrow (0,1) \rightarrow (1,1)$, defines a learning path with two transitions. These consist of learning b, then learning a. The second chain, $(0,0) \rightarrow (1,0) \rightarrow (1,1)$ defines a learning path with the transitions occurring in opposite order: a, then b. The other two ability posets, $a \rightarrow b$ and $b \rightarrow a$, each eliminate one of the alternate learning orders, reducing the potential learning paths to one.

As the number of abilities in a poset increases, the number of learning paths linking two nonadjacent states may also increase. The potential increase depends on and is inversely related to the number of prerequisite relations that constrain the lattice. This poset-lattice framework for ability specification thus constitutes a flexible foundation on which relatively complex ability structures can be formed and for which alternative potential learning paths linking ability states can be characterized.

TASK STRUCTURES

During the performance of a task, an individual occupies one or more task performance states. These states are distinct from ability states. In the example discussed in the section "What is an ability," three tasks were specified (A, B, and C) and three corresponding abilities defined (a, b, and c). Task C consisted of the two subtasks, A and B. In the earlier discussion, our main intent was to define the abilities in terms of successful task performance in a one-to-one fashion. As a consequence, we did not elaborate the performance structure of task C.

Suppose that task C was defined so that subtask A had to be completed before subtask B could be initiated for example, "Add 5 to the sum of 17 and 13." In this case subtask A is to find the sum of 17 and 13, whereas subtask B is to add 5 to 30. We can denote this subtask relation as a poset, $A \rightarrow B$. If we continue to follow the earlier discussion and identify subabilities a and b with the performance requirements for subtasks A and B,[6] then there is no obvious

[6]For purposes of this illustration we ignore the possibility that bringing together subsidiary tasks in a composite one adds new ability requirements. In general, creating composite tasks raises questions about the integration of component skills, that is, whether more than the mere presence of all the components is necessary for successful (integrated) task performance. We mention this possibility in our listing of future tasks at the end of this chapter and address this issue in a forthcoming manuscript (Haertel and Wiley, in preparation).

need to assume that there is any prerequisite structure relating ability a to ability b. That is, it is not unreasonable to assert that some individuals have neither ability (0,0), some have b without a (0,1), some have a without b (1,0), and some have both (1,1).

The task performance, on the other hand, is structured. Since the result of subtask A is required before subtask B can be undertaken (i.e., $A \rightarrow B$), there are only three possible combined performance end states: subtask A (and therefore also subtask B) not successfully performed, subtask A successfully and subtask B not successfully performed, both subtasks successfully performed. If we denote task-performance states (i.e., patterns) in a similar fashion to ability states, then these three states are $\{(A,B): (0,0), (1,0), (1,1)\}$. The subtask dependency has implied that the task-performance end states form a chain. We note that, in terms of process rather than end state, the performer passes through a series of intermediate performance states from preperformance to the actual performance end state as the task is being performed.

Even though there is not a one-to-one relationship between ability states and task-performance end states, the relation is still strong, as the ability state determines the task-performance end state. In fact, the relation is a function, because each ability state corresponds to one and only one performance end state.[7] To clarify this, we set out the relational structure connecting ability states to task-performance states for the case of two abilities (a,b) specifically linked to the performance requirements of two subtasks (A,B), such that a is required for A and b for B.

In Table 14.2, rows correspond to ability states and columns correspond to task performance states. The columns are subdivided into three panels, where the first (antichain) denotes subtasks A and B, and the second and third panels represent sequential dependency of B on A and of A on B, respectively. The columns within each of these panels denote all of the task-performance states included within the corresponding structure. The rows of the table (Table 14.2) are also divided into three panels, each corresponding to a particular ability structure. The first (antichain) represents an ability structure where there is no sequential dependency between abilities a and b, and the second and third panels represent ability structures with sequential dependency of b on a and of a on b, respectively. Thus, within the table, each row-and-column combination represents the relation between an ability state within an ability structure and a particular task performance state within a task structure. The task-performance end state that a given ability state leads to is demarked by a "1" and remaining table entries are "0."

---

[7]The ability state determines the task performance end state in the sense that it completely determines the underlying capability of the performer to reach a given end state. The degree of success observed in an actual task realization may not always coincide with the performer's underlying capability, due to extraneous influences on both the task performance and the observation and scoring of that performance. Both false-positive and false-negative errors may occur.

TABLE 14.2
Relation of Ability States to Task Performance End States for Two-Ability Posets
and Two-Subtask Structures

Ability structure	ab	Antichain (A,B)				Chain (A→B)			Chain (B→A)		
		00	10	01	11	00	10	11	00	01	11
Antichain											
(a,b)	00	1	0	0	0	1	0	0	1	0	0
	10	0	1	0	0	0	1	0	1	0	0
	01	0	0	1	0	1	0	0	0	1	0
	11	0	0	0	1	0	0	1	0	0	1
Chain (a→b)											
	00	1	0	0	0	1	0	0	1	0	0
	10	0	1	0	0	0	1	0	1	0	0
	11	0	0	0	1	0	0	1	0	0	1
Chain (b→a)											
	00	1	0	0	0	1	0	0	1	0	0
	01	0	0	1	0	1	0	0	0	1	0
	11	0	0	0	1	0	0	1	0	0	1

The most generally informative of task structures is that which comes about from an antichain of subtask performances, that is, when any subtask performance combination is possible. This task structure assures that all ability states are distinguishable, regardless of their prerequisite relations. It can also be seen that when the task structure matches the ability structure, there is a one-to-one relationship between ability and task performance states. However, if the task structure constrains the performance states in a way that does not match the constraints on the ability states, then there will be two or more distinct ability-state combinations leading to the same task-performance end state. This in turn implies that the task cannot be used to distinguish among those ability-state combinations.

This loss of information is illustrated in the above table. Note that either of the chain subtask dependency structures (i.e., $A{\rightarrow}B$ or $B{\rightarrow}A$) permits only three possible performance states. Assuming all four ability states, two of these must be confounded in one performance state. In the case of $A{\rightarrow}B$, ability state (0,1) is not distinguishable from state (0,0). Even where the number of ability states is equal to the number of task performance states, information will be lost if the task structure does not match the ability structure. Note, for example, that for task structure $B{\rightarrow}A$ with ability structure $a{\rightarrow}b$, performance state (1,0) is not realizable and two ability states, (1,0) and (0,0), are confounded.

In general, when a task structure results in a confounding of ability states, full identification of states requires multiple tasks.[8] An appropriate combination

---

[8]An ability-state combination is *identifiable* using a collection of one or more tasks if and only if it implies a set of task-performance end states distinct from the set implied by any other possible

of tasks taken together can distinguish all ability states, even if each separate task confounds some states. For example, all four of the antichain-induced set of ability states can be identified if two tasks having structures $A \rightarrow B$ and $B \rightarrow A$ are both performed. The four combined performance states[9] of both tasks correspond to the four underlying ability states.

The simple example we have given to illustrate the relation between ability states and task performances assumes explicit assessment of subtask performance. Detailed assessment of distinct subtasks could involve the classification of performance using multiple subtask criteria and could result in performance scorings that are partially ordered rather than merely dichotomous or graded. Obviously, the more complex the task structure is, in terms of both numbers of embedded subtasks and goal aspects, the greater is the amount of information that can be extracted.

Scoring is the process of converting raw task performances into ability-relevant information. At one extreme, all the features of a performance are collapsed into a simple dichotomy: successful versus unsuccessful performance. This was illustrated in the earliest version of our two-ability, two-subtask example, given in the preceding section. There, the performance state corresponding to the (1,1) ability state was scored as successful (1) and each of the other states were scored as unsuccessful (0), resulting in the mutual confounding of these latter states. In this section, the more articulated version of the ability-state/performance-state relation confounded states because of task structure, not scoring. Thus, scoring can only *add* to whatever confounding takes place because of the task structure and its relation to the ability structure.

We note that for any of the task structures given earlier, the (1,1) state is always identified. Thus, regardless of task structure, it is always possible to score complete success versus any thing less than that. Consequently, task structure is really irrelevant if dichotomous scoring is used. Clearly, such scoring sacrifices additional information and increases the number of separate tasks needed to identify the ability states. In an ability domain with k abilities, if the abilities form an antichain, $2^k - 1$ dichotomously scored tasks are possible and at least k selected tasks are required to identify all the ability states.

At the other extreme, a scoring method may distinguish among all of the separate performance states available for a given task. As shown by the example, the number of performance states and the confounding structure of these states for assessing ability depend on the task structure and its relationship to the ability structure. Such scoring clearly depends on a method of performance

---

ability-state combination. *Full identification* means that all possible ability-state combinations are identifiable, that is, that any two ability-state combinations can be distinguished from one another on the basis of the task-performance end states they imply.

[9] Note that in combining the two "chain" tasks, even though three states (for $A \rightarrow B$), are combined with three states (for $B \rightarrow A$), only four combined states are realizable.

recording that preserves information about success with respect to the separate subtask performances.

Formalization of Task Structures

The simple example we have elaborated involved two abilities and a task with two corresponding subtasks. Viewed in isolation from the abilities underlying this task, we found three different task structures based on two ways of combining subtasks. One of these did not constrain the performance relations of the two subtasks, and the other two linked the tasks by making the result of one task a precondition for initiating the other.

A closer consideration of these task structures suggests a distinction between two forms of order relations between subtasks. The strong form, *contingency,* means that one subtask cannot be attempted until after some other subtask has been completed successfully, typically because the contingent subtask requires some information or other product of the prerequisite subtask performance. The weak form, *succession,* means that one subtask cannot be attempted until after some other subtask has been attempted, but not necessarily completed successfully. Note that contingency implies succession, but not conversely. Succession relations among subtasks may arise as a consequence of task administration procedures, and may be implicit or explicit in the task specification. Changing succession relations may change a task. As an instance, computer-administered and paper-and-pencil forms of some tests may differ in that on the paper-and-pencil version, examinees are free to skip around from item to item and return to earlier items, whereas in the computer-administered version, items must be attempted in a fixed sequence.

The relations of contingency and succession cover most but not all forms of serial dependency among tasks. Consider, for example, the procedure for establishing a ceiling on the Peabody Picture Vocabulary Test–Revised, where the test administration is ended after some specified number of consecutive subtasks are failed. This gives rise to a situation in some sense intermediate between contingency and succession, where subtasks are presented in a fixed order ignoring success or failure (succession), but only until failures become frequent enough to trigger task termination (contingency). More generally, adaptive testing may entail subtask dependencies that cannot be simply characterized as either contingency or succession. We have not as yet attempted to formalize such cases.[10]

Other task structures may involve relations that are cumbersome to specify

---

[10]There are also important cases where one subtask is to be undertaken only after some other subtask has been attempted and has been *unsuccessful.* For example, an emergency-room physician should generally perform a tracheotomy only after less drastic means of restoring a patent airway have been tried and failed.

in terms of pairs of subtasks. For example, three subtasks A, B, and C might be related in such a way that A and B were independent of each other, but C was contingent on successful performance of either A or B, not necessarily both. More generally, a given subtask might be contingent on successful performance of at least one out of a set of two or more subtasks. This kind of structure would arise if any one of the possible prerequisite subtasks yielded some common information or other product required for the subsequent subtask. It defines a nonbinary relation among subtasks that we refer to as *set-contingency*. In this example, C is set-contingent upon A and B.

The fact that subtasks, by definition, occur during distinct segments of time implies that they are strictly (temporally) ordered in any task realization. This observation gives rise to the possible subtask relation of *adjacency*. Two subtasks are *adjacent* if no other subtask(s) may be interposed between them. In combination with the rules already presented, the notion of adjacency gives rise to six distinct, nonisomorphic rules for combining two subtasks: (a) unordered, that is, no constraints; (b) adjacent-unordered, or simple adjacency, that is, subtasks may be performed in either order but no other subtasks may intervene; (c) succession, that is, one subtask must occur at some point subsequent to the other; (d) adjacent-succession, in which one task must immediately follow the other; (e) contingency, in which one task must occur at a point subsequent to successful completion of the other; and (f) adjacent-contingency, in which one task must occur immediately following successful completion of the other. *Binding* is a generalization of simple adjacency pertaining to a set of two or more subtasks, which specifies that once one of the set is attempted, all must be attempted before proceeding to any subtask not in the set. (For just two subtasks, binding is the same as simple adjacency.)

Clearly, the range of task structures enabled by these various relations does not exhaust all those that are possible. As already observed, adaptive or interactive assessments may entail subtask selection rules too complex to be accommodated in this framework. Moreover, up to this point we have only considered contingency relations among subtasks that were dichotomously scored. The number of relations that might be defined among a given set of subtasks increases rapidly as subtask scoring is elaborated beyond a simple judgment of success versus failure. Different degrees of partial success on one subtask may depend in complex ways on degrees of partial success on one or more other subtasks. Nonetheless, we believe that the relations of succession, contingency, set-contingency, adjacency, and binding, together with nonordering, are sufficient to characterize the structure of a great number of widely used tasks.[11]

Task structures induce performance-state patterns in the same way that ability

---

[11]Elsewhere (Haertel & Wiley, in preparation), we elaborate a theory of task concatenation that simplifies this framework by combining contingency with performance order constraints.

posets induce ability-state patterns, but the different means of task combination permit a richer class of structures than that of the ability structures. The two simplest ways of combining subtasks, unordered and contingent, are sufficient to construct an analogue performance-state structure corresponding to each ability-state pattern. Each of these analogue structures is a distributive lattice. However, in addition to these task-performance structures, others may be created by imposing other constraints on subtask relations. For example, a task with four subtasks, say, *A, B, C,* and *D,* could be created in several stages. First, *A* and *B* could be combined as subtask *A→B,* that is, *B* could be contingent on *A.* Similarly, *C* and *D* could be combined as subtask *C→D.* Finally, these two combined subtasks could be again combined. This final combination could take place as unordered, that is, the *A→B* and the *C→D* subtasks could be performed in either order. With no further constraints, these subtask relations give rise to a set of performance states that form a distributive lattice. If the states are indexed by subtasks in alphabetical order—for example, 1010 means *A* and *C* were successfully completed but *B* and *D* were not—then the performance structure is

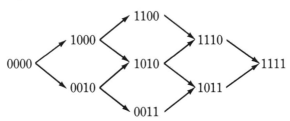

Suppose, however, that subtask pairs (*A,B*) and (*C,D*) were adjacent-contingent. If the task performer is required to successfully finish one *complete* subchain (i.e., all of either *A→B* or *C→D*) before beginning the other, then a different structure results:

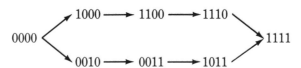

This lattice is not distributive and does not correspond to a set of subtask dependencies that can be expressed as a unique poset.[12]

The intent of our analysis of task structures is to create an "algebra" of task combination that can be used to create complex task structures. These

---

[12]Note that the structure as displayed does not have arrows representing all of the "order" relations among the performance states: for example, 0010 < 1110, but there is no arrow from 0010 to 1110. Thus, the lattice-order relations do not directly conform to the performance paths. This makes task-performance structures more difficult to represent unambiguously than ability structures.

structures can then be linked to ability structures to fully articulate the role of task structure and scoring in the identification of ability states from task performance. This work is ongoing.

A FRAMEWORK FOR TESTING

Under current psychometric models, the problem of test design is conceived almost exclusively in terms of error structures. Consideration of item content, if it occurs at all, is atheoretical. For tests with multiple content specifications, cross-classifications of potential item types are created. These take the form of constraints (side conditions) on the error minimization problem to assure representation of content topics or areas. Typically, within categories, a unidimensional item pool is assumed, and item selection is aimed at maximizing the precision of inferences from observed data to one or more (continuous) underlying abilities.

As we have already indicated, questions of what abilities are required by test tasks are central to the problem of test design, and logically prior to any consideration of error structure. Such a theoretically grounded analysis of test content only becomes possible, however, after an appropriate framework for abilities has been developed. Because a test is a collection of particular tasks (e.g., exercises or items), our analysis of tasks and abilities provides such a content framework. From specifying the abilities required for a particular task, two consequences flow: (a) It is possible to form the ability-state lattice for these combined abilities. (b) A mapping can be established between this lattice and the set of potential performance states for that task. This mapping constitutes a ''content'' analysis of the task.

Just as an ability-state lattice is determined by the combined abilities underlying test performance, a performance-state ''lattice'' is determined by combining the performance state sets for the tasks constituting the test. (As explained and illustrated in the preceding section, this latter structure need not, in general, conform to the mathematical definition of a lattice.) It is then possible to specify precisely which ability states are confounded and which are distinguishable from these combined task-performance states. This specification allows the resolution of two outstanding problems.

First, it clarifies what abilities a test can potentially measure, and what ability states are actually distinguished using a specific task or set of tasks and a given method of scoring. It does this by enabling the accounting of the ability states that map into distinct performance-state patterns. Note that a scoring scheme is just a further mapping from performance-state patterns into a (typically) smaller set of scores or score profiles.

Second, the content analysis opens an expanded range of possibilities for complex tasks. Performances on these tasks need not be dichotomously scored. In fact, the performance assessments need not even be graded. Any partially ordered set of performance states can be used in assessing ability states. Thus, the information content in complex task performances can be fully utilized.

To date, we have most closely investigated the problem of test design for one limited but important case: That in which each test task (item) is dichotomously scored, all test tasks are unordered (i.e., there are no contingencies among test tasks), and each test task can be performed successfully by exactly those examinees who have mastered all of its prerequisite abilities. This is equivalent to saying that items are dichotomously scored and independent of one another, and that for each particular item, there is only one set of abilities that is both necessary and sufficient to solve it. Within the general framework we are developing, these assumptions appear highly restrictive, but in fact they are much less restrictive than the assumptions of unidimensionality and conditional independence typically made for multiple-choice tests. Space does not permit a full discussion of even this limited case, but an illustration may be informative. Note that in this limited case, a performance state for an item is either correct or incorrect, denoted "1" or "0," respectively. A *performance state pattern* is an item response pattern, denoted by a vector of ones and zeros indicating which items an examinee answered correctly.

Illustrative Analysis for 10 Multiple-Choice Items

A systematic subsample of 2,089 fourth-grade examinees was taken from the Anchor Test Study norming sample (Loret, Seder, Bianchini, & Vale, 1974), and tabulations were made of their responses to 10 selected reading comprehension items from the Metropolitan Achievement Tests, Form F, Elementary Level (Durost, Bixler, Wrightstone, Prescott, & Balow, 1970). Students failing to respond to item 45, the last item of the 10 selected and also the last item on the test, were excluded from the sample. The items used were numbers 1, 3, 12, 16, 21, 24, 34, 35, 40, and 45. Each successive pair of these items is based on a different passage. (Five passages in all are represented.) The 10 items represent a range of item difficulties from .32 to .92.[13] Of the 1,024 possible (correct/incorrect) response patterns to these 10 items, 356 occurred in the sample. Nearly half of these, 163, were produced by only one examinee, and another 124 occurred four or fewer times. The most frequent pattern, getting all 10 items correct, was produced by 226 examinees, or 10.8% of the sample. The all-incorrect pattern was the 26th most frequent, produced by 11 examinees. The 24 most frequent patterns, together with the all-incorrect pattern, accounted for 1,273 examinees (60.9%).

---

[13]These are proportions of the 2,089 examinees answering items 45 and 1 correctly. The sample weights derived for the original Anchor Test Study were ignored in the analysis reported here.

As discussed later, examinees' manifest responses give imperfect information about their underlying abilities, due to carelessness, guessing, and other sources of misclassification. For purposes of this analysis, it was assumed that the highest-frequency response patterns represented actual underlying performance-state patterns, and that lower-frequency patterns arose due to false-positive or false-negative responses from examinees who in fact conformed to one of the (high-frequency) patterns. Under the assumptions stated above concerning the ability requirements of the items, it is readily shown that the set of potential performance-state patterns must be closed under intersection (Haertel & Wiley, in preparation). In a set of just three items, for example, if performance-state patterns 110 and 011 both occurred, then the pattern 010 would also have to be possible. This closure property provided a basis for deciding how many of the high-frequency manifest patterns to accept as representing true (error-free) patterns. If the set of k most frequent patterns is examined (augmented with the all-correct and all-incorrect patterns if either of them is not included), it can easily be determined what additional patterns not in the set may be obtained as intersections of patterns that are in the set. The number of additional patterns required to close the set may be viewed as a function of k, the number of patterns taken initially. The values of this function for the Anchor Test Study data are shown in Table 14.3.

It is immediately apparent that accepting the 25th most frequent pattern, 1101111111, produced by 12 examinees, greatly increases the number of unobserved or lower-frequency performance state patterns that must be inferred. On the basis of this analysis, the 24 highest-frequency patterns together with the pattern 0000000000 were taken as the initial set of true patterns. These were augmented with the six additional patterns required for closure. All six of these additional patterns were in fact observed, although with lower frequencies. The 31 patterns taken to represent underlying performance states are shown in Fig. 14.1, organized into a lattice.

From the structure shown in Figure 14.1, it is easy to determine the minimum number of dichotomous abilities that must underlie the observed performance states. That minimum number may always be realized under the assumption that any combination of abilities is possible (i.e., that the ability poset is the antichain). Assuming the antichain ability poset, the most parsimonious set of ability requirements for the 10 items is as shown in Table 14.4.

Without attempting to explain the underlying theory, the mechanics of obtaining these item-ability assignments are quite simple. A distinct ability is associated with each performance-state pattern that has just one arrow exiting from it in the lattice diagram, and this ability is assigned to just those items for which the state in the association pattern is ''incorrect'' (0). For example, the pattern 0000000000 was associated with a, and so ability a was assigned to all ten items. The pattern 1110111000 was associated with b, and so ability b was assigned to the fourth, eighth, ninth, and 10th items, numbers 16, 35, 40, and

TABLE 14.3

Number of Additional Patterns Required for Closure Under Intersection,
as a Function of Number of Highest-Frequency Patterns
(Illustrative Anchor Test Study data).

No. of highest-frequency patterns included	No. of patterns added	No. of highest-frequency patterns included	No. of patterns added
1	0	21	5
2	0	22	8
3	0	23	7
4	0	24	6
5	0	25	35
6	0	26	35
7	0	27	62
8	1	28	69
9	3	29	68
10	2	30	67
11	2	31	66
12	1	32	65
13	4	33	64
14	3	34	63
15	3	35	63
16	4	36	62
17	5	37	61
18	8	38	60
19	7	39	59
20	6	40	59

45. If prerequisite relations among abilities were permitted, then the number of abilities that must be assumed will remain the same or increase, although the ability requirements of items may be simplified. If the strongest (i.e., most restrictive) possible set of prerequisite relations among abilities is assumed, then the number of abilities that each item must be assumed to require is minimized. The most restrictive ability poset and the corresponding minimal item-ability requirements are as shown in Fig. 14.2.

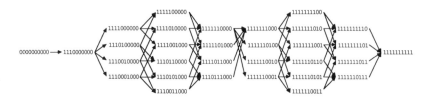

FIG. 14.1. Hypothetical Performance Slate Lattice for Ten MAT Items.

TABLE 14.4
Hypothetical Ability Requirements for Ten MAT Items

Item	Abilities Required
1	a
3	a
12	a
16	ab
21	ac
24	ad
34	ae
35	abcdf
40	abcdg
45	abcdh

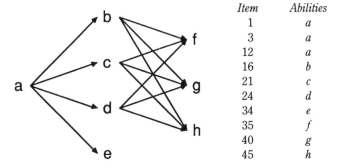

Item	Abilities
1	a
3	a
12	a
16	b
21	c
24	d
34	e
35	f
40	g
45	h

FIG. 14.2. Alternative ability configurations for 10 MAT items.

Intermediate degrees of structure in the ability poset would correspond to item ability requirements of intermediate complexity.

Statistical Models for Test Task Performance

As already stated, test task responses are subject to misclassification. Individuals who possess all of the abilities that an item requires may respond incorrectly, and those who lack one or more requisite abilities may sometimes produce correct responses. Examinees may even be observed to succeed on some tasks and fail on others requiring exactly the same abilities. Thus, when the problem is taken up of inferring abilities from manifest task performance, observed success or failure must be treated as a fallible indicator of the examinee's underlying ability state, even when there is a direct correspondence of the underlying performance states to distinct ability states. The example just presented addressed the problem of fallible manifest responses by the somewhat naive expedient of accepting high-frequency response patterns as error-free. Although this approach was satisfactory for the purpose of illustrating how ability structures could be derived from task performance-state structures, it does not lead in any straightforward way to a characterization of the distributions of these ability-state combinations in the population of examinees. A more sophisticated procedure would explicitly model the response process, augmenting the ability and performance-state structures discussed above with a probabilistic misclassification structure.

This augmentation leads on to the outline of a procedure for recovering ability structures from manifest task performances, beginning with statistical models that are special cases of Lazarsfeld's latent-class model. (For prior uses of these models in testing, see Haertel, 1984a, 1984b, 1990a, 1990b; Macready & Dayton, 1980; Wiley, Haertel, and Harnischfeger, 1981.) Each "true" performance-state pattern is associated with a distinct latent class, and an error structure is specified, which determines the conditional probabilities of observing each possible manifest response pattern for examinees conforming to each performance-state pattern.[14] Fitting the latent-class model would yield estimates of proportions of examinees conforming to each possible performance-state pattern, possibly including performance-state patterns not actually observed.

After recovering true performance-state patterns from manifest responses via latent-class analysis, one would next infer the corresponding ability-state patterns. (This step was not explicit in the example presented earlier.) Ideally, the derivation of ability-state patterns would be heavily conditioned by substantive knowledge about both the structure of the tasks used and the relations among the abilities they required. As with factor analysis, analysis of covariance structures, or any other method that may be used for inferring the abilities underlying individual differences in human performance, it is likely that a great variety of distinct models will be consistent with the data obtained.

Once the ability-state lattice was obtained, the analysis might proceed along the lines of the example presented above. One could recover the structure of abilities by inverting the ability-state lattice to the poset. Given the defined ability structure, the associated ability-state patterns, the mapping from ability states to task performance states, and the error (misclassification) structure relating true task performance states to manifest responses, one could then use individuals' manifest response patterns to estimate, using empirical bayes methods, the probabilities of their conformity to possible ability-state patterns.

CONCLUSIONS

This chapter has attempted to lay out a new basis for understanding human abilities and their relation to task performance. It exhibits some of the foundations

---

[14]An alternative model might relate manifest response pattern probabilities directly to underlying ability-state patterns, bypassing the true performance-state patterns. This approach could offer greater flexibility by permitting error structures that differed for examinees in separate ability states, even if those ability states mapped onto the same performance-state pattern.

of a research program that we believe is required in order to move the assessment of such abilities beyond the current limitations of testing practice. These limitations (a) prevent, for broad-range assessment, the precise definition of ability aggregates in terms of the micro-structure of component abilities; (b) preclude the analysis of learning within the same framework as the assessment of ability; (c) inhibit the appropriate use of complex tasks for multicriterial assessment; and (d) interfere with the design of tests with sharply defined ability requirements.

As discussed in the body of this chapter, these limitations can be overcome within the framework we have exposited. Surely, much further work remains to be done to further develop and fully exploit this new framework. An eclectic listing of future directions for theory development includes:

- Formalizing the "algebra" of task performance-state structures.
- Expanding and elaborating the analytic framework for linking ability and task structures.
- Characterizing highly integrated skill structures.
- Elaborating and implementing procedures for parameterization and estimation of misclassification structures.
- Elaborating and exhibiting a new theoretical framework for test design and analysis.

These further theoretical developments should both enable and depend on:

- Performing task-ability analysis of commonly used school tasks, complex tasks currently used for research on cognition, and historically important psychological tasks.
- Analyzing existing tests to exhibit their strengths and shortcomings.
- Developing new tests, including performance exercises, in the light of this framework.

ACKNOWLEDGMENTS

Order of authorship is alphabetical. We have collaborated fully and contributed equally in work presented. We are grateful to our editors, especially Robert Mislevy, and to our discussant, Henry Braun, for their insightful comments and suggestions.

REFERENCES

Birkhoff, G. (1967). *Lattice theory* (3rd ed., Vol. 25). American Mathematical Society Colloquium Publications. Providence, RI: American Mathematical Society.

Burton, R. R. (1982). Diagnosing bugs in a simple procedural skill. In D. Sleeman & J. S. Brown (Eds.), *Intelligent tutoring systems* (pp. 157-183). New York: Academic Press.

Falmagne, J.-C., Koppen, M., Villano, M., Doignon, J.-P., & Johannesen, L. (1990). Introduction to knowledge spaces: How to build, test, and search them. *Psychological Review, 97,* 201-224.

Haertel, E. H. (1984a). An application of latent class models to assessment data. *Applied Psychological Measurement, 8,* 333-346.

Haertel, E. H. (1984b). Detection of a skill dichotomy using standardized achievement test items. *Journal of Educational Measurement, 21,* 59-72.

Haertel, E. H. (1990a). Using restricted latent class models to map the skill structure of achievement items. *Journal of Educational Measurement, 26,* 301-321.

Haertel, E. H. (1990b). Continuous and discrete latent structure models for item response data. *Psychometrika, 55,* 477-494.

Haertel, E. H., & Wiley, D. E. (in preparation). *Ability and task performance structure: A theory with selected applications.*

Macready, G. B., & Dayton, C. M. (1980). The nature and use of state mastery models. *Applied Psychological Measurement, 4,* 493-516.

VanLehn, K. (1990). *Mind bugs: The origins of procedural misconceptions.* Cambridge, MA: MIT Press.

Wiley, D. E. (1990). Test validity and invalidity reconsidered. In R. Snow & D. E. Wiley (Eds.), *Improving inquiry in social science* (pp. 75-107). Hillsdale, NJ: Lawrence Erlbaum Associates. Also as *Studies of Educative Processes,* No. 20, Northwestern University, 1987.

Wiley, D. E., Haertel, E. H., Harnischfeger, A. (1981, May). Test validity and national educational assessment: A conception, a method, and an example. *Studies of Educative Processes,* No. 17. Evanston, IL: Northwestern University.

Comments on Chapters 11–14

Henry I. Braun
Educational Testing Service

The impetus for developing a new generation of tests does not stem simply from a desire to accomplish the same ends more perfectly or more efficiently. Rather, it arises from a reconceptualization of the purpose of testing, the nature of the information produced through testing, and the audience for that information. In brief, testing is seen as a means for developing an elaborated portrait of an individual that facilitates decisions in an ongoing learning process.

Classical test theory and its successor, item response theory, are now generally regarded as inadequate to the task principally because they rely on a trait theory of psychology that overly simplifies the structure of human abilities. Moreover, for the most part these are models of status that provide precious little information on the likelihood or direction of change (learning). This failing, though not logically inherent in the models, is empirically true, principally because of the powerful effect certain statistical considerations have had on test design.

The contributions to this volume describe approaches to both test design and to test analysis; for the most part they are grounded more firmly in contemporary views of the structure of knowledge, the nature of human ability, and the mechanisms of learning. The consequent increase in complexity sometimes seems daunting, particularly because of the interdisciplinary nature of much of the discussion. Nonetheless, the effort is worthwhile because the ultimate goal is a body of theory and methods that should be immensely more valuable to the world of education.

The preceding four chapters differ substantially in scope. The ones by Bejar and by Haertel and Wiley take a broader, more theoretical perspective, and those by Yamamoto and Gitomer and by Carroll are more narrowly focused. I propose to discuss them in this order (rather than in the order of presentation) with the hope that I can in this way better elucidate the connections between them.

Bejar's chapter (chapter 13) is both rich and provocative. He argues that an important component of a new paradigm for educational measurement is a principled approach to item development based on a generative grammar that also provides direct links to a psychometric model. This "strong" version of response generative modeling (RGM) would have very desirable consequences that are discussed at length.

The key benefits of RGM are likely to be improved construct validity, enhanced utility, and greater operational efficiency (especially in the context of computer-based testing). Through the discipline of the cognitive analysis that must underlie RGM and the evaluation of proposed grammars, construct validity is built in, as it were, rather than being a hoped-for consequence of a vaguely defined process. Moreover, the grammatical structure facilitates interpretation of test performance and provides a defensible basis for generalization. Finally, an explicit grammar of some kind appears to be a necessary condition for automated scoring of open-ended responses.

The latter point deserves some comment. Bejar seems to imply that the grammar used in item generation can also serve as the foundation for computer-based scoring of open-ended responses. Although that may be true in some cases, a different grammar may be required when the solution space includes very complex elements. For example, consider item types that call on the examinee to write an essay interpreting the main idea of a passage, or to outline the solution process to a problem in Newtonian mechanics. The grammar that describes the (restricted) universe of passages or problems being contemplated will not be sufficiently rich to capture the universe of potential responses. At the least, the grammar needed to support scoring would have to accommodate a much larger set of structures and relations. On the other hand, the generative grammar and the scoring grammar would ordinarily be strongly linked.

Bejar also states that RGM "implies that we have a complete understanding of the underlying response process." This statement should be qualified, I believe, to take into account the possibility of different response processes, particularly in more complex response sets. More specifically, the aim should be to characterize the components of different potential response processes at a level of detail commensurate with the kind of inferences to be drawn from the results of the test.

It is important to remember that because responses to questions are fallible indicators of abilities, it is rare that reliable conclusions can be drawn from a single item. Useful interpretations generally will require consideration of the responses to a number of related items. Consequently, the generative grammar and the solution grammar should facilitate the analysis of both questions and responses, each linked to a theory of performance.

For the most part, Bejar works within the framework of IRT and illustrates the psychometric links of RGM by a mapping from the item to the difficulty parameter. Of course, such a mapping cannot be done without a great deal of empirical work, involving at the least the calibration of a "basis set" of items from which the full map can be constructed. For purposes of amassing validity evidence, it may be sufficient for the theory to suggest ordinal relations among items.

Bejar does acknowledge, however, that for diagnostic assessment, IRT models are not adequate because they are not designed to support representations that are useful in that setting. In my view, the labor involved in RGM is only fully justified if we have measurement models that can indeed take advantage of the wealth of information inherent in RGM. For example, to say that one item is "harder" than another only tells us something that is true on average over the population. It may well be the case, for recognizable subgroups of the population, the order of difficulty is reversed. Moreover, when considered in conjunction with performance on other related items, and with the insights derived from RGM, the implications for learning are very different for these two groups. Thus, RGM should not be viewed primarily as a means of making IRT more useful (though it could play such a role) but rather as a motivation for the development of more refined measurement models.

Bejar has performed a great service by bringing together evidence on RGM from many different domains, and his review suggests that RGM is not easy to accomplish. Nonetheless, this program of research is worthwhile not only because the goal has merit but also because we have much to learn along the way.

The chapter by Haertel and Wiley (Chapter 14) contributes to the RGM program by providing the framework from which appropriate grammars can be constructed. In a sense, the authors go beyond RGM since their goal is to "allow for the characterization of both status and change in ability (learning)." The emphasis on transitions between states is a welcome one because it focuses attention on a somewhat neglected area of educational measurement.

Essentially, Haertel and Wiley present a vocabulary and grammar to facilitate the characterization of the structure of abilities and tasks. What is particularly noteworthy about their approach is that it deals explicitly with the different kinds of relations that can occur among sets of abilities (or sets of tasks). Such a framework is essential to the effective cognitive analysis of performance.

In setting out the structure of abilities, however, it is important that the boundaries between ability states (particularly in the case of polytomous abilities) not be too rigid. An appropriate specification of ability states may well depend on the context and purpose of the assessment. The structures described in this chapter appear to be well suited for describing the learning that occurs within a single conceptual framework. It remains to be seen whether these structures can also describe the qualitative reorganization of knowledge that some researchers believe takes place during certain critical periods.

Formally, diagnosis is defined as a mapping from an observable performance state to an unobservable ability state. This has certain consequences for test design: If the goal is to distinguish between different ability states (because they have different instructional implications), the set of tasks comprising the test must be sufficiently rich.

To my mind, this is not the most challenging problem. The greater difficulty lies in linking the formal structure of tasks and abilities with the calculus of probabilities. This is absolutely necessary because an examinee's performance is only a fallible indicator of his or her true condition. Consequently, we must make inferences about the examinee's ability state from a set of responses that are contaminated by deviations from an ideal pattern. These inferences take the form of posterior probabilities (in the sense of Bayes), attached to each possible state. As more information becomes available, the task of updating these probabilities is a nontrivial one, even in moderately simple settings (see Mislevy, chapter 2, this volume, and the references therein). How to deal with the more complex structures described by Haertel and Wiley has not yet been worked out.

It is essential that we not succumb to the expedient of employing some informal calculus of evidence to avoid the hard work of doing it right. The method presented by Haertel and Wiley of using the more common response patterns as a set of ideal types is suggestive but, as they themselves acknowledge, is not a substitute for a more formal analysis.

The chapter by Haertel and Wiley constitutes only an extract of a much larger body of work dealing with the representation of ability structures and its implications for educational measurement. The disciplined approach they have taken holds great promise and we must all look forward to the resolution of the outstanding problems they mention at the end of the chapter. Most important, it will be interesting to see this theory applied in realistic situations requiring test development and analysis.

The chapter by Yamamoto and Gitomer (chapter 11) describes the application of a relatively new psychometric model to data obtained from a test of understanding of the function of certain types of electronic logic gates. Yamamoto and Gitomer state that the test was one for which "item demands were explicitly defined, item characteristics were manipulated systematically, and a cognitive error analysis revealed that examinees did make consistent types of errors across subsets of items that shared identifiable characteristics."

Although Yamamoto and Gitomer do not engage in a discussion of test design to facilitate cognitive diagnosis, it is evident that this test would be included within the RGM framework and ought to be amenable to some of the analysis proposed by Haertel and Wiley. Because the ability structure is rather simple, inferences from response patterns to useful diagnoses would be easy if there

were no "noise" in the data. As I indicated earlier, the presence of noise neces-
sitates the use of statistical methods to recover the underlying "signal." In my
view, the HYBRID model represents a way station between conventional IRT
and the measurement models of the future. Important subsets of the response
space are characterized in terms of ideal response patterns that are, in turn,
associated with different latent classes in the statistical model. An IRT model
is then postulated to account for the remaining variation.

In this application, five classes are used. Approximately 25% of all examinees
(nearly 30% of those who made at least one error) were assigned to one of
the latent classes. Clearly, with more time and effort, further classes could be
identified and added to the model. Ideally, the IRT component should be eliminated completely, replaced by an exhaustive set of latent classes with clear diagnostic interpretations. For the present, that may be impractical in all but the
simplest settings. Nonetheless, the critical element in this endeavor is to build
a rich library of performance patterns that can be associated with different ability states. The psychometric characteristics of individual items are of secondary
importance compared to the part each item plays in the interpretation of different response patterns.

One of the grand goals of the new test theory is to communicate more effectively with various audiences. The chapter by Carroll (chapter 12) shows how,
under certain conditions, we can extract more useful information from conventional tests using standard IRT.

Behavioral anchoring depends on constructing a set of person characteristics functions in conjunction with establishing on a single scale the difficulties
of a set of representative items. As a consequence, once we know that an individual falls at a particular point on the scale, we also know the likelihood of
success with each of the representative items. To the extent that these items
carry substantively meaningful connotations, behavioral anchoring adds considerable interpretive value to the test score.

The use of the person characteristic function should eliminate the confusion
that sometimes occurs with other forms of behavioral scaling. In the example
cited by Carroll, the National Assessment of Educational Progress (NAEP) Reading Proficiency Scale, statements of the level of competence associated with
particular points of the scale are provided along with typical tasks. At that level,
individuals are expected to have at least an 80% success rate, whereas individuals
at the next lower scale point are expected to have no more than a 50% success
rate with the same tasks. Unwary readers occasionally try to impute the overall success rate in the population for a particular task. Use of the person characteristic function would prevent such unwarranted inferences.

The utility of behavioral anchoring rests heavily on how well the IRT assumptions are satisfied as well as on the overall design of the test. In this context,
it may be instructive to recall the example in the chapter by Yamamoto and
Gitomer. The inclusion of five latent classes greatly clarifies the item charac-

teristic curves that describe the performance of the examinees who do not fall into one of the classes. It may be that a combination of the HYBRID model and behavioral anchoring could yield extremely useful results for all examinees.

As described by Carroll, behavioral anchoring is oriented toward describing current status. For this reason it is well suited to enhance the value of account-ability assessments. Whether it can also play a role in instructional assessment will depend greatly on the nature of the domain and the structure of the test. In fact, Carroll avows that he knows of no instance in which behavioral anchor-ing makes reference "to the level of cognitive processing involved in correct response at a given item-difficulty level." There is no reason to believe that this is due to a structural limitation of the method rather than to a paucity of tests constructed to support this level of interpretation.

Fortunately, this is the exact direction in which the work described by Bejar and by Haertel and Wiley is moving. We ought to be able to apply behavioral anchoring techniques to tests designed to support instruction. If that indeed proves to be the case, we will find ourselves in the happy situation of building tests that can properly satisfy more than one master.

I believe we are now at a critical point in the history of educational measure-ment. The public and its representatives have demonstrated increased concern with issues of assessment. Within the education community itself, there are many voices arguing for new forms of testing that would yield more useful data. At the same time, there is considerable interest in moving to computer-based test-ing. The convergence of these three movements imparts enormous momen-tum to the drive for a new generation of tests.

The high stakes and public visibility associated with assessment for account-ability places great pressure on test developers to demonstrate construct valid-ity. The demands for richer (and different kinds of) information leads to a reconceptualization of the nature of assessment and of test construction. Many of the chapters in this volume, and those by Bejar and by Haertel and Wiley in particular, represent attempts by educational researchers to meet these challenges.

In implementing computer-based testing with automated scoring of open-ended responses, the great utility of these more formal approaches to assess-ment design will become evident. From an operational point of view, it is this third movement that will most justify the investment in the foundational work for RGM and the algebra of tasks and abilities. Although much remains to be done, we are fortunate to be able to build on the solid efforts described in this volume.

Author Index

K

Kacmerek, R. M., 33, *35*
Kadane, P., 249, *268*
Kahneman, D., 198, *216*
Kane, M. T., 48, *70*
Katz, B., 342, *355*
Kaufer, R., *36, 70*
Kaufman, D. R., 214, *217*
Kegl, J., 337, 340, *355*
Kelley, T. L., 22, 25, 36
Kelly, F. J., 269, *274*
Kerr, M., 327, *353*
Kershaw, R. C., 108, *121*
Kibler, D., 339, *354*
Kiely, G. L., 80, *97*, 120, *123*
Kieras, D. E., 345, *355*
Kilpatrick, J., 243, *267*
Kintsch, W., 155, *179*
Klahr, D., *15, 36, 241*
Klassen, D., 86, *96*
Klavans, J. L., 337, *352*
Klopfer, L. E., 224, *240*
Kolen, M. J., 339, *355*
Koppen, M., 359, *384*
Kotovsky, K., *15*, 332, 335, *355, 356*
Kuder, G. F., 22, *36*
Kyllonen, P. C., 2, 3, 5, 11, *15, 16*, 31, 52, 54, 59, *70*, 329, 351, *355, 356*

L

La Claire, L, 109, *122*
La Hart, C., 100, *121*
Laird, N. M., 25, *36, 295*, 279
Lajoie, S., 8, *15*, 221, *241*
Lamon, S., *37, 241*
Lansman, M., 3, *15*
Larkin, J., 243, 244, 246, 249, *267, 268*, 348, *355*
Lauritzen, S. L., 32, *36*
Lave, J., 200, *216*, 349, *355*
Lazarsfeld, P. F., 31, *36*, 79, 80, *96*, 114, *122*, 246, *268*, 276, *295, 354*
Lawley, D. N., 23, *36*
Lee, D., 327, *353*
Lesgold, A., 1, 8, 10, *14*, 28, *36, 179*, 220, 221, *241, 242*, 346, *353, 355*
Lesh, R. A., *37, 241*
Levin, I., *295*

Levine, H. G., 204, *216*
Lewis, A. B., 255, *268*
Lewis, M., 155, *179*
Lewis, R., 200, 203, *215*
Lidg, C. S., *14*
Lin, Y-G., 8, *16*
Lincoln, M., 347, *357*
Lindquist, E. F., 269, *274*
Linn, R., *14, 38, 121, 122*, 269, *274, 321*, 352, *356*
Livingston, C., 345, *352*
Lodewijks, H., *15, 70*
Loef, M., 345, *352*
Loevinger, J., 51, *70*, 324, *355*
Lohman, D. F., 1, 2, 3, 4, 8, 9, *14*, 29, 31, *36, 38*, 52, 54, 55, 57, 58, 59, 65, *70*, 328, 347, 350, *356*
Lord, F. M., 22, 23, 24, 28, *35, 37*, 44, 45, *70*, 79, *97*, 113, *122*, 142, 144, 146, *150*, 223, 233, *241*, 258, *268*, 275, *295*
Lorge, I., 302, *322*
Lytle, E. G., 340, *352*

M

Macalalad, A., 108, *121*
Mac Leod, C. M., 20, *36*
Macready, G. B., 31, 32, *37*, 238, 239, *241*, 276, *294, 384*
MacRury, K., 102, 117, *122*
Madaus, G. F., 223, *240*
Magder, S., 214, *217*
Mandinach, E. B., 10, *17*
Mandler, J. M., 8, *15*
Markman, E. M., 199, *216*
Marshalek, B., 4, 5, *15, 16*, 351, *356*
Marshall, S. P., 8, *15*, 29, *37*, 160, 164, 178, *179*, 269
Marshall, S. R., 344, *355*
Marton, F., 8, *15*, 221, 224, 226, 227, *241, 242*
Maslow, A. P., *321*
Masters, G. N., 33, *37*, 104, 113, 118, 231, 233, *241, 242*, 272
Matz, M., 120, *122*
Mayer, R., 8, *15*, 249, 255, *268*, 339, 355
Mayhew, J., 332, *355*
McClelland, J., *180, 217*, 326, *356*

Subject Index

A

Ability-state pattern lattices, 368–370
  learning transitions and paths, 370
Ability structures, *see also* schema, 155–177,
  269–271
  theory relations among ability, 367–368
Ability structures and cognition, 359–361,
  367–370
  goals, subgoals, and subtasks, 362–363
Ability, what is it? 363–367
  abilities with more than two states,
  366–367
  ability states, 365–367
  concatenated abilities and tasks, 364–365
Achievement tests, constructing measures
  of, 222–227, *see also* Tests, 27–28,
  206–210, 377–382, and testing,
  377–382
  building achievement tests around key concepts, 224–227
  constructing measures of achievement,
  230–233
  constructing ordered outcome categories,
  227–229
  conventional achievement testing, 222–223
  partially ordered states, 233–237

Application of HYBRID to a test of cognitive
  skills, 275–293
  analysis of electronic gates problems,
  283–291
  estimation of model parameters, 278–283
  HYBRID model of IRT and latent classes,
  277–278
  introduction to HYBRID, 276–277
Applications of IRT, 86–93
  mental health admissions example, 86–90
  risk of eating disorders example, 90–93
  tests need not be long, 93–96
  trace lines, how do we estimate them?
  84–86

B

Behavior, *see* performance, 172–177
Behavior scaling, procedures for, 301–304
  applicability of behavior or scaling, 301–302
  framing of behavior scaling statements,
  302–304
  levels of cognitive processing, 304
  specifications of items, tasks, 303
  task or content parameters, 304
  verbal description of competency, 303–304